second edition

TEACHING STUDENTS WITH LEARNING AND BEHAVIOR PROBLEMS

DEBORAH DEUTSCH SMITH
University of New Mexico

PRENTICE HALL, ENGLEWOOD CLIFFS, NEW JERSEY 07632

Library of Congress Cataloging-in-Publication Data

Smith, Deborah Deutsch.
  Teaching students with learning and behavior
problems.

    Rev. ed. of: Teaching the learning disabled. c1981.
    Bibliography.
    Includes index.
    1. Learning disabled children--Education. 2. Special
education. I. Smith, Deborah Deutsch. Teaching the
learning disabled. II. Title.
LC4704.S62 1989   371.9   87-32859
ISBN 0-13-894189-0

Editorial/production supervision and
  interior design: *Marjorie Shustak*
Cover design: *Bruce Kenselaar*
Cover photo: *Jeffrey Myers, Four by Five, Inc.*
Manufacturing buyer: *Peter Havens*

Previously published under the title *Teaching the Learning Disabled.*

Printed in the United States of America

10 9 8 7 6 5 4 3 2

ISBN 0-13-894189-0

Prentice-Hall International (UK) Limited, *London*
Prentice-Hall of Australia Pty. Limited, *Sydney*
Prentice-Hall Canada Inc., *Toronto*
Prentice-Hall Hispanoamericana, S.A., *Mexico*
Prentice-Hall of India Private Limited, *New Delhi*
Prentice-Hall of Japan, Inc., *Tokyo*
Simon & Schuster Asia Pte. Ltd., *Singapore*
Editora Prentice-Hall do Brasil, Ltda., *Rio de Janeiro*

To—

Jim, who went to Dunkin' Donuts
Steve, who planned his first novel
Bella, who sat and watched
Puffer, who with great relief offered his critique.

Contents

PART III   ACADEMIC INTERVENTION

12   Transition Education   *302*

Author Index   *333*

Subject Index   *345*

Preface

In some respects, it seems like such a short time ago that I wrote my first college text. That book, *Teaching the Learning Disabled,* was intended to guide special education teachers in designing and implementing better instructional programs for their students. In the seven years since that book was released, the amount of research conducted concerning better instructional practices for students with handicaps has been staggering. We definitely know more today about how and what to teach students who are unable to succeed in regular education programs without very special assistance. Hopefully, the same statement can be made seven years hence.

The field—its researchers, curriculum and materials developers, teachers, parents, and students—has made remarkable progress over the past years. Special education curricular options are expanded and diverse. More instructional methods, procedures, and tactics have been developed and verified through research. Improved ways to sequence instruction are available to teachers. Each of these allows for a better match of students' abilities and learning styles with the instructional program. This text strives to present to special educators information about best practices of instruction. By providing information that is grounded in research, the ultimate hope is that teachers will find their jobs more exciting and successful, and that students will profit more from school.

Some unique features have been incorporated throughout this text. References and suggested readings, for example, are grouped by topic at the end of every chapter. Computer assisted instruction is integrated into each chapter where such information is relevant. The same is true for curriculum-based assessment and evaluation. Consistent organizational format is found within each of the three parts of the book. In the chapters that provide information about instructional interventions, graphic schema provide a framework for organizing the material presented and conceptualizing the skill domain.

Part I introduces the reader to generic teaching and classroom skills that all special education teachers should possess. Information is provided about some common characteristics (for example, learned helplessness, inactive learning, and attention deficits) of learners with special needs. Information about critical teaching skills and competencies is also provided. The process whereby individual education programs are developed is discussed in detail. Evaluative methods and curriculum-based assessments used to determine teachers' and programs' effectiveness are also discussed thoroughly.

Part II presents the newest available information about social behavior. A comprehensive section detailing techniques for managing disruptive behavior in a variety of settings begins the discussion. Next, techniques for teaching students a variety of social skills (for example, coping, social interaction, social comprehension, and decision making) are discussed.

In Part III, specific attention is paid to remediation of academic skills. Reading, mathematics, written language, and spoken language are the topics of entire chapters where many direct instructional techniques are presented in a practical manner. The methods presented have been verified through considerable research, and are simple enough for teachers to implement in their classrooms. This section of the text also provides teachers with information about how to teach their students critical study skills so that they might gain more knowledge and information from traditional content courses found in middle and secondary schools. The latest information about transition from school to adult life concludes the book.

Acknowledgments

Although a single name appears on the binding of this book, there are many people who contributed in important ways to its creation. First, I would like to thank the Regents and the President of the University of New Mexico for granting me a sabbatical leave of absence that allowed me the opportunity to think and learn my field once again. Thanks and appreciation are also due to my dean, David Colton, for his unending support throughout this project. I also owe my gratitude to the Special Education Department, its staff and faculty, who assisted me in preparing this manuscript. In particular, I wish to express my sincere thanks to Pamela Livingston for her editorial assistance; her keen perception about how words are used to convey clearer meanings make this text easier to read. Also, thanks are owed to Delilah Yao for typing the most difficult components of the manuscript: the reference lists and tables. The University of New Mexico is most fortunate to have an excellent media department staff, who prepared many of the graphics included in this text. In particular, I want to acknowledge the fine work of Jay Nelson, Paul Gonzales, and David Kress, who took the extra time necessary to produce such outstanding work.

A number of experts in various content areas gave selflessly of their expertise to improve this text. Their feedback and critiques made the content included here more accurate and precise. Thanks go to Dr. Diane Rivera for her input on the mathematics chapter, Dr. Jo Tomason for her help with the chapter about the Individualized Educational Program, and Drs. Eloy Gonzales, Henry Pepe, and Billy Watson for their assistance in clarifying those issues surrounding the assessment process. Also, thanks must go to Dr. Jerry Chaffin, who helped with the sections on computer applications and arranged for the sample screens to be used as figures in this text.

I would like to take this opportunity to thank those who contributed to and enhanced this book. My deepest appreciation goes to Carlene Van Etten, Dr. Chris Marvin, and Dr. Ginger Blalock, whose chapters about reading, language, and transition strengthen and broaden this text. Clearly, this book is better because of their efforts, for their depth of knowledge in those areas strengthened immeasurably the material presented. My sincere gratitude is extended to these fine scholars and practitioners.

The next individual I must thank saved my sanity throughout this project. Without Tom Pierce—who kept his sense of humor, searched for missing volume numbers and missing articles, coped with the library and its staff, handled the permissions, and attended to so many details—this project would have been impossible for me to complete.

Finally, but certainly not least, I wish to thank my family. Throughout my career, there has always been one person who understood the difficulties of achieving, the family sacrifices that are the price to pay, and the efforts that are required to put forth one's best. My deepest thanks and appreciation go to the man who allowed me a room of my own, Dr. James O. Smith. To my son, Steven, thank you for understanding why Mom couldn't. I also thank him as a contributor to this book; his work on study skills (which he could apply more to his own schoolwork) serves as a great example of notetaking.

The text you are about to read is the product of the combined efforts of many people. We all wish you good reading!

DDS

1

Teaching and Learning

Today's educational system provides many different options for students, particularly for students with special needs. Depending on their abilities to profit from the regular education curriculum, their academic and behavioral characteristics, and their ultimate goals, students are placed in classes that can best meet their academic and social needs. Regardless of their placement, teachers need to adjust their educational methods to help students attain their potential. Teachers must understand the learning characteristics of all their students and possess knowledge about both academic content and teaching methods. This text aims at helping teachers gain the skills necessary to be effective instructors who develop positive learning environments where students can gain those academic and social skills needed in life.

LEARNER CHARACTERISTICS

All children differ in temperament, cognitive abilities, personality, and experience. These factors, and many others (motivation, support at home, past education), contribute to success in school. Children with special needs, regardless of their categorical identification, present their teachers with difficulties in learning abilities and styles. These difficulties affect students' learning as well as their adjustment at school. In this section, a few characteristics, commonly observed in children with special needs, are discussed. These characteristics influence how individually tailored instructional programs need to be developed. It is important to remember that learner characteristics can be changed positively so that students benefit maximally from the learning opportunities present at school.

Academic Learning

A primary characteristic of most students with special needs is that they are academically behind their normal counterparts. By high school, many of these students are more than six years behind their normal counterparts in achievement (Deshler & Schumaker, 1986). For many of these youngsters, the tactics and strategies found in Part III of this text will facilitate their learning academic tasks. With careful, systematic, and direct instruction, most can achieve at least grade-level performance or functioning. However, recent research has shown that some of these students possess various characteristics that greatly hinder their learning. These characteristics can be altered, and the results can be substantial. Some of those learning characteristics (learned helplessness, inactive learning, attention deficits, attribution, and an inability to generalize learning) are discussed briefly here.

Attribution

Attributions are the internal justifications that individuals devise to explain their success or failure at a task. School failure may result not only in academic deficits, but also in motivational deficits. After repeated experiences with failure, many students come to expect failure. This expectation becomes outwardly directed, viewed as something beyond one's control. Such individuals may be afraid to respond, take risks, or actively engage in learning. They come to believe that their failure is due to a lack of ability. In turn, this results in lowered expectations and a belief that they cannot succeed. Eventually, such individuals meet their own expectations. They do not believe in themselves and do not try to learn. This situation is frequently called *learned helplessness*. Such students expect to fail.

Students oriented toward mastery tend to find ways to overcome failure (using different strategies, asking for help, studying harder). Students who expect academic failure are more passive, and often attribute success to luck rather than to their abilities or effort. In some ways, special education teachers may contribute to students' learned helplessness through their educational planning (Kleinhammer-Tramill et al., 1983). When teachers direct the entire school day, select students' rewards for achievement, make tasks too easy, and offer too much assistance, students do not become self-directed. They are less likely to persist on difficult tasks and follow them through to completion. Therefore, many do not learn that their efforts can achieve success.

To help conceptualize motivation and attribution, Grimes (1981) developed a useful schema that describes student motivation as it relates to success and attribution. Table 1.1 presents her comparison of high achievers with low achievers and describes their attribution on a number of factors.

Table 1.1
Student Motivation as Related to the Attributional Process

	TYPE OF ACHIEVEMENT RELATED TO EXPECTATIONS OF SOCIETY AND SCHOOLS	TYPE OF ADULT FEEDBACK / ATTRIBUTION MADE BY CHILD	TYPE OF AFFECT ASSOCIATED WITH INTERNAL EVALUATION OF PERFORMANCE	CHILD'S UNDERSTANDING OF HIS ROLE IN CAUSE-EFFECT RELATIONSHIPS	EXPECTATIONS AND PROBABILITY OF SUBSEQUENT BEHAVIOR
High Achiever	Success is positively valued by our society. Success is defined by schools as desirable.	Positive feedback from adults. The child receives positive labels such as smart, gifted, etc. Child accepts and internalizes positive labels. The cause of success is attributed by the child to ability and effort.	The positive affects of pride, accomplishment and competence is associated with successful performance. The child self-reinforces his performance with internal positive self-statements. The child's self-concept is enhanced.	The child perceives that his effort determines positive outcome. Energy is seen as a means of solving problem.	The child has expectancy of success for future performance. Increased probability of future success serves as an incentive to work harder.
Low Achiever	Failure is negatively valued by our society. Failure is defined by schools as undesirable.	Negative feedback from adults. The child receives negative labels such as slow, learning problems, etc. Child accepts and internalizes negative labels. The cause of failure by the child is attributed to lack of ability.	The negative affect of frustration, shame, indifference, and incompetence is associated with failure. Internal statements of the child are primarily negative reflecting his lack of ability. The child's self-concept is decreased.	No causal relationship is perceived between effort and outcome by the child. Therefore, the child considers effort a waste of energy. Energy is spent on avoiding the task.	The child has expectancy of failure in future. Increased probability of failure. Therefore, no incentive to expand effort.

Source: L. Grimes (1981). Learned helplessness and attribution theory: Redefining children's learning problems. *Learning Disability Quarterly, 4,* p. 92. Used with permission.

On a more positive note, attribution can be changed (Borkowski, Weyhing, & Turner, 1986). Students can come to recognize that their efforts do result in success, but for those who have experienced considerable school failure, this process is intensive and prolonged.

When attempting to change students' attributions, teachers should be task-specific, discussing actual performance and how it can be improved. Students need to be given good strategies and procedures to improve their performances and should be reinforced for using them. Aponik and Dembo (1983) suggest that students can be taught to break down problems and tasks into smaller units (by using task analysis techniques) so they are manageable and more easily solved. This increases the likelihood of success. Self-management procedures and strategy training (discussed later, in Chapter 4) engage students more actively and help students to learn that they, and their efforts, are responsible for successful experiences. When students achieve success, teachers should discuss with them the factors that contributed to their accomplishment.

Inactive Learning

Possibly due, in part, to attribution, many students with special needs are called "inactive learners" (Torgesen & Licht, 1983). Inactive learners are less active and organized in their approach to memory and other academic tasks, and they seldom plan for such tasks. They seem to have no useful strategies to help them remember or study. In this regard, many recent research studies, particularly in the area of strategy training (see Chapter 11 on study skills for more information), are helpful. It appears that students can engage in self-questioning strategies to become more actively involved in learning. Also, teachers can plan activities that require students' active, rather than passive, involvement. Instead of relying on lectures and teacher-directed activities, lessons and units can be planned where youngsters need to discover, think, solve problems, and develop a product. Students who participate in the development and implementation of their educational programs become more active learners. For example, Kosiewicz, Hallahan, and Lloyd (1981) found that when a student was allowed to choose his teaching technique, he became a more active learner and improved his academic achievement more than when the teacher selected the teaching tactic. Such procedures are discussed in the self-management sections of this text.

Clearly, students need to become more actively involved in the curriculum and their school programs. When they take more interest in learning, learning becomes more meaningful. They find purpose for their learning, which might not have been as obvious as before.

Attention

Many students with special needs have what some call "attention deficits." These students do not attend to the task to be learned or may pay attention to the wrong features of tasks they are asked to complete. Many of these students are also observed as being distractible. There is evidence that attention deficits can be corrected or lessened through educational procedures.

For example, rewarding students for remembering particular features of assigned tasks can lead to improved attention and academic achievement. Using advance organizers to help students focus their energies and attention on the important information to be learned in content classes has proven beneficial. Providing students with strategies they can use and apply in academic situations (test taking, note taking) helps to focus attention. Actively involving students in their academic programs and procedures and providing more drill and practice activities that key students to relevant cues have proven effective. Attention deficits are now seen by some as relating to task persistence, motivation, attribution, and passivity. As instructional interventions are selected, the learning style of each student must be considered and addressed.

Stages of Learning

All learners pass through various stages of learning every time they master and integrate a new skill. These stages must be anticipated and planned for by those managing students' educational programs. During the 1960s, much to the surprise of some researchers, it was discovered that rewards are not *always* effective. Ayllon and Azrin (1964) and Hopkins (1968), for example, found reinforcement unsuccessful initially. Instructions had to be first used to get the target behavior to a level at which rewards were effective.

Smith and Lovitt (1976) designed a research project specifically to study this phenomenon. They found that when students had to learn how to solve computational arithmetic problems, reinforcement was ineffective. When they had to compute problems more quickly, however, reinforcement contingencies were influential. Since then, a number of studies have shown that certain instructional procedures are best applied in particular situations (see references and suggested readings at the end of this chapter).

Equivocal results of past research might be due to the different entry levels of the research subjects. One way to conceptualize students' entry levels is to relate those to their stages of learning. Today, many educators recommend that the students' stage of learning be considered when selecting instructional methods and the evaluation procedures that check those methods' effectiveness.

At present, five stages of learning have been identified. Future research will certainly lead to finer classifications of these stages and better guidelines for teachers to use to plan students' educational programs. These five stages of learning are acquisition (initial and advanced), proficiency, maintenance, generalization, and adaption (problem solving). A simplified linear diagram of these stages and students' learning levels appears in Figure 1.1. These stages are applicable while students are learning skills and increasing their performance levels.

During *acquisition,* the learner could enter the learning process at 0%, indicating no knowledge of how to perform the task accurately. After a period of

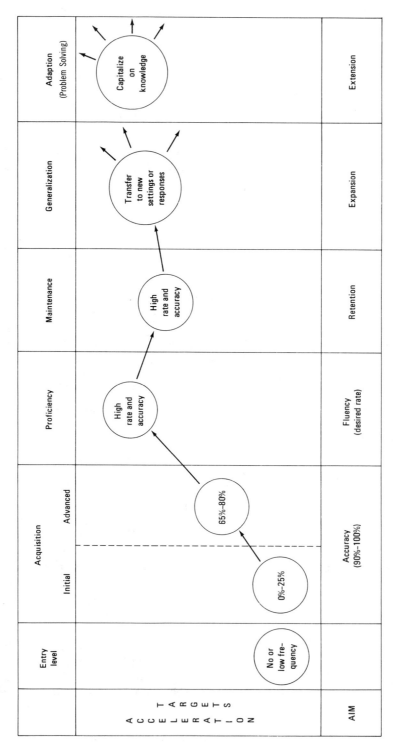

Figure 1.1 Stages of learning that lead to ultimate mastery through continual increases in a skill's frequency.

instruction, some learners indicate that they can perform the task or skill accurately (90–100%); they have passed through the acquisition stage of learning. Others, however, need further direct instruction, at the advanced acquisition phase, to attain sufficiently high levels of accuracy to indicate mastery.

During the acquisition stage, the aim is for the individual to learn how to perform the skill accurately. This, however, is not where the educational process should stop. The individual must also be able to perform the skill quickly enough to execute it automatically. During the *proficiency* stage of learning, the aim is for the learner to perform the task with both quality (accuracy) and sufficient quantity (speed). The tactics used differ from those used in the acquisition stage; they direct the learner to increase speed of performance.

There are some very important reasons why proficient levels of performance are necessary targets. For example, if a student can correctly form the letters of the alphabet but does so too slowly, he or she will not be able to complete assignments that require writing as a basic tool (written composition, spelling tests) on time. Thus, the student who writes slowly might not be able to keep up with the teacher's dictation of spelling words on weekly tests. Low spelling scores might be the result of slow writing, not poor spelling ability. This situation exists with most academic and vocationally related tasks.

Once proficient levels of performance are achieved, the learner enters into the *maintenance* stage of learning. The hope is for the learned behavior to remain at the high levels of the two previous stages. Retention of learning is important to all teachers and their students. For some students this is the most frustrating stage of learning; often learned skills are not retained once direct instruction is withdrawn. For this reason, many teachers set aims in the proficiency situation slightly higher than necessary, so some loss in speed can be accepted. For individuals who tend not to retain desired speed of performance, teachers must plan for maintenance by periodically evaluating retention and implementing direct intervention on an infrequent basis.

After maintenance comes a period of *generalization,* in which the learned behavior should occur in all situations that are appropriate, regardless of the setting. For many students, skills learned in the classroom do not appear automatically in other settings without direct instruction. For example, a youngster who has demonstrated mastery of specific language and grammatical skills might speak appropriately in the classroom, but not on the playground or at home. Another student might have mastered a learning strategy that helps him to write better themes, but does not apply that skill when asked to write reports in history or English classes. For these students, direct instruction is necessary in various settings to guarantee generalization. For most students with special needs, teachers cannot merely hope that generalization will occur. For students who seem to generalize without direct instruction from the teacher, only periodic *probes* (spot checks) need to be conducted to ensure that they transferred their learning to other settings.

Another type of generalization, response generalization, is important to teachers and their students. When some students are taught to borrow in mathematics, for example, they do so in all situations requiring that process (23 − 7 =) (422 − 79 =). Others do not generalize to other response classes, and direct instruction must be provided for each different instance. For these students generalization must be programmed. Possibly the skill of generalizing should be taught.

The last stage of learning is often referred to as *adaption.* This stage requires the student to capitalize on previous learning and to extend knowledge and skills already acquired. In new situations, the learner must be able to *problem solve* to determine what the appropriate response actually is. It is important to teach students to extend their knowledge and skills. Students need to be flexible and able to make decisions based on previous learning. Problem solving is a neglected area in many students' educational programs and needs to be integrated throughout the school years.

Teachers need to be aware of these stages of learning, for the entry level of each student should influence the selection of instructional tactics and accountability systems. Tactics that are most efficient and effective in one stage of learning might not be suitable in another. The measurement systems chosen for the purpose of evaluating instruction differ depending on the stage at which the student is functioning (more details are given in Chapter 3). Because of the importance of this phase on curriculum-based assessment, placement, and educational decision making, these stages of learning and their influence on instruction are stressed throughout this text.

Social Skills

Many students with special needs do not exhibit good social skills. (Chapter 5 is devoted exclusively to this topic.) Either these youngsters do not possess the skills or they do not use those skills required for interpersonal interactions. They are not socially competent. For many, this lack lowers their social status and can affect their lives while in school, at home, and on the job. Social skills training has not been a priority in special education classes until recently. For those students deficient in social skills, education and training aimed at developing social competence must become a part of their curriculum.

Disruption

Students with special needs are often more disruptive than are their normal counterparts. They disturb the learning environment for themselves and their peers. They follow the classroom and school rules less frequently. As discussed in detail in Chapter 4, there are many reasons for this. These students might be frustrated with the academic content presented to them. They might not understand the explicit and implied rules at school. They might purposely seek to destroy the learning environment. Regardless of the reason, many students with special needs are disruptive. According to Drabman and Patterson (1981), this contributes to lowered social status for these youngsters, which, in turn, could result in more inappropriate social behavior.

High rates of disruption also contribute to lowered academic achievement. The relationship between achievement and the amount of time spent engaged in learning (responding time) is great. If students do not spend time learning, they will not learn. This is particularly true for students with handicaps. Students who spend a substantial amount of time away from the learning task do not learn as much. As discussed in Chapter 4, disruption can be reduced or eliminated through the systematic application of various intervention strategies.

The relationship between disruption and academic learning is well-documented. During the 1970s considerable research was conducted and techniques were developed to reduce inappropriate or disruptive classroom behaviors. It was thought that if disruption were eliminated, students' academic achievement would improve. This did not occur.

What, then, is the relationship between academic performance and the reduction of disruption? Reduction in disruption alone does not guarantee collateral increases in attention-to-task or academic improvement. However, when students are reinforced for increased academic output, disruption decreases (Ayllon & Roberts, 1974; Ferritor et al., 1972).

LEARNING ENVIRONMENT CHARACTERISTICS

Research done by the Kansas University Institute for Research in Learning Disabilities (KU-IRLD) has sparked an awareness of regular education's expectations for all learners. Because of that research, there is a better understanding of the *setting demands* of secondary school classes. This is important information for educators, and it must be considered as students with special needs are prepared for and placed in regular education classrooms and least restrictive environments for some or all of their school days. The KU-IRLD work should stimulate others to study what setting demands also exist in elementary classes.

Before the KU-IRLD research information was available, most special educators realized that for their students to be tolerated and accepted in regular education classrooms, the students would have to subscribe to certain behavioral rules and codes. Such rules and codes stipulate that students refrain from disturbing the learning environment (follow directions, not wander around the classroom, talk when called upon, not display outbursts of temper). Special education teachers also understood that students being mainstreamed into regular education classes should be close to grade level in subject achievement. They should be able to perform within the academic achievement range of their normal counterparts. Therefore, students who could not meet the behavioral or academic expectations of the regular education class were viewed as not yet ready to attend those classes. Only students who were close to grade level in a particular subject and could control their behavior were considered for regular education placements.

The findings from KU-IRLD indicate that special educators might not be adequately preparing students with special needs to succeed in the mainstream.

Before the KU-IRLD studies, special education practitioners had not considered other, more subtle demands expected in regular education. For example, Moran (1980) found that secondary content classes require students to listen to quickly delivered lectures in which teachers provided few advance organizers and few checks for students' understanding. In such content classes, students are expected to take notes independently. Link (1980) found that secondary teachers expect students to be able to follow oral and written directions, skim reading passages, locate information found in textbooks, recall information for tests, locate answers to questions, and take notes. For mid-schools, Schumaker, Sheldon-Wildgen, and Sherman (1982) found that for the majority of the time, students are expected to work independently reading and writing. Robinson, Braxdale, and Colson (1985) promote preparing mid-school students with special needs for the transition to secondary schools. They maintain that students need to be able to work with textbooks written above grade level, take notes in classes that depend primarily upon lectures, complete homework, study independently, take tests, monitor errors, and participate in class discussions when appropriate. Some strategies for teaching students such study skills are found in Part III of this text.[1]

The skills just described are not typically taught in most special education classes. Also, they are not the typical setting demands of special education. If students are to make better transitions to regular education from special education, the scope and sequence, as well as the content, of special education classes needs to be broadened. Students with special needs must overcome skill deficits, behavioral deficits, and social skills deficits and learn to cope with the setting demands of regular education. For those who are unable to meet the setting demands of secondary classes, deliberate curriculum tracking into vocational and career educational programs may be a more appropriate alternative.

TEACHER SKILLS

Teachers of students with special needs serve in a variety of roles. They teach youngsters who have great individual differences. Some may present social skills deficits; most possess academic skill deficiencies. Besides their teaching duties, these teachers often consult with parents and other teachers, participate in assessments of students, write and manage individualized program plans (see Chapter 2), and conduct inservice training activities. The roles filled by special education teachers are numerous and important to students, their families, and the school district. But, first and foremost, special education teachers' purpose is to educate students with special needs.

To do this, they must have the knowledge necessary to teach content and

---

[1]For in-depth teacher training on strategies to teach students study skills, contact Dr. Fran Clark, University of Kansas, Institute for Research in Learning Disabilities, 223 Carruth-O'Leary Hall, Lawrence, KS 66045.

be proficient in educational methods through which they can impart that content to their students. The primary purpose of this text is to help teachers teach by providing suggestions for a variety of methods that both research and clinical practice have shown to be effective and efficient. Throughout this book, teaching strategies, procedures, and tactics that improve students' social and academic skills are presented. First, a discussion of the overriding critical teaching skills might be useful.

Critical Teaching Skills

Although specific procedures that serve to remediate specific deficit areas are discussed later in this book, there are some general teaching skills that are important for teachers to use throughout the school day, regardless of the topic of instruction. A number of different researchers and educational experts have attempted to identify those key variables or behaviors that excellent (master) teachers use. Many of the skills that are identified by these experts overlap, but it is useful to study each list.

Kea (1987) and Deshler and Schumaker (1986) identified teacher behaviors that they believe enhance the quality or intensity of classroom instruction, particularly at the secondary school level. Although they found that many middle and secondary resource room teachers fail to use them, they believe the following teaching skills are critical to good instruction:

1. Provide positive and corrective feedback.
2. Use organizers throughout the instructional session.
3. Ensure high levels of active academic responding.
4. Program youth involvement in discussions.
5. Provide regular reviews of key instructional points and checks of comprehension.
6. Monitor student performance.
7. Require mastery learning.
8. Communicate high expectations to students.
9. Communicate rationales for instructional activities.
10. Facilitate independence.

In another attempt to identify those variables that differentiate excellent teachers, Rosenshine (1983, 336–37) lists the following behaviors relied on by elementary teachers.

1. Structure the learning.
2. Proceed in small steps but at a brisk pace.
3. Give detailed and redundant instructions and explanations.
4. Provide many examples.
5. Ask a large number of questions and provide overt, active practice.
6. Provide feedback and corrections, particularly in the initial stages of learning.
7. Divide seatwork assignments into smaller assignments.

8. Provide for continued student practice so that students have a success rate of 90–100% and become rapid, confident, and firm.

Teachers must also use language that is understandable to their students. If the teacher's rate of speech is too fast, if vocabulary is beyond the understanding of the students, or if the syntax is too complex, students will not gain meaning from the educational experience. They will not be able to follow the teacher's directions because they do not comprehend what is being said to them. They will not gain meaning from lectures that are too complex. In Chapter 6, considerable discussion about teachers' language is provided. Matching students' cognitive comprehension skills with the language intended to deliver information is an important teacher skill.

Beyond these skills, teachers must develop a style, a way for them to be comfortable with the students they teach. Teachers need to enjoy their working relationships with students. In turn, students should come to respect and enjoy their teachers. Learning does not have to be dull and routine. Teachers need to keep these critical teaching behaviors in mind, but they also need to diversify educational experiences and to add occasional elements of fun into the learning environment. This can be accomplished by allowing students to work on interesting topics and solve problems.

Teacher Competencies

Recent discussion has focused on the competencies that should be expected from special education graduates. In particular, the Teacher Education Division of the Council for Exceptional Children and the Council for Learning Disabilities have devoted considerable time and energies on this issue. In this discussion of teachers' skills, it is useful to get an overview of those skills that experts believe special education teachers should possess. Although prepared for teachers of students with learning disabilities, the competency areas and statements formulated by Hudson et al. (1987) found in Table 1.2 is useful to all teachers. The competency areas are applicable to all special education teachers and show the depth of knowledge and skills required of special educators.

Computer Literacy

The recent availability of microcomputers in school settings has influenced how students are taught and what they are taught. As society becomes more and more technology-based, so too will our schools. Microcomputers can be used in five general ways in school settings: the delivery of instruction, supplemental activities, word processing, programming, and data management.

Students can learn academic tasks by means of the computer (computer-assisted instruction). Reading and mathematics units, for example, are taught through software that contains independent instructional programs and does not require a teacher. Other materials provide students with opportunities for

Table 1.2
Competency Areas and Statements for Teachers of Students with Learning Disabilities

COMPETENCY

General/Social Knowledge

1. Knowledge of normal range of individual differences and deviations in human growth/development (e.g., discuss normal language development and possible deviations).
2. Knowledge of the way normal children learn basic academic skills and difficulties encountered by LD (learning disabled) students.

Planning/Evaluation

3. Plan remedial instruction for small groups/individuals based on data showing discrepancy between LD student's performance and school's goal.
4. Plan lessons and activities based on diagnostic information about each student's specific learning deficit, such as focusing attention on learning task.
5. Select/design materials and activities that match LD student's learning needs and lesson objectives (e.g., modify mode of presentation or demonstration of knowledge or simplify language/reading level).
6. Plan sequence of instruction which enables LD student to meet lesson objectives and reach long-term goals (i.e., task analyze objectives, provide for maintenance and generalization skills).
7. Plan continuous evaluation of LD student's achievement, basing decisions about changes on data collected.

Curriculum Content

8. Awareness and ability to implement specialized academic programs for LD student (e.g., corrective reading programs or parallel alternate curricula for secondary LD students).
9. Knowledge of affective curricula for specific LD with social/interpersonal deficits.
10. Implement programs which help LD students engage in self-monitoring, predicting outcomes, and other deliberate attempts at studying/learning.

Clinical Teaching Strategies

11. Select appropriate clinical strategies for individual LD students (e.g., does LD student learn decoding better in context or isolation?).
12. Apply direct instruction, using appropriate feedback, to teach mastery of basic skills.
13. Involve LD students as active respondents in learning tasks rather than passive recipients of instruction (e.g., teach LD student questioning strategy to increase comprehension of main ideas).
14. Decrease impulsive behavior, and increase problem-solving techniques.

Behavior Management

15. Implement behavior management system to increase appropriate and decrease inappropriate behaviors.
16. Prevent behavior problems in class by management of simultaneous activities (e.g., room arrangement, engineered classroom, self-correcting activities).

Source: P. J. Hudson, C. V. Morsink, G. Branscum, and R. Boone (1987). Competencies for teachers of students with learning disabilities. *Journal of Learning Disabilities, 20* (4), pp. 232–34. Used with permission.

drill and practice. These programs support ongoing, traditional instruction. Some word-processing programs are simple for even preschoolers to use and have helped older students to write better themes and reports. With the availability of microcomputers, students are learning to write their own software programs (through Logo and BASIC programming techniques). For teachers and administrators, microcomputers can aid in student data management and record keeping.

The advantages of the microcomputer and its related technology are great. However, for maximal use and integration into the classroom, teachers must become computer literate (know how to use computers). They must be able to evaluate the quality of the software materials and learn to link these programs with the curriculum. Clearly, this competency will become increasingly important as more equipment and software become available.

Consultation Skills

Special educators serve a number of different constituents: students, parents, teachers, administrators. They are the advocates for students with special needs, the managers of students' individualized educational plans (IEPs) and entire educational programs, and the facilitators of mainstreaming. These educators must work with large numbers of regular educators to communicate the progress of their students, coordinate services, and assist in developing programs for their students outside the special education classroom. To accomplish these tasks effectively, special educators need to develop skills in consultation, negotiation, and professional communication.

COMMUNICATING WITH OTHER PROFESSIONALS

Teachers of exceptional children must work with many people to achieve the fulfillment of a total, appropriate educational program for each handicapped child. Ultimately, it is not just parents and special educators who must work together, but myriad diverse persons, often from many disciplines, who must coordinate their efforts. Who should orchestrate the services of specially trained personnel such as speech clinicians, recreational therapists, private tutors, counselors, doctors, regular educators, and other specialists? In many instances, the special education teacher is the person who must coordinate services so that they complement each other. This requires very special interpersonal and organizational skills, which are certainly necessary for all teachers of students with special needs. Unfortunately, a list of these specific skills and an educational curriculum does not now exist; until such time, teachers must at least be cognizant of these critical responsibilities.

Regular Educators

As mainstreaming comes closer to its full realization, the role of the teacher of students with special needs becomes more complex. Whether the teacher is a resource or self-contained classroom teacher, coordination of efforts between the special and regular education program must be carefully planned. The regular classroom teacher and all those who provide supplemental services (librarian, music teacher, art teacher, and physical education teacher) must be actively involved in the development and attainment of specific goals and objectives for each student for whom they share responsibility (Wiederholt, Hammill, & Brown, 1978).

The recognition of different goals and objectives for individual students is a departure from regular educators' usual operating procedures. The inclusion of students with special needs in their programs requires a change of attitude and methodology. They must individualize instruction, allow for greater individual differences, and incorporate evaluation procedures into their instructional plans. Special education teachers can help regular educators modify their instructional programs. They can offer assistance in the development of specific instructional goals and objectives that include criterion statements. They can suggest classroom management techniques and aid in the selection of instructional materials that will ease mainstreaming efforts.

This assistance will only be accepted, however, if the special educator understands regular educators' new dilemma (Hawisher & Calhoun, 1978). Suggestions must be offered in such a way that the regular educators are not offended or insulted. Suggestions must be realistic and possible to implement when there are thirty youngsters, all with different needs, in the class. Brown et al. (1979) point out that mutual trust, open communication, genuineness, and a positive regard must exist between the regular and special educator if a truly cooperative working relationship is to be fostered.

COMMUNICATING WITH PARENTS

Many educators hold a peculiar view of parents, particularly those of handicapped youngsters. These parents are often approached as though they are ignorant and hostile, and sometimes even as though they are stupid. These same people could be the doctors, lawyers, merchants, and clerks from whom these educators, when not functioning in the role of teacher, seek advice. Somehow many teachers seem to feel that once the role of parent is assumed, all intelligence is lost. Some parents do need counseling and training to live and work better with their handicapped child, but many do not. It is fallacious to assume that once an individual takes on the role of parent all competence disappears. If a teacher conveys this attitude to a parent, communication and cooperation are difficult. The teacher must enter into a new, open relationship with another adult who shares a common concern—the handicapped student. Decisions about how cooperative the parent will be and whether the parent needs counseling or specific training to deal effectively with the child should be made not *a priori*, but after a number of contacts have been made.

The teacher should remember that the needs and concerns of each parent are different. There are two general groups of parents of handicapped youngsters. One has long been aware that their children have learning problems, and they have long since learned to cope with and resolve their often-experienced feelings of hostility, anger, denial, guilt, and helplessness. Parents who have recently discovered that their children have educational difficulties have a much different perspective of school from those who work in the educational system. If teachers know how long a parent has known about a child's handicap, communication can prevent rather than create crises.

When parents are involved in their child's education, three positive outcomes should become apparent: exchange of information, growth in their parental role, and a productive relationship between teacher and parents. The onset of parental involvement should come early in the child's educational career. Certainly, if special education placement is being considered by school personnel, the parents should at least be informed, if not active, participants in the decision-making process.

In the not so distant past, many teachers believed that their only responsibility was to teach the established curriculum. This responsibility began at 8:30 a.m. and ended at 3:00 p.m. A corollary of this parochial logic was adhered to by many special education teachers: Handicapped students were their sole obligations. These youngsters were their responsibilities; no other teacher in the building was or should have been truly concerned about the welfare or education of "their children." Such beliefs and educational practices are now relegated to history. No longer can teachers live and work in isolation and no longer can youngsters be thought of as "belonging" to one person.

The education of America's younger citizens, particularly those receiving services from special education, is a team effort. *All* those who live and work with a handicapped youngster must be active participants in the educational process. Parents, diagnosticians, regular and special educators, and those who deliver supplemental services (physical education, music, art, speech, and language) must now become partners to ensure an appropriate education for each student. This sound premise, though often tumultuous, is not advocated just by educational leaders but is mandated by federal law (refer to Chapter 2 for review). Whether the special education teacher is ready for broadened horizons, ready for public scrutiny, or ready to work with many diverse people does not matter. This is the new reality of life in the special education classroom.

EFFECTIVE TEACHING

Students with handicaps typically must be taught specific strategies that enable them to learn. Unlike many of their counterparts, these students do not learn incidentally; their teachers must plan for their instruction deliberately. Throughout this text, suggestions are made about ways to teach students in direct and systematic ways. Here, several important points about effective instruction are highlighted and should be kept in mind as the material found later in this text is read.

Instructional Time

The more time students spend in learning, the more they learn. A strong relationship exists between the amount of time allocated to academics—the amount of time students engage in academic tasks—and achievement. Instructional time is the actual time teachers provide direct instruction to their students. The less instructional time (absences, transitional activities, nonacademic activities) students receive, the less students achieve academically (Rieth, Polsgrove, & Semmel, 1979). When achievement is a concern, even quality of instruction may be a less important variable than instructional time.

How much instructional time do students receive at school? Rosenshine (1980) categorized classroom activities into three broad types: academic (reading, mathematics, science, social studies), nonacademic (music, art, physical education, story time, sharing), and noninstructional (transitions before and after breaks, housekeeping tasks, waiting). Although this study included only average elementary students (bright and slow students were not included), the results (presented in Table 1.3) reveal how much instruction does and does not occur in many regular education classroom settings.

On the average, 58% of the school day is allocated to academic activities, 23% to nonacademic activities, and 19% to noninstructional activities. More time allocated for academics does not lead to less engagement time (attention-to-task) from students. Teachers who scheduled more time for instruction did not see their students tire or become less interested in academic tasks. There does not seem to be a correlation between more work time and students' drop in attention. Rosenshine also found seatwork to be the predominate form of instruction (66% for reading and 75% for math), and student engagement time is less for seatwork assignments than for teacher-led activities.

Other studies report less instructional time occurring in classrooms than Rosenshine found. For example, Rieth, Polsgrove, and Semmel (1979) discuss studies where academic responding time was extremely low. In one study, fifth-graders spent less than eight minutes responding orally or in writing to questions asked by the teacher or on written exercises or tests. In contrast,

Table 1.3
Instructional Time in Elementary Schools

CATEGORY	GRADE 2		GRADE 5	
	Time Allotted	*Time Engaged*	*Time Allotted*	*Time Engaged*
Overall academics	2'15"	1'30"	2'50"	1'55"
Reading	1'30"	1'04"	1'50"	1'20"
Mathematics	36"	26"	44"	35"
Nonacademics	55"		1'50"	
Noninstructional	44"		45"	

Source: Adapted from Rosenshine (1980).

students spent more than 50% of class time engaged in transitional activities. In another study they cited, inner-city students averaged no more than twenty seconds in directed reading per day. Thurlow et al. (1983) found that students spend about 45 minutes per day in academic responding. These findings are worrisome. If students are to learn academic material, they must respond to the material. How can students learn to read, if given neither the opportunity to do so, nor direct guided instruction aimed at improving reading skills?

In special education, the amount of instructional time also relates to the amount of time the teacher has to spend teaching. Sargent (1981) conducted an interesting time-utilization study to determine how resource teachers spent their school day. The results are found in Table 1.4.

Table 1.4
Mean Percentages for Time Use Variables

DAILY ACTIVITY	ESTIMATED TIME USED	ESTIMATED TIME NEEDED	MEASURED TIME USE
Direct instruction	63.67	69.86	51.48
Consulting with staff	7.13	10.93	8.51
Consulting with parents	3.73	7.71	3.6
Conducting inservice	1.25	4.08	0
Preparation for instruction	12.08	17.6	16.38
Staffings	5.05	6.45	2.8
Assessment and evaluation	7.68	13.83	8.82
Work with IEPs	5.92	9.15	1.38
Record keeping	5.38	7.72	3.77
General school duties	3.1	3.6	9.22

Source: L. R. Sargent (1981). "Resource teacher time utilization: An observational study," *Exceptional Children, 47,* 422. Used with permission.

It appears that the demands on resource room teachers extend beyond classroom instruction. If they spend only 51% of their time on instruction, and some of that time is lost to noninstructional and nonacademic activities, the amount of time their students engage in academic learning might be very small. Students with special needs require more direct instruction than their normal counterparts and might be receiving less because of their teachers' other duties and their own tendencies to disrupt more and pay less attention to academic tasks. Clearly, teachers must set as a goal for all students an increase in instructional time allocation and engagement. To accomplish this will require a restructuring of the school day and reallocating more time for instruction.

Direct Instruction

Just as students need to be taught for them to learn, they need to be taught well for efficient learning to occur. Classrooms where the principles of direct instruction are used can be typified as being academically focused where instructional objectives are sequenced and ordered, task oriented, using materials that are sequenced and structured, setting clear goals for the students, and continuously monitoring student performance. All these principles are incorporated throughout this text. It is important to recognize that direct instruction is not only logically sound, but has been verified through research and practice. In particular, the Follow-Through Project compared many different educational models (Rosenshine, 1979; Rhine, 1981). The results indicated that the direct and behavioral models proved far superior in student achievement.

Direct instruction incorporates the systematic application of a variety of instructional techniques and tactics (see Chapters 4 and 7 for reviews). It requires ongoing evaluation of student performance to ensure that the educational procedures scheduled are effective for each student (see Chapter 3). It involves careful identification of students' skills and entry behaviors (stages of learning) and encourages individually tailored programs (see Chapter 2) for each child. Direct instruction involves teacher-directed activities with controlled practice, active learner responses, and opportunities for high success. Within the direct instruction model, several instructional techniques characterize the model.

Teachers using direct instruction tend to use praise, reinforcement, corrective feedback, modeling, and precise instructions. They tend to set clear goals and objectives for their students. They select instructional procedures and materials that maximize active student involvement. Finally, these teachers make educational decisions based on data gathered on a frequent basis from students interacting with the curriculum.

Individualized Instruction

Research evidence (Bloom, 1984) is clear: one-to-one instruction is far superior to group methods. Individualized instruction does not require students to work alone or in pairs. It does, however, require students who are grouped to be at the same entry level (or stage of learning). In other words, grouped students need to have the same prerequisite knowledge. It does imply that instruction programs are tailor-made for each student.

Individualized instruction is not unsupervised or guided independent study; rather, it is instruction planned for and delivered based on where the student is in the curriculum. Individualized instruction not only matches students with the specific topic of instruction but also with teaching tactics that have the highest probability of success based on the students' previous success with a particular intervention or their stage of learning. Typically, to use individualized instruction, educators use structured, task-analyzed curricula. The student is carefully placed in the curriculum through a process of curriculum-based assessments where students' exact skills and knowledge are identified. Throughout this book, ways to implement individualized instruction are discussed.

SUMMARY

The educational system is required, by law, to provide students with handicaps an appropriate education. The ultimate questions are these: What constitutes an appropriate education for an individual? and Where can that education best be delivered? Today, professionals and parents from both special and regular education are debating these issues. Regardless of the debate, there can be no uniform answers. Students with special needs are unique and different from each other. They possess different learning styles, abilities, and characteristics.

Students with special needs frequently profit best from individualized instructional programs that account for such differences. For many of these students, it is only through total individualization that they can receive an appropriate education. Others require individualized instruction for only one academic area. An important consideration as individualized educational programs are planned is the student's entry level. Determining the stage of learning a student is in for a particular task or skill can help teachers select teaching tactics that have the highest probability of success. Considering these stages also helps teachers remember that simply acquiring a skill is not the complete mastery necessary for integrated use of that skill.

Where students with special needs should receive their education is of great concern. This must be determined from data about where the student learns best. One factor to consider is whether the student can cope with the demands of the regular education setting or whether the setting can be modified to suit his or her needs. Before placing students, teachers must determine whether students can meet the behavioral and academic expectations of the environment.

The teachers who provide special education must possess many special skills and competencies. They must be proficient in using the critical teaching skills discussed in this chapter. They must use their instructional time efficiently, and must match their language to the students abilities to understand oral and written communication. Other skills, however, extend beyond teaching. Today, teachers must be able to work collaboratively with educators and professionals from other disciplines, and they must be able to form partnerships with parents. Special educators face many demands on their time and expertise, but their most important task is ensuring that each student with a handicap receives the best education possible.

STUDY AND DISCUSSION QUESTIONS

1. List some of the common characteristics of students with special needs. Discuss how these characteristics influence how instruction should be planned for them.
2. Discuss the stages-of-learning theory and how it relates to educational programming.
3. Describe the relationship between disruption and academic learning.
4. List five skills that you believe are critical for teachers to possess. Explain why you believe that these are the most important.
5. Describe the main components of direct instruction.

REFERENCES AND SUGGESTED READINGS

Learner Characteristics

KEOGH, B. K. (1983). Individual differences in temperament—A contribution to the personal, social, and education competence of learning disabled children. In J. D. McKinney and L. Feagans (eds.). *Current topics in learning disabilities.* Norwood, NJ: Ablex.

SCHUMAKER, J. B., SHELDON-WILDGEN, J. S., & SHERMAN, J. A. (1982). Social interaction of learning disabled junior high students in their classrooms: An observational analysis. *Journal of Learning Disabilities, 15,* 355–358.

Learned Helplessness and Attribution

APONIK, D. A., & DEMBO, M. (1983). LD and normal adolescents' causal attributions of success and failure at different levels of task difficulty. *Learning Disability Quarterly, 6,* 31–39.

BORKOWSKI, J. G., WEYHING, R. S., & TURNER, L. A. (1986). Attributional retraining and the teaching of strategies. *Exceptional Children, 53,* 130–137.

CANINO, F. J. (1981). Learned-helplessness theory: Implications for research in learning disabilities. *Journal of Special Education, 15,* 471–484.

ELLIS, E. S. (1986). The role of motivation and pedagogy on the generalization of cognitive strategy training. *Journal of Learning Disabilities, 19,* 66–70.

GRIMES, L. (1981). Learned helplessness and attribution theory: Redefining children's learning problems. *Learning Disability Quarterly, 4,* 92–100.

KLEINHAMMER-TRAMILL, P. J., TRAMILL, J. L., SCHREPEL, S. N., & DAVIS, S. F. (1983). Learned helplessness in learning disabled adolescents as a function of noncontingent rewards. *Learning Disability Quarterly, 6,* 61–66.

PALMER, D. J., DRUMMOND, F., TOLLISON, P., & ZINKGRAFF, S. (1982). An attributional investigation of performance outcomes for learning-disabled and normal-achieving pupils. *Journal of Special Education, 16,* 207–219.

PEARL, R. (1982). LD children's attributions for success and failure: A replication with a labeled LD sample. *Learning Disability Quarterly, 5,* 173–176.

PEARL, R., BRYAN, T., & HERZOG, A. (1983). Learning disabled and nondisabled children's strategy analyses under high and low success conditions. *Learning Disability Quarterly, 6,* 67–74.

PFLAUM, S. W., & PASCARELLA, E. T. (1982). Attribution retraining for learning disabled students: Some thoughts on the practical implications of the evidence. *Learning Disability Quarterly, 5,* 422–426.

TOLLEFSON, N., TRACY, D. B., JOHNSEN, E. P., BUENNING, M., FARMER, A., & BARKE, C. R. (1982). Attribution patterns of learning disabled adolescents. *Learning Disability Quarterly, 5,* 14–20.

Inactive Learning

KOSIEWICZ, M. M., HALLAHAN, D. P., LLOYD, J. (1981). The effects of an LD student's treatment choice on handwriting performance. *Learning Disability Quarterly, 4,* 281–286.

LENZ, B. K., ALLEY, G. R., & SCHUMAKER, J. B. (1987). Activating the inactive learner: Advance organizers in the secondary content classroom. *Learning Disability Quarterly, 10,* 53–67.

TORGESEN, J. K. (1982). The learning disabled child as an inactive learner: Educational implications. *Topics in Learning and Learning Disabilities, 2,* 45–52.

TORGESEN, J. K., & LICHT, B. G. (1983). The learning disabled child as an inactive learner: Retrospect and prospects. In J. D. McKinney & F. Feagans (eds.), *Current topics in learning disabilities,* Vol. 1. Norwood, NJ: Ablex.

WONG, B. Y. L., & JONES, W. (1982). Increasing metacomprehension in learning disabled and normally achieving students through self-questioning training. *Learning Disability Quarterly, 5,* 228–240.

Attention

PELHAM, W. E. (1981). Attention deficits in hyperactive and learning-disabled children. *Exceptional Education Quarterly, 2,* 13–23.

TARVER, S. G. (1981). Underselective attention in learning-disabled children: Some reconceptualizations of old hypotheses. *Exceptional Education Quarterly, 2,* 25–35.

TORGESEN, J. K. (1981). The relationship between memory and attention in learning disabilities. *Exceptional Education Quarterly, 2,* 51–59.

WALKER, N. W. (1985). Impulsivity in learning disabled children: Past research findings and methodological inconsistencies. *Learning Disability Quarterly, 8,* 85–94.

Stages of Learning

AYLLON, T., & AZRIN, N. H. (1964). Reinforcement and instruction with mental patients. *Journal of the Experimental Analysis of Behavior, 7,* 327–331.

BRUNI, J. V. (1982). Problem solving for the primary grades. *Arithmetic Teacher, 29*(6), 10–15.

DESHLER, D. D., ALLEY, G. R., WARNER, M. M., & SCHUMAKER, J. B. (1981). Instructional practices for promoting skill acquisition and generalization in severely learning disabled adolescents. *Learning Disability Quarterly, 4,* 415–421.

GARNETT, K., & FLEISCHNER, J. E. (1983). Automatization and basic fact performance of normal and learning disabled children. *Learning Disability Quarterly, 6,* 223–230.

HARING, N. G., LIBERTY, K. A., & WHITE, O. R. (1981). *Field initiated studies: An investigation of phases of learning and facilitating instructional events for the severely/profoundly handicapped.* Final Project Report, Project No. 443CH70564, Grant No: G007500593. Washington, DC: Bureau for the Education of the Handicapped.

HOPKINS, B. L. (1968). Effects of candy and social reinforcement, instructions, and reinforcement schedule learning on the modification and maintenance of smiling. *Journal of Applied Behavior Analysis, 1,* 121–129.

NAGEL, D. R., SCHUMAKER, J. B., & DESHLER, D. D. (1986). *Learning strategies curriculum: The FIRST-letter mnemonic strategy.* Lawrence, KS: Excel Enterprises.

SMITH, D. D., & LOVITT, T. C. (1976). The differential effects of reinforcement contingencies on arithmetic performance. *Journal of Learning Disabilities, 9,* 11–29.

Social Skills and Disruption (also see Chapters 4 and 5)

AYLLON, T., & ROBERTS, M. D. (1974). Eliminating discipline problems by strengthening academic performance. *Journal of Applied Behavior Analysis, 7,* 71–76.

DRABMAN, R. S., & PATTERSON, J. N. (1981). Disruptive behavior and the social standing of exceptional children. *Exceptional Education Quarterly, 1,* 45–55.

EPSTEIN, M. H., & CULLINAN, D. (1983). Academic performance of behaviorally disordered and learning disabled pupils. *The Journal of Special Education, 17,* 304–307.

FERRITOR, D. E., BUCKHOLDT, D., HAMBLIN, R. L., & SMITH, L. (1972). The non-effects of contingent reinforcement for attending on work accomplished. *Journal of Applied Behavior Analysis, 5,* 7–17.

SMITH, D. D. (1984). *Effective discipline.* Austin, TX: Pro-Ed.

Characteristics of the Learning Environment

LINK, D. P. (1980). *Essential learning skills and the low achieving student at the secondary level: A rating of the importance of 24 academic abilities.* Unpublished master's thesis. Lawrence: University of Kansas Institute for Research in Learning Disabilities.

MORAN, M. R. (1980). *An investigation of the demands on oral language skills of learning disabled students in secondary classrooms* (Research Report No. 1). Lawrence: University of Kansas Institute for Research in Learning Disabilities.

ROBINSON, S. M., BRAXDALE, C. T., & COLSON, S. E. (1985). Preparing dysfunctional learners to enter junior high school: A transitional curriculum. *Focus on Exceptional Children, 18,* 1–12.

SCHUMAKER, J. B., & DESHLER, D. D. (1984). Setting demand variables: A major factor in program planning for LD adolescents. *Topics in Language Disorders, 4,* 22–44.

SCHUMAKER, J. B., DESHLER, D. D., ALLEY, G. R., & WARNER, M. M. (1983). Toward the development of an intervention model for learning disabled adolescents: The University of Kansas Institute. *Exceptional Education Quarterly, 4,* 45–74.

Teacher Skills

CENTRA, J. A., & POTTER, D. A. (1980). School and teacher effects: An interrelational model. *Review of Educational Research, 50,* 273–291.

DESHLER, D. D., & SCHUMAKER, J. B. (1986). Learning strategies: An instructional alternative for low-achieving students. *Exceptional Children, 52,* 583–590.

HELLER, H. W. (1983). Special education professional standards: Need, value, and use. *Exceptional Children, 50,* 199–228.

HUDSON, P. J., MORSINK, C. V., BRANSCUM, G., & BOONE, R. (1987). Competencies for teachers of students with learning disabilities. *Journal of Learning Disabilities, 20,* 232–236.

KEA, C. D. (1987). An analysis of critical teaching behaviors as applied by secondary special education teachers. Chicago: Presentation, Council for Exceptional Children's Annual Convention.

NATIONAL JOINT COMMITTEE ON LEARNING DISABILITIES. (1987). Learning disabilities: Issues in the preparation of professional personnel. *Journal of Learning Disabilities, 20,* 229–231.

NEWCOMER, P. L. (1982). Competencies for professional in learning disabilities. *Learning Disability Quarterly, 5,* 241–252.

ROSENSHINE, B. V. (1979). Content, time, and direct instruction. In P. L. Peterson and H. J. Walberg, *Research on teaching: Concepts, findings and implications.* Berkeley, CA: McCutchan.

ROSENSHINE, B. V. (1983). Teaching functions in instructional programs. *The Elementary School Journal, 83,* 335–351.

TEACHER EDUCATION DIVISION, COUNCIL FOR EXCEPTIONAL CHILDREN (1986). *The val-*

idation of quality practices in personnel preparation for special education. Reston, VA: Council for Exceptional Children.

Effective Schools

LINDSEY, R. B. (1984). *Effective schools.* Unpublished manuscript. Los Angeles: Region D, Los Angeles Unified School District.

MACKENZIE, D. E. (1983). Research for school improvement: An appraisal of some recent trends. *Educational Researcher, 12,* 5–17.

ROWAN, B. (1983). Research on effective schools: A cautionary note. *Educational Researcher, 12,* 24–31.

Computer Literacy and Use

BLACKHURST, E. (1984). *Functions, competencies, and tasks to be developed in the special education microcomputer training program.* Lexington: Special Education Department, University of Kentucky.

COSDEN, M. A., GERBER, M. M., SEMMEL, D. S., GOLDMAN, S. R., & SEMMEL, M. I. (1987). Microcomputer use within micro-educational environments. *Exceptional Children, 53,* 399–409.

GOLDMAN, S. R., & PELLEGRINO, J. W. (1987). Information processing and educational microcomputer technology: Where do we go from here? *Journal of Learning Disabilities, 20,* 144–154.

GOLDMAN, S. R., SEMMEL, D. S., COSDEN, M. A., GERBER, M. M., & SEMMEL, M. I. (1987). Special education administrators' policies and practices on microcomputer acquisition, allocation, and access for mildly handicapped children: Interfaces with regular education. *Exceptional Children, 53,* 330–339.

LIEBER, J., & SEMMEL, M. I. (1985). Effectiveness of computer application to instruction with mildly handicapped: A review. *Remedial and Special Education, 6,* 5–12.

Parent Involvement

KROTH, R. L. (1985). *Communicating with parents of exceptional children* (2nd ed.). Denver: Love.

KROTH, R. L., OLSON, J., & KROTH, J. (1986). Delivering sensitive information (or, please don't kill the messenger!). *Counseling and Human Development, 18,* 1–11.

Consultation

BROWN, D., WYNE, M. D., BLACKBURN, J. E., & POWELL, W. C. (1979). *Consultation: Strategy for improving education.* Boston: Allyn & Bacon.

CAPLAN, G. (1970). *The theory and practice of mental health consultation.* New York: Basic Books.

HAWISHER, M. F., & CALHOUN, M. L. (1978). *The resource room: An educational asset for children with special needs.* Columbus, Ohio: Merrill.

IDOL-MAESTAS, L. (1983). *Special educator's consultation handbook.* Rockville, MD: Aspen Press.

IDOL, L., PAOLUCCI-WHITCOMB, P., & NEVIN, A. (1986). *Collaborative consultation.* Rockville, MD: Aspen Press.

PARSONS, R. D., & MEYERS, J. (1984). *Developing consultation skills.* San Francisco: Jossey-Bass.

ROSENFIELD, S., & RUBINSON, F. (1985). Introducing curriculum-based assessment through consultation. *Council for Exceptional Children, 52,* 282–287.

WIEDERHOLT, J. L., HAMMILL, D. D., & BROWN, V. (1978). *The resource teacher.* Boston: Allyn & Bacon.

Effective Teaching

BICKEL, W. E., & BICKEL, D. D. (1986). Effective schools, classrooms, and instruction: Implications for special education. *Exceptional Children, 52,* 489–500.

MORSINK, C. V., SOAR, R. S., SOAR, R. M., & THOMAS, R. (1986). Research on teaching: Opening the door to special education classrooms. *Exceptional Children, 53,* 32–40.

Instructional Time

KAVALE, K., & FORNESS, S. R. (1986). School learning, time and learning disabilities: The disassociated learner. *Journal of Learning Disabilities, 19,* 130–138.

RIETH, H. J., POLSGROVE, L., & SEMMEL, M. I. (1979). Relationship between instructional time and academic achievement: Implications for research and practice. *Education Unlimited, 1,* 53–56.

RIETH, H. J., POLSGROVE, L., & SEMMEL, M. I. (1981). Instructional variables that make a difference: Attention to task and beyond. *Exceptional Education Quarterly, 2,* 61–71.

ROSENSHINE, B. V. (1979). Content, time, and direct instruction. In P. L. Peterson and H. J. Walberg, *Research on teaching: Concepts, findings and implications.* Berkeley, CA: McCutchan.

ROSENSHINE, B. V. (1980). How time is spent in elementary classrooms. In C. Denham and A. Lieberman, *Time to learn.* Washington, DC: National Institute of Education.

SARGENT, L. R. (1981). Resource teacher time utilization: An observational study. *Exceptional Children, 47,* 420–425.

THURLOW, M., GRADEN, J., GREENER, J., & YSSELDYKE, J. (1983). LD and non-LD student's opportunities to learn. *Learning Disability Quarterly, 6,* 172–183.

Direct Instruction

ELLIS, E. S. (1986). The role of motivation and pedagogy on the generalization of cognitive strategy training. *Journal of Learning Disabilities, 19,* 66–70.

HARING, N. G., & GENTRY, N. D. (1976). Direct and individualized instructional procedures. In N. G. Haring and R. L. Schiefelbusch (eds.), *Teaching special children.* New York: McGraw-Hill.

RHINE, W. R. (1981). *Making schools more effective: New directions from follow through.* New York: Academic Press.

RIETH, H. J., POLSGROVE, L., & SEMMEL, M. I. (1981). Instructional variables that make a difference: Attention to task and beyond. *Exceptional Education Quarterly, 2,* 61–71.

ROSENSHINE, B. V. (1979). Content, time, and direct instruction. In P. L. Peterson and H. J. Walberg, *Research on teaching: Concepts, findings and implications.* Berkeley, CA: McCutchan.

WHITE, O. R. (1986). Precision teaching—Precision learning. *Exceptional Children, 52,* 522–534.

Individualizing Instruction

ALBERTO, P., JOBES, N., SIZEMORE, A., & DORAN, D. (1980). A comparison of individual and group instruction across response tasks. *Journal of the Severely Handicapped, 5,* 285–293.

BLOOM, B. (1984). The 2 Sigma problem: The search for methods of group instruction as effective as one-to-one tutoring. *Educational Researcher, 6,* 4–16.

HARING, N. G., & GENTRY, N. D. (1976). Direct and individualized instructional procedures. In N. G. Haring and R. L. Schiefelbusch (eds.), *Teaching special children.* New York: McGraw-Hill.

KNOWLES, C. J., AUFDERHEIDE, S. K., & McKENZIE, T. (1982). Relationship of individualized teaching strategies to academic learning time for mainstreamed handicapped and nonhandicapped students. *The Journal of Special Education, 16,* 450–456.

2

The Individual Educational Program Process

In 1975 Congress enacted Public Law 94-142, The Education for All Handicapped Children Act, and reaffirmed this law in 1986 through Public Law 99-457, The Education of the Handicapped Act Amendments. These laws entitle all youngsters with handicaps to an appropriate education and include many safeguards with the aim of providing the best educational services possible to students with handicaps. The implications of these laws are far-reaching and have direct impact on the entire educational system. They have changed drastically traditional roles and responsibilities of parent and school personnel (administrators, diagnosticians, counselors, and teachers).

P.L. 94-142 requires that all handicapped children and youth from ages 3 to 21 be provided with appropriate educational services. P.L. 99-457 adds provisions for educational funding to parents and their children who are between the ages of birth and 3 years. These laws require that each state submit documented evidence that efforts were made to locate every handicapped preschool and school-aged person in each state. The laws state that every handicapped student is entitled to participate in activities enjoyed by nonhandicapped youngsters (transportation, counseling, recreation, physical education, employment, special interest groups, athletics, and clubs). Also, they require that before placement in special education and related services, youngsters receive full, nondiscriminatory, individual evaluations (tests administered in the child's native language by properly trained personnel).

For every school-aged student identified as handicapped, an *individual educational program (IEP)* must be developed, implemented, and evaluated. For each

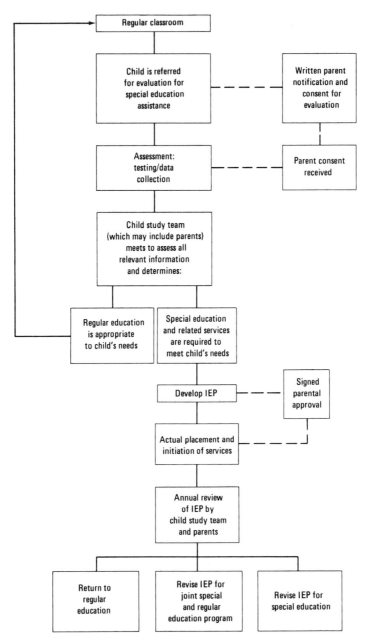

Figure 2.1 Flow chart for the individualized education program process.

preschooler under the age of 3, the *individualized family service plan* (*IFSP*) must include instruction for the child and the family. A role for parents is included in these IFSPs, so they can be active and knowledgeable in assisting in their child's progress. The components of the IEP and IFSP are specified in the law, as are the steps to follow that qualify youngsters for these special services. The IEP necessitates the writing of a set of goals and objectives for each student, as well as meetings with teachers, parents, and other school officials. Also, a check-and-balance system is guaranteed by the option of due process hearings that may be initiated by either parents or school officials. When properly implemented, the individualized educational program process results in improved educational programs for all handicapped students.

To be able to fulfill the requirements of P.L. 94-142 and 99-456 and implement the IEP process, teachers must not only be knowledgeable about the process, but also must possess specific knowledge (assessment instruments and procedures, curriculum content) and skills (writing behavioral goals and objectives, conducting task analyses). Therefore, this chapter provides information about the IEP process, how to write an IEP, and the skills needed to complete these activities.

The IEP process specifies procedures to be followed by school personnel from the initial referral for special educational services to the evaluation of services provided to those eligible for them. The flow chart found in Figure 2.1 illustrates the steps and intended sequence of the IEP process required by the law.

REFERRAL

Children are referred for special education services in a variety of ways for a variety of reasons. Not every student referred qualifies for assistance from specially trained personnel. Although some might argue that all children should receive the benefits of special education (reduced class size, individualized instruction), these services are expensive and are intended for those who are handicapped. Some parents know that their child will need special education before that child starts school (for example, parents of students with severe handicaps). Preschoolers whose language development is delayed usually are identified as potential students for the speech and language therapist before kindergarten. However, most students who receive special services are referred initially by the regular classroom teacher. Sometimes the referral occurs very early in a student's academic career; other times, referral does not occur until middle elementary grades. Although not as common, some students are not identified until mid- or high school, when the curricular and setting demands become most difficult.

The referring teacher notifies the principal and the special services committee about a student who is having difficulties in school. This special services committee, sometimes referred to as the appraisal and review committee or the child study team, should be composed of relevant school personnel. Permanent committee members should be the school's special education resource room teacher(s), principal, counselor, and school psychologist. Rotating members are the child's classroom teacher, the child's parents, and the social service agency representatives who deal with the child and the family. If, after consultation, the committee decides that a formal evaluation of a referred student is warranted, a written notification of the referral and request for permission to evaluate is sent to the child's parents.

The primary referring agent, usually the regular classroom teacher, should indicate to the special services committee the reasons for the referral and provide some data or justification. Information from general screening instruments, from classroom academic performance in relation to classmates, and from observations about social behavior problems should accompany a written request for referral. After reviewing the referral request and considering other information from additional school personnel (supplemental service teachers such as the physical education teacher, the music teacher, or the art teacher), the special service committee may decide that a formal evaluation or assessment is necessary.

DIAGNOSIS

Because special education is expensive and is intended for those students whose handicap requires a specially designed program of instruction, students must qualify for these services. There is a range of special services available. Some students need only limited, special support services (speech or language therapy, adapted physical education) and can remain with their class for a regular academic education. Others require intensive educational and social programs that utilize the expertise of many highly trained specialists.

Currently, most diagnostic information relies heavily on standardized tests. Although there continues to be considerable debate about the appropriateness and usefulness of standardized assessment instruments, the major issues are not resolved, and traditional testing procedures are used nationally. It is important for all special educators to know about traditional assessment instruments and procedures, whether they believe in their merits or not. If teachers are to be active, participating members in the IEP process, they must be cognizant of commonly used evaluation methods, their purposes, and appropriate uses. (See references and suggested readings section for more detailed information.)

Purposes of Assessment

There are many different categories of diagnostic tests and procedures. Each of these is used in one or several ways to identify and serve students who are handicapped. Within the IEP process these assessments might be used for referral, identification, classification, placement, instructional decision making, or program evaluation.

In most states, for students to be placed in special education classrooms, they must meet their state's standards for a particular categorical classification (learning disabilities, behavioral disorders, mental retardation, visually impaired, hearing impaired). For example, to qualify for services from a learning disabilities teacher, the student must (1) be of average or above-average intelligence, (2) be behind academically (often specified as two or more years behind), and (3) be without physical impairments, retardation, or severe behavioral disorder. Many states also include a fourth category specifying that a student must be weak in any one or a combination of psychological processes such as memory, auditory processing, visual processing, or conceptualization.

Therefore, for these students, tests of various types are included in their diagnostic batteries: intelligence, overall academic achievement (and usually several specific achievement tests), acuity, and often learning style. For students with mental retardation, adaptive behavior scales are also included, and for students with learning disabilities a classroom observation often is a required component of the identification process.

To assist in placement decisions, many school districts now also require that direct and daily measurements (curriculum-based assessments) be included. These are very useful for instructional decision making and are discussed later in this chapter and throughout this text. Some (Meyen & Lehr, 1980) also suggest that students' educational histories (previous placements, procedures that were effective, class sizes) be used as data that contribute to placement decisions. Once all the assessment information is collected, the special services committee must evaluate its completeness. If further data are needed, they may request additional testing or referral to other diagnostic specialists (for example, the medical profession).

After a complete formal assessment, many students return to the regular education program and do not receive specialized services because they do not meet the qualifications. For students identified as handicapped, however, placement decisions must be made. A variety of service delivery options are available in most school districts: itinerant teachers, resource rooms, and partially self-contained and self-contained classrooms. The special services team decides what kind of service delivery option is most suitable for each student, and what additional special services are required for the implementation of a complete and appropriate educational program. For example, many students require specialized assistance from language developmentalists or recreational therapists. The appropriateness of these services to the student's educational needs must be considered. If warranted, they must be guaranteed.

The student's parents must be informed of the evaluation results and the ensuing decisions and recommendations about their child's educational program. Parents are to be included in the IEP meeting (at which their child's individual education program for the academic year is developed). They must be notified of the date, place, and time of the meeting. If they cannot attend, parent conferences, telephone calls, and home meetings may be used instead. In most cases, parents and schools are in agreement and share their concerns and program recommendations. Parents do have the right to challenge the committee's evaluation or program recommendations. In instances where agreement cannot be reached between the two parties, a due process hearing may be called; decisions are then made by an impartial hearing officer.

The Assessment Debate

Critics (Ysseldyke, 1986; Ysseldyke, Algozzine, & Epps, 1983) of standardized diagnostic tests cite many reasons for their dissatisfaction with traditional assessment methods. Many tests are discriminatory, and their results are biased toward youngsters from affluent backgrounds and against those from multicultural or bilingual families.

Standardized test scores represent typical (or expected) growth patterns of students from different geographical regions. For example, when a student's pre- and postperformance on a standardized achievement test is evaluated, a comparison can be made between that individual's past and present performances. The scores are evaluated against an often ambiguous national norm or average. If, according to a test's scoring system, a student gained only eight months over a period of a year, some would say that the student was behind and did not progress according to expectations on the material tested. Certainly the student did not progress as much as the nation's average student. If, however, an entire school district's average growth rate for that period of time was only eight months, then, our sample student's growth rate was equal to the growth rate of the peer group.

Caution must be taken when evaluating student progress against the national norm. In one school district, a learning disabilities "epidemic" raged. Close examination of all students' scores determined that the district's average was two years behind the national norm. Therefore, all those children two years "behind" actually were "average," and only those children four years below the national average should have been considered for assistance from the learning disabilities specialists because of severe academic deficiencies.

Also, Ysseldyke (Ysseldyke et al., 1983; Ysseldyke et al., 1982) believes that diagnostic tests do not guarantee accurate identification of those who are handicapped and those who are not. His findings indicate that regular education teachers refer students who bother them to diagnosticians who then find ways to classify students as handicapped so they can receive special education services or be removed from the regular education classroom. The entire diagnostic process also has been criticized on the basis of cost-effectiveness. Some school districts may even spend more money in the referral, identification, and placement process than they do educating students in classrooms.

The debate about assessments of school-aged children has raged for years. At the center are some important issues: What is the purpose of the diagnosis? Who should do the diagnosis? Who should interpret the results of the diagnosis? Does testing violate a child's right to privacy? What is a nondiscriminatory test? Quick and easy answers to these questions are not available. Interpretations of the meanings of these questions and their implications vary from school district to school district and state department of education to state department of education. One gauge or perspective, however, can be offered for the testing issue: Standardized tests can only be justified if they are useful to the school system, the teacher, the parent, *and* the child.

INSTRUCTIONAL DECISION MAKING

Once students are identified as handicapped and are declared eligible for special education, decisions must be made regarding the educational program that they will receive. The IEP requires that goals and objectives be specified for every special service that each student will receive. The student's yearly instructional program needs to be specified and sequenced. The student's performance levels should be stated in detail. Rather than merely indicating students' scores on achievement tests, information about their exact performance in classroom materials should be provided. The IEP also requires evaluation of students' programs and the instructional interventions used to promote academic and social growth (see Chapter 3). The following, then, are some of the prerequisite skills teachers must possess before they approach the task of initiating the IEP process.

Behavioral Goals and Objectives

For more than two decades, teachers have specified the desired products of their instruction in terms of child-change information. Instruction is more efficient and coordination of services is facilitated when goals and objectives are specified. Behavioral goals usually are global and are composed of specific objectives. The crucial elements of any behavioral statements are precise wording and outcomes described in such a way that reliable measurement and evaluation are guaranteed. Therefore, the behavior must be defined precisely and in observable terms with criteria for mastery noted. An example of a poor behavioral goal is: "Johnny and his classmates will like each other better." Although worthy, this statement is not precise, is not suitable for reliable measurement, and does not include a provision for mastery. Without more specificity, independent observers will not be able to measure or collect data on the behavior of interest. Table 2.1 provides a list of behavioral goals and objectives that are stated appropriately and include mastery or criteria statements.

Task Analysis

For instruction to be efficient, behavioral goals and objectives must be sequenced; that is, their order of presentation must be determined. Lists of goals and objectives can be helpful to teachers as they decide what will constitute students' instructional programs. Without a sequence, however, no indication is available regarding *when* an objective becomes the target of instruction. The purpose of a task analysis is to determine the priority of goals and objectives and provide a plan for the sequence of instruction.

Table 2.1
Behavioral Goals and Objectives

Overall goal: to understand and use time
Immediate goal: to tell time using a standard clockface with arabic numerals

ABBREVIATED OBJECTIVE	BEHAVIORAL STATEMENT		CRITERION
Hand discrimination	2.01 The student is able to point to and name both the hour and minute hand	2.01	with 100% accuracy within 15 seconds
Hour hand	2.02 The student is able to identify all hour hand placements	2.02	with 100% accuracy
	2.02.01 The student is able to identify the hour for exact hour hand placements	(.01–	within 10
	2.02.02 The student is able to identify the hour for any hour hand placement	.02)	seconds
Minute hand	2.03 The student is able to identify all minute placements	2.03	with 100%
	2.03.01 The student is able to identify the minute for minute hand placements on any interval of five	(.01–	accuracy
	2.03.02 The student is able to identify the minute for exact minute hand placements	.03)	within 10 seconds
	2.03.03 The student is able to identify fractions of hours using the minute hand (e.g., quarter after)		
Combination of hour and minute hand	2.04 The student is able to identify the correct time using both the hour and minute hand	2.04	with 100% accuracy
	2.04.01 The student is able to identify the time for the "o'clock" times	(.01–	within 10
	2.04.02 The student can identify the time for all intervals of five	.04)	seconds
	2.04.03 The student is able to identify the exact time		
	2.04.04 The student can identify the time for fractions of the hour		

Teachers do not have to conduct task analyses for every skill they teach. In fact, valuable teacher time should not be spent conducting unnecessary task analyses. For students who profit from the standard mathematics sequences used as outlines for elementary basal texts, the sequence of instruction already is determined through the combined efforts of researchers and professionals from that discipline. In some cases, the mathematics textbook does not include an area that particular students need to master. For example, the use and understanding of time is a very important area, often neglected or inadequately programmed in mathematics texts. In such instances, teachers should search for already available instructional materials. Only if appropriate instructional programs are not available should teachers create their own sequences and materials. The time and expertise involved in the development of good instructional materials often is far beyond what an already busy teacher can justify expending.

Teacher-made task analyses are necessary at other times also. Sometimes, instructional programs are available for every goal and objective necessary for a particular student. For example, a program was found for each mathematics area identified for instruction for an entire academic year (computation, time telling, change making, and problem solving). After considerable searching, the teacher located twenty specific instructional programs. Because they were from a variety of sources, the order in which they should be taught had to be determined by conducting a task analysis.

There are various ways to structure the task analysis process. Some processes specify the interventions to be used as well as the sequence of instruction to follow when teaching a skill. Some systems are quite complex and complicated. For the purpose of guiding teachers in their instructional planning, simple systems that provide an outline or blueprint of the instructional sequence is sufficient. When sequencing instructional units, for example, only a skeletal outline of the proposed ordering of objectives is necessary. When developing an IEP, the teacher should flush out behavioral goals and objectives from the abbreviated outline found in the task analysis.

The Lattice System

The lattice system was originated by Myron Woolman in 1962 to organize training activities for the military. Later, teachers and researchers (Bricker, 1972; Smith, Smith, & Edgar, 1976; Smith & Snell, 1978) found the lattice system useful for organizing and sequencing educational activities. A procedural lattice diagramming the technical steps followed to construct a lattice is shown in Figure 2.2.

The lattice system requires the graphic display of the instructional sequence. To use the lattice system for task analysis, the teacher requires some knowledge of the rules for this system plus competence in the subject matter. The teacher first identifies the skill to be developed as precisely and specifically as possible. The words used need not be as complete or thorough as those used in behavioral objective statements, but the implied intent must be recognizable to the users. The entry behaviors (those prerequisite skills expected of the student before the instructional program is initiated) must be specified. The actual skill to be taught is then broken down into small teaching units or component parts. This is accomplished by having the person conducting the task analysis execute the steps identified over and over until the sequence is crystallized.

Once the cell components (the precise behaviors the task or skill is composed of) are identified, the lattice is constructed. The terminal behavior (the achievement of the goal) is stated concisely and placed in a box or cell in the far right-hand corner. The major subgoals leading to the completion of the terminal behavior are placed in the ridgeline. The ridgeline is the stairstep section of the lattice that reads left to right and leads the reader to attainment of the terminal behavior or goal. The enroute objectives are those behaviors that make up each subgoal and are placed below their appropriate ridgeline box.

Some rules or conventions are followed as lattices are constructed so that communication is consistent among lattice readers. The lines connecting the ridgeline boxes form right angles (with the angle at the top) and are arranged in such a way that the ridgeline's first box (the first subgoal to be taught) is the lowest and the terminal behavior is the highest. Whenever possible, the enroute objective boxes are connected to each other and the appropriate subgoal box

36

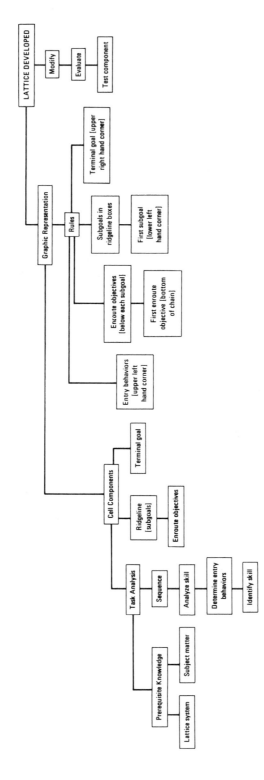

Figure 2.2 Procedural lattice for lattice development. (*Source:* D. D. Smith, J. O. Smith, & E. Edgar. A prototypic model for developing instructional materials for the severely handicapped. In N. G. Haring and L. J. Brown [Eds.], *Teaching the severely handicapped.* New York: Grune & Stratton, 1976, p. 159. Reprinted by permission.)

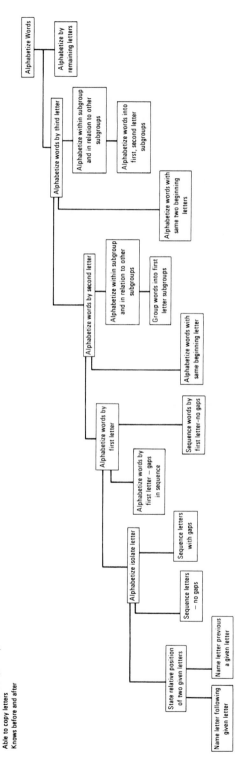

Figure 2.3 The lattice system applied to a sample skill—alphabetizing. (*Source:* National Institute of Education Grant OEG-0-70-3916 [607] under the direction of Norris Haring.)

with straight lines. When two enroute objectives are not necessarily sequential, they may be placed next to each other, and each connects directly with the subgoal box.

It is important to remember that lattices are only blueprints for instruction. They do not necessarily indicate what instructional techniques or aids will be used. They do, however, outline the instructional sequence planned and can be useful as a year's set of goals and objectives is arranged for particular students. As an example, a lattice of the simple skill of alphabetizing is found in Figure 2.3, and lattices of entire curriculum sequences are found in each of the chapters about academic content areas in Part III of this book.

Curriculum-Based Assessment

Teachers need to know exactly where to place students in the curriculum. They need to know which skills in that curriculum students have mastered and which they have not. They need to know at which stages of learning the students are functioning for each skill being taught at school. In reading, for example, teachers need to know in which basal reader each student should be placed for instructional purposes. Although achievement test results indicate grade-level scores, the correlation between these scores and actual reading placement is low (Eaton & Lovitt, 1972; Hansen & Eaton, 1978). These test scores are not helpful in pinpointing exact placement or determining types of errors that need to be corrected.

The best way to make these important instructional decisions is to try the student out in the materials that are to be used in the classroom. Allow the student to read from several different readers, take data (reading rate scores, correct percentage scores for comprehension) for each reading session, and place the student in the highest grade-level reader where the student obtained reasonable scores (see Chapter 8 for more details). This placement period usually also reveals students' error patterns, stage of learning, and other information useful in the selection of intervention procedures that should lead to the most efficient learning.

Once instruction begins, these same curriculum-based assessment techniques serve as evaluation tools. Because they are applied frequently (e.g., three days per week or even daily), a continual indication of the effectiveness of the teaching tactics selected is available. The next chapter in this text provides considerable detail in the methods of these assessment and evaluation techniques.

PARENT INVOLVEMENT

Communicating with parents was discussed at length in Chapter 1. It is important to remember that the IEP requires parent participation. Parents should be present at the IEP meeting and, as much as possible, should participate in the entire process. This means that the IEP should *not* be written and finalized before meeting with the student's parents. Teachers must remember that parents are important resources, and a positive relationship with parents is critical to the overall growth of their children.

Once the IEP is written, communication and dialogue with the parents should continue. Although formal parent conferences are held several times a year at most schools, more frequent communication can lead to joint partnerships between school and home. Parents can become instructional resources that teachers can use to help with students' acquisition, maintenance, and generalization of social and academic skills at school.

EVALUATION/ACCOUNTABILITY

Evaluation and accountability are mentioned only briefly here because these issues are the topics of considerable discussion in the next chapter and throughout this text. However, it is important to remember that the IEP process does require evaluation. Each student is to have a set of annual goals and objectives that are monitored periodically to determine whether progress is being made toward the attainment of the stated goals and objectives. Various tests and assessment procedures can facilitate program evaluation (criterion-referenced tests, achievement tests), but the best methods to ensure accountability are through the curriculum-based assessments of direct and daily measurements.

It is through this kind of sensitive information about students' progress that teachers can plan and make decisions about classroom organization and instruction. This evaluation system allows teachers to know when an objective is met, when to reinstruct particular topics, when to terminate daily instruction, when one tactic is no longer effective, and when a specific kind of tactic is needed. This kind of information only results from sensitive, ongoing, and reliable measurements. With daily or frequent classroom and student evaluation, teachers have immediate documentation of their effectiveness. For these reasons, the evaluation procedures based on applied behavior analysis are useful for judging the effectiveness of student progress. Therefore, they are emphasized throughout this book.

WRITING THE IEP

Once the special services committee decides that a child is eligible for special education and related services, the IEP must be written. P.L. 94-142 and P.L. 99-457 require that this be completed prior to providing special education and related services. The IEP is a communication, management, and administrative

Table 2.2
Information That Must Be Included in the IEP

AREA	SPECIFICATIONS
I. Present functioning levels	1. A statement of the child's present levels of educational performance should be provided for at least each of the following areas: a. Academic achievement b. Social adaptation c. Prevocational and vocational skills d. Psychomotor skills e. Self-help skills
II. Annual goals	1. Annual goal statements should be included for each of the areas listed above. 2. These should describe the educational performance levels expected at the end of the year. 3. They should be individually tailored for each student in line with information provided for present functioning levels.
III. Short-term behavioral objectives	1. Short-term behavioral objectives should be developed for each of the annual goals. 2. These should be measurable intermediate steps leading to the attainment of the stated goals. 3. Appropriate criteria and evaluation procedures must be delineated to indicate whether the short-term objectives have been achieved.
IV. Special and related services	1. A description of the kind of education services required should be included. 2. A justification for the type of special education class placement is required (resource room, partially self-contained, etc.). 3. A listing of specialized related services must be included (language therapy, physical education, etc.). 4. Projected dates for the initiation and anticipated duration of service should be provided.
V. Regular education	1. A description of the extent to which the student will participate in regular education programs must be included. 2. Care must be taken to ensure that the student receives an appropriate education in the least restrictive setting possible.
VI. Responsibility	1. Individuals responsible for implementing and monitoring the student's IEP must be designated.
VII. Evaluation	1. Methods and procedures to be used to review each IEP must be specified. 2. A schedule for review must be indicated. 3. Reviews must take place at least annually.
VIII. Parent involvement	1. The parents of the student should be encouraged to help develop the IEP goals and objectives. 2. They must be aware of the content of the IEP. 3. They must demonstrate approval of the IEP by signing it.

tool. Although it provides guidelines for the content of a student's educational program, it need not be an instructional plan.

Parents should be encouraged to participate actively in the development of the goals and objectives included in their child's IEP. They must be at least aware of its content and indicate their approval by signing the IEP. The intent is that parents' involvement in their child's educational program will continue after the approval of the IEP. Unfortunately, some parents' interest and concern stop at this point. Once they have signed the IEP, their legal commitment is completed. If, however, a more complete educational program is to be implemented, parents and teachers should work together throughout the academic year. Some authorities (Goldstein et al., 1980) suggest that for this to occur, many parents will need special training.

A number of requirements for the IEP and its content are specified in the law. Table 2.2 indicates the items that must be included in each IEP. A portion of one student's IEP, shown in Figure 2.4, delineates only one goal area, mathematics. For most students, a substantial number of goals and their ensuing objectives are necessary.

As specified by law, the IEP is developed by a team of people consisting of the student's teacher(s), an agency or school representative who is qualified to supervise the provision of special education, the student's parent(s) or guardian(s), and (if appropriate) the student. Although some school districts do not insist that the student's teacher(s) for the coming academic year be present, it is advantageous for their input and involvement to come at the beginning, when the development of a student's yearly program is being planned. The teacher is the one who must implement the IEP, select educational programs and materials, write daily lesson plans, and evaluate student progress toward the goals and objectives stated in the IEP. Since the teacher is the one person best able to monitor the delivery of related services, his or her involvement is critical in the early developmental stages. Competent specialists can facilitate the development of IEPs and should insist on participation. Also, if the student attends regular education classes, that teacher should be included to maintain consistency within the total program for the child.

Implementation of the IEP begins the first day the student comes to class. Related services specified in the IEP should be initiated according to the schedule indicated. Continual monitoring of goals and objectives is advisable, even necessary, if efficient progress is to be made. Each day throughout the school year, the attainment of the IEP goals and objectives should be of utmost concern to all those concerned with the educational performance and progress of the student. The responsibility is onerous, but the result can be rewarding.

Although the law does not mandate continual evaluation of student performance (evaluation and review are only necessary annually), without frequent information about the influence of the program planned, there is a higher probability that the student will fall short of the stated goals. The law does mandate the each student's goals and objectives be monitored and that criteria for mastery be indicated.

At the time of the required annual review, decisions about placement, related services, and development of new goals and objectives are made. For some students, return to regular education is appropriate; for others, continuation of special education and related services is required to maintain growth.

Figure 2.4
Sample individualized educational program plan form with individualized program goals in one subject area.

Carleen Jones   September 15
(Student's Name)   (Date)

6/15/79   9
(Birthdate)   (Age)

Ms. Rivera   Valley Vista
(Teacher)   (School)

September 2
(Date of Last Assessment)

Prioritized Annual Goals:
1. Articulation deficits will be remediated.
2. Computational arithmetic skills (addition, subtraction, and multiplication facts and processes like carrying and borrowing) will be mastered.
3. Decoding skills in reading will be mastered.

Description of Student's Program:
Special Education Resource Room, Regular Education 4th grade, and Speech Therapy.

Strengths:
Carleen relates well with her peers and does not display any social behavior problems.

She follows instructions and seems to benefit greatly from individualized instruction.

Weaknesses:
She has an articulation problem that interferes with her oral language, which results in her hesitancy to speak before the group.

She is several grade levels behind in reading and does not demonstrate sufficient word attack skills.

She is behind her classmates in computational arithmetic and has not mastered many basic facts.

Committee Members Present:

Mr. Petre	Ms. Pepe (Reg. Ed.)
(Diagnostician)	(Teacher)
Mr. & Mrs. Jones	Mr. Martinez
(Parent or Guardian Advocate)	(School Representative)
Mr. Porec—Speech	Ms. Rivera (Sp. Ed)

Computational Arithmetic

(Area)

Carleen Jones

(Student's Name)

September 15

(Date)

ANNUAL GOAL: To demonstrate mastery of computational facts from three computational areas (addition, subtraction, and multiplication) and to demonstrate mastery of process problems for two computational areas (addition and subtraction).

REVIEW DATES: 11/15   2/15   4/15

Short-term Objectives	Methods, Materials, and Procedures	Person Responsible	Start Date	Target Date	Date Objective Met	Comments and Revisions
1. Sandra will demonstrate mastery of all addition facts by meeting the criterion of correct rate (CR) score of 25 and an error rate (ER) score of 0.	Teacher-made worksheets, flash cards, error drill, freetime reinforcement.	Ms. Rivera	9/15	10/15		
2. Sandra will demonstrate mastery of all subtraction facts by meeting the criterion of CR at 25 and ER at 0.	Teacher-made worksheets, language master, error drill, freetime reinforcement.	Ms. Rivera	10/15	12/15		
3. Sandra will demonstrate mastery of all multiplication facts by meeting the criterion of CR at 20 and ER at 0.	Teacher-made worksheets, crib sheet, certificate from regular education teacher.	Ms. Rivera and Ms. Pepe	1/15	3/15		
4. Sandra will demonstrate her ability to compute addition problems that require carrying by achieving three consecutive scores of 95% or better.	Teacher-made worksheets, teacher demonstrations, certificate of success.	Ms. Rivera	10/1	11/5		
5. Sandra will demonstrate her ability to calculate subtraction problems that do not require borrowing by achieving three consecutive scores of 95% or better.	Teacher-made worksheets, demonstrations, response cost for errors (minutes from recess).	Ms. Rivera	11/5	11/25		
6. Sandra will demonstrate her ability to calculate subtraction problems that require borrowing without zeros in the minuend by achieving three consecutive scores of at least 95%.	Teacher-made worksheets, demonstrations, reinforcement of special privilege.	Ms. Rivera	11/26	12/20		
7. Sandra will demonstrate her ability to compute subtraction problems that require borrowing with zeros in the minuend by obtaining three consecutive correct percentage scores of at least 95%.	Teacher-made worksheets, demonstrations, peer tutoring, certificate of success from regular education teacher.	Ms. Rivera and Ms. Pepe	1/15	2/25		

SUMMARY

Over the past thirty years, special education has changed the face of regular education. To many, the changes brought about by special education were made slowly; to others the changes were achieved too quickly. Possibly no other single piece of legislation effected as many changes as quickly across the whole of the United States as P.L. 94-142. The IEP process mandated by this law has far-reaching implications for all of education.

One important implication of the IEP process is the increased visibility and participation of children with handicaps in schools. More teachers, both regular and special, now work with handicapped learners. Since most of these students spend at least part of each school day with their normal counterparts, both the teachers and students who fully participate in regular education programs must adjust to and accommodate for individual differences.

The implications of the IEP process have even more impact for special educators. The IEP process requires more curriculum planning, more specification for each student's goals and objectives, and more accountability through the evaluation and monitoring of progress. Although few would question the merit of developing individualized goals and objectives for every student, Buckley and Walker (1978) do offer one caution. They warn that specified goals and objectives can become self-fulfilling prophecies that, if set too low, could hinder students from achieving their maximum potential.

In addition, this process has forced many special educators to form a partnership with the parents of their students, an unheard of venture in the recent past. These new relationships have direct bearing on the type and quality of the instructional program for each youngster.

Also, the IEP process has made the entire educational system more aware of the multiple educational needs of handicapped learners. No longer are these students viewed as the sole domain of the special education teacher. They are now pupils of professionals from a myriad of disciplines within the school system. This has forced the special education teacher into assuming new, complex roles (advocate, multidisciplinary team leader, evaluation coordinator).

Clearly, many changes have been made over the past few years. Most were mandated by federal law and implemented by local school districts. The IEP process has been a jolt to many, but it has initiated the realization of appropriate educational services as the guaranteed right of all students with handicaps.

STUDY AND DISCUSSION QUESTIONS

1. What is the purpose of the IEP?
2. What components must be included in the IEP?
3. Discuss the issues that surround the assessment debate.
4. Write a set of behavioral objectives for Travis, a fourth grader who frequently disrupts class during silent reading time and is a poor independent reader.

5. Construct a lattice for one of the following skills: washing your hands, drinking from the water fountain, brushing your teeth, putting on a jacket. (These simple skills were selected because they are easy to analyze. For first attempts at task analysis or latticing, motor and self-help skills are less frustrating than more cognitive or conceptual skills.)

REFERENCES AND SUGGESTED READINGS

The IEP

SHRAG, J. A. (1977). *Individualized educational programming (IEP): A child study team process.* Austin, TX: Learning Concepts.

TORRES, S. (ed.) (1977). *A primer on individualized education programs for handicapped children.* Reston, VA: The Foundation for Exceptional Children.

TURNBULL, A. P., STRICKLAND, B. B., & BRANTLEY, J. C. (1982). *Developing and implementing individualized educational programs.* Columbus, OH: Charles E. Merrill.

TURNBULL, A. P., STRICKLAND, B. B., & HAMMER, S. E. (1978a). The individualized educational program. Part 1. Procedural guidelines. *Journal of Learning Disabilities, 11,* 40–46.

TURNBULL, A. P., STRICKLAND, B. B., & HAMMER, S. E. (1978b). The individualized educational program. Part 2. Translating law into practice. *Journal of Learning Disabilities, 11,* 67–72.

WHITE, R., & CALHOUN, M. L. (1987). From referral to placement: Teachers' perceptions of their responsibilities. *Exceptional Children, 53,* 460–468.

Behavioral Goals and Objectives

BUCKLEY, N. K., & WALKER, H. M. (1978). *Modifying classroom behavior: A manual for classroom teachers* (rev. ed.). Champaign, IL: Research Press.

CARR, R. A. (1979). Goal attainment scaling as a useful tool for evaluating progress in special education. *Exceptional Children, 46,* 88–95.

MAGER, R. F. (1984). *Preparing instructional objectives* (2nd ed.). Belmont, CA: Lake Management Training.

POPHAM, W. J., & BAKER, E. L. (1970). *Planning an instructional sequence.* Englewood Cliffs, NJ: Prentice Hall.

Task Analysis

Lattice System

BRICKER, W. A. (1972). A systematic approach to language training. In R. L. Schiefelbusch (ed.), *Language of the mentally retarded.* Baltimore, MD: University Park Press.

BUDDE, J. F. (1972). The lattice systems approach: Systems technology for human development. *Educational Technology, 12,* 75–79.

BUDDE, J. F., & MENOLASCINO, F. J. (1971). Systems technology and retardation: Applications to vocational habilitation. *Mental Retardation, 9,* 11–16.

SMITH, D. D., SMITH, J. O., & EDGAR, E. (1976). A prototypic model for developing instructional materials for the severely handicapped. In N. G. Haring and L. J. Brown (eds.), *Teaching the Severely Handicapped.* New York: Grune and Stratton.

SMITH, D. D., & SNELL, M. E. (1978). Classroom management and instructional planning. In M. E. Snell (ed.), *Systematic instruction of the moderately and severely handicapped*. Columbus, OH: Charles E. Merrill.

SMITH, J. O., & SMITH, D. D. (1974). Research and application of instructional material development. In N. G. Haring (ed.), *Annual report: A program project for the investigation and application of procedures of analysis and modification of behavior of handicapped children* (National Institute of Education, Grant OEG-0-70-3916, 607). Washington, DC: National Institute of Education.

SNELL, M. E., & SMITH, D. D. (1983). Developing the IEP: Selecting and assessing skills. In M. E. Snell (ed.), *Systematic instruction of the moderately and severely handicapped* (2nd ed.). Columbus, OH: Charles E. Merrill.

WOOLMAN, M. (1962). *The concept of the program lattice, a working paper*. Washington, DC: Institute of Educational Research.

Assessment

HERON, T. E., & HEWARD, W. L. (1982). Ecological assessment: Implications for teachers of learning disabled students. *Learning Disability Quarterly, 5*(2), 117–125.

MEYEN, E. L., & LEHR, D. H. (1980). Evolving practices in assessment and intervention for mildly handicapped adolescents: The case for intensive instruction. *Exceptional Education Quarterly, 1*(2), 19–26.

SWANSON, H. L., & WATSON, B. L. (1989). *Educational and psychological assessment of exceptional children: Theories, strategies, and applications* (2nd ed.). St. Louis: Mosby.

Debate

EATON, M. D., & LOVITT, T. C. (1972). Achievement tests vs. direct and daily measurement. In G. Semb (ed.), *Behavior analysis and education—1972*. Lawrence: University of Kansas Press.

EAVES, R. C., & McLAUGHLIN, P. (1977). A systems approach for the assessment of the child and his environment: Getting back to the basics. *Journal of Special Education, 11*, 99–111.

HANSEN, C. L., & EATON, M. D. (1978). Reading. In N. G. Haring, T. C. Lovitt, M. D. Eaton, & C. L. Hansen, *The fourth R: Research in the classroom*. Columbus, OH: Charles E. Merrill.

SHINN, M. R., TINDAL, G. A., SPIRA, D., & MARSTON, D. (1987). Practice of learning disabilities as social policy. *Learning Disability Quarterly, 10*, 17–28.

YSSELDYKE, J. E. (1986). Use of assessment information to make decisions about students. In R. J. Morris & B. Blatt (eds.), *Special education: Research and trends*. New York: Pergamon Press.

YSSELDYKE, J. E., & ALGOZZINE, B. (1981). Diagnostic classification decisions as a function of referral information. *Journal of Special Education, 15*, 429–435.

YSSELDYKE, J. E., ALGOZZINE, B., & EPPS, S. (1983). A logical and empirical analysis of current practice in classifying students handicapped. *Exceptional Children, 50*, 160–166.

YSSELDYKE, J. E., ALGOZZINE, B., SHINN, M., & McGUE, M. (1982). Similarities and differences between low achievers and students labeled learning disabled. *Journal of Special Education, 16*, 73–85.

Curriculum-Based Assessment

BLANKENSHIP, C. S. (1985). Using curriculum-based assessment data to make instructional decisions. *Exceptional Children, 52*, 233–238.

DENO, S. L. (1985). Curriculum-based measurement: The emerging alternative. *Exceptional Children, 52*, 219–232.

DENO, S. L., MIRKIN, P. K., & WESSON, C. (1984). How to write effective data-based IEPs. *Teaching Exceptional Children, 16*(2), 99–109.

DUFFEY, J. B., & FEDNER, M. L. (1978). Educational diagnosis with instructional use. *Exceptional Children, 44,* 246–251.

GERMANN, G., & TINDAL, G. (1985). An application of curriculum-based assessment: The use of direct and repeated measurement. *Exceptional Children, 52,* 244–265.

GICKLING, E. E., & THOMPSON, V. P. (1985). A personal view of curriculum-based assessment. *Exceptional Children, 52,* 205–218.

TUCKER, J. A. (1985). Curriculum-based assessment: An introduction. *Exceptional Children, 52,* 199–204.

UTLEY, B., ZIGMOND, N., & STRAIN, P. S. (1987). How various forms of data affect teacher analysis of student performance. *Exceptional Children, 53*(5), 411–422.

WESSON, C., FUCHS, L., TINDAL, G., MIRKIN, P., & DENO, S. L. (1986). Facilitating the efficiency of on-going curriculum-based measurement. *Teacher Education and Special Education, 9*(4), 166–172.

WESSON, C. L., KING, R. P., & DENO, S. L. (1984). Direct and frequent measurement of student performance: If it's good for us, why don't we use it? *Learning Disability Quarterly, 7,* 45–48.

WHITE, O. R. (1986). Precision teaching: Precision learning. *Exceptional Children, 52*(6), 522–534.

3

Evaluation of Instruction: Curriculum-Based Assessment

Children are sent to school to gain knowledge and enhance their abilities. They are expected to learn how to perform academic tasks, interact with others in socially appropriate ways, and develop skills to make them productive members of society. Achievement of these overall goals is the awesome responsibility of teachers. Whether they are appropriate goals for schools to assume is not for debate here. It seems, however, that society has charged the schools and the educational system with the obligation of meeting these somewhat ambiguous yet certainly ambitious goals for each and every individual. The taxpayers' concern with allocation and dispersement of revenue for education, the courts' and state legislatures' demands for the establishment of minimum competency levels, and the implementation of P.L. 94-142 (99-457) requiring accountability in education—all emphasize society's concern about education and the educational process.

Monitoring the learning of students is not an impossible task. In fact, evaluation of student performance has been typical school routine for many years. Traditionally, students' progress is measured at the beginning and at the end of each school year and before each grade report. This noncontinuous system, however, does not provide teachers with feedback about the effectiveness of teaching procedures. For those students who make adequate progress in school, traditional evaluation procedures may be sufficient. For students with special needs, more precise evaluation methods are necessary.

Recommendations about frequent, direct evaluation of student performance in the classroom are neither new nor novel. Olson (1935) stressed the importance of measuring children's behavior in the classroom to ensure greater precision in the discovery of relationships between the environment and student behavior. He advocated systematic measurement and precise record keeping for use with children possessing undesirable behavioral deviations. Certainly the collection of information about target students and their behavioral repertoires should be an integral part of the instructional process.

Although it is possible to measure almost every classroom and student occurrence, it is unreasonable to expect this of teachers who must work within current teacher-student ratios and financial constraints. There are times, however, when social behavior or academic learning is problematic for every student and specific instruction is required. In these instances, teachers must be certain that the instructional activities planned and implemented are effective.

Standard measurement procedures should be employed so that evaluation becomes the collection of facts, not just the interpretation of subjective feelings about the learning situation. In many instances, teachers cannot trust their judgment about changes in student performance. Often, adults accommodate to students' behavior rather than the behavior changing or improving. For example, at the beginning of the school year, Ms. Smith had great difficulty understanding Freddie's speech. He would arrive at school chattering about something that happened yesterday afternoon or on the morning bus ride to school. His enthusiasm was apparent, but Ms. Smith could not understand a word Freddie uttered. Unable to converse, she sent him to his seat to begin his schoolwork. Ms. Smith made a referral to the speech and language specialist, but it was several weeks before an assessment could be scheduled. During that time, Ms. Smith felt that Freddie's speech and language were improving greatly and considered withdrawing the referral. One day the principal visited her class, and Freddie ran up to greet him. The principal could not understand a word of the conversation. So Freddie's speech had not improved—Ms. Smith's listening skills had. Educational decisions need to be made from factual information collected in a frequent and systematic fashion. Without such data, grave errors about students' educational programs will occur.

Evaluation procedures need to be sensitive to the learning situation so that immediate feedback about the influence of instructional procedures can be obtained. Students cannot afford to lose instructional time because of prolonged use of ineffective techniques. This kind of teacher accountability is warranted whether mandated by society or not.

Standard and sensitive evaluation procedures need not be expensive in teacher time or effort. They should be easily incorporated into teaching situations, and a variety of persons (pupils, aides, and volunteers) should be able to implement them. This chapter provides an overview of evaluation procedures that have been in use in classrooms for over two decades. Guidelines for choosing data collection systems are included, as are methods for analyzing and evaluating the product (data) of the evaluation process.

DATA COLLECTION

The purpose of collecting information on student performance is to evaluate the teacher's and student's progress toward achieving goals and objectives. To justify the time spent measuring, the data collected must be meaningful. Therefore, the information gathered should relate directly to the target behavior. If oral reading is the current behavior of concern, words read orally by the student in his or her assigned reader should be the behavior measured.

Direct measurement of the specified behavior alone, however, does not guarantee meaningful data. Student performance must be evaluated across time. This means that direct data should be gathered daily or at least frequently. For teachers who do not see the student daily, measurement of the target behavior should occur each time the student receives instruction.

The data gathered must be of equivalent or comparable scale, in order that one day's performance can be judged against other days' performances to assess whether progress has been made. To have equivalent data, several factors must be constant. First, the behavior measured must remain the same across time. If rate of oral reading is the target behavior, the child should read orally from comparable passages each day—not oral reading on Monday, silent reading on Tuesday, oral reading comprehension on Wednesday, and so on. These other reading targets might also need to be assessed frequently, but they are separate targets, not interchangeable ones. The measurement system chosen must also remain constant. If reading rate is the appropriate measurement system, it must be used consistently. The interspersing of one system with another renders all the data meaningless.

To determine whether the scheduled instruction was responsible for changes in student performance, it is important to keep other situational variables as constant as possible. For example, if a child is asked to read orally in the morning one day, after lunch the next day, and before recess the following day, the changes in that student's oral reading might not be due to the materials presented or the instruction given. Likewise, if the location of the student's reading desk is changed daily, variations in performance might be more attributable to those moves than to actual change in reading ability. Naturally, everything cannot be held constant. The health of the student or the events that happened the previous evening or during the morning on the way to school can affect the way a student performs at school. Frequent measures of performance, however, place those variables in perspective, and an accurate picture of the student's abilities in target areas becomes apparent.

It is important to choose a measurement system that adequately reflects the target behavior, is sensitive to changes in performance, and can be implemented with relative ease. A number of different measurement systems are available. They render different kinds of information and are applicable to specific situations. The remainder of this chapter discusses the advantages and disadvantages of each measurement system.

Anecdotal Logs

Historically, teachers kept information about their students through anecdotal logs. Most often such records were kept in diary format through an abbreviated narrative; naughty or otherwise unacceptable social behavior was noted at the end of the school day (see Figure 3.1 for an example).

Although attempts were made to keep daily records of student behavior, the value of the information was questionable. Noted at the end of the day, the recollections of a tired teacher over a six-hour period had to be trusted. The accuracy and detail of these records were suspect at best, for they relied on the teacher's memory and subjective feelings. Although the reliability of the measurement is in doubt, a busy teacher can use this system initially. The teacher should note occurrences of certain behaviors to determine whether their frequency is sufficient to warrant the scheduling of a complex data collection system.

Antecedent Behavior Consequence (ABC) Analysis

A more sophisticated form of anecdotal record keeping is available for monitoring social behavior as it naturally occurs. The ABC analysis method lends some structure and organization to the collection of observational information. Instead of relying on recollection at the end of a school day or an academic period, the teacher is required to keep a record of classroom or playground events *as they occur*. The notations are organized on a time basis. Events that antecede the

Figure 3.1 Anecdotal records for recording behavioral information.

target behavior are noted in the first column of a prepared form (see Figure 3.2). The behavior of concern for a target student is marked in the middle column, and events occurring subsequent to the behavior under consideration are indicated in the last column.

This system is helpful when teachers are attempting to specify exactly what problem behavior should be considered for remediation. For example, often a teacher indicates that a student is "aggressive," but is not certain about the forms the student's aggression takes, the frequency of such acts, the victims of the aggression, or what events tend to stimulate these episodes.

After watching an aggressive student on the playground for several days and keeping a record of his behavior using this format, one teacher was able to define the behavior more precisely. Bill's aggression, for example, was composed of distinct components: not following the rules of the game, hitting and kicking others, and swearing. By counting the number of times each of these categories of behavior occurred, the teacher had a rough estimate of the frequency of occurrences and which was the most prevalent.

Student's Name _Steve S._   Period _Reading_

Teacher's Name _Mrs. Tidall_   Observation Time _10:10 – 10:25_

Antecedent	Behavior	Consequence
John whispers to Steve	S. Clowns	Class laughs
Class still laughing	S. tells joke	Class laughs
Teacher tells S. to stop	S. laughs	Class quiets down
Teacher tells S. to sit in hall	S. leaves class	

Figure 3.2 ABC analysis reporting form.

The ABC analysis method of note taking also yields additional useful information. Other children who are directly or indirectly involved in the target student's acts of aggression can be identified. For example, Bill only exhibited aggressive behavior when Tom and Susie were present, and Pete most frequently was the victim. Information about other students who might be contributing to the situation is helpful to the teacher in taking steps to reduce aggressive occurrences in the future. Also, certain environmental situations tend to be present when the aggressive acts occur. In Bill's case, the probability of trouble increased when he was playing baseball. The variables contributing to problematic behavioral episodes are almost infinite in number, but being cognizant of their presence and their interactive capabilities certainly facilitates the selection of an appropriate intervention strategy.

Both forms of anecdotal notes, the traditional log and the ABC analysis, are useful initially to pinpoint and define social behaviors. However, both methods are too cumbersome to implement for a long period of time because they require the teacher to make records of behavior in longhand and do not allow for quick review of behavioral changes noted for days, weeks, or months of student performance. Once the target behavior is identified, the teacher should select a measurement system (described shortly) to evaluate changes in student performance.

Curriculum-Based Assessment and Evaluation

Although this chapter is largely about curriculum-based assessment and the tools needed to implement this system, a few words about its role in instructional placement are warranted. Both anecdotal records and ABC analyses help the teacher decide what behaviors should be the targets of instruction. Both systems are used before direct instruction is initiated on some social behavior. Neither, however, is useful in academic situations, for they cannot determine at what place reading instruction should begin, which arithmetic facts students know, or how well a student can write a term paper.

With curriculum-based assessment, the teacher uses material from the students' curricula to determine where students should be placed and what their educational goals should be. In this system, the pupil over several days, reads from several basal readers, answers various computations from the four arithmetic operations, writes a story, or solves several problems. The teacher graphs students' data for easier analysis, studies and places them in the curriculum, and begins instruction.

As discussed in Chapter 2, this system has many advantages over the more traditional, standardized achievement and criterion-referenced test results, namely, less loss in instructional time, development of assessments relate directly to educational placements and decision making, and educational goals and objectives that are more apparent. Chapters about academic remediation in this text include curriculum-based assessment procedures for that content.

Frequency

The simplest system of data collection is frequency. Frequency data indicate the number of times a behavior occurred and are gathered by merely recording each time the behavior is observed. Teachers can collect such data by making hatch marks on an index card taped to a convenient place; data can be collected by aides, volunteers, peers, or the target student. Many situations lend themselves well to the frequency system. For example, the number of disruptive acts, talk-outs, out-of-seats, correct math problems, correct spelling words, and instances of tardiness can all be measured by the collection of frequency data.

Frequency data should not be used in all situations. Systematic measurement devices are needed to translate behavioral occurrences so that one day's performance can be compared with another's, and so that how often the behavior occurs across time can be determined. By merely counting the frequency of the behavior, however, commonality of the data is not guaranteed. Let's suppose that Liz talks back to the music teacher a lot. The teacher decides to count how many times this happens. According to the teacher's data, Liz talked back five times on Monday, Tuesday, and Wednesday, four times on Thursday, and three times on Friday. Can the teacher accurately say that Liz's performance has improved? That is impossible to determine from the data provided, for there is no indication whether session time was held constant. If music period lasted for fifty minutes on Monday, forty minutes on Tuesday and Wednesday, twenty minutes on Thursday, and only ten minutes on Friday, Liz's behavior did not improve across the week. In fact, she was even worse on Friday than Monday! This example demonstrates that if frequency data are to be kept, session time must be held constant.

A corollary is also true. If the number of correct responses is the target of interest, the number of opportunities to respond must be held constant (rather than session time). If frequency data are used in this situation, the only way to determine whether spelling accuracy increases is to keep the number of spelling words dictated the same each time.

Duration

Sometimes the important question is not "How many times does a certain behavior occur?" but rather "How long does the behavior last?" To illustrate this point, two students' tantrums were compared. Both students had two tantrums during the entire school day. One student's tantrums lasted a total of two minutes. In this case, the teacher decided that for the present no direct action was warranted, but the student's tantrums would be monitored periodically to be certain that neither the frequency nor the duration warranted remediation. The second student presented another problem. He also had an average of only two tantrums each day, but the average time spent having tantrums over a week was forty-five minutes daily. Although this student did not have a high frequency of tantrums, the duration was high and indicated a need for remediation. In some cases, both the frequency *and* duration of a social behavior are of concern. When this occurs, both aspects of the target behavior can be measured concurrently.

Duration data are not difficult to obtain if the teacher has a stopwatch. Each time a tantrum begins, the teacher or a classmate of the target child starts the watch. When the tantrum ceases, the watch is stopped. Without erasing the time accumulated, when another tantrum begins the stopwatch is started and the process repeated until the observation period is completed. The amount of time the student spent having tantrums and the day's data are revealed by merely reading the stopwatch.

As with frequency data, a major precaution must be considered when duration data are kept. For the same reasons that either number of opportunities or session time must be held constant in the frequency situation, session time must remain the same for all data collection sessions. If data are kept for the whole day or even for the morning, the time is of sufficient length so that the teacher need not be concerned that each daily recording session is equivalent to the minute. When duration data cannot be collected over an entire school day, morning, or afternoon, a precise observation time (for example, thirty minutes) should be established.

Percent

When neither frequency nor duration data can be collected appropriately because situational variables cannot be controlled, it is necessary to translate the data into a ratio so comparisons can be made from one day's data to another. If the number of spelling words included on each test is the same, frequency data (counting number of correctly spelled words) are appropriate. If, however, the number of words presented varies per test, the raw data must be converted to an equivalent form. A comparable situation exists for duration data. When observation time cannot be held constant, the raw data must be translated into another form to ensure that the data have meaning and can serve to evaluate and reflect changes in student performance accurately across time. Percent scores (percent correct, percent of occurrence) can serve this purpose.

Percent Correct

This measurement system gives an indication of quality or accuracy of performance. Percent correct does not give information about the quantity or amount of work completed, but is a very appropriate measurement system to select when the accuracy of student performance is of concern.

Percent correct scores are calculated by using the following formula:

$$\frac{\text{number of correct responses}}{\text{number of correct and incorrect responses}} \times 100 = \text{percent correct}$$

For example, the percent correct score for one day's spelling test is determined by dividing the number of correctly spelled words by the total number of words on the test, multiplied by 100 (to remove the decimal point). Kyle spelled four words correctly on a fifteen-word test. The percent correct score was calculated by dividing 4 by 15 and then multiplying the quotient by 100 and putting a percentage sign after the product. In this case, the correct percentage score was 27%.

The number of opportunities to respond affects the score a student can obtain, as does the student's performance. If there are only five questions on one social studies quiz and thirty questions on the next quiz, a student who misses only one question on each test receives vastly different percentage scores (80% and 97%, respectively). To remedy this situation, some teachers make certain that all quizzes are of sufficient length so that scores are not biased as in the above example.

Percent of Occurrence

When session time cannot be or is not held constant while duration data are collected, the raw data must be transformed into a ratio so the data can be compared with each other. Therefore, in these instances two different kinds of information must be gathered for each session: the length of observation time and the total amount of time the student engaged in the target activity. The desired percentage score is obtained by using the following formula:

$$\frac{\text{number of minutes engaged in target behavior}}{\text{session time}} \times 100 = \text{percent of occurrence}$$

It should be remembered that although session time may vary from day to day when this type of percentage score is used, it is advisable to keep the observation times comparable and not allow great fluctuations.

Rate

Speed of performance is important for almost everything adults do, particularly in job situations. Unfortunately, it is an area that special education teachers often neglect because they are so concerned with instilling student accuracy. In many academic situations, however, indication of accuracy is not sufficient to evaluate a student's true academic progress. It is possible to get every item attempted on a test correct, but fail academically because assignments are not completed on time. Students who are learning to become better silent readers, for example, must be able to read passages accurately and also quickly enough to keep up with classmates. In these instances, both *accuracy* and *speed* (quality and quantity) of student performance are of vital importance.

Percent correct scores give an indication of the quality of a student's performance. Rate provides a measure of quantity, and correct rate and error rate

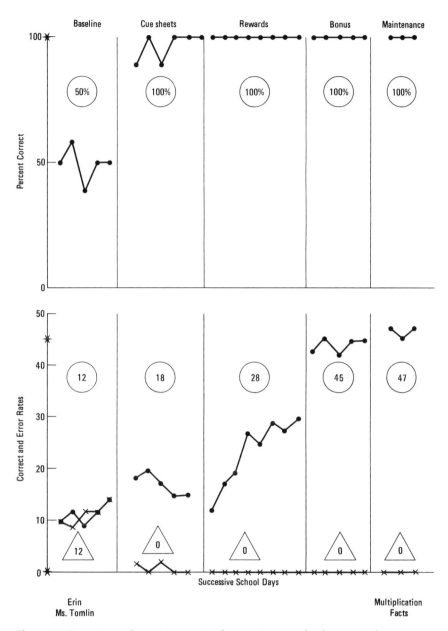

Figure 3.3 Comparison of percent correct and error rate scores for the same task.

scores together show the quality *and* quantity of student achievement. As shown in Figure 3.3, percentage scores show only one aspect of student performance. Once a student achieves 100%, a ceiling is reached. It appears that the student cannot improve anymore. When reviewing the rate graph of Erin's performance on the same multiplication fact worksheets, it is clear that her speed of performance is unsatisfactory even though her percent correct scores are 100.

Rate is a measurement system that gives an indication of speed of performance. In oral reading the teacher can hear each word read. In silent reading the teacher is not able to determine how accurately the student read each word in the passage; a test of comprehension has to serve this purpose. By calculating reading rate, however, it is possible to assess students' proficiency or speed of reading. This is accomplished by dividing the number of words read during a silent reading session by the time it took to complete the passage.

There are two ways to determine the amount of time it took a student to complete a passage. One is to have the students write on a page the times they began and concluded the passage, then subtract the start time from the stop time. Another is to provide them with stopwatches and have them start the watch when they begin reading and stop the watch when they complete the passage. The time indicated on the stopwatch face is the amount of time it took to complete the passage. The number of words read is obtained by either counting the words in the section or using a text with precounted passages.

Correct Rate and Error Rate

In the example provided, it is impossible to gain information about the quality and quantity of performance by using one measurement system. Percent of comprehension questions answered correctly and rate of silent reading had to be the measures used. For many academic areas, however, it is possible to gain an indication of speed of performance and accuracy through the use of one measurement system. Correct and error rates, when used together, provide the teacher with an indication of quality and quantity of student performance. Oral reading, calculation of math facts, assembly-line tasks, and other job skills lend themselves well to the application of the correct and error rate measurement system.

Unlike percent correct, in which only one score per evaluation session is sufficient, two scores per session are required for correct and error rate. With percent, the correct percentage score is inversely related to the incorrect percentage score. A perfect score is always 100% and never more than that; it is impossible to obtain a correct percentage score of 150%. Therefore, if the correct percentage score is 90%, the error percentage score is 10%. If the correct percentage score is 60%, the error percentage score is 40%. Correct and error rate scores are not so related. Error rate scores for an entire school week can be zero and the correct rates can be different each day (Monday's correct rate was 30, error rate was 0; Tuesday's correct rate was 45, error rate 0; Wednesday's correct rate 46, error rate 0; Thursday's correct rate 42, error rate 0; Friday's correct rate 55, error rate 0). Although it might be impossible for a correct rate to go above a certain level, that is a function of the target area and not the measurement system itself. For example, it is possible to read silently at a rate of 300 words per minute, to read orally at a correct rate of 175, and calculate math facts at 75 per minute. One might even surpass these scores, while one cannot surpass 100%.

Correct and error rates are calculated by using these two formulas:

$$\frac{\text{number of correct responses}}{\text{session time (minutes)}} = \text{correct rate}$$

$$\frac{\text{number of incorrect responses}}{\text{session time (minutes)}} = \text{error rate}$$

Since the correct and error rate measurement system is employed commonly in oral reading, that situation is used for illustration. Jennie was a poor reader and her teacher decided that until substantial changes in her reading skills were noted, Jennie's reading progress would be monitored daily. Each day Jennie read orally to her teacher from her assigned basal text for five minutes. As Jennie read, the teacher marked those words read incorrectly in her copy of the text. At the conclusion of the session, the teacher counted the number of errors made and the number of correctly read words. On one day, Jennie read a total of 205 words correctly and made 15 errors. These raw data were calculated into correct and error rate scores by dividing by five minutes (session time). Therefore, the correct rate for this day was 41 (205 ÷ 5 = 41 correct words per minute) and the error rate was 3 (15 ÷ 5 = 3 incorrect words per minute).

Both scores were necessary to evaluate Jennie's progress because they are not dependent on each other (the knowledge of one score does not yield the information necessary to determine the other). It is possible for her correct rate scores to increase, decrease, or stay the same while her error rate scores stayed the same, decreased, or increased. Figure 3.4 shows possible variations in correct and error rate score patterns.

The independence of correct rate and error rate scores is important to consider when evaluating student performance. Figure 3.4 also illustrates this point. Correct rate scores are indicated by dots; error rate scores are indicated by Xs. The top row of graphs (A, B, and C) display data that indicate student improvement. In case A, the student's error rate scores are remaining the same. In case B, the reverse is true; the student is making fewer errors while not showing any change in correct performance. Case C is what every teacher wishes for: overall improvement in both measures of performance. In the middle row of graphs (D, E, and F), the students are not improving at all. In case D, both sets of scores are remaining static. In case E, both correct and error rate scores are accelerating at approximately the same pace; the student is merely doing his or her work faster. In the last graph, case F, the student is slowing down across time, but proportionally. The quality of performance has not improved as overall production has vastly decreased. The bottom row of examples (cases G, H, and I) are all those instances teachers hope not to see. In case G, correct rate scores are remaining static as the error rate scores are accelerating, and in case H, the student's error rates are remaining the same but correct rates are rapidly

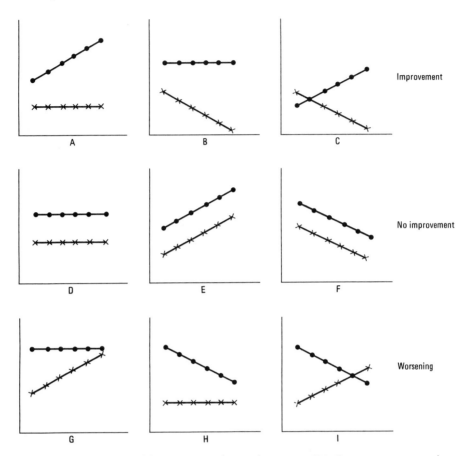

Figure 3.4 Patterns of possible correct rate (dots) and error rate (Xs). Correct rate scores and error rate scores are not reciprocal; one set of scores may decrease, while the other set may also decrease, stay at the same level, or increase. In the top row all three graphs indicate improvement, although the data patterns differ. In the second row all three graphs indicate no improvement. In the bottom row performance is worsening.

decelerating. The last example is every teacher's nightmare. The student started out on the first day of measurement performing the task relatively well, but across time performance deteriorated so that by the final day the student's error rate score exceeded the correct rate score.

The importance of examining both scores should become apparent as one looks only at the correct rates for case E. The correct rate scores were increasing and one might feel that the student's performance was improving. When the error rate scores are evaluated, however, the contrary is found to be true. If one were to study the error rate pattern that appears in case F, one might feel that the student's performance was improving, for the error rate scores are decreasing. When the correct rate scores also are considered, however, one can see that the student is not getting any better at all. From these examples one can see that although correct and error rate information are gathered simultaneously, they are not dependent measures: Both are needed to evaluate accurately student performance when quality and quantity (proficiency) of student performance is of concern.

Observational Recording

This data collection system was designed to evaluate social behavior through the observation of the actions and interactions of students. Only a brief discussion follows because these procedures require the use of outside personnel and are too complex for busy teachers to implement alone. Readers who require more details about observational measurement systems should refer to the reference and suggested reading list in this chapter. Although classroom teachers are not likely to select one of these complex systems, they should be aware of their existence and characteristics, for situations might arise warranting their use.

Basically, there are two versions of observational recording systems: continuous and sampling. In the continuous system, data are kept for a period of time and everything occurring in that period is recorded through the use of observational codes. This system provides a complete "transcript" of the behavioral incident that transpired during the prescribed time. The difficulties involved with collecting and analyzing the voluminous amount of data generated using this system are enormous. Computerized data collection systems are available in which a data collector can enter information about the target environment into a tape recorder, which allows for computerized analysis later.

Time sampling procedures have been used and refined over a long period of time. Olson and Cunningham (1934), in their review of time sampling techniques, indicate the prevalence of the use of this observational measurement system during the 1920s and 1930s. The sampling method does not require the recording of all the incidents, but rather records the events during slices of time. In these cases, fixed time samples might be used. For example, an hour can be divided into twelve five-minute intervals. At the end of every five minutes, the teacher could count the number of children out of their seats. The number of children out of their seats each of the twelve times that the teacher counted is averaged to arrive at the day's data.

Since the teacher is not able concurrently to collect the data and teach, outside personnel are necessary to ensure that the data are collected accurately and reliably. One suggestion is to seek help from a neighboring college's psychology or special education department, after gaining permission from the administration.

Summary of Data Collection Systems

Table 3.1 summarizes those data collection systems teachers are most likely to employ. They range in sophistication from frequency to rate and can be applied appropriately in social and academic situations.

Table 3.1
Summary of Data Collection Systems

MEASUREMENT SYSTEM	DEFINITION	FORMULA	LIMITATIONS
Frequency	The number of occurrences; how often the behavior occurs	Count or tally	Session time or number of opportunities must be held constant.
Duration	The total amount of time the individual engaged in an activity; how long the behavior lasts	Cumulative time; time of each episode added together	Session time must be held constant.
Percent correct	The proportion or ratio between correct and incorrect responses	$\dfrac{\text{no. of correct}}{\text{no. of correct} + \text{incorrect}} \times 100$	Data are biased by the number of opportunities—only an indication of accuracy with no indication of quantity or speed of performance.
Percent of occurrence	The ratio between the amount of time the student engaged in the target activity and session time	$\dfrac{\text{no. of minutes engaged in the target activity}}{\text{session time}} \times 100$	Data are biased if some sessions are very short in length.
Rate	The speed at which an activity is performed, transposed into a per minute score	$\dfrac{\text{no. of responses}}{\text{time}}$	Sheer rate provides no indication of quality of performance, only quantity.
Correct rate and error rate	The number of correct and error responses made per minute	$\dfrac{\text{no. of correct responses}}{\text{session time}}$ $\dfrac{\text{no. of error responses}}{\text{session time}}$	Correct rate and error rate cannot be used alone; both scores must be kept per session.

DATA ANALYSIS

One important component of the evaluation process is the analysis of data collected on student performance. While the data are being gathered, the teacher must be able to judge the effectiveness of those procedures scheduled in light of student progress. Many different ways to analyze data are now available to the teacher and researcher. Some of these methods are simple to execute; others are not. Since the purpose of this chapter is to help teachers and other school personnel evaluate the success or failure of events planned at school, sophisticated research designs are not discussed here (see this chapter's reference and suggested reading list for other sources).

For school personnel to evaluate instruction, steps must be taken beyond the mere collection of data. The data collection and the intervention application must be submitted to some structure, which involves selecting an appropriate evaluation design and submitting the teaching process to that format. This allows for precise teacher judgment based on student performance and systematically observed changes.

Evaluation Designs

One important key to the evaluation of instruction is the structure to which the learning situation is submitted. First, the teacher must be fully aware of those events that might be functioning in the school situation. Although a vast number of events can contribute to student performance, a determination must be made of those variables that, when manipulated, will achieve the desired aim: enhanced student performance. To facilitate the teacher's efforts in identifying those events contributing to undesirable situations and those encouraging student progress, a number of evaluation designs are simple to employ and provide the teacher with the needed information.

It is important to note that all of the designs discussed require certain information from the teacher. The target student(s) must be identified and the target behavior(s) selected. This can be accomplished through the structured observation methods described in the ABC analysis section, by using checklists, criterion-referenced tests, or collecting some preliminary data. This prebaseline or predesign implementation period, which need only last a few days, can save the teacher a substantial amount of time and facilitate the selection of the most advantageous evaluation design.

Reversal or ABAB

Although a number of variations of this design have been developed and refined over the years, the basic format remains as it was outlined by Baer, Wolf, and Risley (1968). Usually, there are four basic elements or phases of this design: *baseline, intervention, return to baseline,* and *return to intervention.*

The purpose of the baseline phase is to assess the target behavior over time.

By measuring or collecting data on the target behavior during the usual class-room routine for a period of time, the teacher learns about the nature of the target, its components, and functioning level. This usually takes anywhere from three to five data days. The data gathered during the baseline phase can help the teacher select the intervention strategy having the highest probability of producing the desired changes in the target behavior.

The second phase of the reversal design is the intervention condition. Each day during this phase, the teacher teaches in about the same way. If instruction is selected as the intervention strategy, it is provided every day that the conditions prescribed are in effect. Changes in the intervention strategy should not be made haphazardly. For example, on day three, feedback should not be added; on day four, reinforcement should not be scheduled. The first intervention should be given a chance to operate. If, after four or five data days, the amount of change in the target behavior is not sufficient, a new phase is implemented that adds to the first intervention or substitutes a different strategy.

If the first intervention strategy produced the desired changes in student performance, a return-to-baseline condition (removal of the intervention) usually is scheduled to be certain that the desired changes were influenced by the intervention and not some yet unidentified environmental factor. When this design is selected, it is assumed that the target behavior will reverse or return to the performance levels of the initial baseline period. Typically, social behaviors (talking out, out of seat, aggression, and disruption) fluctuate in this manner. Once verification (that the intervention was the cause of the changes in the target behavior) is obtained by a return of the scores to the approximate levels of the first baseline phase, the intervention procedures are reapplied. A graph of data submitted to an ABAB design is shown in Figure 3.5.

Modified Reversal Design

The reversal design is adapted by many teachers for academic or learning situations. In the instances just described, performance levels are expected to return to the initial levels when the intervention is withdrawn. When learned behavior is the target (acquisition of sight words, spelling words, or math facts), the hope is that when the intervention is withdrawn, the learned behavior will not return to the poor performance levels of the baseline period, but rather remain at mastery levels of performance. In these situations, application of the reversal design is not appropriate. A variation, however, is helpful to teachers and students as they monitor progress in the acquisition of specific skills. In this modified version of the reversal design, the initial baseline and intervention phases are similar to those described earlier. In the baseline condition, an assessment of student performance is made; in the second condition an intervention is scheduled. If criterion for mastery is achieved in the second condition, the intervention is discontinued to determine whether the student can perform the task without the help offered during intervention. If the student can again demonstrate mastery of the learned behavior, performance is monitored on a weekly posttest basis to

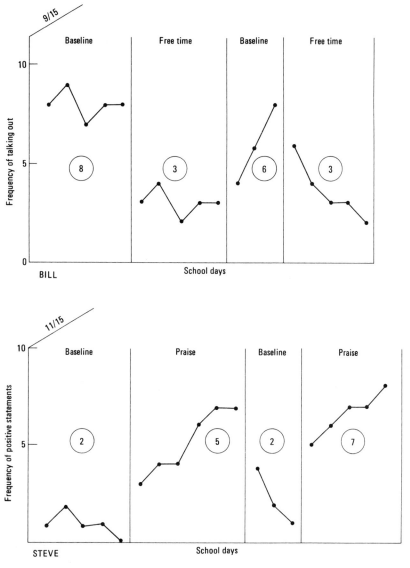

Figure 3.5 These graphs show expected patterns for data gathered by the reversal design. In each graph the dots represent daily frequency scores. Each phase is labeled. The score of central tendency (median) for each condition is circled.

ensure that learning is maintained over time. An example of this version of the reversal design is found in Figure 3.6. In this instance, the procedures are reversed (no instruction, instruction, no instruction), but the data do not reverse (low, high, high).

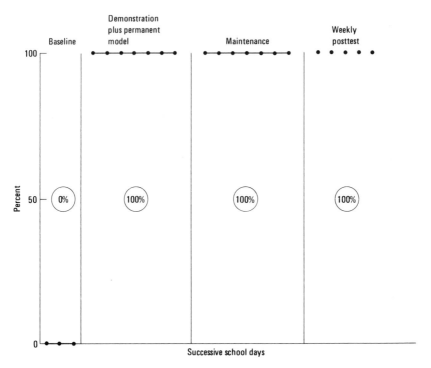

Figure 3.6 This graph illustrates the desired pattern for the data collected when a modified reversal design is used. The dots represent each day's percent correct score. Each phase is labeled to indicate what procedures were in effect, and the median score for each phase is circled.

Changing the Criterion

Another variation of the modified reversal design is the changing criterion design. As with all modified reversal designs, the expectation is for the data gathered during the return-to-baseline condition not to revert to the original undesirable state. The changing criterion design is comprised of a baseline phase, an intervention phase of several parts, and a maintenance or return-to-baseline phase. Within the intervention condition, a number of minor changes are scheduled: the criterion for acceptable performance becomes more stringent as the target behavior improves. This design incorporates an intervention technique (see the go-no go contingency section of Chapter 7) into the design format.

To use oral reading as an example, Kevin's initial performance level was far below that of his classmates. A changing criterion design was selected for him. During the baseline condition, he obtained an average correct rate score of twenty words per minute. His classmates all read around eighty correct words per minute. In the initial period of the intervention condition, the teacher set a correct rate aim of thirty. On any day Kevin did not achieve this aim, he received no reinforcement; he only received a reward when he obtained a correct rate score above twenty-nine. After he demonstrated achievement of this objective for three days, the aim score was increased to a correct rate of forty. For Kevin, after several conditions, it became apparent that he needed to improve his error rate as well as his correct rate scores. Figure 3.7 illustrates the changing criterion design as applied in the example.

Figure 3.7 A changing criterion design.

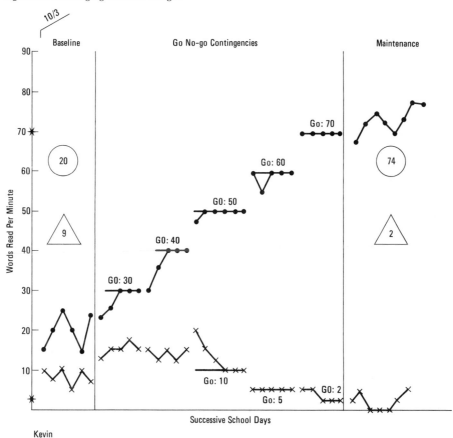

Task Analysis

This design is selected most appropriately when a behavioral checklist, criterion-referenced test, or teacher-made instructional sequence is followed. This graphing system allows for the monitoring of the mastery of each component of a complex task or skill. In the example in Figure 3.8, the skill of subtraction was first submitted to a task analysis. The components of subtraction were identified, sequenced, and placed along the vertical axis of the graph. Weekly checks were

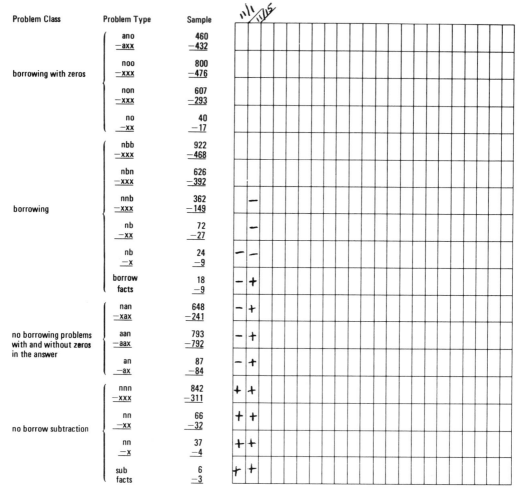

Figure 3.8 A task analysis design.

made on the student to determine whether mastery (90%) was achieved for each class of problems. Those classes in which mastery was achieved were given a plus, those not meeting the aim score were given a minus, and those not yet tested were left blank. The overview of skill attainment illustrated by this kind of graphic display can be useful to both teacher and student as evaluation of progress made toward the mastery of an entire skill is monitored.

Multiple Baseline

As the name of this design implies, more than one measurement of performance is kept at a time. Measurements on several targets are begun at the same time, but intervention is scheduled first for one target, then another, and so on. The general format for this design is shown in Figure 3.9. There are several varia-

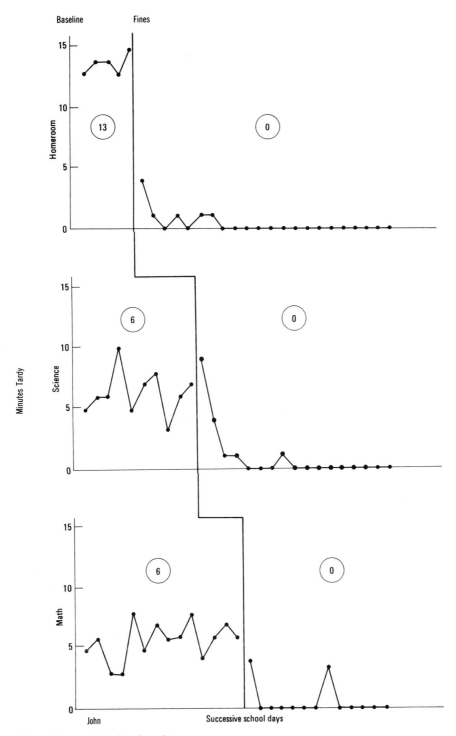

Figure 3.9 A multiple baseline design.

Table 3.2
Summary of Classroom Designs

DESIGN	DEFINITION	DIAGRAM	LIMITATIONS
Reversal (ABAB)	A teaching and research design that contains at least four phases and alternates treatment with baseline conditions.	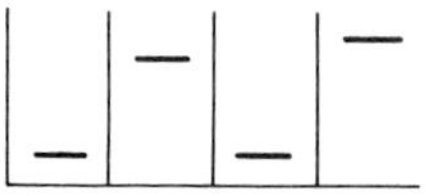	Proof of intervention's effectiveness questionable when data do not reverse as in learning situations.
Modified Reversal	A teaching design that contains at least three conditions with the treatments reversing (no instruction, instruction, no instruction), but data do not.		No experimental or research control unless many replications are conducted.
Changing Criterion	A modified reversal design where during treatment the behavior is shaped toward goal.	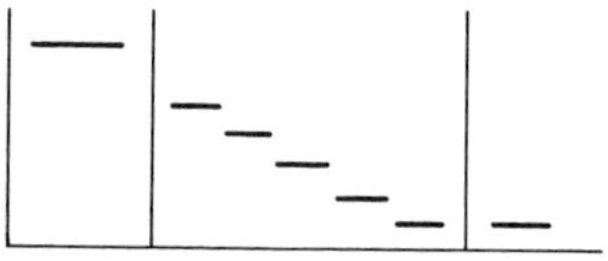	No experimental or research control unless many replications are conducted.
Task Analysis	A system of probing skills that belong to a sequence; an overview of related performance.	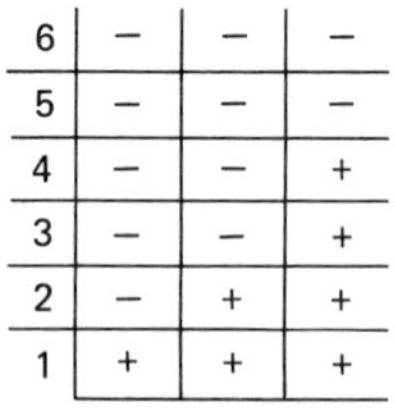	Provides no record of individual skill mastery and how it was achieved.

Task Analysis diagram:

6	−	−	−
5	−	−	−
4	−	−	+
3	−	−	+
2	−	+	+
1	+	+	+

Multiple Baseline

DESIGN	DEFINITION	DIAGRAM	LIMITATIONS
Setting	Data taken on the same behavior for the same pupil in at least three settings. Intervention is staggered.	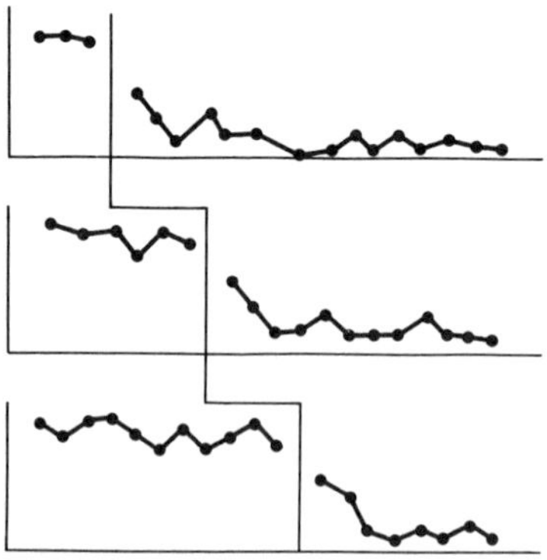	Loss of instruction time for last setting intervened in and no experimental control if generalization occurs.

Table 3.2   *(Continued)*

DESIGN	DEFINITION	DIAGRAM	LIMITATIONS
Skills	Data taken on the same pupil in the same setting for at least three different skills. Intervention is staggered.		Experimental or research control is lost if generalization occurs.
Pupils	Data on the same behavior in the same setting for three youngsters. Intervention is staggered.		No instructional reason to delay instruction, better to group them.

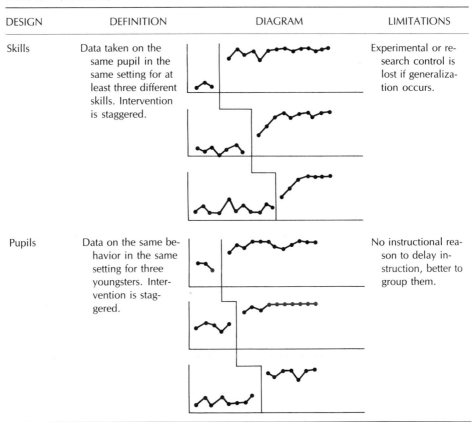

tions of the multiple baseline design, across individuals, settings, or target behaviors.

One commonly used variation of this design follows a student across settings. For example, some high school students were frequently tardy in reporting to their various classes. The teachers discussed this problem and found that John was tardy to homeroom, science, and math class too often. The teachers decided that action must be taken. All the teachers involved measured the amount of time that John was late to each class every day (see Figure 3.9). From the data, it was determined that John was late to homeroom most often. Together, the teachers decided that homeroom tardiness would be targeted first. For every minute that John was late to homeroom, he missed a minute from gym (an activity greatly important to John). Once his tardiness decreased for homeroom, the procedure was scheduled for science. Finally, it was applied to math.

Multiple baseline designs frequently are used in across-setting situations. The following are clusters of settings that might be used for multiple baseline applications in school situations: recess, hallway, and lunchroom; resource room, regular classroom, and home; before morning recess, after morning recess, and after lunch. For many students, it is most advantageous to target intervention first in one setting, then in another, and finally in all situations where the behavior or skill is of concern. This seems to be more acceptable to students and more manageable for teachers than attempting to handle remediation efforts in all situations initially.

The multiple baseline design also is useful when monitoring several behaviors or skills at the same time, as when a student is learning to compute subtraction problems requiring borrowing. The teacher presents the student each day with three sheets of borrowing problems, each containing problems of different types. After a baseline period on all three pages, intervention (demonstration and instruction) is scheduled for one of the three. Once some improvement is noted on the targeted page, instruction is given for the second class of problems. Finally, instruction is provided for all three pages until mastery is achieved for any or all of the pages.

In the last variation of the multiple baseline design, the performance of several students who present a common problem is monitored concurrently. Remediation efforts are aimed first at only one of the students. Progressively, each student receives direct intervention until all are being helped simultaneously. This version of the multiple baseline design is least desirable in classroom settings, for it is usually more convenient to group youngsters with common problems and schedule their interventions concurrently.

Summary of Classroom Designs

The evaluation designs presented here are arranged to give structure to the teaching situation so that student and teacher performance may be subjected to some objective scrutiny. Each has distinctive features that allow for differences in teaching situations. Table 3.2, which reviews each of these designs, could be used as a guide as designs are selected to match an individual's learning situations with evaluation procedures.

Data Calculations

Once data are gathered, it is necessary to perform several calculations to render the data more meaningful. When the effectiveness of an intervention strategy is being evaluated, comparative scores can be useful. It is important to be able to compare a student's performance in one condition to the next, so that a judgment about whether or not a procedure should be discontinued can be made. The following discussions center on those calculations that give the data referents.

Central Tendency

There are three different ways to calculate central tendency for the data within a condition: mean, median, and mode. The mode is the score occurring most often and one that serves no purpose for the evaluation of student performance.

The mean and median are, however, useful measures. The mean is the average score (total of all scores within a condition divided by the number of scores). The median is the middle score by rank order: with practice, it is very simple to determine. First, count the number of scores in the condition. Divide that by two to determine which place is in the middle. Using rank order (not temporal sequence), count until that place is reached. The score in the middle place is the median. See Figure 3.10 for examples.

Another way to determine the median score follows the same general theme, but instead of a raw data sheet (and the actual scores), the graphed data are used. In this second method, the teacher again counts the number of scores in a phase, but then uses the horizontal lines on the graph to help determine the rank order of the scores. See Figure 3.10 for an example.

A score representing central tendency, *either* a mean *or* median, should be calculated for each set of scores for every condition. If correct and error rate scores are the measures used, then two scores of central tendency are calculated for each condition.

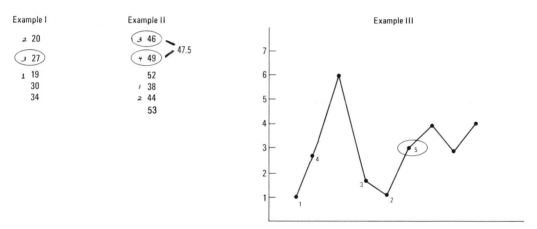

Figure 3.10 Calculating medians. In Example I there are five scores; the third (27) score is the median. In Example II there are six scores; the median (47.5) is half way between scores 3 and 4. In Example III there are nine scores; the fifth score (3) is the median.

Trend

Although no details are given here about precise ways of calculating trend lines, it is important to include consideration of the trend or direction of the data as part of the evaluation process. Data can follow three basic trends: increasing, decreasing, or flat. One reason that it is not sufficient to use only the mean or median is illustrated in Figure 3.11. In A, the median scores for each condition are the same—18; the profile shown is that which most people envision when the medians or means are the same for two conditions. The two conditions shown in B also have the same median scores, but the trends and interpretation of the data are different. In C, an entirely different point is made. If one considers only the

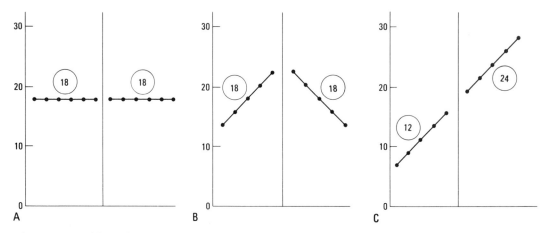

Figure 3.11 Possible combinations of data trends and middle scores and their relation to interpretation of results. It is important to note the central tendency (mean or median) for each condition, but the trend of the data should also be considered. In A, no improvement across conditions was noted. In B, the central tendency scores for both conditions are the same, but the trends of the data are different: in this case, the student's performance worsened. In C, the student's performance improved across conditions; the trend indicates that the improvement continued during the second condition. The intervention scheduled during the second condition cannot be credited for the improvement indicated by the changes in central tendency scores.

central tendency scores for each condition, it is possible to conclude that the student improved greatly from one condition to the next. When the *trend* is considered, however, it becomes apparent that there is no improvement at all, only a maintenance of the trend initiated in the first condition. Both the scores of central tendency and the trend or direction of the data must be considered before declaring a tactic successful, because of the changes noted from one condition to the next.

Aim Scores

There are two general types of aim scores possible for individual students: long term and short term. The long-term goal for a student might be to read fast enough to keep up with classmates in the in-class reading assignments in social studies, since the student's present functioning level is far below that level. Therefore, several goals (and aim scores) are established for this student: one that is attainable in the near future and one that is the ultimate aim. In fact, as student performance improves, a number of short-term aims might be established in the course of reaching the final goal.

Sometimes aim scores are referred to as levels of mastery. In percent situations, teachers often demand three days above 90% before moving the student to a new task. Some even require three consecutive days at 100%. Why these particular criteria are used, no one knows. Keeping some pupils from learning new skills because they cannot obtain three consecutive 100% scores does not seem pragmatic. The teacher should judge what the aim score should be for an individual and what information should be learned. It is important, however, for the teacher to make such a determination before or at the time instruction is initiated.

Aim scores also are used in rate situations. Many refer to these aim scores as *desired rates.* In general, students should be able to function with their classmates. One way to determine aim scores is to test the skills of sample students from the regular classroom to which the student is returning or is a member. If members of the regular class calculate math facts at a rate of 40, the target student should be able to do about the same. Otherwise, the student cannot succeed in this situation.

Criteria for Change of Phase

There should be two different criteria for concluding a condition: failure of a tactic or attainment of the aim score. It is vital to instructional planning to know when a tactic is insufficiently effective or totally ineffective. Sometimes an intervention does not work for a particular student; after four days of very little or no change in the data, another intervention should be scheduled. In some cases, an intervention is effective for awhile, but then ceases to be. In such instances, it is important to know when substantial change is not occurring so that another intervention can be added to the first or scheduled alone. Although no precise rules exist, some guidelines are available. After a condition is at least five days long and the last two days' scores fall below the scores obtained on the two previous days, a new intervention should be selected. Of course, other guidelines can be developed. The important point is that guidelines be established so that ineffective procedures are not followed too long.

Needless to say, when criterion for mastery or the aim score is reached and maintained for several days, new procedures should be implemented. If the aim score is reached during an intervention condition, it is advisable to discontinue the intervention procedures to determine whether the student can remain at the desired levels of performance without the help of the intervention procedure. If the preestablished aim score level is maintained, it is time to move on to the next step in the instructional sequence.

DATA DISPLAY

Data gathered on student performance are easier to evaluate if transformed into a visual display as they are collected. When data are presented graphically, analysis becomes obvious and evaluation almost automatic. In fact, performance has been shown to improve when graphs are shown to students.

Data should be graphed when collected and not after long intervals. Many times the need to change intervention strategies becomes apparent only when the data are displayed visually. Time lost because data were not analyzed cannot be justified.

Raw Data Form

As data are being collected, scores describing student performance (math worksheets, spelling tests, pages of creative writing) can soon be overwhelming; it is advisable to transpose the data to one sheet of paper for easy reference. The same is true for other products of student performance that do not leave a permanent record (oral reading, social behavior, and oral language). In these cases, it is even more important that data be stored in a convenient place in an orderly fashion. A sample data sheet is shown in Figure 3.12. Other versions can be developed to suit individuals and specific learning situations better.

Figure 3.12 Sample raw data sheet.

Student's name

Subject area

Teacher's name

Specific target

Date D/M/Y	D A Y	Number		Percent Correct	Time	Rate	
		Correct	Error			Correct	Error
/ /	M						
	T						
	W						
	T						
	F						
/ /	M						
	T						
	W						
	T						
	F						
/ /	M						
	T						
	W						
	T						
	F						
/ /	M						
	T						
	W						
	T						
	F						

Setting Up a Graph

Student performance data are displayed most conveniently on a graph. Several different kinds of graph paper are available. The most commonly used is the standard arithmetic graph paper available in most bookstores. Some teachers prefer using semilogarithmic graph paper when charting rate data, but as can be seen in Figure 3.13, an arithmetic grid is acceptable for graphing rates. Standard

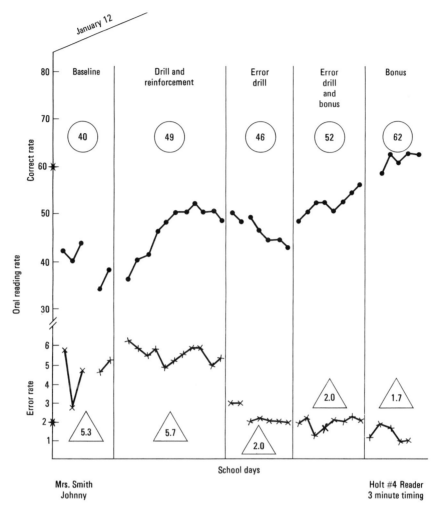

Figure 3.13 An oral reading rate graph where the vertical axis is broken and different scale units are used for the correct rate (dots) and the error rate (Xs) scores. The aim scores for each are indicated by stars on the vertical axis. Each condition is labeled to indicate the procedures in effect. Also, central tendency scores for each condition are noted. Because daily correct rate and error rates were calculated, two central tendency scores appear for each condition. The correct rate central tendencies are circled; error rates are shown inside large triangles.

procedures to follow when setting up a graph, such a labeling the axis and noting preestablished criteria, are discussed in the following sections.

The Vertical Axis

The scores are shown on the *ordinate*, or vertical axis (a line that goes up and down). The axis must be labeled with the name of the measurement system used (frequency, duration, percent correct, rate per minute), and hatch marks should be noted so quick reference can be made as a specific score is plotted (for example, 25, 50, 75, and 100 for percent; 5, 10, 15, and 20 for frequency).

If rate is the measure chosen, a special arrangement of the vertical axis is often required. If a student's correct and error rate scores are close together, there is no need for any change in the vertical axis. Most often, the correct rate scores cluster in one area of the graph and the error rate scores in another. Using the typical arrangement of a graph, changes in correct rate scores are clearly visible.

Error rate scores can present a different problem, however. A number of plots are possible between a score of one and zero (.2, .1, .5). Without some adjustment of the vertical axis, changes in error rate performance go unnoticed. For this reason, many teachers break the vertical axis into two parts: one for the correct rate scores, and one for the error rate scores. The correct rate axis must be deep enough to allow for change in performance, both positive and negative. Therefore, it is advisable to get an estimate of a student's correct rate performance before the graph is made. Allowance must be made so that some decrease and a substantial amount of change in the desired direction can be noted.

The arrangement of the vertical axis for error rate scores is determined by looking at student performance and the scores possible. First, if a student is making about ten errors per minute initially, room must be left for scores of ten and slightly above that level. Also, a place to enter a zero score and room for those scores that can fall below one and above zero (.5, .2) must be provided. A sample rate graph is shown in Figure 3.13.

The Horizontal Axis

Session days are represented on the *abscissa* (a line that goes across the page). This axis is labeled in accordance with the frequency of data collection. If the teacher is in a resource room and sees the student only three times a week, the abscissa is labeled "Session days." If data are collected daily, the horizontal axis is labeled "School days." Some teachers like to see the days of each week cluster together. To accomplish this, the horizontal axis is labeled "Successive calendar days," and day lines are held for Saturday and Sunday although they are never used.

Once the abscissa is labeled, the days are represented by vertical lines that cross the horizontal axis. If "School days" is the label chosen, the lines representing Monday, Tuesday, Wednesday, and so on, always represent those days. If a student was absent on Monday, that day line is left open and Tuesday's data are plotted on the next line, the line designated for Tuesday.

Other Labels

It is necessary to have the following information clearly visible on every graph so that one student's chart is not confused with another's, or math is not thought to be reading. The teacher's name should be on the graph. If more than one person teaches the student, their names should appear somewhere on the chart

also. The homeroom teacher's name always should be noted to facilitate compila-
tion of a student's graphs for any given year. Besides the names of the teacher(s)
and the student, information about the target behavior sufficient to distinguish
one graph from another is necessary. In some cases a brief notation like "oral
reading from the Holt #4 reader" is enough; in other situations more information about the target behavior and materials used is needed.

The date for the first data plot should be indicated on the graph. Often it is
desirable to indicate the day line that stands for the first data day of each month.

Along the vertical axis additional data notations can appear. It is helpful to
both student and teacher to mark the short-term aim score on the graph by
placing stars on the vertical axis at the levels of the aim scores. The notations and
aim scores for both correct and error rates appear on the sample graph shown
in Figure 3.13.

Entering Data on Graph

As mentioned earlier, it is important that data be plotted immediately upon
collection and calculation so that continual evaluation of student performance
can occur.

Plotting Conventions

Data plots are placed on a graph in such a way that the scores fall directly *on* day
lines (vertical lines) and at the appropriate gradients as indicated on the vertical
axis. The score of 12% is placed on the day line for the day on which it was
collected at the correct level for 12 percent—between the 10% and 15% designated places.

Plots are connected within a phase or condition. When a student is absent,
that day line is left blank and the plots preceding and subsequent to the absence
are *not* connected. No-chance days (hearing screening test, fire drill, field trip,
teacher lost the data) are noted on the graph by a blank day line, but the data
before and after a no-chance day *are* connected.

If Saturday and Sunday day lines are included in a graph, they are left
blank, because no data are collected on these days. In this situation, Friday and
Monday plots are *not* connected, so a week's set of data cluster together visually.
If the graph is labeled "School days," there are no day lines to represent Saturday and Sunday, and the Friday and Monday data plots *are* connected.

If correct rate and error rate are used as the measures of performance, two
plots appear on each day line: one for correct rate and one for error rate. To
distinguish these two sets of data, a dot is used to indicate correct rate and an X is
used for the error rate score. When connecting the plots, the rules provided
above hold, but correct rate plots are connected to the other correct rates, and
the error rates are connected to error rates. An example is provided in Figure
3.13.

A change in condition is indicated by a solid vertical line drawn between the two day lines that represent the last plot for one condition and the first plot for a new condition. This line is referred to as a *phase change line* and serves to separate the data from two different conditions. To facilitate the visual separation of the data from two phases, plots are *not* connected across phase change lines. Also, each phase is labeled so the teacher quickly can recall the procedures used in each different phase.

Central Tendency

Scores to indicate central tendency, either the mean or median, must be calculated for each condition and each set of scores. After the calculations are completed at the conclusion of each phase, the score is entered on the graph centered within the phase, but not in such a way that it covers the data. Usually it is written in the center of a phase and a large circle drawn around it. If correct rate and error rate scores are used, there are two central tendency scores per phase. The correct rate central tendency score is placed in a large, open circle; the error rate central tendency score is placed in a large, open triangle.

Checklist

To ensure that all the steps necessary to construct a meaningful evaluation graph are completed, a checklist is provided in Table 3.3. This checklist also serves as a summary of this section (Data Display) of the chapter.

SUMMARY

This chapter has served as an overview of the steps teachers follow to evaluate the influence of the intervention strategies they select for individual students. These evaluation procedures test such influences by judging the amount of progress made or not made in a given situation. Teachers follow a general sequence of steps, although clearly not linear, as they establish the structure necessary to evaluate instruction. A general delineation of those steps follows.

Prebaseline

During this initial stage of the evaluation process, answers to some fundamental questions are sought. What are the behaviors of concern and in need of remediation? Which and what level of materials should be utilized? Which measurement system should be selected? Which evaluation design might be most appropriate?

Answers to these critical questions are found through systematic observation and testing. An ABC analysis might be used when social behavior is under consideration. A criterion-referenced test or task analyzed skill-sequence checklist might answer initial material and placement questions for academic situa-

Table 3.3
Checklist for Constructing Evaluation Graphs

DONE

———

1. Set up graph.
  ——— a. Draw abscissa line (horizontal axis).
  ——— b. Draw ordinate line (vertical axis).
  ——— c. Label abscissa.
  ——— d. Label ordinate.
  ——— e. Note target (spelling, etc.; indicate material used).
  ——— f. Note teacher's name.
  ——— g. Note student's name.
  ——— h. Date graph.
  ——— i. Note aim score(s).
2. Calculate data.
  ——— a. Set up raw data sheet.
  ——— b. Calculate scores.
3. Plot data.
  ——— a. Place plot(s) on appropriate day line.
  ——— b. Connect plots for successive data days.
  ——— c. Do not connect plots if student was absent.
  ——— d. Connect plots for no-chance days.
  ——— e. Note phase changes with a solid vertical line.
  ——— f. Label phase.
4. Analyze data.
  ——— a. Calculate either mean or median scores by condition.
  ——— b. Enter sores of central tendency on graph for each phase.

tions. Trying out several curriculum materials with the student also might be beneficial. Once the target behavior is identified and the level of the student's performance determined, the selection of the measurement and evaluation design is facilitated.

Before formal data collection procedures are implemented, a number of other details must be handled. First, a consistent time and place for data collection must be established. Formats for data collection and analysis must be designed. A raw data sheet must be developed. A graph should be set up to reflect the needs of the data system used.

Baseline

During this and all of the conditions that follow, data are collected and plotted regularly and frequently. Systematic and frequent assessment of the student's performance is conducted to obtain knowledge about the characteristics of the target behavior. The initial performance levels of the student are judged against a long-range aim score, and a short-term aim is established. The final decision about the intervention strategy to try first is made after observing systematically the student's performance. Criteria for change of phase are set. Once the teacher feels confident that an understanding of the student and his or her performance characteristics has been achieved, a central tendency score is calculated and the baseline phase terminated.

Intervention Conditions

During instructional conditions, the student is learning to perform a target assignment at more desirable levels of performance or is learning not to exhibit undesirable behavior. A specific intervention procedure is applied systematically and consistently each day of instruction. Again, evaluation data are collected, plotted, and analyzed to ensure that desired changes in student performance continually occur. If a tactic loses its effectiveness, and meets the criteria for change of phase, another tactic is added to the first, or a new strategy is scheduled. The changes in procedures are submitted to the same evaluation system.

If a reversal design was selected, return-to-baseline conditions are established. After several days the effective procedures are reinstituted, and it is hoped, desired changes in student performance reoccur.

Once the desired change is achieved, the aim score or mastery criterion reached, and a score of central tendency calculated, the intervention procedures are discontinued.

Maintenance

The last phase of the implementation of daily or frequent data collection is designed to ensure maintenance or retention of the desired level of performance without the intervention strategy. Can the student perform the task on his or her own? This is the ultimate test of the teaching procedures implemented. Once the student again demonstrates mastery or achievement of the aim score, frequent testing of the target behavior can be stopped.

Posttest

After the target skill is learned and maintained, it is important to be certain that it remains at the desired levels. Therefore, weekly posttests are recommended for awhile followed by monthly posttests for the remainder of the school year. It is important to monitor student performance, for the monitoring process in and of itself can facilitate retention.

DISCUSSION AND STUDY QUESTIONS

1. What are the purposes of evaluating instruction?
2. Describe each of the various data collection systems presented in this chapter and provide a classroom application for each.

3. Give three reasons for graphing data collected on student performance.
4. List the designs used in classrooms that structure classroom evaluations. Briefly describe a classroom situation for each design.
5. Create a percentage and a rate (daily session time was held constant at five minutes) graph for Heather's multiplication fact performance, which follows:

Aim: 100%; CR 40, ER 1

Date	# Correct	# Wrong	Phase
10/2	30	5	
	35	10	
	25	5	Baseline
	30	10	
	35	10	
10/9	25	10	
	25	5	
	40	5	
	40	5	Cue sheet
	55	2	
	55	0	
	50	0	
10/17	100	2	
	125	0	Cue sheet
	150	0	and
	185	1	rewards
	200	0	
	200	0	
10/24	210	0	
	220	0	Maintenance
	215	0	

REFERENCES AND SUGGESTED READINGS

Evaluation of Instruction

BRANDSTETTER, G., & MERZ, C. (1978). Charting scores in precision teaching for skill acquisition. *Exceptional Children, 45,* 42–48.

FREDERICKS, B., BALDWIN, V., MOORE, W., TEMPLEMAN, T. P., & ANDERSON, R. (1980). The teaching research data-based classroom model. *Journal of the Severely Handicapped, 5*(3), 211–223.

HARING, N. G., & GENTRY, N. D. (1976). Direct and individualized instructional procedures. In N. G. Haring & R. L. Schiefelbusch (eds.), *Teaching special children.* New York: McGraw-Hill.

JENKINS, J. R., MAYHALL, W. F., PESCHKA, C. M., & TOWNSEND, V. (1974). Using direct and daily measures to increase learning. *Journal of Learning Disabilities, 7,* 605–608.

MARTIN, G., & PEAR, J. (1983). *Behavior modification: What it is and how to do it* (2nd ed.). Englewood Cliffs, NJ: Prentice Hall.

OLSON, W. C. (1935). The diagnosis and treatment of behavior disorders of children. In the Thirty-fourth Yearbook of the National Society for the Study of Education (eds.), *Educational diagnosis*. Bloomington, IL: Public Schools.

UTLEY, B. L., ZIGMOND, N., & STRAIN, P. S. (1987). How various forms of data affect teacher analysis of student performance. *Exceptional Children, 53*(5), 411–422.

WESSON, C. L., KING, R. P., & DENO, S. L. (1984). Direct and frequent measurement of student performance: If it's good for us, why don't we do it? *Learning Disability Quarterly, 7,* 45–48.

WHITE, O. R., & HARING, N. G. (1980). *Exceptional teaching* (2nd ed.). Columbus, OH: Charles E. Merrill.

WHITE, O. R., & LIBERTY, K. A. (1976). Behavioral assessment and precise educational measurement. In N. G. Haring & R. L. Schiefelbusch (eds.), *Teaching special children*. New York: McGraw-Hill.

ZIGMOND, N., & MILLER, S. E. (1986). Assessment for instructional planning. *Exceptional Children, 52,* 501–509.

Applied Behavior Analysis

General

ALBERTO, P. A., & TROUTMAN, A. C. (1982). *Applied behavior analysis for teachers: Influencing student performance* (rev. ed.). Columbus, OH: Charles E. Merrill.

BAER, D. M. (1975). In the beginning, there was the response. In E. Ramp & G. Semb (eds), *Behavior analysis: Areas of research and application*. Englewood Cliffs, NJ: Prentice Hall.

SALZBERG, B. H., WHEELER, A. J., DEVAR, L. T., & HOPKINS, B. L. (1971). The effect of intermittent feedback and intermittent contingent access to play on printing of kindergarten children. *Journal of Applied Behavior Analysis, 4,* 163–171.

SULZER-AZAROFF, B., & MAYER, G. R. (1977). *Applying behavior-analysis procedures with children and youth*. New York: Holt, Rinehart and Winston.

Research Techniques and Designs

BAER, D. M., WOLF, M. M., & RISLEY, T. R. (1968). Some current dimensions of applied behavior analysis. *Journal of Applied Behavior Analysis, 1,* 91–97.

CAMPBELL, D. T., & STANLEY, J. C. (1973). *Experimental and quasi-experimental designs for research*. Chicago: Rand McNally.

COOK, T. D. & CAMPBELL, D. T. (1979). *Quasi-experimentation: Design & analysis issues for field settings*. Chicago: Rand McNally.

DREW, C. J. & HARDMAN, M. L. (1985). *Designing and conducting behavioral research*. New York: Pergamon Press.

HERSEN, M., & BARLOW, D. H. (1984). *Single-case experimental designs: Strategies for studying behavior change* (2nd ed.). Elmsford, NY: Pergamon Press.

KERLINGER, F. N. (1979). *Behavioral research: A conceptual approach*. New York: Holt, Rinehart and Winston.

OLSON, W. C., & CUNNINGHAM, E. M. (1934). Time-sampling techniques. *Child Development, 5,* 41–58.

SIDMAN, M. (1960). *Tactics of scientific research: Evaluating experimental data in psychology.* New York: Basic Books.

TAWNEY, J. W., & GAST, D. L. (1984). *Single subject research in special education.* Columbus, OH: Charles E. Merrill.

4

Generic Interventions that Improve Social Behaviors

Many educators associate the notion of improving youngsters' social behaviors with the reduction of classroom disruption. Concern about students who disrupt the learning environment is justified. Even the smallest disruption, if it continues, can inhibit or impair the learning of an entire class. Generally, minor disruptions can be reduced or eliminated by applying simple interventions or changes in the educational routine. But some maladaptive behaviors do not respond to intervention strategies. While the numbers of students who engage in maladaptive behaviors are small, constituting possibly 0.1 to 7% of the total school population (Macomb Intermediate School District, 1981), the learning environment for an entire school can be affected negatively. Educational programs that foster positive learning environments must be put into place for all students in our schools.

As educators attempt to reduce disruption by putting various disciplinary actions into place, a constant vigil must be kept to ensure that interventions selected do not alter a positive, free educational climate where students can explore, discover, and learn. Sometimes, because they are not fully informed, teachers select interventions that are too severe or require too much time to implement, when other tactics would have sufficed. Smith (1984) developed the Intervention Ladder (see Figure 4.1) as a guide for reducing disruption in school settings. According to Smith, the intervention should be matched to the infraction, and tactics lower on the Intervention Ladder are sufficient to reduce most disruptions at school. Finally, less intrusive or severe tactics should be tried first. In this chapter the Intervention Ladder concept is explored. In the next chapter,

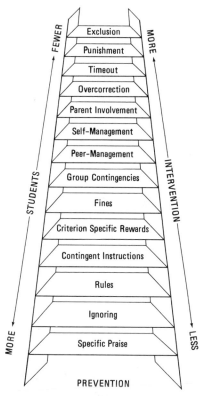

Figure 4.1 The Intervention Ladder (*Source:* D. D. Smith (1984). *Effective Discipline.* (Austin: Pro-Ed, Inc.), p. 2. Used with permission.)

the development of social skills, often deficient in students with special needs, is discussed in some detail.

PREVENTION

Before implementing any direct intervention program aimed at reducing conduct problems, educators should study and analyze the situation. Many conduct problems can be avoided by simple preventative measures. Often, simple changes (such as altering the seating arrangement, implementing a more flexible academic schedule) will reduce disruption and eliminate having to institute disciplinary programs. Although preventing conduct problems could be viewed as an intervention, here such concepts serve as the floor or foundation for the Intervention Ladder and are considered the basis upon which interventions are placed.

School conduct problems occur for several major reasons. Students might be bored with the academic materials presented to them. If the material is too easy, students are not challenged and find other ways to interest themselves. Some students engage in disruptive activities because they are frustrated with academic programs they find too difficult. Others come to school with a well-developed ability to disrupt the learning environment for themselves and others. For these youngsters the academic material is neither too difficult nor too easy. For whatever reasons, they are simply unmotivated to become active participants in the learning process or in activities arranged for the group. Still others seem unable to meet the behavioral expectations of the classroom routine. They are not necessarily unmotivated—in some instances their motivation may be high; rather, their inability to conform often prevents their successful participation in the class.

The relationship between students' abilities and the academic tasks presented to them is strong. Center, Dietz, and Kaufman (1982) found that there is a strong correlation between task difficulty and inappropriate behavior. For students who misbehave because the instructional material is either too difficult or too easy, simply adjusting the curricular demands will eliminate most of the disruption that these students create.

Researchers have also found a strong relationship between academic productivity and disruption. During the 1970s, several groups (Ayllon & Roberts, 1974; Ferritor et al., 1972) found that when students were reinforced for increased academic output, they paid more attention and the number of academic assignments completed increased. The by-product was a decrease in disruption. However, when attending was reinforced, the students looked as if they were paying attention, but academic productivity did not increase. Similar findings were also noted by Lloyd et al. (1981). Educators should be encouraged by these findings. When students are actively involved in their academic learning, disruption and conduct problems are reduced without direct intervention.

For students who misbehave because they are not motivated by learning or typical school events, sometimes making school more interesting and exciting will reduce their conduct problems. Some of these students are "inactive learners" who need to become more involved in their school programs. If educators were to arrange more school activities that mandated increased student involvement, many of these youngsters might become more interested in school, and thereby less disruptive. Many of these students do not participate in team sports, do not belong to school societies and groups, and are detached from school events. For these students, teachers might plan instructional activities (class plays, group assignments that result in a product, mock TV news productions of historical events) that encourage youngsters to become more actively involved in learning.

Consistency in teachers' expectations of school and the consequences for varying from those expectations is important. School personnel need to communicate specifically and carefully, so youngsters understand what is expected of them in a variety of different school situations. For consistency, school personnel must also communicate with each other. All members of the school community—parents, maintenance staff, administrative staff, students, and teachers—must have a common understanding of what constitutes expected and acceptable behavior in the classroom, lunchroom, playground, hallway. Often, when parents and school personnel discuss what behaviors are expected from students in various school situations and come to agreement, schoolwide behavior improves. The reason for this is probably that all those who come into contact with students at a particular school are consistent in their expectations and make those expectations clear to the students.

Some students need direct intervention to decrease their disruptive behavior. For them, the tactics found on the Intervention Ladder will need to be implemented. It is important to remember, however, that tactics found lower on the ladder should be tried first, for they are less serious, are less intrusive upon the learning environment, take less of the teacher's time to implement, disrupt positive learning environments least, and often are effective.

PRELIMINARY INTERVENTIONS

Praise

Praise—complimenting or verbally rewarding others for their accomplishments—is a simple, natural human act that can bring about substantial changes in performance. Unfortunately, it is underused in many classroom settings. This form of teacher attention and feedback has been studied for many years. Gilchrist (1916) found that in English classrooms the praised group of learners' achievement far surpassed that of another group admonished for poor work. According to Kennedy and Willcut (1964) in their review of praise and blame as incentives in the classroom, the influence of praise was studied carefully as early as 1897 by Binet and Vaschide. Despite almost 100 years of research indicating that praise is a very powerful tactic, teachers—particularly those at the upper grade levels—do not use it. The few studies (White, 1975; Thomas et al., 1978) that have investigated the influence of praise more recently have shown that first and second grade teachers tend to use praise, but upper-level teachers do not. By eighth grade, students might hear only four approving statements from their teachers in a forty-minute period. By high school, praise is used almost not at all. These findings are disturbing. How can a learning environment be considered positive when students are not praised for their achievements?

Praise and a teacher's attention can produce remarkable changes in students' social and academic performance. One need only watch a group of kindergarteners react when their teacher praises one of them for being ready to begin group time. Praise is effective when it is specific and tailored to the age and personality of the person. Teachers cannot praise tenth grade students in the same way they do first graders. Older students might not respond favorably to a teacher who praises them publicly, but a private word can mean a great deal. To be effective, praise needs to be precise. Rather than saying, "Heather, you had a good day today," a statement such as, "Heather, I liked the way you came in from all recesses quietly and on time today," will prove to be more effective in improving Heather's transition from play to work. Praise can serve as a reward for proper conduct, and also as a reminder and feedback about a teacher's expectations for students. Before scheduling elaborate programs aimed at changing minor conduct problems, teachers should examine their own rates of attention (praise) to determine whether they could be altered to produce more positive changes in their students' performances.

Ignoring

When someone's attention is important to an individual or group, behavior can be changed by either the systematic application or withdrawal of attention. Praise is a common form of the application of a teacher's attention. Ignoring is its converse. The landmark study that clearly demonstrated the power of adult attention on nursery school children's behavior was conducted more than twenty years ago (Allen et al., 1964).

That work showed that behavior correlates with the application and withdrawal of teacher attention. When the teacher attended to a preschooler while he played alone, the amount of time that child played alone increased. When the teacher paid attention to him when he was playing with other youngsters, he increased his participation in group play. These findings led to a long series of systematic research studies that showed that human attention is important to individuals and influences their behavior. As with praise, however, ignoring is effective only when it is consistently applied. The person applying the tactic must be important to the individual whose behavior needs improvement, and this person must persist in carrying out the tactic in all circumstances. For example, adult attention is extremely important to younger children. That is why those teachers see immediate, and often dramatic, changes when they praise or ignore their students. However, as children get older, the attention of the peer group increases in importance, and the teacher's influence lessens. That is why ignoring older youngsters when they are tardy, talk out of turn, or clown around is ineffective.

Ignoring, particularly when paired with rewards such as praise, can reduce classroom disruption. It can be applied by an adult or peer group (as discussed later in this chapter). Of course, there are instances when ignoring is not the appropriate tactic. It is inappropriate, for example, when the attention of significant others (peers) cannot be controlled or when the student's behavior is dangerous or harmful to the learning environment or to other individuals. Ignoring is a subtle tactic, and might not produce change fast enough for some situations. Breaking school windows, threatening others, or fighting will probably not be influenced quickly enough by ignoring. In such cases, more stringent procedures found higher on the Intervention Ladder will need to be applied.

Rules

Some students do not conform to teachers' expectations for classroom settings because they do not understand what is required of them. They do not understand the demands of the setting. Often, educators assume that youngsters know how they are supposed to act in particular situations. They feel that all students should know they are to be quiet and work on their assignments independently during seatwork time, come to class on time, and listen and take notes during lectures. The codes of school conduct are often implied and not delineated carefully. In some school situations, students learn about the existence of a rule only when they break it and are punished for the infraction. A discovery method for learning school rules and codes of conduct is inefficient.

Also, usually rules of conduct are inconsistent. In some cases the rules change; in others the range of tolerance or the limits of acceptable behavior vary. Some teachers allow considerable freedom of movement or noise during class time; others do not. To conform to different settings and different teachers' styles requires considerable discrimination skills. Such skills are often lacking in students with special needs. Establishing classroom rules and having discussion sessions about them can facilitate a better understanding of school expectations and lead to increased compliance for many youngsters.

Experience and reason provide educators with some guidelines about rules and how they should be developed. Rules are best developed with the entire group through guided discussion. The list of rules developed should not be too long. Rather, rules should be broadly stated so they encompass many situations ("Work quietly so you do not disturb others"). They should be positively stated. Instead of a list of "Don'ts," a list of "Remembers" is more effective.

MODERATE INTERVENTIONS

Contingent Instructions

The establishment of rules usually reduces many instances of classroom disruption but does not result in their elimination. Some students might not understand the implication of the rules set, others might have forgotten a rule, and still others may break rules simply to be disobedient. When a rule is broken or unacceptable behavior occurs, there must be a consequence. For minor or infrequent violations, the consequence should be mild. For major infractions, more serious measures need to be taken. Instructions should be considered when the violation is minor. In some cases, instructions could take the form of a reminder about the rule, a description of the unacceptable behavior, and suggestions about more suitable ways to behave in similar situations. In other cases, mild reprimands—a form of instructions—might be effective. Research findings do provide teachers with some guidelines about the application of reprimands. They should be given quietly, individually, and immediately after (or during) the infraction. The key to the effective use of instructions is for them to be simple, precise, and directly relating to the message.

Probably because instructions are delivered unclearly in many instances, they have resulted in inconsistent results. Many teachers doubt the power of instructions, but they can be quite influential, even in serious situations. In one such case (Roberts & Smith, 1977), a preschooler's aggressive behavior during recess changed positively. John was a particularly large child whose rate of hitting, biting, kicking, and hurting others was very high (see Figure 4.2). He presented a clear danger to the other children in his group. When he hurt another child, his teachers ignored him and attended to his victim. This was ineffective, as indicated by the average number of aggressions (almost twenty) each thirty-minute recess period. During the intervention period, after each act of aggression a teacher held John by the shoulders, looked him in the eye and said, "Don't hit." The instructions were effective. To be certain that the instructions caused the improvement in performance, during one condition, after each aggression the teacher still held John by the shoulders and gained eye contact, but said, "Birds fly." Because the undesirable behavior began to return to rather high levels, one can assume the instructional component brought about the improvement. This was verified by the further improvement noted when the instructions were reinstituted. Clearly, instructions are powerful if carefully applied. In this case, the age of the subject might have contributed to the project's success, but by no means should instructions not be considered when teachers are searching for tactics that have a probability of changing student performance.

Figure 4.2 Number of individual acts of aggression by John across baseline and intervention phases. Contingent instructions were administered during intervention phases. (*Source:* M. B. Roberts & D. D. Smith (1977). The influence of contingent instructions on reducing inappropriate behavior of preschool children. *School Applications of Learning Theory: SALT,* 9(3), p. 33. Used by permission.)

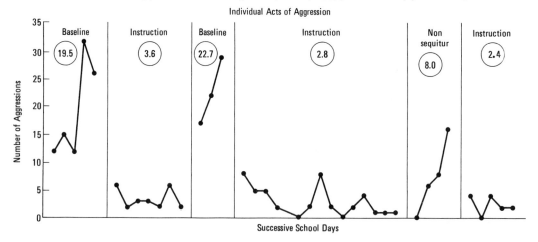

Criterion-Specific Rewards

Rewarding students for improvement in their academic or social skills can come in a variety of forms ranging from concrete or tangible representations of improvement to earning privileges, freetime, or honors. Rewards can be very effective in encouraging students of all ages to conform to classroom and school rules and to improve socially and academically as individuals and as members of groups.

The deliberate use of reinforcement procedures was introduced into classroom settings more than twenty years ago. Although reinforcement has gained in popularity and use since then and the number of variations are now almost infinite, it is not a new discovery. Itard, in 1802, incorporated reinforcement procedures in his remediation program to normalize Victor, the Wild Boy of Aveyron. Although Itard relied heavily on shaping procedures, he used contingent rewards (milk) and praise to reinforce Victor's development of specific skills.

Reinforcement can be defined as the application of an event that increases the likelihood that the behavior it follows will occur again. Reinforcement is applied after a behavior occurs and is functionally related to an increase in frequency of that behavior. An event is a reinforcer only if it causes an increase in the target behavior. What might be a reinforcer for one student might not be for another. Except in the case of primary reinforcers (food, sleep, water), it cannot be assumed that any tactic is a reinforcer. Data must be kept to determine this.

Many teachers like to reduce undesirable behavior by rewarding a behavior that is incompatible with it (*counterconditioning*). For example, students cannot be out-of-seat when they are in their seats; they cannot be talking-out-of-turn when they are quiet. Many situations occur in classrooms where alternative behaviors can be rewarded. Teachers should try to reinforce positive behavior before they implement unpleasant tactics that center on inappropriate conduct. In many cases, direct intervention on the inappropriate or undesirable behavior is necessary. It is advisable, however, first to use a positive procedure so the classroom atmosphere can be as free from negative occurrences as possible.

Selecting Rewards

Most rewards used in school situations are termed secondary reinforcers, for their value must be learned. Events such as freetime, for example, are not naturally reinforcing; the teacher must arrange for students to learn their reinforcing value. Students will not work for library time if they do not know what library time is or that it can be fun and interesting. Many of the events that are highly motivating in school can be used as positive reinforcers, but first students must be aware of their reinforcing value. This can be accomplished through discussions or periods where students can try out potential reinforcers.

Rewards offered to students do not need to be expensive, tangible, or complicated. Because the selection of rewards (reinforcers) is key to the effective use of reinforcement procedures, students should be active participants in the selection of those items or activities that they strive to earn. Probably the best way to select reinforcers is to ask students what they would like to earn as rewards for their accomplishments.

Smith (1984) did just that. Of interest is the finding that middle and high school students (see Table 4.1) often said they would prefer privileges over material goods. In fact, many of the rewards suggested were inexpensive, and some were even tasks many teachers prefer not to do themselves. One reward that has great appeal because of its flexibility and easy fit into the school routine is freetime.

Those activities the student likes to engage in follow those activities the student does not like. "Finish your vegetables, then you may have dessert" and "Complete your arithmetic assignment, then you may work on your art project" are examples of the application of the *Premack Principle*. Premack (1959), through a series of laboratory studies, formulated this hypothesis: *high-strength activities can serve as reinforcers for low-strength activities.*

The first deliberate application of this principle in a classroom situation was probably conducted by Homme et al. (1963). The 3-year-old nursery school students who participated in this study spent an inordinate amount of time running and screaming. This distracted from the "academic" routine. During the intervention condition, children were allowed to run and scream for a period of time contingent upon how long they sat in their chairs, paid attention to the

Table 4.1
Rewards Suggested by Students

Working with a friend in the hall	Reading a magazine
Collecting the lunch money	Obtaining legal hall passes
Taking attendance	Running errands for the teacher
Taking the attendance cards to the office	Taking notes to other teachers
Running off dittos and collating papers	Taking good work to the principal or counselor
Early dismissal	Freetime for special projects
Writing something on a ditto master and running it off	Extra recess
	Stickers on a behavioral report card
Sitting at the teacher's desk to do the assigned seat-work	Lunchtime basketball games, with the teacher serving as referee
Viewing noneducational video tapes on Friday afternoon	Popcorn during educational films
	Special parties
Extra shop or gym time	Field trips
Special picnic lunches or food treats	Special art projects
More assemblies	Listening to the radio
Working on games or puzzles	Decorating the bulletin board
Typing on a typewriter	Being a group leader
Extra library time	Leading the class to the library
Helping the class line up at the door	

Source: D. D. Smith (1984). *Effective Discipline* (Austin: Pro-Ed, Inc.), p. 49. Used with permission.

teacher, and engaged in organized activities. In other words, an organized schedule was imposed on the situation. The children were still allowed to engage in their favorite activities, but this was contingent upon behavior the teaching staff considered most desirable.

The most common application of the Premack Principle in classroom situations is freetime. When contingent freetime is used, students earn minutes to spend in activities of their choice contingent upon appropriate behavior or desirable academic performance. Usually there are a number of freetime activities from which the student can choose (working on an art project, leisure reading, working puzzles, or playing quietly with a friend). It is advisable, however, to allow students to work on freetime activities only during time they have earned. If a student can engage in these activities at any time (earned or not), the incentive for earning minutes of freetime, and thereby improving performance, diminishes.

The incorporation of freetime into the school situation has several advantages. First, the activities used during freetime can be natural to the school setting, not requiring the use of expensive or outside materials; monetary or tangible rewards need not be used. Second, students learn to manage leisure time for themselves. This is an important aspect for many students whose school routine is so established that they do not learn how to manage independent activities and leisure time in constructive ways. For some students, freetime can prove to be a valuable learning experience in itself.

The rewards that students work for must be highly desirable to them. Individuals' tastes and preferences change. What is important to third graders might not be to ninth graders. What is important to students one week might not be the next. Therefore, students should be allowed to work for a variety of rewards and participate in their selection.

Schedules of Reinforcement

When teachers use reinforcement, they typically apply a schedule that organizes and systematizes the earning of rewards. A number of different types of schedules are available that assist in this process. *Fixed ratio (FR) schedules of reinforcement* are used when the individual receives a unit of reinforcement after a specified number of occurrences of a target behavior. This is probably the most common schedule of reinforcement used in academic situations, for it allows the teacher to count the number of correct responses made by a student, apply the ratio, and deliver the specified amount of reinforcement.

One form of a fixed ratio schedule, used only in the early acquisition stages, is the *continuous reinforcement schedule (CRF)*. Here, each time Sue begins her seatwork on time, the teacher praises her. For each ten-minute period that Michael works quietly and independently, a star is placed on a chart. Every time Monica comes to class on time without disruption, she earns a point.

Although continuous reinforcement is quite useful at first, the frequency of reinforcement should be reduced as soon as possible. There are several important reasons for *leaning* (reducing) the schedule of reinforcement from continuous to intermittent. First, the application of a CRF schedule of reinforcement is very expensive in teacher time, requiring a considerable amount of one-to-one attention. Second, CRF schedules are subject to extinction: if reinforcement is given each time the target behavior occurs, when the reinforcement is withdrawn, the desirable behavior tends to disappear and the frequency drops to zero. The last reason for only using CRF schedules initially is a phenomenon referred to as *satiation.* When one reinforcing event is used again and again, its power is often lost. The student who is praised over and over again soon becomes bored with praise and the tactic no longer serves it original purpose. CRF schedules tend to overuse specific tactics and soon meet with the phenomenon of satiation. Therefore, although CRF schedules of reinforcement often are initially highly effective in building a positive set of behaviors for a youngster, it is advisable to move to a less frequent delivery system as soon as possible.

Most youngsters do not need a CRF schedule. For them, earning a unit of reinforcement for every five or ten correct or appropriate responses is sufficient to motivate them to improve their performance. In social situations, fixed ratios might be used when the teacher is counting the number of academic periods a student does not disturb others, play periods free from fights, or offers to help a peer.

One difficulty with FR schedules is that reinforcement is earned even for unsatisfactory performances. Although not many units of reinforcement are earned, even minimum performance levels allow the student reinforcement. If John behaved appropriately in only two academic periods, even if four was the aim, he would receive a reward when FR schedules are in place. To accommodate unsatisfactory behaviors, a slightly more sophisticated tactic may be added to the FR schedule. When *differentially reinforcing higher rates of responding (DRH) schedules* are applied, reinforcement is earned only when the student's scores surpass a specified level—the central tendency score of the previous condition or current functioning level. Because of its confusing name, this schedule of reinforcement is often referred to as a *go-no go contingency.* As its name clearly implies, reinforcement is received for really good work or it is not received at all.

A comparable schedule of reinforcement used to decrease rather than increase students' performances is called *differentially reinforcing lower rates of responding (DRL)* and is often paired with a DRH schedule.

Go-no go contingencies can be used in a variety of social situations as well. They can be applied to increase the number of times a student shares while decreasing the number of unkind statements made toward others. They can be set up to encourage the number of homework assignments turned in on time or the amount of litter left in the lunchroom. The advantage of these schedules of reinforcement centers on the clear indication of the range of behavior that is deemed acceptable.

To help with the determination of what schedule of reinforcement to put into place, formulas and guides for their application are found in Figures 4.3 and 4.4.

Fixed Ratio Reinforcement System

Steps to follow

1. Determine current functioning level
2. Determine short-term aim score
3. Decide reward you want to give for achieving aim score
4. Calculate ratio of reinforcement (aim score ÷ reward)

Example 1:

Previous mean rate = 25
Desired rate = 2 × 25 = 50
Reward for achieving aim = 5
Ratio = 50 ÷ 5 = 10:1

Rate	Calculate	Reward
20	20 ÷ 10 =	2
30	30 ÷ 10 =	3
40	40 ÷ 10 =	4

Example 2:

Previous mean rate = 35
Desired rate = 2 × 35 = 70
Reward for achieving aim = 10
Ratio = 70 ÷ 10 = 7:1

Rate	Calculate	Reward
25	25 ÷ 7 =	3
35	35 ÷ 7 =	5
45	45 ÷ 7 =	6
55	55 ÷ 7 =	8
65	65 ÷ 7 =	9
75	75 ÷ 7 =	10

Figure 4.3 A list of steps to follow and two examples of the implementation of fixed ratio schedules.

Fixed ratio point systems are fairly easy to arrange and manage. Figure 4.3 provides a formula to follow to arrive at the desired ratio, and two examples of its implementation. First, the mean or median score from the previous condition (or baseline) must be determined. This current level of functioning is the basis for determining the amount of improvement attainable. The short-term aim score then must be set in accordance with the student's current functioning level. In the examples provided, the aim score or desired rate was calculated by requiring a doubling of the current functioning level (central tendency score from the previous condition). The teacher then arbitrarily decided that any day the aim score was reached was worth a specific number of reinforcement units. In Exam-

DRH or Go-No Go Contingency

Steps to follow

1. Determine current functioning level
2. Determine short-term aim score
3. Decide reward you want to give for achieving aim score
4. Calculate ratio of reinforcement (aim score ÷ reward)

Example 1:

Previous mean rate = 25
Desired rate = 2 × 25 = 50
Reward for achieving aim = 5
Ratio = 50 ÷ 5 = 10:1
Below 25 no reward

Rate	Calculate	Reward
20	below 25	0
30	30 ÷ 10 =	3
40	40 ÷ 10 =	4

Example 2:

Previous mean rate = 35
Desired rate = 2 × 35 = 70
Reward for achieving aim = 10
Ratio = 70 ÷ 10 = 7:1
Below 35, no reward

Rate	Calculate	Reward
25	below 35	0
35	35 ÷ 7 =	5
45	45 ÷ 7 =	6
55	55 ÷ 7 =	8
65	65 ÷ 7 =	9
75	75 ÷ 7 =	10

Figure 4.4 A list of steps to follow and two examples of DRH schedules of reinforcement.

ple 1, the teacher decided that reaching the aim score was worth five units of reinforcement; in Example 2, it was worth ten. By dividing the aim score by the amount of reinforcement decided upon in step 3, the fixed ratio of reinforcement was determined. That ratio becomes a constant for that intervention condition and is used each day to determine the number of units of reinforcement the student earned for that day's performance.

The DRH or go-no go contingency system merely adds to the fixed ratio situation. Reinforcement is only given to the student if the daily score surpasses a certain level. When fixed ratio schedules are applied, reinforcement (although not much) is given to the student even when performance levels are not desirable (see Figure 4.3). This does not happen when a DRH schedule is applied. The fixed ratio is calculated and implemented as described above, but now reinforcement is earned only when the student's score surpasses a specified level: the central tendency score of the previous condition or current functioning level. Steps to follow and two examples of a DRH reinforcement schedule are provided in Figure 4.4

Multiple ratio schedules of reinforcement are slightly more difficult to establish initially, but they are the most sophisticated form of reinforcement delivery systems used in classrooms. The logic behind their implementation is that greater levels of improvement should be worth more units of reinforcement. In the schedules of reinforcement described here, the same ratio is applied regardless of how much improvement is made by the student. The go-no go contingency feature accounts for unsatisfactory performance, but the ratio is applied consistently at all levels. The multiple ratio schedule allows little reinforcement when small amounts of improvement are achieved and substantial reinforcement for greater amounts of improvement.

When following a multiple ratio schedule, teachers set bands of performance that earn set levels of reinforcement. For example, a student might earn no reinforcement for asking the teacher for assistance properly (raising hand, using a complete sentence, making the request specific) only twice in a school day. He could earn five points for anywhere from three to five such questions and ten points for six or more proper requests for assistance.

In many social situations, the number of correct responses is not as important as the amount of time spent engaged in the proper activity in the desired manner. In these cases, another type of reinforcement schedule is more useful: one that is based on time rather than on number of responses.

The *fixed interval (FI) reinforcement schedule* allows for reinforcement for every selected period of appropriate behavior. FI schedules usually are applied to improve social behavior, on task behavior, study time, or "attending." A kitchen timer can be used to indicate when the fixed time period has passed and reinforcement should either be received or not. For example, Sue needed to increase the amount of time she spent in her seat calculating problems in her arithmetic workbook. The teacher selected a FI schedule of 5:1. For each five-minute time period over the twenty-minute arithmetic study time planned for each day, Sue could earn one point. Each point was exchangeable for an extra minute of recess time. A total of four extra minutes of recess could be earned each day. A kitchen timer was set for five minutes. If she was in her seat working on her assignment during the five-minute segment, she received one point. If she was out of her seat during that segment, she did not receive a point. The timer was then reset and another five-minute segment was initiated.

With both the ratio and interval schedules of reinforcement, schedules may be either fixed or variable. In the fixed situations, as just described, the time period used or the number of responses required are constant. In some cases, better performance is noted when students are not as certain about reinforcement delivery. Then, variable schedules are more useful.

The *variable interval (VI) schedule,* as with most interval schedules, usually is used for social behavior. As with the fixed interval, reinforcement is delivered according to segments or amounts of time, but each time segment differs from the next.

One common application of a variable interval schedule is the "timer game" (see page 102). A kitchen timer is set to ring *on the average* of every five minutes (a schedule of 5 : 1). Sometimes it will ring after one minute, sometimes after nine minutes, sometimes after three minutes, and so on. Anyone in his or her seat working on the assignment when the bell rings receives a point. Anyone not behaving appropriately when the bell rings does not receive a point. At the end of the period, the team or student with the most points wins. Because of the unpredictability of when reinforcement can be earned, students tend to behave consistently better throughout the entire period.

Variable ratio (VR) schedules of reinforcement are similar to fixed ratio schedules, but here once a ratio is determined, an average of that number is applied per session. VR schedules can also be applied when the maintenance of social behaviors is of concern. Peggy's maintenance of excellent behavior in social studies class could be encouraged with a VR schedule. Here, she might not know which days of "perfect" behavior in social studies earn her reinforcement and which days do not.

Fines

As students can be reinforced or rewarded for improvement, they could lose privileges when their performance is unsatisfactory. Fines, often referred to in the research literature as *response cost,* usually are tied to rewards. As a student can earn a privilege through good behavior, that student can lose that privilege because of poor behavior. As with rewards, the schedule for fines should be predetermined, and not set during or immediately after the infraction when tempers and feelings might result in fines too stringent.

In many school situations, students are given privileges even when they do not earn them. For example, attendance at school plays, assemblies, field trips, and sporting events are allowed, regardless of student deportment. Participation and attendance in such activities or specially arranged events could be earned or lost depending on students' behavior. One caution must be raised, however. Some events and activities are not enjoyable to all youngsters. Students who do not want to participate might misbehave purposely to avoid having to attend a school event.

Also, teachers must be careful not to levy fines that negate the possibility of earning a privilege early in the reward period. For example, on Monday each child in the sixth grade was given one card that served as a pass to view on Friday a video recording of the book they were reading. Any child who displayed improper conduct in the hallway during period change was fined that card. Throughout the week, behavior during period change grew worse because those youngsters who were fined on Monday had lost all chance of attending the video. They had no reason left to behave properly. Each day, the number of such children increased, and disruption increased to a level greater than it was originally. When fines are used, students must not lose the incentive to keep working.

Group Contingencies

Group contingencies are tactics that are liked by teachers as well as students, for they can be arranged as classroom games. For this reason, they are sometimes called "good behavior games." In 1975, Litow and Pumroy classified group contingencies into three types: dependent, independent, and interdependent. In the dependent group contingency situation, the class receives reinforcement if a classmate earns it for them. When the independent version is used, a group goal is stated, but students earn reinforcement for themselves as they meet the goal set for the group. When interdependent group contingencies are applied, the behavior of the whole class determines whether reinforcement is received.

Dependent group contingencies have proven to be effective strategies to employ if the behavior of one student is in need of modification. Several precautions should be taken, however, before this contingency system is employed. Target individuals should be capable of earning reinforcement for the group, for if they are not, their peers might inflict severe penalties on them because they failed and the group was denied its due reward.

Independent contingencies eliminate the competitive element present in many group contingency situations. Students can, with the assistance of the teacher, keep track of their own inappropriate behavior during an academic period. Students whose daily score is below the group goal can leave for recess five minutes early; those who exceed the goal must stay in the classroom and continue working.

The most commonly used group contingencies are interdependent, in which the behavior of the group determines whether the group receives reinforcement. In one of the first published reports about the effectiveness of an interdependent contingency. Sulzbacher and Houser (1968) demonstrated its simplicity and power. This intervention was selected because the children engaged in acts that greatly bothered the teacher (using and talking about what these researchers referred to as the "naughty finger"). During intervention, the teacher placed a flip chart at the front of the room. On it were cards with the numbers 10 to zero. The first card showing was the number 10. This indicated that the students had 10 minutes of a special recess at the end of the day. For each transgression a card was flipped, revealing a lower number and indicating that the class lost one minute from their special recess time. Even on the first day of intervention a substantial reduction in the frequency of this behavior was noted. The nice feature of this technique is that the teacher is not required to spend much time managing a complex record-keeping system.

When interdependent group contingencies are used, it is important, however, for the teacher to be certain that the children involved are capable of the requisite behavior. If not, undue pressure could be placed on the individual who causes the group to lose its opportunity for reinforcement. When one child consistently ruins the chances for the group, an individual contingency program could be arranged for that pupil, while the others participate in the group contingency. Also, the teacher must plan for the possibility that several students might actually enjoy subverting the program for the group. If this occurs, the teacher must make special arrangements for the subversive students. Interdependent group contingency programs can be quite effective, particularly when the peer group's attention and reactions are the reasons that undesirable behavior occurs.

Educators have found that interdependent group contingencies can influence a variety of behaviors ranging from general disruption and classroom noise to tardiness. They have reduced the number of off-topic comments in group discussion time by tallying appropriate and inappropriate comments with different colored pencils. That difference could either result in earning or losing different levels of rewards. Those teachers have used listening to popular music while working, free activity periods (justified because of the savings in instructional time regained when the contingency was in effect), extra minutes of physical education, or additional art or science time.

Behavior games are an interesting version of group contingencies that students find fun and motivating. Originated by Barrish, Saunders, and Wolf (1969), behavior games, typically, divide a class into one or more teams. Each time a team member violates a rule (talking out of turn, out-of-seat), that team receives a point. At the end of the period, the team with the fewest points wins the game that might or might not result in a reward or privilege. If all teams have too few points, no team wins. All teams that surpass a certain number of points win the game. The Timer Game, developed by Broden et al. (1970), follows a similar format, but here a kitchen timer is used. Using a variable interval schedule, possibly 5 : 1, the clock is set to ring at different times, averaging every five minutes. In this way, the students cannot predict when the bell is going to ring. When it does ring, each team gets a point if all members are engaged in the proper activity (studying, completing assignments). At the end of the game, teams with points beyond a minimum set by the teacher win the game. Using both the Good Behavior Game and Timer Game formats, teachers have found that behavior control can be accomplished without the aversive aura that some interventions possess.

Peer Management

Using children to help each other is not a new concept. In fact, as early as the first century, the Romans used tutoring as an integral part of the instructional process. Educators are most familiar with peer management as it is applied in tutoring situations (discussed in detail in Chapter 7). However, behavioral management, which uses a one-to-one, tutoring format, and environmental restructuring, relies on an entire group, can be applied to the improvement of student's social behavior. These two techniques are discussed in the next sections.

Behavioral Managers

Peers can help classmates improve their social behavior by establishing a situation much like tutoring. As in other tutoring arrangements, however, educators must consider a number of factors. The children need to be carefully selected. The tutor, referred to as the behavioral manager in social situations, needs to be matched with the other youngster(s). The behavioral manager selected cannot be too powerful or too authoritarian. Some mutual respect between the youngsters should exist or be fostered. The behavioral manager needs to be trained. Those students need to be proficient in the skill they are assigned, and be able to follow through with the program designed by the teacher. Behavioral managers need to know how to use instructions as well as feedback, praise, and reinforcement procedures. They also need defined space in which to work. Finally, behavioral managers need to be rewarded for their efforts, possibly through a dependent group contingency arrangement.

A clever use of a classmate serving as a behavioral manager was reported by Lovitt et al. (1973). The students, two 9-year-old learning disabled youngsters, usually sat near each other in class. One of the students tended to engage in inappropriate and distracting verbal behavior, which the authors generically referred to as "bathroom language." During the intervention condition, the peer manager, upon inappropriate language from his classmate, said, "I don't like you when you say _____." Then he picked up his schoolwork and moved to another desk, away from the other child. Within a short period of time, the frequency of this type of language dropped to zero and remained at that level. Most likely the use of a classmate as the behavioral manager (rather than the teacher) created a positive atmosphere for both boys and released the teacher from interfering in the situation.

When carefully monitored, peers can effectively be used as behavioral managers to help develop a more positive classroom environment. Since in many situations peers encourage inappropriate behavior, it seems worthwhile to encourage them to develop more positive behavior in each other.

Environmental Restructuring

In many situations, inappropriate behavior occurs because the peer group encourages it and reinforces its maintenance. If, after a treatment program, the environment that originally reinforced the undesirable behavior is not altered, the likelihood of that behavior reoccurring is increased. The "class clown" only engages in silly behavior because he is reinforced by the peer group: They laugh at his antics, pay attention to him, and like his jokes. Through discussion sessions, modeling, role playing, and considerable practice, the class can learn not to react or reinforce inappropriate behavior from a peer. The peer group can also learn to praise proper conduct of a misbehaving or inappropriate peer. This is not easy to accomplish, and takes considerable time. In some situations, however, it might be well worth the effort, for all parties involved can learn that they too are responsible for the behavior that occurs in their classroom or at their school.

Self-management

Self-management procedures have received considerable attention from researchers and teachers lately. These procedures encourage students to become actively involved in their educational programs. For those who could be called inactive learners, these procedures might serve to change their overall orientation to learning and school. Besides being excellent interventions that help to improve students' behavior, they also teach valuable skills needed in life. They help students learn to manage their time, control their behavior, and develop independence. There are three general types of self-management procedures: self-regulation, self-evaluation, and self-reinforcement. These procedures may be used independently or as an entire treatment package.

Self-regulation

The aim of self-control tactics is for individuals to monitor their own behavior. For example, in some instances students determine when and how much study time they need to increase academic performance. In other instances they do not engage in inappropriate behavior because they know which situations precipitate those events and seek to avoid them.

These procedures are usually employed when the target is to reduce undesirable behavior patterns. A series of activities are employed, with controlled relaxation as one of the usual components. One example of a self-control strategy for aggression is called the *turtle technique* (Robin, Schneider, & Dolnick, 1977). The student delays responding or reacting and assumes the turtle position (eyes closed, fists clenched, and head on desk), which relaxes him or her and restrains the aggression. The child then relaxes and thinks of alternative ways to deal with the situation.

Many self-control instructional programs include the following targets: anticipating consequences, appreciating feelings, and managing frustration, inhibition, and delay. These are important skills for all individuals to master, but for those who seem unable to regulate their own behavior, they are critical.

Self-evaluation

There are many components of self-evaluation. Sometimes they are used together as an intervention package, and sometimes only one component is utilized. One form of self-evaluation allows students to correct their own work. *Self-correction* can be useful to busy teachers (because teacher time is saved) and students receive useful and immediate feedback about the accuracy of their work. Many teachers have found that students' accuracy of correcting their assignments is high when the students' papers are periodically checked. Also, this encourages students to be more actively involved in their learning, a by-product of which is less inappropriate behavior in class.

When *self-recording* or *self-monitoring* is implemented, students keep records on their own behavior. Simple frequency measurements are easy for youngsters to use, and in many cases the mere act of keeping data on their own behavior causes positive changes in performance. When *self-reporting* is used, students are required to report to the teacher and sometimes to the class about their performances. Also, many students enjoy and are further motivated by a tactic that is referred to as *self-graphing*. Here, students are responsible for their own evaluation graphs (see Chapter 3), and many educators report substantial improvement in a variety of behaviors when students produce a visual display of their improvement.

Recently, self-monitoring has received considerable attention from researchers. Its use has resulted in increased amounts of attention to task (Hallahan, Marshall, & Lloyd, 1981; Kneedler and Hallahan, 1981; Lloyd et al., 1982) and, thereby, reductions in disruption. Kneedler and Hallahan (1981) also found that students do not have to be accurate in their self-recording for the procedure to be effective.

Self-reinforcement

When this procedure is used, the students rather than the teacher determine the reinforcement schedule and the rewards that are earned for improvement. One of the first studies of this kind (Lovitt & Curtiss, 1969) showed that students can determine their own reinforcement schedules. In that study, student performance was much better under conditions where they determined the reinforcement schedule than when the teacher set the schedule. Although there has been considerable debate about whether self-imposed contingencies are better than teacher-imposed arrangements, it appears that self-reinforcement is superior. In one study (Dickerson & Creedon, 1981), students performed better in the self-reinforcement condition than they did when the teachers were in control. They also noted an excellent by-product of this tactic: the students reminded each other to be quiet and do their assignments and actually praised themselves and each other for improvement.

Many educators who use self-management procedures strongly recommend that all three types—self-regulation, self-evaluation, and self-reinforcement—be used together. Each procedure has considerable power, and together they tend to cause even greater improvement. There are many advantages of self-management. It encourages active involvement that frequently results in students maintaining their improvement for longer periods of time. Once implemented, it saves a teacher considerable time, for the students are responsible for much of their educational programs. This frees the teacher to work individually with students and oversee the class's progress without being bogged down with time-consuming tasks.

Parent Involvement

In the section about preventing behavioral problems in the classroom, at the beginning of this chapter, discussion was provided about including parents in their children's educational programs at schools. Discussion about communicating and working with parents is also found in Chapter 1. Interchange between parents and school personnel should be ongoing. However, asking parents to be involved in the direct intervention of school-related problems should be reserved until other methods, such as those previously described, are tried.

Parents and educators can serve as partners in students' educational programs. Parents have successfully participated in school-based reinforcement programs. Parents could determine part of their children's weekly allowances based on weekly behavioral reports from their teachers. For improved behavior at school, parents could provide their children with extra allowances, more time reading a bedtime book, extra minutes of television, or a special dinner. They also could take the children to a weekend movie, a sporting event, or some other special activity.

There are several important considerations for parents who are arranging a reinforcement system at home. Parents must be able to deliver the reward; a reward earned but not received can result in worsened performance. Many parents need to be guided in their decision making about what is a reasonable reward. Some parents who use fines are too harsh. Parents need guidance in determining the severity of fines. Throughout school-home intervention plans, educators need to supervise the program and be certain that ongoing communication exists.

MORE SERIOUS INTERVENTIONS

Overcorrection

Overcorrection procedures have gained considerable popularity in schools recently because they have an educational component, students must take responsibility for their actions, and they are effective. There are two kinds of overcorrection, *positive practice* and *restitution*. Positive practice overcorrection requires the student to "overpractice" an extreme form of the desired behavior. Table 4.2 gives some examples of positive practice and how it might be implemented.

The form of overcorrection that has drawn the most attention from educators and parents is restitutional overcorrection. The notion of restitution is

Table 4.2
Examples of Positive Practice Overcorrection

UNDESIRABLE ACT	POSITIVE PRACTICE PROCEDURE
1. Nailbiting	Hold hands at side for one minute
2. Noisy classroom transition	Spend the recess period practicing coming to class quietly and beginning assignment independently
3. Autisticlike gestures	Hold hand stiff for fifteen seconds
4. Poor spelling on a composition assignment	Look up all words spelled incorrectly in dictionary and write a paragraph about each word
5. Use of slang words	Practice using correct words in phrases
6. Agitation and disruption	Required relaxation
7. Talking out of turn	Raise hand and wait for teacher to call on student during five-minute practice sessions

supported in many phases of society today, particularly in the court system. Victims are being repaid for losses incurred from crimes. Those who litter are required to pick up litter along roadways. In school situations, restitutional overcorrection requires the individual to restore the environment to an improved state. Table 4.3 lists examples of the implementation of this tactic.

Restitutional overcorrection has several advantages. First, individuals are responsible for their actions. For example, if Jeremy disrupts the class by throwing over desks and scattering books around the floor, he must restore the learning environment, whereas with other procedures, Jeremy might be punished for his actions, but others are left with the task of replacing the classroom furniture. Second, because the offending student is not removed from the classroom, that individual does not lose instructional time.

Although overcorrection is an appealing tactic, it is aversive and rather negative. Educators need to remember that there are many other tactics lower on the Intervention Ladder that should be tried before overcorrection procedures.

Table 4.3
Examples of Restitution Overcorrection

UNDESIRABLE ACT	RESTITUTION PROCEDURE
1. Throw and overturn furniture	Restore whole room to a pleasant appearance, straighten furniture, dust and clean whole room
2. Break or destroy others' property	Earn money needed to purchase replacements
3. Write on desk	Clean all desks in class
4. Write obscenities on wall	Paint whole wall
5. Steal	Return item stolen and an additional item
6. Chew objects	Cleanse mouth with antiseptic
7. Throw rocks on playground	Pick up litter and rocks to clear ground

Timeout

Timeout might well be one of the most controversial tactics found on the Intervention Ladder, largely because of this tactic's frequent misuse and misapplication. As with reinforcement, the use of timeout can be documented as early as the 1800s when Itard tried to teach the wild child, Victor (Lane, 1976). An isolation technique is also described by Olson (1935, pp. 378–79):

> In general, the careful teacher attempts to avoid situations in which a child is given the feeling of being cut off from a group. An occasional child, however, may "go to pieces" so completely as to disrupt either the comfort or activities of his associates in a room. Nursery school teachers, in particular, have found it highly advantageous to remove such a child from the group to a place where he may relax and acquire control without being a distracting influence or attracting the attention he may be seeking. In some instances special rooms have been set aside for this purpose. The isolation technique must be used skillfully in order to be an educational experience for the child, gradually modifying him in the direction of greater control. This goal may be defeated if the child regards the treatment simply as punishment and develops a feeling of antagonism toward the teacher.

Timeout did not gain widespread use until the 1970s, and it has been used most extensively in special education. Simply, timeout is the removal of an individual from an environment that is reinforcing and maintaining inappropriate behavior. There are three forms of timeout. At its mildest, *contingent observation,* a youngster is removed from a group activity for not participating properly, but may still watch the activity from a removed vantage point for a short period of time. The advantage of this tactic is that the student does not lose instructional time and can watch others participating appropriately.

The next form of timeout is referred to as *exclusion timeout* and requires that the student be removed from the learning activity. The educational components are missing, for the student cannot observe the appropriate performance of his or her peers. A disruptive student might be excused from music and requested to return to homeroom.

The most severe variation of timeout (and the one most publicized), *seclusion timeout,* necessitates the use of an isolation room. The misbehaving student is removed from the classroom and spends a specified amount of time alone. Upon each act of aggression, for example, a student was instructed to go to the timeout room for a period of three minutes. When seclusion timeout is used, several important precautions must be taken. First, an appropriate place or room must be found. It should be well-lighted, properly ventilated, sizable (at least six feet by six feet), safe, unlocked, and preferably having a window so the student can be observed periodically (Gast & Nelson, 1977a, 1977b). Also, the duration of timeout should be predetermined (anywhere from one to five minutes is usually sufficient). It is advisable for release to be contingent upon good behavior.

Therefore, many educators use an *extension release clause* or a *changeover delay procedure*. This extends timeout for fifteen seconds if the student is misbehaving while timeout is scheduled to end: to be released the student must act appropriately for at least the last fifteen seconds of the timeout experience.

There are many concerns about timeout and its use in school settings. For some students, timeout could be reinforcing, for they are removed from what they might view as an unpleasant situation. For students who find the academic situation frustrating and even punishing at times, timeout may prove to cause increases rather than decreases in the target behaviors. Inappropriateness may increase when timeout is scheduled because it allows the student to escape an aversive situation. When the learning process is not enjoyable and teachers do not compensate for the often boring and repetitious activities they plan for their students, even timeout, a tactic designed to be unpleasant, can become a more attractive alternative to students.

Timeout, particularly seclusion timeout, has received considerable attention from the press and public recently. There are some very undesirable features of seclusion timeout, and careful consideration must be given to the seriousness of the behavioral infraction before it is scheduled. The implementation of timeout is costly to both student and teacher. The student loses valuable instructional time, and the teacher is forced to schedule an intervention that can be difficult to manage.

Because of the furor over seclusion timeout and because of several court actions placed against residential facilities for the handicapped, a number of precautions must be taken before it is implemented. First, an appropriate and safe place must be located. If a room cannot be found where an adult can monitor the actions of the student, another intervention should be scheduled. For the protection of the teacher, the school principal should be consulted next. If the school administration agrees that seclusion timeout is necessary, the parents should be contacted and their permission obtained. Once timeout is initiated, precise records on its use should be kept. A sample data sheet is provided in Figure 4.5. On that sheet the number of times a student goes to the timeout room and the amount of time spent there are noted.

Timeout and its variations can be very effective tools for teachers who are trying to eliminate or greatly reduce behavioral repertoires that interfere with the learning process. Implementation should occur with care and caution. The student's performance should warrant timeout either because it was unaltered by other tactics or because the transgressions are serious.

Punishment

Although most of the tactics discussed in this chapter can be called punishers, for the sake of clarity, punishment here includes those tactics involving the application of aversive consequences. Punishment, then, is the most severe tactic found on the Intervention Ladder. Although no research studies have investigated physical punishment's effectiveness with noninstitutionalized moderately or mildly handicapped students (Polsgrove & Rieth, 1983), its use by school admin-

		Student's name		Target behavior	

Day	Date	Time Timeout Initiated	Total Time in Timeout	Description of Behavior in Timeout

Figure 4.5 Sample record sheet to be posted near the door of seclusion timeout room.

istrators and their staffs is widespread (Rose, 1983). One reason for this could be its effectiveness. It is, however, an aversive tactic with many negative aspects. Children often associate the aversive technique with the person who administers it. Punishment increases the likelihood of the student trying to escape the situation. Its influence does not usually generalize across settings, so often it needs to be applied in all situations in which the behavior occurs. It can even result in overgeneralization, thus decreasing positive behavior. Punishment is not a behavior-building technique, for new skills are not taught through this method.

There are other negative features of punishment that educators need to know. Some children may simply substitute another undesirable behavior for the one that was punished. Punishment can also put fear into the classroom environment; children perform because they are afraid not to. This does not foster a good learning environment where children feel free to explore and discover.

For these reasons, educators should carefully consider whether punishment should be used in school settings. Many other, less aversive procedures are available that do not have such negative potential. The controversy over punishment has raged for years. Olson (1935) stated that punishment has no real place in "modern" schools. He believed that the use of punishment by a teacher was a sign of incompetence and inefficiency and that direct and rewarding consequences were more effective. Despite concerns about the use of punishment, more and more states are approving, through various court decisions, the use of punishment in the schools. The prevalence of its use is unknown. Clearly when it is used, its full impact must be monitored, and those students who are punished should receive rewards for appropriate performances.

Exclusion

Only a brief discussion is given here about exclusion because states and school districts differ greatly in their policies about excluding regular or special students from school. Generally, there are three kinds of exclusion: *in-school supervision, suspension,* and *expulsion.* The first is a mild form of exclusion and requires the student to spend time in a study hall under the supervision of an adult. One might even consider this procedure a form of timeout. In-school suspension has been used in many mid- and high school settings with considerable success in reducing tardiness to classes, hallway disruptions, and various school rule violations. It can be most useful to have a designated room, supervised by a teacher or paraprofessional, for such instances when students lose the privilege of attending an assembly, field trip, or other school event. When an in-school suspension room is always available, teachers do not have to make special arrangements for students who need to be dismissed from a class because they are disrupting their peers' learning or have lost a privilege.

The other two forms of exclusion require the youngster to stay away from school for some defined period of time. Both these procedures have serious ramifications and need to be carefully considered before they are applied. Under these conditions students lose valuable instructional time, and may fall far behind in their academic subjects, which could contribute to further frustration with school and more behavioral problems. Another difficulty with these procedures is that students may not be supervised while they are excluded from school. When this occurs, they might find that being away from school is more reinforcing than is school itself. If this occurs, students might misbehave again when they return to school, so they can be dismissed again. School officials must consider these negative possibilities before they exclude youngsters from school.

SUMMARY

A considerable number of tactics have been presented in this chapter that aim at the reduction or elimination of misconduct or behavioral problems in school settings. Table 4.4 summarizes these tactics and includes some cautions that educators must consider for each. The Intervention Ladder should serve as a reminder that many mild tactics are available. These should be tried before more elaborate, expensive, or intrusive procedures are implemented. Also, for most infractions in school settings those tactics found lower on the ladder will be effective with the majority of youngsters. For those few youngsters who do not respond favorably to those tactics, the procedures that are more complex and

Table 4.4
Tactics to Improve Social Behavior

TACTIC	DEFINITION	CAUTIONS
Specific praise	Students are provided with positive statements and feedback about their appropriate conduct.	The praise must be precise and tailored to the individual's age and interests.
Ignoring	Teacher systematically and consistently does not pay attention to each occurrence of the target behavior.	The attention of the person who does the ignoring must be important to the one who is ignored.
Rules	The entire class (teacher and pupils) determines a code of conduct for all to follow.	Rules should be positively stated and general so the list is not too long.
Contingent instructions	After an occurrence of the target behavior, quietly and on a one-to-one basis, the individual is told specifically not to engage in that activity.	Instructions need to be concise, direct, and delivered during or immediately after the infraction.
Criterion-specific rewards	The student earns a special privilege only for reaching the desired level of the target behavior.	When a student in the class is earning rewards, all students should have the opportunity to earn rewards. Otherwise, they might purposely misbehave to be put on a reinforcement schedule.
Fines	The student loses privileges for engaging in the target behavior.	Students cannot lose, through fines, the opportunity for receiving a reward or privilege too early; the ratio of units of reward needs to be greater than the fines.
Group contingencies		
Dependent	A person earns privileges or rewards for peers by behaving appropriately.	The target student must be capable of earning rewards for other students.
Independent	Individuals earn reinforcement when they achieve a goal established for the group.	The reward established for the group needs to be important to all the group's members.
Interdependent	The class or group earns a special reward when the entire class meets the established goal.	Any student who is unable to meet the group's goal should have a reasonable, individually set goal to meet.
Peer management		
Tutoring	One student proficient in an academic assignment serves in the role of teacher for a classmate who needs additional assistance.	All tutors, and behavior managers, need to be selected carefully, be proficient in the skills they are to teach, be trained to use teaching methods (praise, feedback, reinforcement), and be rewarded for their efforts.

(continued)

Table 4.4   (*Continued*)

TACTIC	DEFINITION	CAUTIONS
Behavior managers	One whose classroom behavior is usually appropriate earns the privilege of becoming the dispenser of praise and rewards for a peer.	They need a program to implement that is carefully designed, and they need to be supervised.
Environmental restructuring	The class is instructed and reinforced for encouraging a classmate's appropriate behavior.	The peer group needs to be prepared through group discussions and role playing so their reactions to a target peer are appropriate.
Self-management		
Self-regulation	Individuals monitor their own behavior, seek to avoid those situations that precipitate inappropriate behavior, and stop that behavior if it is initiated.	Students need to be taught to analyze their own behavior and predict their reactions in various situations through discussions and role playing.
Self-evaluation	Correcting one's own performance, recording the frequency, and graphing the resulting data.	Students need to be taught to collect data on their own performance and graph the results. Teachers need to check periodically for accuracy.
Self-reinforcement	Rewarding oneself for correct behavior.	Students need to be guided to select realistic goals and rewards.
Overcorrection		
Positive practice	Extreme practice of the desired forms of the target behavior.	Short practice sessions (three to five minutes) are sufficient to cause behavior change.
Restitution	When the environment is destroyed or altered, the student must restore it to an improved state.	The restitution must be directly related to the infraction.
Timeout		
Contingent observation	A disruptive student is removed from a group activity, but is still allowed to observe the proceedings.	The observation period need not be long, and the student should be allowed to rejoin the group.
Exclusion	Upon substantial disruption, the student is excused from class.	A supervised place where the student can be sent must be prearranged.
Seclusion	For severe, out-of-control behavior, the pupil is placed in an isolation room.	Permissions of school officials and parents must be obtained. A proper timeout room that meets standard guidelines (size, lighting, ventilation, supervised) needs to be arranged. Data on its use must be collected.
Punishment	An aversive event is applied to a student after an occurrence of an undesired behavior.	The punishment and the person who delivers it can become negatively associated.
Exclusion		
In-school supervision	Student is removed from one or more classes but is required to spend the time in a designated school area.	A room needs to be designated and an adult continually assigned for supervision.

(*continued*)

Table 4.4 *(Continued)*

TACTIC	DEFINITION	CAUTIONS
Suspension	An individual is removed from school for a specified number of days, not usually longer than ten school days.	Plans for supervision of a suspended youngster should be established with the parent.
Expulsion	A student is removed from school either permanently or for an indefinite time, usually exceeding ten school days.	The possibility that an expelled student will find nonschool activities more interesting and rewarding must be considered.

aversive, found higher on the ladder, may prove to be necessary to improve the learning environment for target students and their peers.

STUDY AND DISCUSSION QUESTIONS

1. Explain the concept of the Intervention Ladder.
2. Provide a classroom example of each tactic listed in Table 4.4.
3. Select three tactics from the Intervention Ladder, discuss their major limitations, and indicate the concerns that educators must consider before their implementation.

REFERENCES AND SUGGESTED READINGS

General Social Behavior Remediation

McConnell, S. R., Strain, P. S., Kerr, M. M., Lenkner, D. A., & Lambert, D. L. (1984). An empirical definition of elementary school adjustment. *Behavior Modification, 8*(4), 451–473.

Macomb Intermediate School District. (1981). We're good . . . and getting better! *Idea Series,* 1–6.

Smith, D. D. (1984). *Effective discipline.* Austin, TX: Pro-Ed.

Prevention

Ayllon, T., & Roberts, M. D. (1974). Eliminating discipline problems by strengthening academic performance. *Journal of Applied Behavior Analysis, 7,* 71–76.

Center, D. B., Dietz, S. M., & Kaufman, M. E. (1982). Student ability, task difficulty, and inappropriate classroom behavior. *Behavior Modification, 6*(3), 355–374.

Ferritor, D. E., Buckholdt, D., Hamblin, R. L., & Smith, L. (1972). The non-effects of contingent reinforcement for attending behavior on work accomplished. *Journal of Applied Behavior Analysis, 5,* 7–17.

Lloyd, J. W., Hallahan, D. P., Kosiewicz, M. M., & Kneedler, R. D. (1982). Reactive effects of self-assessment and self-recording on attention to task and academic productivity. *Learning Disability Quarterly, 5,* 216–227.

Praise

BROPHY, J. (1981). Teacher praise: A functional analysis. *Review of Educational Research, 51*, 5–32.

GILCHRIST, E. P. (1916). The extent to which praise and reproof affect a pupil's work. *School and Society, 4*, 872–874.

HELLER, M. S., & WHITE, M. A. (1975). Rates of teacher verbal approval and disapproval to higher and lower ability classes. *Journal of Educational Psychology, 67*, 796–800.

KENNEDY, W. A., & WILLCUTT, H. C. (1964). Praise and blame as incentives. *Psychological Bulletin, 62*, 323–332.

MORSINK, C. V., SOAR, R. S., SOAR, R. M., & THOMAS, R. (1986). Research on teaching: Opening the door to special education classrooms: *Exceptional Children, 53*, 32–40.

THOMAS, J. D., PRESLAND, I. E., GRANT, M. D., & GLYNN, T. L. (1978). Natural rates of teacher approval and disapproval in grade-7 classrooms. *Journal of Applied Behavior Analysis, 11*, 91–94.

THURLOW, M., GRADEN, J., GREENER, J., & YSSELDYKE, J. (1983). LD and non-LD students' opportunities to learn. *Learning Disability Quarterly, 6*, 172–183.

WHITE, M. A. (1975). Natural rates of teacher approval and disapproval in the classroom. *Journal of Applied Behavior Analysis, 8*, 367–372.

Ignoring

ALLEN, K. E., HART, B. M., BUELL, J. S., HARRIS, F. R., & WOLF, M. M. (1964). Effects of social reinforcement in isolate behavior of a nursery school child. *Child Development, 35*, 511–518.

BECKER, W. C., MADSEN, C. H., ARNOLD, C. R., & THOMAS, D. R. (1967). The contingent use of teacher attention and praise in reducing classroom behavior problems. *The Journal of Special Education, 1*, 287–307.

BIRNBRAUER, J. S., BIJOU, S. W., WOLF, M. M., & KIDDER, J. D. (1965). Programmed instruction in the classroom. In L. P. Ullmann & L. Krasner (eds.), *Case studies in behavior modification.* New York: Holt, Rinehart and Winston.

HALL, R. V., FOX, R., WILLARD, D., GOLDSMITH, L., EMERSON, M., OWEN, M., DAVIS, F., & PORCIA, E. (1971). The teacher as observer and experimenter in the modification of disputing and talking-out behaviors. *Journal of Applied Behavior Analysis, 4*, 141–149.

LOVITT, T. C. (1978). *Managing inappropriate behaviors in the classroom.* Reston, VA: The Council for Exceptional Children.

LOVITT, T. C., LOVITT, A. O., EATON, M. D., & KIRKWOOD, M. (1973). The deceleration of inappropriate comments by a natural consequence. *Journal of School Psychology, 11*, 148–154.

MADSEN, C. H., JR., BECKER, W. C., & THOMAS, D. R. (1968). Rules, praise, and ignoring: Elements of elementary classroom control. *Journal of Applied Behavior Analysis, 1*, 139–150.

SAJWAJ, T., TWARDOSZ, S., & BURKE, M. (1972). Side effects of extinction procedures in a remedial preschool. *Journal of Applied Behavior Analysis, 5*, 163–175.

WILLIAMS, C. D. (1959). The elimination of tantrum behavior by extinction procedures. *Journal of Abnormal and Social Psychology, 59*, 269.

ZIMMERMAN, E. H., & ZIMMERMAN, J. (1962). The alteration of behavior in a special classroom situation. *Journal of the Experimental Analysis of Behavior, 5*, 59–60.

Rules

DUKE, D. L. (1980). *Managing student behavior problems.* New York: Teachers College, Columbia University.

EMMER, E. T., EVERTSON, C. M., SANFORD, J. P., CLEMENTS, B. S., & WORSHAM, M. E. (1984). *Classroom management for secondary teachers.* Englewood Cliffs, NJ: Prentice Hall.

EVERTSON, C. M., EMMER, E. T., CLEMENTS, B. S., SANFORD, J. P., & WORSHAM, M. E. (1984). *Classroom management for elementary teachers.* Englewood Cliffs, NJ: Prentice Hall.

LONG, J. D., & FRYE, V. H. (1977). *Making it till Friday: A guide to successful classroom management.* Princeton, NJ: Princeton Book Company.

LOVITT, T. C. (1978). *Managing inappropriate behaviors in the classroom.* Reston, VA: Council for Exceptional Children.

Contingent Instructions

O'LEARY, K. D., KAUFMAN, K. F., KASS, R. E., & DRABMAN, R. S. (1970). The effects of loud and soft reprimands on the behavior of disruptive students. *Exceptional Children, 37,* 145–155.

ROBERTS, M. B., & SMITH, D. D. (1977). The influence of contingent instructions on the social behavior of a young boy. *School Applications of Learning Theory, 9,* 24–42.

VAN HOUTEN, R., NAU, P. A., MCKENZIE-KEATING, D. E., SAMEOTO, D., & COLAVECCHIA, B. (1982). An analysis of some variables influencing the effectiveness of reprimands. *Journal of Applied Behavior Analysis, 15,* 65–83.

Criterion-Specific Rewards

AYLLON, T. (1963). Intensive treatment of psychotic behavior by stimulus satiation and food reinforcement. *Behavior Research and Therapy, 1,* 53–61.

AYLLON, T., & AZRIN, N. H. (1964). Reinforcement and instructions with mental patients. *Journal of the Experimental Analysis of Behavior, 7,* 327–331.

BIRNBRAUER, J. S., BIJOU, S. W., WOLF, M. M., & KIDDER, J. D. (1965). Programmed instruction in the classroom. In L. P. Ullmann & L. Krasner (eds.), *Case studies in behavior modification.* New York: Holt, Rinehart and Winston.

DEITZ, D. E. D., & REPP, A. C. (1983). Reducing behavior through reinforcement. *Exceptional Education Quarterly, 3,* 34–36.

FULLER, P. R. (1949). Operant conditioning of a vegetative human organism. *American Journal of Psychology, 62,* 587–590.

GIRARDEAU, F. L., & SPRADLIN, J. E. (1964). Token rewards in a cottage program. *Mental Retardation, 2,* 345–351.

HEWETT, F. M. (1967). Educational engineering with emotionally disturbed children. *Exceptional Children, 33,* 459–467.

HEWETT, F. M., TAYLOR, F. D., & ARTUSO, A. A. (1969). The Santa Monica project: Evaluation of an engineered classroom design with emotionally disturbed children. *Exceptional Children, 35,* 523–529.

KAZDIN, A. E. (1982). The token economy: A decade later. *Journal of Applied Behavior Analysis, 15,* 431–445.

LANE, H. (1976). *The wild boy of Aveyron.* Cambridge, MA: Harvard University Press.

RASCHKE, D., STAINBACK, S., & STAINBACK, W. (1982). The predictive capabilities of three sources for a promised consequence. *Behavior Disorders, 7*(4), 213–218.

SCHULTZ, C. B., & SHERMAN, R. H. (1976). Social class, development, and differences in reinforcer effectiveness. *Review of Educational Research, 46,* 25–59.

Freetime

BRODEN, M., HALL, R. V., DUNLAP, A., & CLARK, R. (1970). Effects of teacher attention and a token reinforcement system in a junior high school special education class. *Exceptional Children, 36,* 341–349.

COWEN, R. J., JONES, F. H., & BELLACK, A. S. (1979). Grandma's rule with group contingencies—A cost-efficient means of classroom management. *Behavior Modification, 3,* 397–418.

EVANS, G. W., & OSWALT, G. L. (1968). Acceleration of academic progress through the manipulation of peer influence. *Behavior Research and Therapy, 6,* 189–195.

HOMME, L. E., DEBACA, P. C., DEVINE, J. V., STEINHORST, R., & RICKERT, E. J. (1963). Use of the Premack principle in controlling the behavior of nursery school children. *Journal of the Experimental Analysis of Behavior, 6,* 544.

LOVITT, T. C., GUPPY, T. E., & BLATTNER, J. E. (1969). The use of a free-time contingency with fourth graders to increase spelling accuracy. *Behavior Research and Therapy, 7,* 151–156.

OSBORNE, J. G. (1969). Free-time as a reinforcer in the management of classroom behavior. *Journal of Applied Behavior Analysis, 2,* 113–118.

PREMACK, D. (1959). Toward empirical behavior laws. I. Positive reinforcement. *Psychological Review, 66,* 219–233.

Fines

POLSGROVE, L., & RIETH, H. (1983). Procedures for reducing children's inappropriate behavior in special education settings. *Exceptional Education Quarterly, 3,* 20–33.

RAPPORT, M. D., MURPHY, H. A., & BAILEY, J. S. (1982). Ritalin vs. response cost in the control of hyperactive children: A within subject comparison. *Journal of Applied Behavioral Analysis, 15,* 205–216.

SINDELAR, P. T., HONSAKER, M. S., & JENKINS, J. R. (1982). Response cost and reinforcement contingencies of managing the behavior of distractible children in tutorial settings. *Learning Disability Quarterly, 5,* 3–13.

WALKER, H. M. (1983). Applications of response cost in school settings. *Exceptional Education Quarterly, 3,* 47–55.

Group Contingencies

BARRISH, H. H., SAUNDERS, M., & WOLF, M. M. (1969). Good behavior game: Effects of individual contingencies for group consequences on disruptive behavior in a classroom. *Journal of Applied Behavior Analysis, 2,* 119–124.

BRODEN, M., HALL, R. V., DUNLAP, A., & CLARK, R. (1970). Effects of teacher attention and a token reinforcement system in a junior high school special education class. *Exceptional Children, 36,* 341–349.

LITOW, L., & PUMROY, D. K. (1975). A brief review of classroom group-oriented contingencies. *Journal of Applied Behavior Analysis, 8,* 341–347.

SPELTZ, M. L., MOORE, J. E., & McREYNOLDS, W. T. (1979). A comparison of standardized and group contingencies in a classroom setting. *Behavior Therapy, 10,* 219–226.

Dependent

EVANS, G. W., & OSWALT, G. L. (1968). Acceleration of academic progress through the manipulation of peer influence. *Behavior Research and Therapy, 6,* 189–195.

Independent

BROOKS, R. B., & SNOW, D. L. (1972). Two case illustrations of the use of behavior-modification techniques in the school setting. *Behavior Therapy, 3,* 100–103.

Interdependent

GREENWOOD, C. R., SLOANE, H. N., JR., & BASKIN, A. (1974). Training elementary aged peer-behavior managers to control small group programmed mathematics. *Journal of Applied Behavior Analysis, 7,* 103–144.

HERMAN, S. H., & TRAMONTANA, J. (1971). Instructions and group versus individual reinforcement in modifying disruptive group behavior. *Journal of Applied Behavior Analysis, 4,* 113–119.

RETTIG, E. B., & PAULSON, T. L. (1975). *ABC's for teachers: An inservice training program in behavior modification skills.* Van Nuys, CA: Associates for Behavior Change.

SAIGH, P. A., & UMAR, A. H. (1983). The effects of a good behavior game on the disruptive behavior of Sudanese elementary school students. *Journal of Applied Behavior Analysis, 16,* 339–344.

SCHMIDT, G. W., & ULRICH, R. E. (1969). Effects of group contingent events upon classroom noise. *Journal of Applied Behavior Analysis, 2,* 171–179.

SULZBACHER, S. I., & HOUSER, J. E. (1968). A tactic to eliminate disruptive behaviors in the classroom: Group contingent consequences. *American Journal of Mental Deficiency, 73,* 88–90.

WILSON, C. W., & HOPKINS, B. L. (1973). The effects of contingent music on the intensity of noise in junior high home economics classes. *Journal of Applied Behavior Analysis, 6,* 269–275.

Peer Management

DOUGHERTY, B. S., FOWLER, S. A., & PAINE, S. C. (1985). The uses of peer monitors to reduce negative interaction during recess. *Journal of Applied Behavior Analysis, 18,* 141–153.

FOWLER, S. A. (1986). Peer monitoring and self-monitoring: Alternatives to traditional teacher management. *Exceptional Children, 52,* 573–581.

GRAUBARD, P. S. (1969). Utilizing the group in teaching disturbed delinquents to learn. *Exceptional Children, 36,* 267–276.

GRIEGER, T., KAUFFMAN, J. M., & GRIEGER, R. M. (1976). Effects of peer reporting on cooperative play and aggression of kindergarten children. *Journal of School Psychology, 14,* 307–312.

KERR, M. M., STRAIN, P. S., & RAGLAND, E. U. (1982). Teacher-mediated peer feedback treatment of behaviorally handicapped children. *Behavior Modification, 6*(4), 277–290.

LAZERSON, D. B. (1980). "I must be good if I can teach!"—Peer tutoring with aggressive and withdrawn children. *Journal of Learning Disabilities, 13,* 152–157.

LOVITT, T. C., LOVITT, A. O., EATON, M. D., & KIRKWOOD, M. (1973). The deceleration of inappropriate comments by a natural consequence. *Journal of School Psychology, 11,* 148–154.

SAINATO, D. M., MAHEADY, L., & SHOOK, G. L. (1986). The effects of a classroom manager role on the social interaction patterns and social status of withdrawn kindergarten children. *Journal of Applied Behavior Analysis, 19,* 187–195.

SIEGEL, L. J., & STEINMAN, W. M. (1975). The modification of a peer-observer's classroom behavior as a function of his serving as a reinforcing agent. In E. Ramp & G. Semb (eds.), *Behavior analysis: Areas of research and application.* Englewood Cliffs, NJ: Prentice Hall.

➤ SOLOMON, R. W., & WAHLER, R. G. (1973). Peer reinforcement control of classroom problem behavior. *Journal of Applied Behavior Analysis, 6,* 49–56.

➤ STRAIN, P. S. (1981). Peer-mediated treatment of exceptional children's social withdrawal. *Exceptional Education Quarterly, 1,* 93–105.

SURRATT, P. R., ULRICH, R. E., & HAWKINS, R. P. (1969). An elementary student as a behavioral engineer. *Journal of Applied Behavior Analysis, 2,* 85–92.

Self-Management

BORNSTEIN, P. H. (1985). Self-instructional training: A commentary and state-of-the-art. *Journal of Applied Behavior Analysis, 18,* 69–72.

KAROLY, P., & KANTER, F. H. (1982). *Self-management and behavior change: From theory to practice.* New York: Pergamon Press.

LOVITT, T. C. (1973). Self-management projects with children with behavioral disabilities. *Journal of Learning Disabilities, 6,* 138–150.

MEICHENBAUM, D. (1977). *Cognitive-behavior modification: An integrative approach.* New York: Plenum Press.

➤ O'LEARY, S. G., & DUBEY, D. R. (1979). Applications of self-control procedures by children: A review. *Journal of Applied Behavior Analysis, 12,* 449–465.

➤ POLSGROVE, L. (1979). Self-control: Methods for child training. *Behavior Disorders, 4*(2), 116–130.

Self-regulation

BOLSTAD, O. D., & JOHNSON, S. W. (1972). Self-regulation in the modification of disruptive classroom behavior. *Journal of Applied Behavior Analysis, 5,* 443–454.

DRABMAN, R. S., SPITALNIK, R., & O'LEARY, K. D. (1973). Teaching self-control to disruptive children. *Journal of Abnormal Psychology, 82,* 10–16.

➤ FAGEN, S. A., LONG, N. J., & STEVENS, D. J. (1975). *Teaching children self-control: Preventing emotional and learning problems in the elementary school.* Columbus, OH: Charles E. Merrill.

PARIS, S. B., & OKA, E. R. (1986). Self-regulated learning among exceptional children. *Exceptional Children, 53,* 103–108.

ROBIN, A., SCHNEIDER, M., & DOLNICK, M. (1977). The turtle technique: An extended case study of self-control in the classroom. In K. D. O'Leary & S. G. O'Leary (eds.), *Classroom management: The successful use of behavior modification* (2nd ed.). New York: Pergamon Press.

➤ ROSENBAUM, J. S., & DRABMAN, R. S. (1979). Self-control training in the classroom: A review and critique. *Journal of Applied Behavior Analysis, 12,* 467–485.

STEVENSON, H. C., & FANTUZZO, J. W. (1984). Application of the "generalization map" to a self-control intervention with school-aged children. *Applied Behavior Analysis, 17,* 203–212.

Self-evaluation

BRODEN, M., HALL, R. V., & MITTS, B. (1971). The effect of self-recording on the classroom behavior of two eighth-grade students. *Journal of Applied Behavior Analysis, 4,* 191–199.

— HALLAHAN, D. P., KNEEDLER, R. D., & LLOYD, J. W. (1983). Cognitive behavior modification techniques for learning disabled children: Self-instruction and self-monitoring. In J. D. McKinney & L. Feagon (eds.), *Current topics in learning disabilities.* Norwood, NJ: Ablex.

HALLAHAN, D. P., LLOYD, J. W., KNEEDLER. R. D., & MARSHALL, K. J. (1982). A comparison of the effects of self versus teacher-assessment of on-task behavior. *Behavior Therapy, 13,* 715–723.

HALLAHAN, D. P., MARSHALL, K. J., & LLOYD, J. W. (1981). Self-recording during group instruction: Effects on attention to task. *Learning Disability Quarterly, 4,* 407–413.

KNEEDLER, R. D., & HALLAHAN, D. P. (1981). Self-monitoring of on-task behavior with learning disabled children: Current studies and directions. *Exceptional Education Quarterly, 2,* 73–82.

Self-reinforcement

BILLINGSLEY, F. F. (1977). The effects of self- and externally-imposed schedules of reinforcement on oral reading performances. *Journal of Learning Disabilities, 10,* 549–559.

DICKERSON, E. A., & CREEDON, C. F. (1981). Self-selection of standards by children: The relative effectiveness of pupil-selected and teacher-selected standards of performance. *Journal of Applied Behavior Analysis, 14,* 425–433.

DICKIE, R. F., & FINEGAN, S. (1977). The long-term effects of self-recording on academic behavior rate in an "emotionally disturbed" boy. *School Applications of Learning Theory, 9,* 38–48.

FANTUZZO, J. W., & CLEMENT, P. W. (1981). Generalization of the effects of teacher- and self-administered tokens to non-treated students. *Journal of Applied Behavior Analysis, 14,* 435–447.

FELIXBROD, J. J., & O'LEARY, K. D. (1973). Effects of reinforcement on children's academic behavior as a function of self-determined and externally imposed contingencies. *Journal of Applied Behavior Analysis, 6,* 241–250.

GLYNN, T. L. (1970). Classroom applications of self-determined reinforcement. *Journal of Applied Behavior Analysis, 3,* 123–132.

LLOYD, J. W., HALLAHAN, D. P., KOSIEWICZ, M. M., & KNEEDLER, R. D. (1982). Reactive effects of self-assessment and self-recording on attention to task and academic productivity. *Learning Disability Quarterly, 5,* 216–227.

LOVITT, T. C., & CURTISS, K. A. (1969). Academic response rate as a function of teacher- and self-imposed contingencies. *Journal of Applied Behavior Analysis, 2,* 49–53.

LOWE, J., & SMITH, D. D. (1979). *Self-management techniques to improve middle school students' math proficiency* (working paper). Albuquerque: Department of Special Education, University of New Mexico.

— RHODE, G., MORGAN, D. P., & YOUNG, K. R. (1983). Generalization and maintenance of treatment gains of behaviorally handicapped students from resource rooms to regular classrooms using self-evaluation procedures. *Journal of Applied Behavior Analysis, 16,* 171–188.

Parent Involvement

KROTH, R. & OTTENI, H. (1985). *Communicating with parents of exceptional children*, 2nd ed. Denver: Love Publishing.

WAGONSELLER, B. R., & McDOWELL, R. L. (1982). *Teaching involved parenting*. Champaign, IL: Research Press.

Overcorrection

CAREY, R. G., & BUCHER, B. (1983). Positive practice overcorrection: The effects of duration of positive practice on acquisition and response reduction. *Journal of Applied Behavior Analysis, 16,* 101–109.

FOXX, R. M., & BECHTEL, D. R. (1983). Overcorrection: A review and analysis. In S. Axelrod and J. Apsche (eds.), *The effects of punishment on human behavior.* New York: Academic Press.

Timeout

BARTON, L. E., BRULLE, A. R., & REPP, A. (1987). Effects of differential scheduling of timeout to reduce maladaptive responding. *Exceptional Children, 53*(4), 351–356.

BRANTNER, J. P., & DOHERTY, M. A. (1983). A review of timeout: A conceptual and methodological analysis. In S. Axelrod and J. Apsche (eds.), *The effects of punishment on human behavior.* New York: Academic Press.

GAST, D. L., & NELSON, C. M. (1977a). Time out in the classroom: Implications for special education. *Exceptional Children, 43,* 461–464.

GAST, D. L., & NELSON, C. M. (1977b). Legal and ethical considerations for the use of timeout in special education settings. *The Journal of Special Education, 11,* 457–467.

LANE, H. (1976). *The wild boy of Aveyron.* Cambridge, MA: Harvard University Press.

MACE, C. F., PAGE, T. J., IVANCIC, M. T., & O'BRIEN, S. (1986). Effectiveness of brief time-out with and without contingent delay: A comparative analysis. *Journal of Applied Behavior Analysis, 19,* 79–86.

OLSON, W. C. (1935). The diagnosis and treatment of behavior disorders of children. In the Thirty-fourth Yearbook of the National Society for the Study of Education (eds.), *Educational diagnosis.* Bloomington, IL: Public Schools.

Punishment

BAER, D. M. (1970). A case for the selective reinforcement of punishment. In C. Neuringer & J. L. Michael (eds.), Behavior modification in clinical psychology. New York: Appleton-Century-Crofts.

HEWETT, F. M. (1967). Educational engineering with emotionally disturbed children. *Exceptional Children, 33,* 459–467.

NEWSOME, C., FAVELL, J. E., & RINCOVER, A. (1983). Side effects of punishment. In S. Axelrod and J. Apsche (eds.), *The effects of punishment on human behavior.* New York: Academic Press.

POLSGROVE, L., & RIETH, H. (1983). Procedures for reducing children's inappropriate behavior in special education settings. *Exceptional Education Quarterly, 3,* 20–33.

RISLEY, T. R. (1968). The effects and side effects of punishing the autistic behaviors of a deviant child. *Journal of Applied Behavior Analysis, 1,* 21–34.

ROSE, T. L. (1983). A survey of corporal punishment of mildly handicapped students. *Exceptional Education Quarterly, 3,* 9–19.

SMITH, J. D., POLLOWAY, E. A., & WEST, G. K. (1979). Corporal punishment and its implications for exceptional children. *Exceptional Children, 45,* 264–268.

WOOD, F. H., & BRAATEN, S. (1983). Developing guidelines for the use of punishing interventions in schools. *Exceptional Education Quarterly, 3,* 68–75.

5

Social Skills

Regardless of the setting (school, home, workplace, leisure-activity), being socially competent enhances individuals' quality of life. Unlike their normal counterparts, individuals with handicaps tend to exhibit the following tendencies in social situations (Schumaker & Hazel, 1984b, p. 492):

> [They] choose less socially acceptable behaviors in a number of situations; they are less able to predict the consequences for their behavior; they misinterpret social cues more often; they adapt their behavior to the characteristics of their listener less frequently; they perform certain verbal and nonverbal social skills at significantly lower levels; and they perform certain inappropriate social behaviors at significantly higher levels.

Although educators have developed and researched many procedures that reduce disruptive classroom behaviors (see Chapter 4 for suggested interventions), the development of positive classroom skills *alone* cannot be equated with the development of social competence. In fact, many youngsters, particularly the withdrawn, do not present conduct problems to their teachers and, therefore, do not receive instructional programs aimed at improving classroom behavior. However, most of these youngsters, and many others, do not develop the social skills necessary for successful social interactions.

Social skills are used in the multidimensional process called social competence. This complex set of abilities facilitates interactions. When effective, social interactions elicit others' positive reactions and reduce the probability that they will respond negatively. The application of social skills must be flexible: different skills must be applied depending upon the situation and social context. The result contributes to acceptance by others.

Deficits in social skills occur throughout all groups of handicapped students. Therefore, issues surrounding the development of social competence are of utmost concern to many educators. Possibly, the importance of developing social skills is more apparent to educators today because of the "mainstreaming" (least restrictive environment) requirement of P.L. 94-142 and P.L. 99-457. As special education youngsters return to regular education for some or all of their educational programs, their deficits in social skills are more obvious. To succeed in these least restrictive environments, students must be able to compete academically *and* socially. Since the initiation of special education, teachers have emphasized academic remediation and improvement. However, social skills development also needs to be a high priority for many students. Social skills training is important because there may be a relationship between poor social skills and juvenile delinquency (Bryan & Bryan, 1986; Schumaker et al., 1982). Schloss et al. (1986) aptly point out that this important area is a set of survival skills, for social competence is important to employment supervisors and relates to job success. Also, Schumaker and Hazel (1984a) believe that for those who do not develop adequate social skills naturally, social interaction difficulties persist through adulthood. For these reasons, educators should include social skills targets in the IEPs of students who do not interact with others successfully.

TOPICS FOR INSTRUCTION

Although a verified taxonomy for social skills training does not exist, considerable research about a variety of skills that fall within the realm of social skills training has been conducted. Also, a number of social skills curricula and instructional programs have been developed recently. These products can assist educators in planning instruction in this important area. Tables 5.1, 5.2, and 5.3 show the topics of instruction included in three well-researched social skills curricula. Analysis of these curricula reveals a vast number of targets for educators to address.

Research about social skills and social competence has focused on clusters of behaviors organized and named differently from those listed in most curricula. Therefore, the lattice found in Figure 5.1 was developed to show another schema for social competence. This lattice is not intended to represent another curriculum model, but rather to organize the research literature so the results can be presented concisely. Throughout these discussions, it is important to remember that recent research (see the suggested readings list at the end of the chapter) has shown that social skills can be taught and peer acceptance improved.

Table 5.1
Stephens's Social Skills Curriculum

SELF-RELATED BEHAVIORS	ENVIRONMENTAL BEHAVIORS
Accepting consequences	Care for the environment
Ethical behavior	Dealing with emergencies
Expressing feelings	Lunchroom behavior
Positive attitude toward self	Movement around environment
Responsible behavior	
Self-care	

TASK-RELATED BEHAVIORS	INTERPERSONAL BEHAVIORS
Asking and answering questions	Accepting authority
Attending behavior	⇠ Coping with conflict
Classroom discussion	Gaining attention
Completing tasks	Greeting others
Following directions	Helping others
Group activities	Making conversation
Independent work	Participating in organized play
On-task behavior	Exhibiting positive attitude toward
Performing before others	others
Quality of work	Playing informally
	Respecting property, own and others

Source: Thomas M. Stephens, *Social Skills in the Classroom* (Columbus, OH: Cedars Press, 1978), pp. 34–38. Reprinted by permission.

Social Cognition

To interact with others effectively, individuals must comprehend each other's messages, those implied and those explicit. They also must understand the social context and situation. Social cognition is the ability to gather information from the social field, process that information, determine its importance, and formulate a direction for positive action. This requires a considerable degree of experience and sophistication, which many persons with special needs do not possess.

To comprehend social situations, individuals also need to understand the emotional state of others. To do this requires an ability to understand other people's viewpoints. In the research literature, this ability is called *role taking*. Role taking relates to social perception because it requires a person to determine what someone else is thinking and feeling. It also forces that individual to "see" things from a different perspective. Role-taking skills can be improved through a number of activities. For example, students can make up several versions of the same story. The "Three Little Pigs" could be told from two perspectives: the pigs' and the wolf's. Role-taking skills are also refined through acting. Students could put on a class play, where extra time in discussion would be spent talking about the characters, their feelings, and emotions.

Table 5.2
The Walker Social Skills Curriculum

AREA I:	CLASSROOM SKILLS
	Listening to the teacher (sit quietly and look at . . .)
	When the teacher asks you to do something (you should do it)
	Doing your best work (follow directions and write neatly)
	Following classroom rules
AREA II:	BASIC INTERACTION SKILLS
	Eye contact
	Using the right voice
	Starting (finding someone to talk to)
	Listening (look at the person and pay attention)
	Answering (saying something after someone talks to you)
	Making sense (talking about the same things)
	Taking turns talking
	Asking questions
	Continuing to talk (keeping the talking going)
AREA III:	GETTING ALONG SKILLS
	Using the polite words (saying nice things at the right time)
	Sharing
	Following rules (everyone plays the game the same way)
	Assisting others (doing nice things for others when they need help)
	Touching the right way
AREA IV:	MAKING FRIENDS
	Good grooming (wash hands and face, brush teeth, clean clothes)
	Smiling
	Complimenting
	Friendship making (starting, taking turns talking, inviting)
AREA V:	COPING SKILLS
	When someone says no (find another way to play)
	When you express anger
	When someone teases you
	When someone tries to hurt you
	When someone tells you to do something you can't do
	When things don't go right

Source: H. M. Walker, S. McConnell, D. Holmes, B. Todis, J. Walker, & N. Golden (1983). *The Walker social skills curriculum: The accepts program.* (Austin, TX: Pro-Ed, Inc.). Used by permission.

Social comprehension, which may be improved by enhanced role-taking abilities, requires the individual to perceive the words used, the tone of voice, and the nonverbal expressions of others. The research evidence is clear: many students with special needs—whether watching a video tape or television show or participating in real-life situations—do not perceive or comprehend social situations well. This might be due to an inability to discriminate social cues, make inferences, or understand the importance of information conveyed implicitly or received subtly in social situations. Evidence from research and clinical practice

Table 5.3
Social Skills for Daily Living

ORIENTATION: BODY BASICS

Kit 1: Conversation and Friendship Skills
Active listening
Greeting
Saying goodbye
Answering questions
Asking questions
Introducing yourself
Interrupting correctly
Conversation
Making friends

Kit 2: Skills for Getting Along with Others
Accepting thanks
Saying thanks
Accepting compliments
Giving compliments
Apologizing
Accepting no
Resisting peer pressure
Responding to teasing
Accepting criticism
Giving criticism

Kit 3: Problem-Solving Skills
Following instructions
Getting help
Asking for feedback
Giving rationales
Solving problems
Persuasion
Negotiation
Joining group activities
Starting activities with others
Giving help

Source: J. B. Schumaker, J. S. Hazel, & C. S. Pederson, *Social Skills for Daily Living* (Circle Pines, MN: American Guidance Service, 1988). Used by permission.

indicates that social cognition is developmental: For many it improves with age; for those who do not gain these skills independently, social cognition can be improved through direct instruction. Therefore, teachers need to consider social cognition targets (sensitivity, perception, comprehension, interpretation) and use opportunities for instruction that arise across the school day. Also, planned lessons aimed at teaching these social cognition skills need to be scheduled for students who have skill deficits in this area.

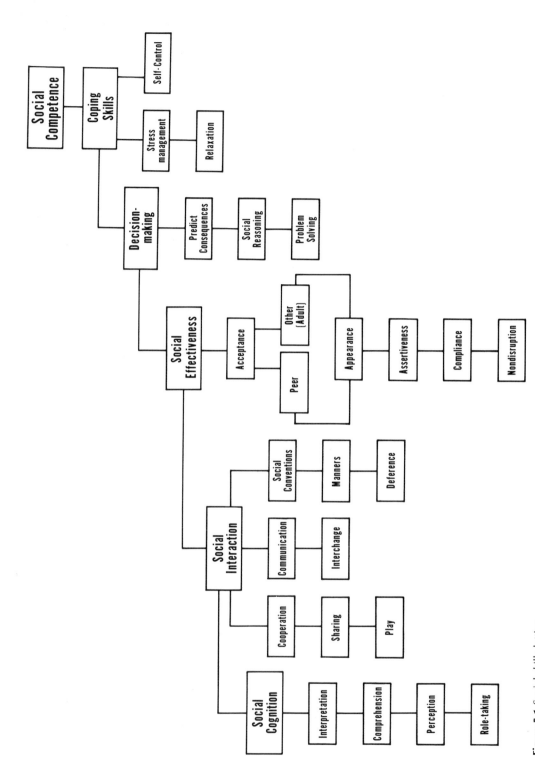

Figure 5.1 Social skills lattice.

Social Interaction

People interact with each other in a variety of ways. Very young children interact with each other primarily through play. In play situations, children learn to cooperate, establish and follow rules, and share. Although play remains a part of people's lives through adulthood, social interaction assumes a greater communicative function (see Chapter 6 for more information) as individuals become older. As with play, communicative interaction requires facility with a number of complex behaviors. Someone must initiate. For those participating, an interchange of giving and taking of turns and persistence to remain on topic is required for the interaction to continue. Then, the interaction needs to be terminated. The communicative situation requires individuals to ask open-ended questions and select and engage in conversational topics.

Social interaction requires complex skills and abilities that interplay with each other. A number of skills contribute to successful social interactions: eye contact, duration and latency of replies, compliance, requesting new behaviors or topics, loudness of speech, gestures, and general affect. Effective social interactions also require individuals to discriminate the proper place and time for their interactions. Engaging in conversation about the games to play at recess is not appropriate during seatwork assignments. Manners and other social conventions also determine the appropriateness of when and how to interact with others. Introductions and greetings vary by the setting and the person. The way one greets an employer is different from the way one greets a friend. In that regard, individuals must learn that interactions with authority figures are different; there is an expectation of deferential respect and attentiveness.

The social context in which interactions occur, and the way they vary, make the mastery of skills that constitute social interaction difficult. These difficulties are compounded for individuals who come from a culture different from the dominant one. McDowell and Murphy (1979) point out that cultural differences must be considered when teaching students social skills. For example, gaining eye contact when participating in a conversation is expected in the dominant culture. It is considered rude in the Navajo and other Native American cultures. This fact raises several questions that have yet to be answered by educators. For example, exactly what social skills should educators teach students from different cultures? Can these students be taught to discriminate cultural settings and the appropriateness of various interaction styles depending on the cultural situation? Who should teach these skills?

Social Effectiveness

Social effectiveness, sometimes referred to as social integration, implies acceptance from peers and others. The product of social effectiveness is social status. This status, particularly from the peer group, is important to most individuals. Peer acceptance requires a number of skills and attributes, such as friendliness, social visibility, outgoingness, social participation, nurturance and reinforcement of peers, kindness, and sensitivity. The result is making and maintaining friendships, an aspect of peer acceptance.

Many students with special needs are not as socially active as their normal counterparts (Deshler & Schumaker, 1983). They go out less frequently, attend fewer sporting events, and participate less in extracurricular activities. Whether social inactivity is a result of social ineffectiveness, or vice versa, it further contributes to lessened acceptance and lowered valuation from the peer group.

Social skills instructional programs (Schumaker, Hazel, & Pederson, 1988; Hazel et al., 1981; Walker et al., 1983) typically include components on how to make friends. Interestingly, a relationship exists between having friends and social status and grooming (being neat and clean, dressing). The importance of good grooming skills was identified in a study conducted by Schumaker, Wildgen, and Sherman (1982). They found that students with special needs tend to be less able in a number of factors relating to appearance (pleasant facial expression, posture, grooming, clothing neatness, general attractiveness) than their regular education counterparts. Other behaviors like verbal and nonverbal interactions (such as smiling, complimenting others, initiating conversations, and taking turns) also seem to relate to social effectiveness.

Another factor that contributes to social effectiveness for school-aged youngsters is their classroom behavior. Drabman and Patterson (1981) maintain that disruptive students are less popular than are those who follow rules and behave according to teacher's expectations for the class. This may be one reason why many exceptional students are not valued by their peers. These authors suggest that once such inappropriate behavior is reduced or eliminated (see Chapter 4 for suggestions for remediation), these students' social status also improves.

Another aspect of social effectiveness—assertiveness—is beginning to come to the attention of researchers. Although in the extreme it is not a positive characteristic, assertiveness is a valuable social skill. There are many facets of assertiveness, and each has some social benefits. For example, students must know when and how to say "no" to peers or others who demand the participation in or submission to an inappropriate behavior. Avoiding being a victim requires assertion. Assertion can also be helpful, according to Combs and Slaby (1977), to complain about unsatisfactory services, return goods, refuse unreasonable demands, make rightful claims to goods or services, and stand up for one's rights. Assertiveness, like other social skills, can be developed through direct instruction (as described in the teaching tactics section of this chapter).

Social effectiveness requires proficiency in the skills discussed in this section as well as those identified under the topic of social cognition. Merely interacting with others does not guarantee effectiveness, nor does the possession of the skills discussed in these two sections. Students must decide when to use and apply them at the appropriate times and places.

Decision Making ✷

Although many students seem to understand what is deemed acceptable behavior at school and in society, they seem unable to choose socially acceptable behaviors in specific situations. According to Schumaker and Hazel (1984b), many youngsters are unable to solve social problems. When a situation is described, they cannot identify the problem. They cannot provide options for handling the situation or predict the consequences for the solutions they suggest. They cannot arrive at the best way to behave or react in situations similar to the one presented to them. Bryan and Bryan (1986) maintain that many youngsters with special needs tend to select antisocial behaviors, particularly when pressured by their peers. The link between juvenile delinquency and mild handicaps might relate to poor decision-making skills and inabilities to solve social problems.

Problem solving, as discussed throughout this text, is an area in which many students need considerable instruction. Whether solving a mathematical problem or a problem in a social situation, these students are unable to arrive at appropriate solutions. Meichenbaum (1979) believes that problem-solving deficits "include selecting the first solution the child thinks of without developing alternatives or examining consequences, thus failing to conceptualize alternative options of action" (p. 24). He believes that children need to develop social reasoning skills, where they develop alternate solutions to simple conflict situations and predict the consequences of their solutions. He suggests that training sessions can take the form of group games where children are encouraged to think and reason rather than elicit set responses. Table 5.4 shows the components of social problem-solving training advocated by Meichenbaum. These steps should be helpful to teachers as they design instructional programs for students deficient in these important skill areas.

Table 5.4
Meichenbaum's Components of Problem-Solving Training

Prerequisite skill	(Pre)	Look for signs of upset, or "not so good," feelings.
Problem definition	(1)	Know exactly what the problem is.
Goal statement	(2)	Decide on your goal.
Impulse delay	(3)	Stop and think before you act.
Generation of alternatives	(4)	Think of as many solutions as you can to solve your problem.
Consideration of consequences	(5)	Think of the different things after each solution.
Implementation	(6)	When you think you have a really good solution, try it.
Recycle	(Post)	If your first solution doesn't work, be sure to try again.

Source: D. Meichenbaum, Teaching self-control. In B. B. Lahey & A. E. Kazdin, eds., *Advances in Clinical Child Psychology: vol. 2.* (New York: Plenum Press, 1979), p. 10. Used by permission.

Coping Skills

The broad area of coping skills has not received the attention of researchers, yet it is an area that needs to be studied, particularly as it pertains to the social competence of individuals with special needs. For example, stress management and anxiety control are areas that all people, whether handicapped or not, find important in our increasingly complex society.

One aspect of coping—self-control—has been the topic of considerable research over the last decade. Self-control, one component of self-management, was discussed in some detail in the preceding chapter. Therefore, it is only mentioned here as an important set of intervention procedures that help reduce high rates of inappropriate social behavior. Self-control relates to social competence in several additional ways. Once individuals learn how to perform and apply various social skills, they must regulate their execution of these skills. They must regulate their own behaviors, resist reacting too quickly, delay gratification, persist with a task until it is completed, and balance their behaviors in conflict situations. The self-management procedures described earlier can be scheduled by teachers and applied by students to master these and related skills.

Social Competence

Social competence is the general construct under which social skills training exists. Social competence can be assigned to individuals who are proficient in and generalize their use of social skills. Deshler and Schumaker (1983, p. 16) maintain the following:

> [A] socially skilled person is able to perceive which situations require the use of social skills, discriminate which social skills would be appropriate, and then perform the skills in a manner that increases the likelihood that the behavior will result in positive consequences.

Social competence, then, is the broad array of skills discussed throughout this section. It is the ultimate goal of social skills training efforts. Although all adults possess varying degrees of social competence, many students with special needs require direct instruction in some or all of the skills that constitute social competence to be independent adults, successful in their interactions on the job, at home, and during leisure activities.

CURRICULUM-BASED ASSESSMENT AND EVALUATION

Educators need to decide which students are in need of social skills training programs and which are not. For those students in need, selected specific skill and performance deficits must be identified, programs implemented, and ongoing evaluation systems put into place.

Gresham (1981) and Schumaker and Hazel (1984a) believe that individuals who do not display social competence fall into several categories. The first they term as a skill deficit. The necessary behavior(s) are not in the repertoire of the individuals. The second group have a performance deficit; the individual possesses the necessary skills, but they are not applied at the appropriate times or places. The third kind is a self-control deficit. In these cases, the individuals do not control their behaviors, and often high rates of aversive behaviors result. Those who have skill deficits could be considered in the acquisition and proficiency stages of learning. In these cases, the goal of instruction is for students to learn the target behavior or groups of behavior so they are mastered at a set level of accuracy and fluency. In the second case, when the individual is capable of performing the desired responses but does not apply them, one could say that the individual is not generalizing previous learning to different settings where the behavior should occur. Students who display excesses of behavior must reduce or eliminate their occurrences (see Chapter 4 for suggested remediation strategies for reducing excesses of social behavior). Therefore, just as with academic behaviors, it appears that the stages-of-learning theory (presented in Chapter 1 and throughout Part III of this text) are relevant to the instruction of social skills.

If the problems identified fall within the classroom behavior (disruption) category, the ABC analysis (see Chapter 3 for details) should facilitate specific identification of instructional targets. Once the behaviors are pinpointed, either frequency, duration, or percentage of occurrence measurement systems should serve to monitor students' improvement across time.

Social skills have also been measured through other ways. Observational methods use behavioral codes ranging from simple to complex. Such systems provide a considerable amount of information. However, they typically only indicate whether a behavior occurred or did not occur within a particular time period. They do not judge the quality of performance. Observational systems usually require an outside observer because teachers busy instructing students cannot simultaneously collect such data.

Another method for assessing skills is to use behavioral checklists. One that has particular relevance to an aspect of social skills training was developed by Hazel et al. (1981) and is shown in Figure 5.2. The advantage of checklists is that they tend to be relatively easy to use and survey a wide range of skills. They help educators remember skills not present in their students' repertoires. Since checklists can be used over and over again, they can be used as ongoing measures of overall student growth. They are not sensitive enough to assess student learning on any subskill listed on the checklist. For this purpose, teachers need to employ one of the direct measurement systems discussed in Chapter 3 (frequency, percentage correct, percentage of occurrence, correct and error rate).

Some educators use sociometric measurement systems to judge students' adequacy in social skills. The most common form, the nomination method, requires classmates to identify each other by certain characteristics. ("Name the

Pre-Test	Post-Test	Did the participant:
————	————	1. Face the person when giving feedback?
————	————	2. Maintain eye contact with the person?
————	————	3. Keep a serious facial expression?
————	————	4. Use a serious voice tone?
————	————	5. Maintain a straight posture?
————	————	6. Ask to talk to the other person for a moment?
————	————	7. Initially give a positive statement or compliment?
————	————	8. Tell how he/she feels or what he/she feels that the other person has done wrong?
————	————	9. Give the other person a reason for changing?
————	————	10. Ask if the other person understood what was said?
————	————	11. Clarify the feedback, if necessary?
————	————	12. Ask how the other person feels (what is the other person's side)?
————	————	13. Give the other person suggestions for changing or improving?
————	————	14. Thank the other person for listening?
————	————	15. Change the topic to something else?
————	————	16. Make a statement of concern or understanding?
————	————	17. Not "put down" the other person?

Figure 5.2 Social skills behavior checklist for giving negative feedback. (*Source:* J. S. Hazel, J. B. Schumaker, J. A. Sherman, & J. Sheldon-Wildgen (1981), *ASSET: A Social Skill Program for Adolescents: Leader's Guide* (Champaign, IL: Research Press), p. 129.)

three classmates you like to play with.") Other sociometric systems ask students to rate their classmates. These indirect measurements can give educators some notion of the overall effectiveness of training programs, but are used infrequently and cannot be used to evaluate the immediate effects of social skills instructional programs. For this purpose, direct measurements of the skills being taught is best.

TEACHING TACTICS

In this section, several topics of instruction were selected to provide examples of how specific social skills can be taught. Because many of the same procedures (modeling, coaching, rehearsal) are used to teach students many different social skills, descriptions are provided only in specific areas to serve as examples of how they can be implemented. Table 5.5 provides a more thorough listing of social skills and suggested remediation procedures that have proven successful through research and practice.

Table 5.5
Social Skills Training Tactics

INSTRUCTIONAL TARGET	STAGE OF LEARNING	POSSIBLE TACTICS
Social cognition		
Interpretation	Acquisition	Role playing
		Coaching
		Discussions
Perception	Acquisition	Role taking
		Acting in dramas
		Role playing
		Retelling stories
		Role taking
		Coaching
Social interaction		
Peer interaction	Acquisition	Modeling
		Group contingencies
		Peer pairing
		Behavioral management
		Dispense reinforcement
		Adult-mediated prompting
		Social praise
Conventions	Acquisition	Self-management
		Self-instruction
		Coaching
		Role playing
		Rehearsal
		Verbal
		Behavioral
		Modeling live film
		Coaching
		Peer tutoring
	Maintenance and	Rationales
	generalization	"Surprise" visits
		Variable reinforcement
Appearance	Acquisition	Modeling
		Instructions
		Coaching
		Group discussions
Assertiveness	Acquisition	Role playing
		Reinforcement
		Coaching
		Modeling
		Peers
		Videotapes
		Adults
		Instructions
		Discussions
		Behavioral rehearsal and feedback

(continued)

Table 5.5   (*Continued*)

INSTRUCTIONAL TARGET	STAGE OF LEARNING	POSSIBLE TACTICS

Compliance	Acquisition	Role playing
		Reinforcement
		Coaching
		Modeling
		  Peers
		  Videotapes
		  Adults
		Instructions
		Discussions
		Behavioral rehearsal and feedback

Decision making
  Problem solving
	Acquisition	Rationales
		Develop alternative solution
		Group discussions
		Role playing
		Rehearsals
		  Behavioral
		  Verbal

Social reasoning	Proficiency	Rationales Role playing Instructions
	Acquisition	Group discussions Role playing

Coping skills
  Self-control
	Acquisition	Self-management
		  (self-regulate, self-evaluate, self-reward)
		Self-instruction
		Goal setting
		Modeling

	Generalization	Self-management
		  (self-regulate, self-evaluate, self-reward)
		Goal setting
		Rehearsal
		  Verbal
		  Behavioral
		Rationales
		Rewards

Cooperation Acquisition

Coaching is a tactic that is used to teach many different social skills. It is discussed only to serve as an illustrative example of how this procedure can be applied. Coaching uses direct verbal instructions, followed by rehearsing the target skill in a nonthreatening situation. According to Gresham (1981), coaching typically uses the following steps:

1. Presentation of rules or standards for the target behavior
2. Rehearsing the skill (behavioral rehearsal) with the coach or peer partner

3. Feedback from the coach on the rehearsed performance
4. Discussions and suggestions for future performances.

To teach young children to cooperate, teachers might arrange a group of toys (blocks) that require cooperative play on the floor. The children are given a task, such as building a castle or fort. Then, the teacher discusses the rules for sharing and might even model the desired behaviors (asking for a block, discussing how the fort should look, talking about where to start building). The youngsters then rehearse or practice sharing in the situation defined by the teacher. While the students are engaged in behavioral rehearsal, the teacher praises the desired behaviors and coaches the youngsters in better execution of their cooperation. Once the task is completed (the fort built), the teacher discusses the activity with the children and suggests other situations where their cooperative skills can be used and practiced.

Social Convention Acquisition

As with coaching, modeling has been used to teach a variety of social skills. It is described here as an example of how it can be effectively used to teach youngsters how to interact in a job interview. Regardless of the skill taught, the relevant features of this procedure remain much the same, regardless of its application.

Modeling social skills comes in two general forms: live modeling and symbolic modeling. In live modeling, one person (perhaps a counselor) role plays the employer interviewing applicants for a position. Another person (possibly the teacher) plays the part of the applicant. To demonstrate a job interview to students, both models need to be experienced with the interview/job applicant situation. In the symbolic modeling situation, video tapes or films of actual interviews are used.

For the situation just described, it is advisable to pair modeling procedures with other procedures. For example, before the demonstration, the teacher should engage the students in a discussion about the importance of job interviews and guide the students to watch for specific behaviors on the part of the applicant (greetings used, deference, tone of voice, gestures, smiling). Afterward, to follow up the observation period, a discussion session that analyzes the demonstration is held. The students then practice the mock interview. Students are paired and take turns being the employer and applicant. Here, they rehearse the good skills they observed and avoid the negative ones. Throughout these practice sessions, the teacher coaches, provides feedback, and praises students for the appropriate application of social conventions.

Gresham (1981) points out that for modeling to be effective, the target student(s) must attend to the model, retain the information presented, have the ability to execute the skill that was demonstrated, and possess the motivation necessary to apply and practice the skill. When modeling and peers are paired, the cautions discussed in Chapter 4 about the selection and use of peers in tutoring must be considered.

Assertiveness Acquisition

Few studies have yet been conducted that study how assertiveness can be developed in children. Assertion relates to social effectiveness and is required in even the simplest situations (asking for objects controlled by others, requesting assistance, seeking a chance to participate). Assertiveness can be taught. Combs and Slaby (1977) describe a teaching process they used with young children. The children were guided in active role playing. A doll was used to serve in the role of protagonist, reacting peer, or teacher. Through discussions and reinforcement for assertive responding, the behaviors shown in Table 5.6 were taught to nonassertive, withdrawn preschoolers.

Table 5.6
Assertiveness Training Targets

TARGET	UNDESIRABLE ALTERNATIVE
Saying: "No hitting."	Hitting back
Holding a toy, and saying: "I'm playing with this now."	Letting a peer grab it
Saying: "Please don't lean on me—I don't like that."	Shoving
Telling a bossy peer: "No, I want to do it my way."	Submitting
Ignoring an insulting comment.	Reacting
Trading or asking peers for an object.	Grabbing
Asking peers for permission to interact.	Barging in
Asking for help in a normal voice.	Whining
Making friendly suggestions.	Making bossy demands

Source: M. L. Combs & D. A. Slaby, Social skills training with children. In B. B. Lahey & A. E. Kazdin (eds.), *Advances in Child Psychology, vol. I* (New York: Plenum, 1977), pp. 39–60.

Social Skills Problem Solving

In one study, Hazel et al. (1982) taught youngsters to improve their social problem-solving skills through a systematic training program. The students were presented with a problem-solving situation where they were required to describe a social problem, generate three solutions to the problem, evaluate the consequences of each solution, choose the best one, and decide how to implement the solution they selected. The researchers cited the following examples of problem situations: talking a parent into a later curfew, not having enough time to complete an assignment. Instruction was presented in role-playing situations where the group leader modeled the skill and the students verbally and behaviorally rehearsed the skill through role playing and group discussion sessions. The final test of skill acquisition was for the students to role play the problem-solving skill with a novel situation. The results of this study indicate that students with cognitive processing difficulties did not learn to solve problems as well as those subjects who did not display such deficits. Students with poor cognitive skills might need more time to acquire and master the abilities to generate different solutions and select ones that best fit a given problem.

Teachers who need to teach students to solve social problems better might use a group of interventions together, as Hazel et al. did. Meichenbaum's problem-solving components (found in Table 5.4) could serve as the framework for lesson plans developed. Actual problems that occur at school might be used as the skills to discuss. The teacher would describe the social problem and lead students in group discussions where the problem is analyzed and possible solutions generated.

✗ Another approach to teaching interpersonal problem-solving skills is presented by Adelman and Taylor (1982). The tactics they used to teach students to

Table 5.7
Initial Steps for Enhancing and Maintaining Motivation to Solve Interpersonal Problems

Such activities as direct discussion, responses to direct questions, sentence completion, Q-sort items, role playing, audiovisual presentation, etc.* are used as vehicles for presenting/eliciting and clarifying the following:

1. Specific times when the individual experiences interpersonal problems (without assigning blame).
2. The form of the problems (again, no judgments are made).
3. The individual's perceptions of the causes of the problems.†
4. A broader analysis of possible causes (e.g., the individual's thoughts about other possible reasons and about how other people might interpret the situation; intervener examples of other perceptions and beliefs).
5. Any reasons the individual might have for wanting the interpersonal problems not to occur and for why they might continue.
6. A list of other possible reasons for people not wanting to be involved in such problems.
7. The reasons which appear to be personally important to the individual and why they are significant, underscoring those which are the individual's most important reasons for wanting not to be involved in such problems.
8. General ways in which the individual can deal appropriately and effectively with such problems (i.e., avoid them, use available skills, and develop new skills).
9. The individual's (a) general desire not to continue to experience interpersonal problems, (b) specific reasons for wanting this, and (c) desire to take some action.
10. The available alternatives for avoiding problems, using acquired skills, and developing new skills.
11. The available options related to activities and objectives associated with learning new skills (e.g., the specific activities and materials, mutual expectations).
12. Specific choices in the form of a mutually agreeable plan of action for pursuing alternatives related to steps 10 and 11.

Any step can be repeated as necessary, e.g., because of new information. Also, once the skill development activities are initiated, some of the above steps must be repeated in order to maintain an individual's motivation over time.

*Videotapes are particularly useful to make points vividly (e.g., to portray others in comparable situations, to present others as models).
†Each step does not require a separate session (e.g., steps 1–3 can be accomplished in one session).

Source: H. S. Adelman & L. Taylor, Enhancing the motivation and skills needed to overcome personal problems, *Learning Disability Quarterly*, 5, (1982), p. 5. Used by permission.

solve social problems are found in Table 5.7. These researchers maintain that students do not solve their interpersonal problems because they are not motivated to do so. Their premise is that students need to be motivated to learn; this motivation needs to be instilled before skill remediation is started. Once students are eager to learn a skill, teaching is less difficult for the teacher. Maintenance and generalization also are enhanced. To increase motivation, they emphasize that the time and effort the student puts into learning a skill is worthwhile, that there is value in the outcome, and that the student's expectations of the results are realistic. This motivational technique, which many teachers call providing *rationales*, clearly is a sound instructional procedure.

Social Skills Generalization

Deshler and Schumaker (1983) report that students do generalize their learning of social skills if they are programmed for this generalization. As with all learning, teachers cannot expect that generalization will occur without direct instructional efforts. In a preliminary report of the field test results of their social skills training program, skills that were taught through role playing and verbal and behavioral rehearsal did generalize to normal school situations. They tested this generalization through the observations of "surprise situations" and found that the trained students generalized their learning well. It appears that generalization was enhanced because once a skill was mastered in the training sessions, the teachers set up surprise situations to test the students' ability to apply the newly learned skill and gave immediate feedback about the adequacy of the students' responses. If, for example, a student is learning to accept criticism, teachers could schedule intermittent testings of this skill to determine if it is maintained and applied in those situations where it should be. Once the skill is mastered in these situations, the student is encouraged to set goals for using this skill outside the testing situation.

Self-control

As stated earlier, self-control and self-management strategies were discussed in some detail in Chapter 4 and are presented again in Chapter 7. Since developing self-control is so important for the attainment of social competence, a set of strategies that can help teachers plan lessons and experiences for students to develop and generalize these skills is presented here. Meichenbaum (1979) presented a helpful hierarchy (see Table 5.8) that organizes the general topics of instruction that should be included when self-control is taught. Whether the particular skill is delaying gratification, controlling one's temper, persisting to complete a task or meet a goal, or participating effectively in an extracurricular school activity, the steps that Meichenbaum outlines are useful to guide the development of complete lesson plans.

The development of social competence is a comprehensive goal that teachers and their students need to address. The training of social skills can occur one

Table 5.8
Meichenbaum's Strategies of Self-control

Strategy 1: Developing and maintaining commitment
  a. Substitute more adaptive self-attributions about nature of problem.
  b. What "if-then" relationships do you see between certain actions and particular outcomes?
  c. Identify and systematically anticipate several positive outcomes of your new behavior.

Strategy 2: Observing one's activities
  a. What do you say to yourself about
    (i) the behavior you want to change?
    (ii) your ability to change it?
    (iii) your progress?
  b. Under what circumstances do you currently engage in the behavior you want to change?
  c. How frequently or how much do you currently engage in the behavior you want to change?

Strategy 3: Planning the environment
  a. Establish a supportive environment: teach family, friends, and/or associates how you would like them to help.
  b. Modify the stimuli or cues that evoke the behavior you want to change.
    (i) External: rearrange your physical environment.
    (ii) Internal: alter undesirable internal cues such as thoughts and images.
  c. Develop a contract that specifies goals, behavior needed to attain those goals, and consequences for success and failure.

Strategy 4: Arranging consequences (behavioral programming)
  a. Self-reward
    (i) Covert: plan positive thoughts to follow successful actions.
    (ii) Overt: plan to give yourself or have someone give you a reward for success (e.g., playing golf on Saturday, a gift).
  b. Self-punishment
    (i) Covert: plan negative thoughts and/or images to follow immediately undesired actions.
    (ii) Overt: withhold a selected pleasant activity (e.g., watching your favorite TV show) or take away something you have (e.g., fine yourself $1 for each occurrence of undesirable behavior).

Source: D. Meichenbaum, Teaching Self-control. In B. B. Lahey & A. E. Kazdin, eds., *Advances in Clinical Child Psychology: vol.2* (New York: Plenum, 1979), p. 26. Used by permission.

by one. However, teachers must retain a vision of the overall construct of social competence if their students are to be competent in those social skills needed for independent adulthood.

SUMMARY

Although many students with special needs are not socially competent, direct instruction aimed at the development of social skills is not typically included in the overall school curriculum. This area is now gaining more attention from researchers, teachers, and instructional materials developers.

Being socially competent requires the use of many sophisticated and, often, subtle skills. Socially competent individuals interact with others well. They understand social situations and other people's feelings and viewpoints. Such individuals understand the conventions of society and can discriminate different social contexts and adapt their behavior accordingly. By understanding different social contexts, they are able to make decisions, gain acceptance from others, and cope well with their environments.

Because many students with special needs are unable to sustain friendships, decide what behaviors are expected and are correct in particular situations, or understand social contexts, they frequently do not adjust well at school or home. This can lead to difficulties in adult life such as problems on the job, as well. Less is known about how to effectively teach social skills to students than is known about more traditional content (e.g., mathematics, reading, written language). Regardless, teachers need to remember that the direct instructional techniques can cause substantial improvement in skills that constitute social competence.

STUDY AND DISCUSSION QUESTIONS

1. Discuss the implications and your suggested resolutions for teaching social skills to students who do not come from the United States' dominant culture.
2. Develop a lesson plan for teaching improved grooming and appearance to middle or secondary students.
3. Describe three ways to teach students social perception.

REFERENCES AND SUGGESTED READINGS

General Social Skills Training

BRYAN, T. H., & BRYAN, J. H. (1986). *Understanding learning disabilities.* Palo Alto, CA: Mayfield.

COMBS, M. L., & LAHEY, B. B. (1981). A cognitive social skills training program: Evaluation with young children. *Behavior Modification, 5,* 39–60.

— COMBS, M. L., & SLABY, D. A. (1977). Social skills training with children. In B. B. Lahey & A. E. Kazdin (eds.), *Advances in child psychology,* Vol. 1. New York: Plenum Press.

— DESHLER, D. D., & SCHUMAKER, J. B. (1983). Social skills of learning disabled adolescents: characteristics and intervention. *Topics in Learning and Learning Disabilities, 3,* 15–23.

DUDLEY-MARLING, C. C., & EDMIASTON, R. (1985). Social status of learning disabled children and adolescents: A review. *Learning Disability Quarterly, 8,* 189–204.

— GRESHAM, F. M. (1981). Social skills training with handicapped children: A review. *Review of Educational Research, 51,* 139–176.

— HAZEL, J. S., SCHUMAKER, J. B., SHERMAN, J. A., & SHELDON-WILDGEN, J. (1981). The development and evaluation of a group skills training program for court-adjudicated youths. In D. Upper & S. M. Ross (eds.), *Behavioral Group Therapy, 1981* (Annual Review). Champaign, IL: Research Press.

HOLLINGER, J. D. (1987). Social skills for behaviorally disordered children as preparation for mainstreaming: Theory, practice, and new directions. *Remedial and Special Education, 8*(4), 17–27.

HOPS, H. (1982). Social-skills training for socially withdrawn/isolate children. In P. Karoly and J. J. Stevens (eds.), *Improving children's competence: Advances in child behavioral analysis and therapy,* Vol. I. Lexington, MA: Lexington Books.

McDOWELL, R. L., & MURPHY, E. D. (1979). Teaching social skills to the behaviorally disordered adolescent. *Journal of Special Education Technology, 3,* 50–55.

PARIS, S. G., & OKA, E. R. (1986). Self-regulated learning among exceptional children. *Exceptional Children, 53,* 103–108.

PEARL, R., BRYAN, T., & DONAHUE, M. (1983). Social behaviors of learning disabled children: A review. *Topics in Learning and Learning Disabilities, 3,* 1–12.

SCHLOSS, P., SCHLOSS, C., WOOD, C. E., & KIEHL, W. S. (1986). A critical review of social skills research with behaviorally disordered students. *Behavioral Disorders, 12*(1), 1–14.

SCHUMAKER, J. B., & HAZEL, J. S. (1984a). Social skills assessment and training for the learning disabled: Who's on first and what's on second? Part I. *Journal of Learning Disabilities, 17,* 422–431.

SCHUMAKER, J. B., & HAZEL, J. S. (1984b). Social skills assessment and training for the learning disabled: Who's on first and what's on second? Part II. *Journal of Learning Disabilities, 17,* 492–499.

SCHUMAKER, J. B., HAZEL, J. S., SHERMAN, J. A., & SHELDON, J. (1982). Social skill performances of learning disabled, non-learning disabled, and delinquent adolescents. *Learning Disability Quarterly, 5,* 388–397.

WALKER, H. M., SHERIN, M. R., O'NEILL, R. E., & RAMSEY, E. (1987). Longitudinal assessment of the development of antisocial behavior in boys: Rationale, methodology, and first year results. *Remedial and Special Education, 8*(4), 7–16, 27.

Social Skills Curricula and Instructional Programs

BROLIN, D. E., & KOKASKA, C. J. (1985). *Career education for handicapped children and youth* (2nd ed.). Columbus, OH: Charles E. Merrill.

GOLDSTEIN, H. (1974). *The social learning curriculum.* Columbus, OH: Charles E. Merrill.

HAZEL, J. S., SCHUMAKER, J. B., SHERMAN, J. A., & SHELDON-WILDGEN, J. (1981). *ASSET: A social skills program for adolescents.* Champaign, IL: Research Press.

MANNIX, D. S. (1986). *I CAN behave: A classroom self-management curriculum for elementary students.* Portland, OR: ASIEP Education Company.

ODOM, S. L., BENDER, M., STEIN, M., DORAN, L., HOUDEN, P., McINNES, M., SHAFTO, F., GILBERT, M., DeKLYEN, M., SPELTZ, M., & JENKINS, J. (1982). *The integrated preschool curriculum: Procedures for socially integrating handicapped and nonhandicapped preschool children.* Seattle: University of Washington Press.

SCHUMAKER, J. B., HAZEL, J. S., & PEDERSON, C. S. (1988). *Social skills for daily living.* Circle Pines, MN: American Guidance Service.

SCHUMAKER, J. B., PEDERSON, C. S., HAZEL, J. S., & MEYEN, E. L. (1983). Social skills curricula for mildly handicapped adolescents: A review. *Focus on Exceptional Children, 16*(4), 1–16.

STEPHENS, T. M. (1978). *Social skills in the classroom.* Columbus, OH: Cedars Press.

WALKER, H. M., McCONNELL, S., HOLMES, D., TODIS, B., WALKER, J., & GOLDEN, N. (1983). *The Walker social skills curriculum: The accepts program.* Austin, TX: Pro-Ed.

Curriculum-based Assessment

ASHER, S. R., & TAYLOR, A. R. (1981). Social outcomes of mainstreaming: Sociometric assessment and beyond. *Exceptional Education Quarterly, 1*(4), 13–30.

HAZEL, J. S., SCHUMAKER, J. B., SHERMAN, J. A., AND SHELDON-WILDGEN, J. (1981). The development and evaluation of a group training program for teaching social and problem solving skills to court-adjudicated youths. In D. Upper & S. M. Ross (eds.), *Behavioral Group Therapy.* Champaign, IL: Research Press.

SCHUMAKER, J. B., & HAZEL, J. S. (1984a). Social skills assessment and training for the learning disabled: Who's on first and what's on second? Part II. *Journal of Learning Disabilities, 17,* 422–431.

Social Cognition

AXELROD, L. (1982). Social perception in learning disabled adolescents. *Journal of Learning Disabilities, 15,* 610–613.

CARTLEDGE, G., STUPAY, D., KACZALA, C. (1986). Social skills and social perception of LD and nonhandicapped elementary students. *Learning Disability Quarterly, 9,* 226–234.

GERBER, P. J., & ZINKGRAF, S. A. (1982). A comparative study of social-perceptual ability in learning disabled and nonhandicapped students. *Learning Disability Quarterly, 5,* 374–378.

JACKSON, S. C., ENRIGHT, R. D., & MURDOCK, J. Y. (1987). Social perception problems in learning disabled youth: Developmental lag versus perceptual deficit. *Journal of Learning Disabilities, 20,* 361–364.

MAHEADY, L., & MAITLAND, G. E. (1982). Assessing social perception abilities in learning disabled students. *Learning Disability Quarterly, 5,* 363–370.

MAHEADY, L., MAITLAND, G., & SAINATO, D. (1984). The interpretation of social interactions by mildly handicapped and nondisabled children. *Journal of Special Education, 18,* 151–159.

PEARL, R., & COSDEN, M. (1982). Sizing up a situation: LD children's understanding of social interactions. *Learning Disability Quarterly, 5,* 371–373.

Role taking

BRUCK, M., & HEBERT, M. (1982). Correlates of learning disabled students' peer interaction patterns. *Learning Disability Quarterly, 5,* 353–362.

BRYAN, T. H., & BRYAN, J. H. (1986). *Understanding learning disabilities.* Palo Alto, CA: Mayfield.

CARTLEDGE, G., & MILBURN, J. F. (1986). *Teaching social skills to children: Innovative approaches* (2nd ed.). New York: Pergamon Press.

Cooperation

BRYAN, T., COSDEN, M., & PEARL, R. (1982). The effects of cooperative goal structures and cooperative models on LD and NLD students. *Learning Disability Quarterly, 5,* 415–421.

Social Interaction

Peer interaction

BRYAN, J. H., BRYAN, T. H., & SONNEFELD, L. J., (1982). Being known by the company we keep: The contagion of first impressions. *Learning Disability Quarterly, 5,* 288–294.

BRYAN, T., WERNER, M., & PEARL, R. (1982). Learning disabled students' conformity responses to prosocial and antisocial situations. *Learning Disability Quarterly, 5,* 344–352.

LA GRECA, A. M., & MESIBOX, G. B. (1981). Facilitating interpersonal functioning with peers in learning-disabled children. *Journal of Learning Disabilities, 14,* 197–199, 238.

LEVY, L. & GOTTLIEB, J. (1984). Learning disabled and non-LD children at play. *Remedial and Special Education, 5,* 43–50.

SAINATO, D. M., MAHEADY, L., & SHOOK, G. L. (1986). The effects of a classroom manager role on the social interaction patterns and social status of withdrawn kindergarten children. *Journal of Applied Behavior Analysis, 19,* 187–195.

Use of peers

HENDRICKSON, J. M., STRAIN, P. S., TREMBLAY, A., & SHORES, R. E. (1982). Interactions of behaviorally handicapped children. *Behavior Modification, 6,* 323–353.

STRAIN, P. S., & ODOM, S. L. (1986). Peer social initiations: Effective intervention for social skills development of exceptional children. *Exceptional Children, 52,* 543–551.

VAN BOURGONDIEN, M. E. (1987). Children's responses to retarded peers as a function of social behaviors, labeling, and age. *Exceptional Children, 53,* 432–439.

Social Effectiveness

DESHLER, D. D., & SCHUMAKER, J. B. (1983). Social skills of learning disabled adolescents: Characteristics and intervention. *Topics in Learning and Learning Disabilities, 3,* 15–23.

DRABMAN, R. S., & PATTERSON, J. N. (1981). Disruptive behavior and the social standing of exceptional children. *Exceptional Education Quarterly, 1,* 45–55.

GARRETT, M. K., & CRUMP, W. D. (1980). Peer acceptance, teacher preference, and self-appraisal of social status among learning disabled students. *Learning Disability Quarterly, 3,* 42–48.

SCHUMAKER, J. B., WILDGEN, J. S., & SHERMAN, J. A. (1982). Social interaction of learning disabled junior high students in their regular classrooms: An observational analysis. *Journal of Learning Disabilities, 15,* 355–358.

Assertiveness

COMBS, M. L., & SLABY, D. A. (1977). Social skills training with children. In B. B. Lahey & A. E. Kazdin (eds.), *Advances in Child Psychology,* Vol. 1. New York: Plenum Press.

HOPS, H. (1982). Social-skills training for socially withdrawn/isolate children. In P. Karoly and J. J. Stevens (eds.), *Improving children's competence: Advances in child behavioral analysis and therapy,* Vol. I. Lexington, MA: Lexington Books.

Decision Making

CARTLEDGE, G., STUPAY, D., & KACZALA, C. (1986). Social skills and social perception of LD and nonhandicapped elementary students. *Learning Disability Quarterly, 9,* 226–234.

SCHUMAKER, J. B., & HAZEL, J. S. (1984b). Social skills assessment and training for the learning disabled: Who's on first and what's on second? Part I. *Journal of Learning Disabilities, 17,* 422–431.

Problem solving

ADELMAN, H. S., & TAYLOR, L. (1982). Enhancing the motivation and skills needed to overcome interpersonal problems. *Learning Disability Quarterly, 5,* 438–445.

BASH, M. A. S., & CAMP, B. W. (1986). Teacher training in the think aloud classroom program. In G. Cartledge and J. F. Milburn (eds.), *Teaching social skills to children*. New York: Pergamon Press.

— HAZEL, S. J., SCHUMAKER, J. B., SHERMAN, J. A., & SHELDON, J. (1982). Application of a group training program in social skills and problem solving to learning disabled and non-learning disabled youth. *Learning Disability Quarterly, 5,* 398–408.

— MEICHENBAUM, D. (1979). Teaching children self-control. In B. B. Lahey and A. E. Kazdin, *Advances in clinical child psychology*, Vol. 2. New York: Plenum Press.

— SCHUMAKER, J. B., HAZEL, J. S., SHERMAN, J. A., & SHELDON, J. (1982). Social skill performances of learning disabled, non-learning disabled, and delinquent adolescents. *Learning Disability Quarterly, 5,* 388–397.

Generalization

ADELMAN, H. S., & TAYLOR, L. (1982). Enhancing the motivation and skills needed to overcome interpersonal problems. *Learning Disability Quarterly, 5,* 438–446.

FOXX, R. M., McMORROW, M. J., BITTLE, R. G., & NESS, J. (1986). An analysis of social skills generalization in two natural settings. *Journal of Applied Behavior Analysis, 19,* 299–305.

SCHLOSS, P., SCHLOSS, C., WOOD, C. E., & KIEHL, W. S. (1986). A critical review of social skills research with behaviorally disordered students. *Behavioral Disorders, 12,* 1–14.

SCHUMAKER, J. B., & ELLIS, E. S. (1982). Social skills training of LD adolescents: A generalization study. *Learning Disability Quarterly, 5,* 409–414.

SCHUMAKER, J. B., & HAZEL, J. S. (1984b). Social skills assessment and training for the learning disabled: Who's on first and what's on second? Part I. *Journal of Learning Disabilities, 17,* 492–499.

Coping Skills

SCHULTZ, E. W. (1980). Teaching coping skills for stress and anxiety. *Teaching Exceptional Children, 13,* 12–21.

Self-control

GRESHAM, F. M. (1981). Social skills training with handicapped children: A review. *Review of Educational Research, 51,* 139–176.

MEICHENBAUM, D. (1979). Teaching children self-control. In B. B. Lahey and A. E. Kazdin, *Advances in clinical child psychology*, Vol. 2. New York: Plenum Press.

6

Language and Learning*

Scenario: Nine-year-old Craig spends many Saturdays at the local soccer field watching other boys kick the black-and-white ball about the field. After weeks of watching, Craig asks the boys if he can play with them. They agree, but soon regret their decision as Craig proceeds to "play" the game by carrying the ball down the field, kicking the ball out-of-bounds, and kicking a field goal into the opponent's net. The boys tell Craig to leave. "You don't know how to play the game," they tell him.

A week later, Craig returns to the soccer field to watch the boys play. He is approached by one of the older boys playing this week. The older player asks Craig if he'd like to join in the game. Craig responds, "I don't know how." The older boy smiles and asks Craig if his legs, eyes, ears, and head work OK. "All my body parts work just fine," answers Craig.

"Then c'mon," the older boy says. "All you need to do is learn the rules. Don't let the ball go outside the white lines, use your feet, don't touch the ball with your hands, and try to kick the ball into the blue net, not the green one."

Craig joins the game and plays happily with the group all afternoon. He makes mistakes, but the group is tolerant, and Craig is never discouraged. Everyone knows Craig is playing according to the rules of the game.

Craig had some of the basic behaviors and abilities necessary to play soccer, but he needed to learn the rules to be socially accepted into the group. He also needed to be given the opportunity to play. Language and learning also involve a set of behaviors and rules that can be likened to a communication game.

Students with special needs, like Craig, often demonstrate inconsistencies

---

*This chapter was written by Christine Ann Marvin, Ph.D.

in their knowledge and use of the behaviors and rules necessary for playing the communication game. These students must be explicitly taught the rules of the game (Simon, 1985). In this chapter, the behaviors and rules used in the communication game are discussed. Transcripts from Craig and other students in special education classrooms are reviewed, so the absence of key communicative behaviors or disregard for established communicative rules can be noted. The importance of learning and using the rules of verbal communication are emphasized in terms of the students' attempts to read, write, and reason. Finally, the role the teacher plays in helping students learn the rules of the communication game at home and at school is evaluated.

THE COMMUNICATION GAME

The communication game is a process that involves at least two players and a message (Cherry, 1957). Figure 6.1 is a simple representation of the communication process. The sender and receiver represent the players in the game, and the message becomes the purpose for the two players' interaction. Communication only occurs if and when the message intended by the sender is the message understood by the receiver.

The sender may generate an idea or thought and then decide to share the idea with someone else. The sender's idea needs to be translated from thought to some code that other people can understand. The codes for communication are frequently referred to as signals and symbols. Once the thought is coded, the sender must then select a mechanism for delivering the coded message. Possible delivery mechanisms include the mouth and voice; sign language; simple arm, hand, or facial gestures; telegraph; or some graphic utensils such as paper and pencil to write or draw.

The receivers in the communication game must have some functional mechanism for receiving the coded message. They might use their ears, eyes, or

Figure 6.1 The communication process/game.

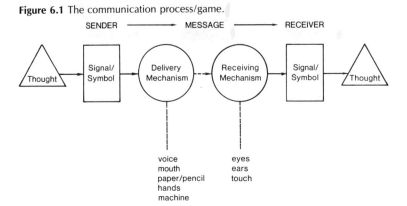

even tactile senses to take the message to the brain. Receivers must also have some knowledge of the signals or symbols the sender used. This knowledge allows receivers to interpret the code, take meaning from the message, and establish a new thought.

A breakdown in the communicative attempt can occur anywhere in the process. If no one has a thought they wish to share, the communication game cannot be initiated. If either the sender or the receiver fails to encode or decode adequately the symbols or signals, the communication of a message does not occur. Finally, if the sender or receiver has a defective mechanism for delivering or receiving the message, communication is impaired. Defective mechanisms for delivering or receiving human communication include permanent disabilities as well as temporary malfunctions. The former includes hearing loss, blindness, paralyzed arms and hands, and the inability to make recognizable graphic markings. The latter includes laryngitis, stuttering speech, visual or auditory misperceptions, and broken equipment such as pencils, typewriters, and telephones.

The coding of thoughts into signals and/or symbols is an important process in the communication game and underlies the relationship of language and learning to communication (Carrow-Woolfolk & Lynch, 1982). *Signals* are simply gestures, vocalizations, or graphic markings that "announce" some immediate event, person, object, action, or emotion. Signals used for communication include snapping your fingers to get someone's attention, winking, smiling, drawing an arrow, and waving hello.

Symbols can represent past, future, and present events, persons, objects, actions, or emotions. They generally are used in combination with one another. *Rules* govern those combinations. Symbols "refer" to some thing rather than announce its presence and can be gestural, vocal, or graphic. Human speech sounds are vocal symbols; the letters of the alphabet are graphic symbols for the speech sounds of a language, and sign language gestures are symbolic movements that represent either the speech sounds (fingerspelling) or specific words and phrases.

Signals, symbols, and the rules that govern their use for the purpose of effective human communication in a given community, are referred to as *language* (Sapir, 1927). Language systems can be vocal or nonvocal. The vocal language system for communication by humans is referred to as *speech*. Reading and writing are nonvocal, graphic language systems for communicating messages. Braille is a nonvocal tactile language system for communication by persons with limited vision. Formal sign language is a nonvocal gestural form of communication used by many hearing impaired and deaf people. Speech, writing, braille, and sign language can all be viewed as symbolic systems for communication, or simply various forms of language. The relationship between signals and symbols and the distinction between speech and language are graphically presented in Figure 6.2.

It is important to note that the nonvocal language systems just described are often based on, or related to, the rules for the vocal language system in a given community (Bellugi & Klima, 1978; Liberman et al., 1980). In French-

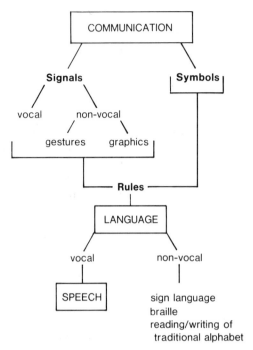

Figure 6.2 Relationship of signals, symbols, speech, and language to human communication.

speaking Canada, written communication reflects the French language; braille and some sign language systems in those communities are related to French speech. In English-speaking Canada, however, the nonvocal systems are representations of the English verbal language.

Regardless of the language form used (verbal, written, gestural), the intent of the process is always to communicate a message between a sender and a receiver. Senders intend to deliver something meaningful; receivers expect to hear, read, or see something meaningful. It is this intent for meaningful exchanges that entices persons to become active participants in a "communication game." Learning the rules for language is extremely important to increasing the opportunities a person has for playing the game with any meaning or pleasure.

Behaviors and Rules

Human communication is composed of vocal, graphic, or gestural behaviors and sets of rules for using those behaviors. Knowledge and use of the rules for combining the signals and symbols allow students to play the communication game to their fullest potential at home and school.

The language of any community (English, Spanish, French, Navajo) is composed of rules for content, form, and use (Bloom & Lahey, 1978). These rules address (1) sound selection and sound combinations, (2) meaning of utterances, (3) word order and word endings, and (4) the appropriate social use of these productions. Rules for a community's language are not taught to children explicitly. Generally, the rules are mastered through observation and trial-and-error processes. As children are exposed to opportunities to hear the language used in social interactions and see the consequences of people's various utterances, they develop an eagerness to try the system. These efforts are mere approximations at first. Over time, they systematically modify their productions and interpretations so that early telegraphic utterances increase in length and meaning. At this point, too, listening becomes far more critical.

When children begin school at age 5 or 6, they can converse with most people about recent events and concrete ideas. As they advance through the grades, children demonstrate abilities for handling discussions about topics taken out of context; that is, they can discuss abstract events of the past or future and concepts that are neither concrete nor visible (Berko-Gleason, 1985). In addition, an increased awareness and appreciation for the rules of the language allow school-aged children to master meaningful reading and writing tasks. Children with special needs, however, may show delays or disorganization in their ability to master the rules of language, either receptively or expressively. A special education teacher can help the student develop a functional use of these rules in classroom interactions and assignments. But what are these rules used so casually, yet considered so important?

A lattice was developed (see Figure 6.3) to present an overview of some major behaviors and rule sets that pertain to the communication game. The behaviors and rules found on the lower end of the lattice are often contained in the subsequent higher rule sets. The lattice illustrates that vocabulary and sentence structures are only behavioral components of communication. The appropriate use of these components for functional social interactions (verbal or written) should be the targeted goal for students.

Teachers must understand the interrelationship of these communication patterns and simultaneously recognize their individual value for effective communication. This knowledge allows teachers to select appropriate activities for teaching the communication game to students with special needs. In the following section, definitions, examples, and discussion are provided about the major rules for human communication.

Speech Sounds

The first set of rules for communication specifies which sounds a community will allow in its language. For example, the German *ach* and Spanish *j* sounds are not heard in English. The English language contains approximately forty-five different vocalizations, while Hawaiian languages contain fewer than half this number. The sound rules of a particular language also govern how these vocalizations can be combined and sequenced. The English language dictates the presence of vowels and limits the number and selection of consonants that can be strung together before or after a vowel. For example, it is feasible that the

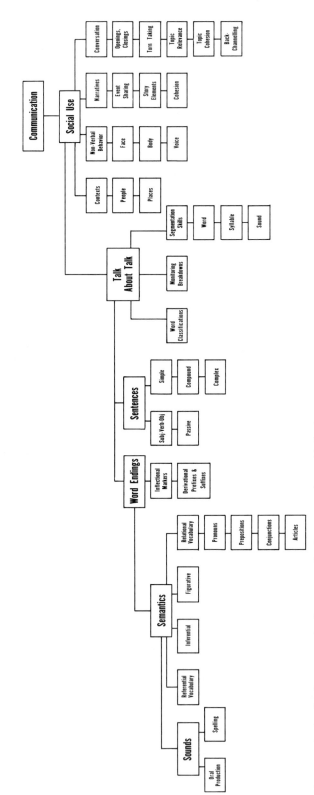

Figure 6.3 Lattice for the communication game using language rules and behaviors.

152

production *staz* could be an English word; the production *blnp,* however, is quite improbable.

Sound rules are upheld in both the verbal and written (spelling) forms of language. Students with special needs who demonstrate problems making or using speech sounds may have difficulty learning to read. An awareness of these sound segments in speech has been correlated to early reading success (Catts & Kamhi, 1986; Liberman & Shankweiler, 1979). Children with sound production difficulties may have problems using a phonics approach for learning to read. Phonics programs encourage students to "sound out" words. Some students with special needs may decode words erroneously by mispronouncing the speech/letter sounds. In addition, students who do not yet know all the sound rules of language may show some creative but erroneous spelling when first introduced to the process of writing (e.g., MSTR/monster, ATE/eighty).

Meaning of Utterances

A second set of language rules pertains to the meaning of spoken or written statements. This set of rules is commonly referred to as semantics. *Semantic rules* encompass more than just individual vocabulary; an entire statement can be judged to be meaningful or not meaningful. The key words of a statement provide information about the dimensions, features, and actions of objects or persons. This is referred to as referential semantics. But the assumed "little" words, and the order of the words in the statement, also play an important part in establishing meaning about relational aspects of words and ideas. Look at the examples in Figure 6.4 and note Craig's semantic errors. His word choices and word combinations are vague and do not successfully convey a clear message. Activities that challenge Craig to be more explicit can help him improve his use of semantic rules.

Teachers need to recognize that meaning can come from what is and what is *not* said explicitly. Most first graders can select pictures to match the words *boat, running,* or *angry.* But at this age, most children are unable to understand quickly statements in which the meaning is inferred. Figure 6.5 gives an example of a short story with one review question. This simple task challenges students to use their knowledge of inferential semantics. Some students with special needs in the third and fourth grades might have trouble with this particular task. Teaching students to predict logical actions and outcomes for real or imaginary events can help develop inferencing skills. Explaining the untold events of characters in stories may also help students see the inferred meaning of a series of statements.

Word Order and Word Endings

Another set of language rules governs the use of word order and word endings. For example, in English, nouns used as subjects are generally followed by verbs. In fact, students come to expect the subject-verb-object word order in almost all statements or written sentences. But some sentences in English do not use this

TEACHER:	What sorts of jobs do you do around your home?
CRAIG:	Picking up the garbage. I'm tired.
TEACHER:	I bet it's been a rough day. I'll tell you what—I'll do your chore for you, but you have to tell me exactly what I have to do. Okay, you tell me what I have to do to take care of your chore.
CRAIG:	You couldn't.
TEACHER:	Let's just pretend.
CRAIG:	It's too hard.
TEACHER:	Explain to me what I have to do.
CRAIG:	You have ta clean blocks.
TEACHER:	I have to clean blocks? What do you mean?
CRAIG:	You have ta chip em with a tool.
TEACHER:	What?
CRAIG:	Have to chip the stuff off. Other people used it and they tore their something off when they built it.
TEACHER:	I don't understand. You told me your chore was taking out the garbage. I don't understand what chipping blocks has to do with taking out the garbage.
CRAIG:	[When the stuff gets] . . . when the garbage can gets full, then I take it out and put it out in the big garbage can, then I bring it back in the house and go play.
TEACHER:	What's the chipping block about? Is this something else you do? Do you help your Dad?
CRAIG:	I do it myself. I chip twenty a day.
TEACHER:	You chip twenty blocks a day? What does that mean?
CRAIG:	There's some stuff on it and you have ta get all that off [so it'll] so the block will be smooth.
TEACHER:	Oh—this is a job you have after school?
CRAIG:	I get $10.00 a day.

Figure 6.4 Word errors in conversation. (*Source:* C. Simon, *Communicative competence: A functional-pragmatic approach to language therapy.* Tucson: Communication Skill Builders, Inc. (1981), p. 79.)

predictable pattern. The sentence, "The man was hit by the truck," is interpreted as "the man hit the truck" by children under the age of 4 or 5 (Bever, 1970). Most students with special needs, like their younger peers, have difficulty understanding the exception to this subject-verb-object rule of English (Wallach, 1977).

Word order rules govern the placement of modifiers in statements. English requires that adjectives in a noun phrase be spoken before the noun, as in "the big ugly bear." Adverbs, on the other hand, usually follow the verb in a verb phrase, as in "he swam fast" and not "he fast swam." Other languages, such as German or Spanish, use different word order rules for noun-verb or adjective placement.

THE RAINY DAY

(Scene: Boy watching rain outside)

Little Boy: I can't go out. I lost my umbrella.
Big Sister: I have an umbrella. You can go with me.

Circle the correct choice:

1. The little boy will stay inside.
2. Big sister will paint.
3. Both children will go outside.

Figure 6.5 Task requiring knowledge of inferential semantics.

In addition to word order, language rules influence the use of prefixes and suffixes to change the meaning of words (Brown, 1973). Nouns can be made plural or possessive by adding the inflectional "s" sound to the end of the word. Verbs can be marked for past or present tense by adding "-ed" or "-ing." Derivational prefixes and suffixes such as "re-," "un-," "de-," or "-able" can alter the meaning of many words (touch → untouchable). But the rules for language also dictate which words can receive a particular prefix or suffix. It is not acceptable, for example, to place the "-ing" suffix on such words as "not," "boy," or "bright." Little words such as "will," "is," "the," "be," and "have" can act like prefixes or suffixes to alter the meaning of statements, when they are positioned appropriately before or after certain words. Look again at Craig's transcript in Figure 6.4; identify any errors related to word order or word endings.

Appropriate Social Use of Language

All the previously mentioned language behaviors and rules are ineffective for functional communication if they are not used according to the accepted social standards of the community. The rules for the social use of language cover style changes for contexts, use of nonverbal behaviors, and appropriate conversational and narrative patterns.

Children learn at a young age to adjust their speech for different people in different settings (Carrow-Woolfolk & Lynch, 1982). They learn to speak politely to adults and respectfully to the police and judges. They also learn the rules for speaking in a church, library, museum, or school. Thank goodness for "rules" that allow children to yell and laugh aloud at ballgames, in parks, and at parties!

Nonverbal behaviors such as the physical distance between conversational partners, the amount of eye contact, and whether or not people touch each other in a conversation are all dependent upon the language rules that exist for social interactions. In English, conversational partners obtain and maintain some eye contact regardless of age, sex, or status. But in Navajo and some Asian languages, eye contact between a child and adult may be viewed as disrespectful (Taylor, 1986).

Many of the social rules for using language influence the construction and maintenance of conversations (dialogues) and narratives (monologues). The rules dictate changes in style and form of language when students communicate socially or "at home" and when they are in a "school" setting. The rules for conversational or narrative discourse may appear obvious and "common sense" for students who are proficient in using the community's language. But the rules are a mystery for many students with special needs.

Language in Conversations

Conversational rules include the use of (1) appropriate opening statements to focus the listener on a given topic, (2) acceptable turn-taking patterns, (3) relevant and cohesive statements, and (4) reasonable judgments about the listener's knowledge of the topic (Carrow-Woolfolk & Lynch, 1982). It is appropriate and expected that conversations open with statements that inform the listener of a main thought. Listeners, including teachers, are often confused when students do not establish a focus early in conversation. The conversational flow is interrupted with either a series of questions or a change in the topic by the listener.

Conversational rules dictate the manner in which students take turns at being the speaker or listener. Most people abide by the unwritten rule that says "Wait for a one- to two-second period of silence; then you can talk." This pause by the speaker usually comes after a drop in voice as a statement is completed, or follows a rising intonation associated with a question. Eye contact with the listener is usually evident during the exchange of speaker roles in one-on-one interactions, but is not necessarily observed in group conversations. Taking a speaking turn too quickly is called interrupting, and may be tolerated socially only in conversations with very familiar persons or groups.

In addition to knowing the rules for when to speak in conversation, competent communicators must know the rules for keeping their turn as speaker (Roth & Speckman, 1984). If listening partners become confused by what a speaker says, they may choose to take the speaker role themselves and change the topic or discontinue the conversation by walking away. What a speaker says in a conversation (or in a written passage) must be relevant to the established topic and the partner's preceding statements. Relevance can be achieved by using vocabulary the partner used; using connection words such as "so," "but," or "and"; or using pronouns such as "he," "they," or "it." By making relevant statements, a person can successfully assume the role of speaker.

Utterances in conversations must also be cohesive if a person wishes to maintain the speaker role for extended periods of time. Cohesiveness refers to the ability to maintain connections between a series of statements. First, second, and third statements (sentences) must be related to one another, as well as to a shared topic and the listener's comments. Random statements cause confusion for the conversational partner and interfere with the delivery of any one message. The transcript in Figure 6.6 shows how Craig failed to use relevant and cohesive statements in two different conversations with his teacher.

Teachers need to play an active listening role when conversing with their students. If students make irrelevant comments or fail to maintain a topic over two or three statements in a conversation, the teacher should inform students (interrupt if necessary) that their comments are not pertinent. Then teachers can redefine the topic and encourage students to continue the conversation. Students can be challenged to practice relevance and cohesiveness during language activities that specifically reward students for maintaining a topic for one, two, or three conversational exchanges.

Finally, conversational rules require the speaker to "size up" his or her listener and adjust the conversation appropriately. Speakers' word choices and organization of their utterances are influenced by what they assume the listeners do or do not know about the topic (Speckman, 1983). More explicit words and detailed statements are needed if the listener has not seen or experienced the event or topic the speaker chooses to discuss. Students with special needs appear to have great difficulty making appropriate assumptions about what their conversational partners already know or don't know (Speckman, 1981). In verbal and written passages, these students frequently remain self-centered and view

Figure 6.6 Examples of poor conversational relevance and cohesiveness.

Sample A

TEACHER: . . . anyway, I'm glad you enjoyed the fair. Let's talk about something else. How do—

CRAIG: Did you ever see the bicentennial state fair?

TEACHER: No, I didn't see that one. Hey, how do you like your new teacher?

CRAIG: She's really O.K. She lets me work on my bulletin board. . . . She also lets me play with the cars.

TEACHER: The cars? Which cars are those?

CRAIG: The model cars in the state fair exhibit. How much do you really like the state fair?

Sample B

CRAIG: . . . but I missed it [an early TV program] 'cuz I went to bed.

TEACHER: That early? You must have had a hard day.

CRAIG: Yeah.

TEACHER: What made it such a hard day?

CRAIG: The raking.

TEACHER: That's hard work isn't it?

CRAIG: Our teacher said, uh . . . whoever wins in checkers—I won—goes to McDonald's.

things only from their own perspective. Teachers need to model the use of explicit words and descriptions, teach students to ask their partners what they know before beginning conversations, and demonstrate vividly for students the negative effect of using pronouns like "he" and "it," without first establishing a referent for the pronoun by name ("John," "the ball").

Rules for conversation include rules for listening as well as rules for speaking. Listeners are expected to "pay attention" and ask for clarification when needed. Attention is demonstrated by body posturing toward the speaker, occasional eye contact, and various forms of vocal or facial feedback (back-channeling) that tell the speaker, "I hear you" or "I agree." Requests for clarification include questions ("What's a . . . ?") or paraphrasing statements ("You mean like . . . ?").

Students with special needs have difficulty using the rules for many of these subtle behaviors in conversation. Teachers may have difficulty conversing with students, or may notice students being ineffective in establishing friendships and lasting interactions. Instructional group activities that focus on the specific use of particular conversational behaviors and rules can be beneficial for these students. Adolescents, in particular, are able to appreciate the need to learn these rules and behaviors, and can be encouraged to practice them in role-playing situations. Prompts and modeling from the teacher throughout the school day can stimulate the students' awareness for these rules and provide "real" opportunities for the students to practice the new conversational skills with peers or adults.

Language in Narratives

Children's stories and attempts to share past events are developmentally influenced by a community's social rules (Mandler et al., 1980). When parents ask children, "What did you do at school today?" they do not want a simple listing of key actions. Instead, most parents expect to hear a series of activities described in order of their occurrence. When teachers ask children, "What's going on in this story (or picture)?" the students are expected to give (at a minimum) descriptions of person/action, object/action, or object/person relationships. Simple one-word labels for objects or actions fail to satisfy the adults.

The ability to tell (or write) a story about imaginary characters, places, or events demands some knowledge of what makes a good story. By the time children are 6 years old, they learn what components to include in a story and how to sequence those elements to make their story complete and interesting (Page & Stewart, 1985). Table 6.1 presents an ordered list of some essential components for a simple story (Stein & Glenn, 1979). When a child omits or reorders any of these elements, his or her story sounds vague and incomplete. As children approach adolescence, they should be able to include greater detail in each component and present multiple episodes sequentially or simultaneously.

A 9-year-old student in Craig's special education classroom told the story shown in Figure 6.7. This student has reported difficulties in reading; she occa-

Table 6.1
Elements for a Simple Story

Setting	Introduction of main characters; sets stage, gives context
Initiating event/beginning	Action that changes the story environment, evokes formation of the goal
Internal response	Goal, serves as motivation for later action
Attempt	Overt actions that are directed toward goal attainment
Consequence/outcome	Result of an attempt (attainment or nonattainment of goal)
Reaction/ending	Emotion, cognition, or endstate expressing protagonist's feelings about goal or generalization to some broader consequence

Source: Adapted from N. Stein & C. Glenn, An analysis of story comprehension in elementary school children. In R. O. Freedle (ed.), *Advances in Discourse Processing, Vol. 2,* New directions in Discourse Processing (Norwood, NJ: Ablex, 1979), pp. 53–120.

sionally ignores the cause-effect relationships established in stories (similar to ones she omits in her verbal productions) and fails to answer comprehension questions accurately. Note the important story elements this student has omitted or transposed. (Note, too, the semantic, word order, and cohesion problems.)

Special education teachers should allow time in reading lessons to discuss the cause-and-effect relationships in stories, should challenge students to predict outcomes, and should encourage students to recall personal experiences that generated feelings like those described for the characters in a story (Garnett,

Figure 6.7 Student's story with notable errors.

I'm not sure . . . and he . . . um . . . he's arm wrestling with these big ol' guys, and he went he bought a truck and he goes all these things and it's in Mexico . . . he . . . um. Then he get to this place and then this guy gets a can of motor oil and he drinks it. (Laugh.) Then they were going to have the arm wrestling "contents" . . . And . . . un . . . and he . . . uh . . . I saw him get some Alka Seltzer and put them in there and dranked it cuz he had an upset stomach from the . . . uh . . . the oil motor, motor oil, whatever it's called. And . . . um . . . he . . . he . . . um . . . whoever was they were talking about cuz they were going to win . . . um I think $20,000 and a big ol' truck, diesel truck. And the he . . . um . . . the . . . he. At the end he was doing this big ol' guy that broke people's arms? And he just got it and slammed it down and he won the big ol' truck and I think $20,000, I'm not sure. And the . . . um . . . he . . . he was . . . um . . . he there was this guy that . . . uh . . . that he . . . he . . . went over there . . . to pick his son from the army. And the he . . . uh . . . he . . . uh . . . um picked him up and brought him to that place and they had the arm wrestling "contents" and then the uh . . . they went to this guy's house. And they um . . . they sol, they stole, um . . . his son from . . . um . . . then he was in his big ol' truck and there was a big ol' . . . uh . . . uh . . . medal gate like about four inches thick of metal and he backed up and he . . . uh . . . broke through it and he I think he got his son I can't remember that then he they were going then when they saw this guy and then his the one that . . . he was going to them $20,000 I mean $5,000 and . . . um a big ol' truck and he didn't want it. And then he . . . um . . . he . . . went over there and won the wrestling "contents" and that all I can remember.

1986). Writing tasks in the classroom might include activities in which students are presented with incomplete stories. Key words or statements can be listed on the board or spaced on lined writing paper to remind students to include a "problem, attempt, outcome, or feeling" in their efforts to complete the story.

Language at Home and at School

The language behaviors and rules expected for classroom interactions differ somewhat from the communication patterns accepted from students at home or on the playground (Wells, 1986). The words and structure of statements, turn-taking patterns, topic choices, and complexity of questions and directives are notably different in social "home" communication and "school" discourse.

Table 6.2 lists some of the rule changes students have to appreciate to succeed in the communication game at school. Some of these differences are often highlighted in kindergarten programs to prepare younger students for the style of communication teachers in upper grades typically use and expect. Most students adapt well to these rule changes by the time they finish first grade. But students with special needs may take longer to understand the need for the changes and have difficulty understanding the teacher's communicative efforts when these style differences are used without explanation.

Communication in the classroom includes both verbal and written interactions. The teacher or a textbook controls the communication focus at school, and students may experience decreased opportunities to talk or initiate new topics. Teachers frequently ask questions to check the students' retention of recently presented material rather than for the purpose of sincerely seeking new information (Tattershall & Creaghead, 1985). Students are delegated to the responder's role most of the time in the classroom and find themselves needing

Table 6.2
Language Differences at Home and School

	HOME	SCHOOL
Form:	Predominantly oral social style	A mix of oral and written formal style
Topics:	Social, curiosity-based	Content, procedures, facts
	Child can select and control topic	Teacher selects and controls topic
	Sharing feelings and experiences	
Focus:	Immediate context	Decontextualized
	Shared frame of reference	Reference to past or future events and abstract ideas
Turn taking:	Frequent between child-child or child-adult	Monologues by teacher
	Assumes speaker role at will	Teacher-child interactions with little child-child interaction
	Directs speech to group, or select individuals	Assumes speaker role by raising hand
		Directs speech to teacher
Questions:	"Real" attempts to seek answers to unknown questions	Rhetorical, or used to "check" new knowledge

more time to think before responding. The questions asked at school often tap thinking skills (reasoning, evaluating, or synthesizing information) seldom used at home. The topics of conversation in the classroom are also different from ones heard at home. They are often about events or objects that are not present and demand the use of explicit vocabulary and lengthy statements. Students, therefore, expend a great deal of mental energy during classroom interactions, trying to organize the explicit, abstract, verbal information they hear or read.

Another difference between the language patterns of home and school is the amount of attention that is directed to the topic of language or talk itself. At home or in social situations, students speak freely and automatically with very little discussion about the words they choose or the structure of their sentences. Occasionally, students might ask someone to repeat a word or chuckle about the difficulty they have in producing some multisyllable words ("cinnamon"). But at school, students are frequently asked to analyze or reflect upon their spoken or written productions (Van Kleeck, 1984). Students are directed to identify the nouns, verbs, syllables, sounds, letters, paragraphs, or clauses in verbal and written passages. Students are asked to recognize sounds or words that sound or look alike. Students are expected to read "for meaning" and seek clarification of unclear passages by rereading a passage or using a dictionary. The students' experiences with language during their first five years of life focus very little attention on these component parts of communication. First and second graders, therefore, spend much time learning to "talk about talk." Students with special needs require even more time as well as guided instruction in this area.

Language in the classroom has been described as generally more abstract and complex than the language used at home (Berlin, Blank, & Rose, 1980). Most students with special needs have difficulty learning when traditional school discourse patterns are used. Therefore, special education teachers need to explain directions more concretely, guide students in interpreting lengthy passages, rephrase questions to less complex forms, and allow some students to express their knowledge in concrete verbal ways before challenging them to demonstrate their knowledge in more typical written formats. (These and other suggestions for adapting teaching behaviors are addressed in the final section of this chapter. In addition, reference lists included at the end of the chapter provide teachers with ideas for maximizing communicative interactions with the students.)

FUNCTIONS OF COMMUNICATION

At the start of this chapter, young Craig learned to use his kicking and running behaviors in a rule-governed manner to gain acceptance among his peers. As Craig continues to play the game in a more organized fashion, he could learn additional rules and behaviors that facilitate more pleasure, acceptance, and success. Ongoing practice and participation in the communication game can provide similar advantages.

Language for Thinking

Through the acceptable use of language, students can foster growth in their knowledge of the world and increase their ability to learn independently. Language is viewed as the medium for establishing new ideas and organizing thoughts (Muma, 1978; Vygotsky, 1962) in that people often think in words and phrases. Experiences that are seen, heard, or felt are presumed to be coded (in words) and then stored in memory (Butler, 1984; Gagne, 1985).

The words of a language can represent a variety of thoughts and references. Words typically represent ideas about objects, relationships, or underlying concepts (Bloom & Lahey, 1978). Students' poor understanding of words, relationships, and concepts can limit their ability to organize information in memory for easy recall and use (Wiig, 1984). On the other hand, students' organization and recall abilities can influence the extent to which they can use words, relationships, and concepts. It is generally accepted that decreased mental ability can influence the learning of language (Miller & Yoder, 1974). But conversely, students with potentially high intelligence can be limited in some thinking and learning abilities without adequate language skills. It is common for students with special needs to be characterized by both their language deficits and their ineffective strategies for learning (Gerber & Bryen, 1981; Wallach & Liebergott, 1984).

This symbiotic relationship that exists between thinking and language demands that special education teachers consider their use of language in the classroom as influential in maximizing students' language-learning potentials. Students with special needs may require repetition or visual cues to appreciate the relatedness of new terms and old ideas held in memory. Teachers should provide repeated opportunities to see, hear, or feel an experience and its associated language. For example, audiotapes can be used to record teachers' instructions and comments and be played back as often as is necessary for students. In addition, students can be encouraged to "think out loud" and talk themselves through classroom directives and activities (Camp & Bash, 1975). Problem solving, inferring, and predicting can all be strengthened through the use of "think out loud" strategies when teachers reflect students' ideas and encourage clarification and reorganization of facts. By explicitly stating the relationship between one activity and another, and allowing students' active involvement with materials while thinking and talking in the classroom, teachers can help students commit new knowledge and words to memory.

Language for Socializing

Language and social skills are believed to be closely interrelated in the communication game (Bates et al., 1983). The use of acceptable language patterns allows young children to move beyond isolated interactions with their parents. Speech can be used to request, comment on, or respond to the actions and objects of other children or adults nearby. Through language, children 4 or 5 years old develop abilities for meeting their needs and desires, nearly independent of parents or primary caregivers.

As children approach adolescence, acceptable language patterns are used to facilitate the young person's access to larger social networks (Donahue & Bryan, 1984). Girls and boys establish same-sex interest groups during their preteen years. Members of these homosexual, shared-interest cliques rely on talking to exchange ideas, exercise leadership abilities, and express preferences for clothes, hobbies, sports, or persons of the opposite sex. Adolescents also acquire language specific to particular activities, such as cheerleading, playing in a band, or participating on a sports team. Adolescent slang, puns, jokes, and private languages (Pig Latin) develop in these cliques or clubs and act to bond the members together. Early heterosexual interactions in adolescence frequently revolve around similar, shared-interest activities; consequently, adolescent girls and boys must learn the various language adaptations and idiosyncrasies pertinent to these activities.

Students with special needs frequently have difficulty understanding or using the language associated with adolescent cliques (Boyce & Larson, 1983). Puns, jokes, and slang terms require adolescents to appreciate the arbitrariness of words and their multiple meanings. Figurative patterns of speech, such as the idiom, metaphor, and simile, are also used by adolescents and require comparable knowledge of words. These and other characteristics of teen-age lingo make it difficult for students with special needs to access or maintain membership in a social network with peers (Donahue & Bryan, 1984). Chapter 5 of this text addresses social skills curricula for students with special needs. In addition to the suggestions provided in that chapter, teachers in special education classrooms need to assist the students in learning the value and meaning of jokes, puns, idoms, metaphors, and slang. Students also need to be taught how to use language effectively to persuade, negotiate, or differ with others. Development of these communication skills allows students access to a social network with their peers.

Language and Literacy

Communicative interactions influence the development of thinking and socializing skills through a variety of verbal and written activities. Some authors suggest that increasing competency with the verbal language of a community contributes to students' understanding of written communication in that language (Menyuk, 1983; Wells, 1986). It is interesting to note that many school-aged students with learning disabilities, who show difficulties with reading and writing, have reported preschool histories that include speech and language problems (Aram, Ekelman, & Nation, 1984; Maxwell & Wallach, 1984; Strominger & Bashir, 1977). These data suggest that some knowledge and proficiency with oral language is important for a student's acquisition of more literate forms of communication.

The differences between an oral and literate style of communication do not simply represent a distinction between speaking and writing. *Oral styles of communication* can be *either* verbal or written. Generally, oral communication occurs with familiar persons in unstructured situations and focuses on concrete topics or questions. Oral styles of communication are less formal than are literate styles and allow for the use of familiar vocabulary, pronouns, slang, and loosely structured sentences. Social conversations and brief written notes are examples of communication in an oral style.

Literate styles of communication, in contrast, are reserved for more formal settings, where persons are less familiar with one another (school or work). An emphasis is placed on learning new information and stresses a need to reason, reflect, and plan. Topics and questions presented in a literate style frequently demand new vocabulary, concise grammar, and thinking in terms of inferences and summarizations. Literate styles of communication may be verbal as in a classroom lecture, or written, in the form of books or compositions.

Since oral and literate styles of communication both utilize verbal and written forms, the two styles can be viewed as a continuum of language activities rather than as a dichotomy (Tannen, 1980; Westby, 1985). Figure 6.8 presents some verbal and written language activities on an oral-literate continuum. Any activity can be viewed as more or less oral, or more or less literate, than another activity by noting the degree of structure and demand for explicitness in the task.

Students with special needs demonstrate delays and difficulties advancing toward literacy. Special education teachers can increase the likelihood of these students successfully using literate language if teachers appreciate the oral and literate aspects of any communication task in the classroom. By providing students opportunities to practice literate styles of communication in verbal forms first, teachers can make the task of reading or writing in literate styles easier. For example, before students are expected to write a book report or answer chapter review questions, teachers can ask students to share their ideas verbally. In this way, students use speech as an advance organizer for preparing their thoughts and selecting appropriate words. Then, as students approach the mechanics of writing, they can concentrate on *how* to write and not worry as much about *what* to write.

Figure 6.8 An oral-literate language continuum. (*Source:* C. Westby, Learning to talk–talking to learn: Oral-literate language differences. In C. Simon (ed.), *Communication Skills and Classroom Success* (San Diego: College-Hill, 1985), p. 197. Used by permission.)

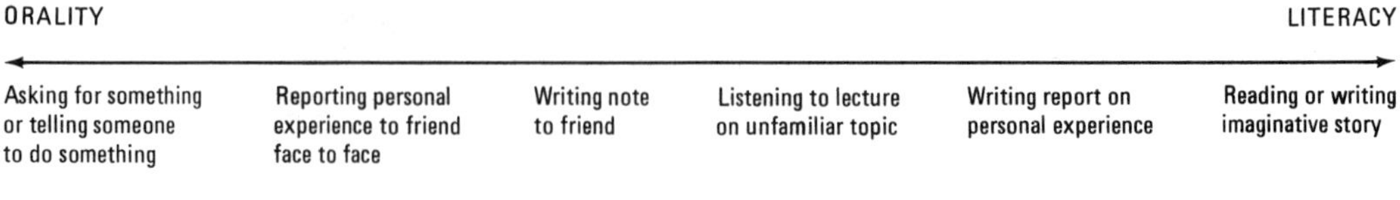

ORALITY   LITERACY

$\longleftrightarrow$

| Asking for something or telling someone to do something | Reporting personal experience to friend face to face | Writing note to friend | Listening to lecture on unfamiliar topic | Writing report on personal experience | Reading or writing imaginative story |

COMMUNICATION IN THE CLASSROOM

Instructional programs in special education classrooms should be designed to provide students an opportunity to learn new concepts and facts, new strategies for thinking and problem solving, and appropriate social-communicative behaviors that allow them to succeed in a social-literate community. Listening, speaking, reading, writing, and even the use of computers are all language skills that can be used for learning in the classroom.

Although the skills listed in Figure 6.9 appear in the order in which they are typically mastered, the development and use of any of these language skills can have bidirectional influences. For example, students can improve their comprehension of the language by imitating the speech of others and noting the effect (meaning) the words have on their listener (Stine & Bohanon, 1983). Writing activities can be used to highlight the relationship between printed graphics (letters or words) and the vocal language symbols they represent (speech sounds and words). Teachers can guide students to manipulate the letters to create a variety of meaningful words and statements. In doing so, students can increase their awareness of print as a communicative medium. They may be more likely, then, to approach reading (like listening) as a process in decoding meaning, rather than simply as an exercise in sounding out letters and words (Johnson, 1985; Wells, 1986).

Computers can foster the students' appreciation of language, in any form, as an arbitrary system of symbols. Students learn to use the keyboard symbols for creating images and statements that represent their thoughts and ideas. Computers can be used in special education classrooms to help students improve vocabulary, reading, and writing abilities. Commercial programs such as *Micro-Soc Thinking Games* or *KIDWRITER, The Storyteller,* and *Computer Courseware for the Exceptional Student* are designed to be used by students in regular and special

Figure 6.9 Bidirectional influences of language behaviors in the classroom.

Listening

Speaking

Reading

Writing

Computers

education classrooms. These computer programs stimulate the students' knowledge of words and sentences for sequencing thoughts, building associations between words, and interpreting new information.

Clearly, learning in any classroom is dependent upon the students' abilities to comprehend and use a variety of language forms. But many students with special needs reportedly have difficulties and delays in using some language behaviors and rules. How, then, can these special students be expected to learn the academics and learning strategies teachers attempt to teach them?

Teacher-Student-Curriculum Interactions

The responsibility for making the classroom a successful learning environment lies with the teacher. Figure 6.10 shows the triadic relationship that exists for the student, teacher, and curriculum material in any academic setting (Gruenewald & Pollack, 1984). Students interact with both the teacher and the printed material many times each day as they participate in classroom activities and complete

Figure 6.10 Language triad in the classroom. (*Source:* From L. Gruenewald & S. Pollack, *Language interaction in teaching and learning* (Austin, TX: Pro-Ed, Inc., 1984), p. 10. Used by permission.)

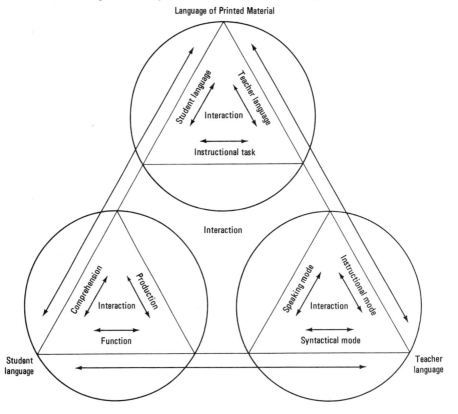

academic tasks. Teachers prepare instructional materials for presentation to students and then discuss the material with students before, during, and after they complete assignments. The triadic members continually interact and influence one another in the processes of teaching and learning. But it is the teacher who has the ability to control many of the interactions within the triad. If teachers recognize their influential position, they can succeed in meeting some important teaching goals in classrooms for students with special needs.

Role of Language in Instructional Goals

Special education teachers have many goals for teaching students with special needs. Foremost is the teaching of academics. Science, history, civics, social studies, and literature as well as math, reading, and writing are just a few of the content areas that may be addressed by special education teachers. Another goal for teaching students with special needs focuses on improved communication skills. Since language is the medium for learning and the foundation for literacy, special education teachers need to address specific language behaviors and rules as part of the curriculum. Objectives that emphasize improved conversational skills in social and classroom settings, narrative skills in verbal and written forms, semantics, and rules for sound and word combinations should be notable components of students' individual education plans (IEPs).

These two instructional goals demand that special education teachers have a working knowledge of language and are sensitive to the role language plays in learning. Teachers need to be aware of each student's language deficits so appropriate adaptations can be made in teachers' verbal instructions and in any printed materials presented to the students. If students demonstrate persistent difficulty managing verbal and written forms of communication, it is the teacher's responsibility to refer them for thorough evaluation by a speech-language pathologist (SLP). When speech-language therapy is recommended, teachers play an important role in reinforcing targeted communicative goals within the classroom and in integrating language targets into the total curriculum. In summary, teachers need to be competent in using language for effective teaching and teaching students to use language effectively.

Using Language for Teaching

By their mere title, special education teachers are expected to do something "special" when they teach. Students with special needs are often referred for special education services because they demonstrate an inability to learn efficiently in academic settings where traditional teaching methods are used. Special education teachers can facilitate learning by monitoring their rate of speech, the complexity of their sentences, and their choice of questions (Gruenewald & Pollack, 1984).

In a study of first, third, and sixth grade teachers, Cuda and Nelson (1976) found that first grade teachers used a rate of speech that was slow but effective for teaching these beginning learners. The average rate of speech for the first grade teachers was 4.5 syllables per second (sps). Third and sixth grade teachers used a faster rate of 5.1–5.4 sps. Special education teachers might consider the advantages of using the slower rate of speech. Students with special needs, like first graders, display difficulty adapting to the language of school. These students can benefit from having added time to comprehend and respond to the complex and abstract questions, directions, and instructions presented by teachers.

In addition, special education teachers should evaluate the content and form of their conversations with students in the classroom. Do most classroom interactions consist of comments, or questions? Extensive questioning certainly challenges students to think. But students with special needs appear to benefit from having teachers comment, describe, demonstrate, and relate new concepts and materials to previously existing information (Gersten, Woodward, & Darch, 1986; Turnure, 1986). After students have an opportunity to synthesize the new material, teachers can proceed with questions to facilitate recall and reorganization of new and old thoughts.

When special education teachers do decide to question the student, they should select their questions thoughtfully (Blank & White, 1986). Some questions demand more thinking than others. Some students may find it difficult to express knowledge they possess about a particular topic, if the question presented to them is too complex. The student may recognize some of the words in the question, but be unsure of what to say. Teachers may erroneously interpret students' inadequate responses to mean the students have "no knowledge" on the topic. By using a different and easier question, teachers may discover students' true knowledge.

A hierarchy of questions and directives is presented in Table 6.3. Questions that require only recall of simple facts (levels 1, 2) are generally easier than are questions that require reasoning, evaluation, or comparisons (levels 3, 4). The higher-level questions demand more thinking, and frequently require more time for students to produce an acceptable answer. If teachers appreciate the thinking complexity of the various questions they use, they can present students with questions and directives that appropriately tap students' knowledge. In time, teachers can challenge students to expand their thinking and answer more complex questions.

The printed materials in classroom curricula are used to introduce students to new facts or challenge students to practice new learning strategies. To meet these goals, teachers should present students with printed academic material that is written in a language form and style that students can understand. The passages, directions, and questions found in many textbooks and workbooks require students to comprehend compound and complex sentences. These materials also require students to think about objects and events that cannot presently be seen, touched, or heard. The complex and abstract nature of many academic materials (Lasky & Chapady, 1976) demands that their language be

Table 6.3
A Hierarchy of Questions and Directives

LEVEL	QUESTIONS/STATEMENTS
Level 1: Matching perception At this level, the simplest level, the child must be able to apply language to what he or she sees in the everyday world identifying, naming, or imitating.	What is this? What did you see? Show me the circle.
Level 2: Selective analysis of perception At this level, the child must focus more selectively on specific aspects of material and integrate separate components in a unified whole, describing, completing a sentence, giving an example, or selecting an object by two characteristics.	What is happening? Find something that is . . . Finish the sentence.
Level 3: Reordering perception The child must restructure or reorder perceptions according to constraints imposed through language (excluding assuming role of another or following directions in correct sequence).	Find the things that are not . . . What will happen next? What would she say?
Level 4: Reasoning about perception The formulations at this level, the most complex level, require the child to go beyond immediate perceptions and talk about logical relationships between objects and events (predicting, explaining, or finding a logical solution).	What will happen if . . . Why should we use that? What could you do?

Source: L. Berlin, M. Blank, and S. Rose, The language of instruction: The hidden complexities. *Topics in Language Disorders and Learning Disabilities, 1,* (1980), 52.

simplified, or augmented if students with special needs are to learn the concept or facts that are presented (Darch & Carnine, 1986; Wiig & Semel, 1984). The complex sentences and implicit words used in many workbooks and texts can be simplified without sacrificing the author's intent. Table 6.4 provides some guidelines for noting semantic and grammatical complexity in spoken and written passages. The classroom directives listed are adapted for easier understanding by students with special needs. The content of the message is conserved. The adaptations made in printed materials can be presented to students verbally ("cross out *collections* and write in *groups*") or, if necessary, in the form of new worksheets.

Special education teachers need to create a match between the student's language and learning abilities and the language used in the classroom (Gruenewald & Pollack, 1984; Wiig & Semel, 1984). By considering the language variables of speaking rate, question difficulty, and semantic and grammatical complexity, special education teachers can make useful changes in both their verbal teaching patterns and in the language used in textbooks and workbooks.

Teaching Students to Use Language

Another teaching goal for special education teachers addresses the students' need to improve basic communication skills. Listening, speaking, reading, and writing require students to interpret and manipulate the symbols of language, so

Table 6.4
Examples of Classroom Language Adapted for Complexity of Message

INSTRUCTION/QUESTIONS	ADAPTATION	FOCUS
(*Math*)		
Ring the accurate answer in each problem.	Draw a circle around the correct answer.	Vocabulary
(*Science*)		
Why are location and motion important to people?	What is motion? Why is it important to people? What is location? Why is it important to people?	High-level question; multiple concepts
(*Math*)		
Write numbers on the second ruler, color it yellow, and cut it out to use in class.	Write the numbers 1–6 on the empty ruler below. Color the ruler yellow. Cut out the ruler. Use the ruler to measure your pencil.	Long sentence; multiple steps; vague pronoun referent
(*Reading*)		
The characters in the story were too upset to do anything constructive when they discovered the burglar. What would you do?	Who were the characters in the story? How did they feel when they found the burglar in the house? What would you do if you found a burglar in your house?	Complex sentence; vocabulary; high-level question

that meaningful communication occurs. Students with special needs, however, require assistance in learning to select, organize, and present their verbal or written words in a meaningful manner (Simon, 1985).

"Communication" should be viewed as an important part of the overall curriculum each week at school. Blocks of time should be designated each day for language objectives, just as time is specified for math, science, and reading. During these language activities, direct instruction techniques can be used to make the behaviors and rules of language explicit. Students should be encouraged to do most of the talking in these activities; listening alone cannot improve students' knowledge and use of language. Teachers can play the role of facilitator and troubleshooter while students engage in verbal games and role playing. Teachers can model correct word choices and combinations or demonstrate the use of appropriate nonverbal behaviors. When students have difficulty or "break down" in the communication task, teachers can prompt students to recall and use targeted behaviors or rules.

Activities that promote talking between students for purposes of reasoning, explaining, and questioning are highly recommended for students with special needs. Many commercially available language programs that provide daily lesson plans for groups of students emphasize the use of language components in social, interactive activities. The *Peabody Language Development Kits (Revised) Levels P-3 (PLDK), Developing Understanding of Self and Others (DUSO-Revised),* and *Classroom Listening and Speaking (CLAS)* include useful activities for students in primary grades. *Let's Talk, Conversations, Communicative Competence,* and *Directing Discourse* provide ideas for adolescents.

Cooperating with the Speech-language Pathologist (SLP)

Because of reported high incidences of language difficulties among children with special needs, many special education programs provide individual or small-group instruction from an SLP for these students. SLPs might remove students from the classroom for structured therapy, or meet with students in the classroom for small-group instruction. Teachers can collaborate with the SLP to help maximize the effect of the language intervention programs. If an SLP conducts language activities in the classroom with large groups of students each week, teachers can use these visits to observe the intervention strategies the SLP uses. Students benefit from the teacher's use of these same strategies to prompt and reinforce targeted behaviors in routine classroom interactions during the rest of the week.

The direct individual or group intervention provided by an SLP or teacher needs to be complemented by teachers' efforts to incorporate the communicative goals into everyday school activities. Throughout the school day, during academic work and interactions, teachers should prompt and reinforce students' use of language patterns that were discussed and practiced in specific language activities with the SLP or teacher. During reading lessons, teachers can point out the story characters' appropriate use of turn taking or relevant statements. The order and value of story elements can be noted during reading assignments as well. Vocabulary that is introduced in the reading passage can be related to terms used previously in science, math, or language lessons.

Classroom Activities

The following activities are suggested for use in the classroom with groups of students. Some are appropriate for times delegated specifically for "language enrichment"; others can be incorporated into reading, social studies, and language arts lessons. (For a more comprehensive presentation of classroom language activities, refer to the list of instructional programs and materials in the references and suggested readings for this chapter.)

Using Explicit Vocabulary and Requests for Clarification

Barrier games, in which speakers and listeners are unable to see each other's materials (referents) are easy to implement in the classroom. "Go Fish" and "Old Maid" card games as well as variations on "do-as-I-say, but-don't-peek" activities are barrier games. Games are especially useful for creating functional communication that demands the use of explicit vocabulary ("the blue, square package in the middle of the table"), consideration of the listener's perspective, effective listening skills, and requests for clarification (Which one? Huh?). Students can take turns being the speaker or listener. The speaker can describe a picture of an item or action that differs only slightly in some way from the other pictures in view. Listeners are challenged to name or select matching pictures. Commercially available products that promote the use of a barrier game concept for language instruction include *Hot Air Balloons, Familiar Objects and Actions,* and *A Sourcebook of Pragmatic Activities.* Picture cards from the *Peabody Picture Collection* can easily be adapted for this kind of activity.

Painting Pictures with Words

Teachers can stimulate students' understanding of question words and can prompt the use of acceptable grammatical constructions by asking students to tell a story about their experiences or about a set of sequential pictures. The teacher can ask questions that elicit detail and qualifying information (Which one? Where was he going? How will he do it?). As the story is being told, the teacher can write or type it for the child. The teacher and student reread the story together and clarify information. Teachers can model more grammatically correct sentences by writing just above students' original entries. Students learn to appreciate the relationship of speech and written text as they proceed to edit the scripts. This activity is especially effective when used for letter writing (to parents or friends) or oral book reports.

Inferring Meaning

Perceptual, logical, and evidence-based inferences can be stimulated by directly challenging students to discuss options for specific situations or facts. Teachers can prepare index cards that contain an inferential prompt on one side and an acceptable inference on the other. Students are assigned to teams or play with partners. Students read the cards aloud and challenge their opponent to report an appropriate inference. For example, one card might read: "On your way to school today, you notice people standing outside a church. Everyone is dressed nicely in dark clothes; a hearse is parked along the curb. You infer . . .". Another card reads: "Three boys are needed for the school play. John and Mike tell you they each got parts. You see a sign outside the auditorium that reads 'Auditions today 3:00.' You infer . . .". The activity can be added to the card decks found in *Pragmatic Language Trivia.*

Sequencing and Maintaining Coherence

To be coherent in conversations, or story telling, students need to appreciate the order of events as well as the pertinence of anything they mention. Students can be challenged to recall the simple sequence of morning activities, directions for getting to the principal's office, completion of a chore, or directions for a familiar board game. Partners can attempt to execute the sequence as given by the student. Teachers can record in writing the verbally presented sequence and ask other students to "follow these directives." Students can monitor their abilities for successfully completing such activities by noting the number of statements that are pertinent and in sequence before an inappropriate or useless statement is noted.

Maintaining and Changing Topics

Students can be encouraged to practice rules for topic maintenance and the appropriate behaviors for switching topics in a conversation. Two students can be assigned to play speaker and listener, respectively. The speaker is given a topic to initiate and pursue. The listener is given a different topic to address. The listener is reminded of some acceptable behaviors for switching topics ("That reminds me, . . ." or "Before I forget, I wanted to tell you . . ."). Students in the audience can monitor (1) the number of consecutive statements "on topic" by speaker, (2) the listener's behaviors for attending to speaker topic, and (3) the listener's behaviors for changing topics (successful and unsuccessful). Similar objectives can be addressed in written activities to encourage the use of appropriate connecting statements at the beginning and end of paragraphs in a composition.

Building Vocabularies

As students learn new words, they modify their understanding of old but related words. The relatedness of old and new words can be made more explicit by asking students to look for synonyms of a word in a dictionary or thesaurus. The target word, and all the synonyms, can be written on index cards and organized in a hierarchy of intensity or quality. For example, the target word "stroll" can be defined by its relatedness to such words as strut, plod, run, prance, gallop, walk, and trudge, according to speed and agility. The words are viewed as degrees of walking and are placed in an appropriate order. Categorical terms can be reinforced in similar ways. Students can group word cards according to some predetermined quality or base word (categorical term). Student groups can practice using these words in sentences by playing an adapted card game. Students are dealt four to five cards. One at a time, students select a word card from their hand and use the word in a sentence. Students who recognize the sentence as containing a synonym for a word they hold in their hand can repeat the sentence using the synonym and gain the right to initiate a new turn.

Problem Solving and Using Conjunctions

Teachers can teach students appropriate use of conjunctions through group discussions. Each day five to ten minutes can be used to pursue solutions or explanations to problems or situations described on typed cards. These cards can be placed in a pocket on the bulletin board or in a container for easy selection. Students take turns each day selecting and reading a problem. Each problem or situation ends with a conjunction prompting related answers. Students are encouraged to discuss possible answers using the given conjunction. Teachers redirect inappropriate answers or request clarification from students. For example, the cards students select might read: "The pencil sharpener broke because . . ."; "If the school closed earlier today then . . ."; "I forgot to ask my dad for permission to use his baseball glove, so . . .".

Teachers can create other activities to address conversational openers, polite forms, relevant statements, or appropriate pronouns, or recognize word or syllable segments. Discussing ideas and plans with the speech-language pathologist can provide insight into the selection of communication objectives and activities.

SUMMARY

Students with special needs often experience difficulties succeeding in academic or routine classroom activities. These difficulties are often related to an inability to effectively use language for learning new information or communicating old knowledge. These students may have problems expressing their ideas orally or in writing; they may demonstrate confusion when trying to understand the teacher's verbal instructions, questions, or comments. Students with special needs may have difficulty using words and phrases to develop and later reorganize ideas about topics presented in science, math, social studies, and physics courses. In addition, these students may fail to develop the necessary competence with language to gain acceptance in social groups, or once accepted, may be unable to maintain membership in the group. The deficits in social skills described in Chapter 5 are very often related to the students' deficiencies in language.

The ability to play the communication game, specifically the ability to follow the rules of oral language, helps students develop competency with more literate forms of communication. Language is a medium for learning. Academic instruction in the classroom uses both oral and written language to convey new concepts and ideas. But written forms of communication are patterned after the oral language rules in a community. The rules that govern spelling and sentence or paragraph constructions in written form are related to the rules which govern intelligible speech and coherent conversations. The purpose of written language is similar to that of verbal language: The function of both is to communicate a message. It is not surprising that the reading and writing difficulties reported for special students are often based in their inadequate ability to communicate orally.

Teachers must learn to appreciate and play the communication game within the context of the classroom. Teachers must assume sole responsibility for its successful use in special education classrooms where students with special needs demonstrate language deficiencies. Teachers must have a working knowledge of the rules of language and be sensitive to the role language plays in learning. They also must be aware of students' deficiencies in language so they can adapt their oral instructions and classroom texts to students' ability to comprehend.

And they must realize that by helping students improve their skills in language, they are also helping students increase their potential to learn. Time must be allotted in each school day for teaching, modeling, and reinforcing correct language for effective and functional communication.

This chapter provided an overview of the elements of language and the specific behaviors and rules that contribute to a successful and enjoyable communication game. Specific suggestions were provided for assessing and adapting both the teacher's speech in classroom instruction and the semantic complexity of printed instructional materials. Finally, activities for promoting improved verbal communication and transferring verbal language skills to written form were provided.

STUDY AND DISCUSSION QUESTIONS

1. Review the continuum of oral and literate activities presented in Figure 6.8. Think of three more activities that commonly occur in classrooms and decide where they fit on the continuum. Be sure to consider such aspects as verbal or written form, amount of structure to the task, and type of audience.

2. Ask a student to tell you a story. Tape record the production and transcribe it verbatim. Does it contain the essential elements for a simple story? What could be different?

3. Select a textbook or workbook to review. Analyze the complexity of one passage, set of instructions, or review questions.

4. Select two students to play a barrier game. Designate one student as the speaker and the other as listener. Position these conversational partners on either side of an opaque wall or screen. The speaker is instructed to describe abstract drawings to the listener. The listener attempts to select the appropriate match from the array of drawings on his side of the screen. Proceed through four or five descriptions. Note the team's success rate. Reverse roles. Discuss the language demands in this activity. What real-life situations demand a similar use of language?

REFERENCES AND SUGGESTED READINGS

General

ARAM, D., EKELMAN, B. & NATION, J. (1984). Preschoolers with language disorders: 10 years laters. *Journal of Speech & Hearing Research, 27*(3), 232–244.

BATES, E., BRETHERTON, I., BEEGHLY-SMITH, M., & McNEW, S. (1983). Social bases of language development: A reassessment. In H. W. Reese & L. P. Lipsett (eds.), *Advances in child development and behavior,* Vol. 16. New York: Academic Press.

BELLUGI, R., & KLIMA, E. (1978). Structural properties of American Sign Language. In L. S. Liben (ed.), *Deaf children: Developmental perspectives,* pp. 43–68. New York: Academic Press.

BERKO-GLEASON, J. (1985). *The development of language.* Columbus, OH: Charles E. Merrill.

BEVER, T. J. (1970). The cognitive basis of linguistic structures. In J. R. Hayes (ed.), *Cognition and the development of language*, pp. 279–362. New York: John Wiley and Sons.

BLOOM, L., & LAHEY, M. (1978). *Language development and language disorders*. New York: John Wiley and Sons.

BROWN, R. (1973). *A first language: The early stages*. Cambridge, MA: Harvard University Press.

BUTLER, K. (1984). Language processing: Halfway up the down staircase. In G. Wallach & K. Butler (eds.), *Language learning disabilities in school-age children*, pp. 60–80. Baltimore, MD: Williams & Wilkins.

CARROW-WOOLFOLK, E., & LYNCH, J. (1982). Learning words: Semantic development. In *An integrative approach to language disorders in children*, pp. 133–151. New York: Grune and Stratton.

CHERRY, C. (1957). *On human communication*. New York: John Wiley and Sons.

GAGNE, E. (1985). *The cognitive psychology of school learning*. Boston: Little, Brown & Co.

GERSTEN, R., WOODWARD, J., & DARCH, C. (1986). Direct instruction: A research-based approach to curriculum design and teaching. *Exceptional Children, 53*(1), 17–31.

McCORMICK, L., & SCHIEFELBUSCH, R. L. (eds.) (1984). *Early language intervention*. Columbus, OH: Charles E. Merrill.

MUMA, J. R. (1978). *Language handbook: Concepts, assessment, intervention*. Englewood Cliffs, NJ: Prentice Hall.

ROTH, F., & SPECKMAN, N. (1984). Assessing the pragmatic abilities of children. Part 1. Organizational framework & assessment parameters. *Journal of Speech and Hearing Disorders, 49*(1), 2–11.

SAPIR, E. T. (1921). *Language: An introduction to the study of speech*. New York: Harcourt, Brace & World.

SCHUELE, C. M., & VANKLEECK, A. (1987). Precursors to literacy: Assessment & intervention. *Topics in Language Disorders, 7*(2), 32–44.

STINE, E., & BOHANNON, J. (1983). Imitation, interactions and acquisition. *Journal of Child Language, 10*, 589–604.

TANNEN, D. (1980). Implications of the oral/literate continuum for cross-cultural communication. In J. E. Alatic (ed.), *Current issues in bilingual education*. Washington, DC: Georgetown University Press.

TAYLOR, O. (1986). Clinical practice as a social occasion. In L. Cole & V. Deal (eds.), *Communication disorders in multicultural populations*. Rockville, MD: American Speech-Language-Hearing Association.

TURNURE, J. E. (1986). Instruction and cognitive development: Coordinating communication and cues. *Exceptional Children, 53*(2), 109–117.

VANKLEECK, A., & SCHUELE, C. M. (1987). Precursors to literacy: Normal development. *Topics in Language Disorders, 7*(2), 13–31.

VYGOTSKY, L. S. (1962). *Thought and language*. Cambridge, MA: M.I.T. Press.

WALLACH, G., & BUTLER, K. (1984). *Language learning disabilities in school-age children*. Baltimore, MD: Williams & Wilkins.

WARREN, S. F., & ROGERS-WARREN, A. K. (1985). *Teaching functional language*. Baltimore, MD: University Park Press.

WELLS, G. (1986). *The meaning makers: Children learning language and using language to learn*. Portsmouth, NH: Heinemann.

WELLS, G. (1981). *Learning through interactions: The study of language development*. Cambridge, England: Cambridge University Press.

WIIG, E. (1984). Language disabilities in adolescents: A question of cognitive strategies. *Topics in Language Disorders, 4*(2), 41–58.

Language in Special Populations

BOUCHER, C. R. (1986). Pragmatics: The meaning of verbal language in learning disabled and non-disabled boys. *Learning Disability Quarterly, 9*(4), 285–295.

CALCULATOR, S. (1985). Describing and treating discourse problems in mentally retarded children: The myth of mental retardese. In D. Ripich & F. Spinelli (eds.), *School discourse problems*, pp. 125–148. San Diego: College-Hill Press.

DONAHUE, M. (1985). Communicative style in learning disabled children: Some implications for classroom discourse. In D. Ripich & F. Spinelli (eds.), *School discourse problems*, pp. 97–124. San Diego: College-Hill Press.

DONAHUE, M., & BRYAN, T. (1984). Communicative skills and peer relations of learning disabled adolescents. *Topics in Language Disorders, 4*(2), 10–21.

FEAGANS, L. (1983). Discourse processes in learning disabled children. In J. D. McKinney & L. Feagans (eds.), *Current topics in learning disabilities*, pp. 87–115. Norwood, NJ: Ablex.

GERBER, A., & BRYEN, D. (1981). *Language and learning disabilities*. Baltimore, MD: University Park Press.

GRIFFITH, P., JOHNSON, H., & DASTOLI, S. (1985). If teaching is conversation, can conversation be taught? Discourse abilities in hearing impaired children. In D. Ripich and F. Spinelli (eds.), *School discourse problems*, pp. 149–178. San Diego: College-Hill Press.

HARING, T., ROGER, B., LEE, M., BREEN, C., & GAYLORD-ROSS, R. (1986). Teaching social language to moderately handicapped students. *Journal of Applied Behavior Analysis, 19*(2), 159–171.

MAXWELL, S., & WALLACH, G. (1984). The language-learning disabilities connection: Symptoms of early language disabilities over time. In G. Wallach and K. Butler (eds.), *Language learning disabilities in school-age children*, pp. 15–34. Baltimore, MD: Williams & Wilkins.

MILLER, J., & YODER, D. (1974). An ontogenetic language teaching strategy for retarded children. In R. Schiefelsbush (ed.), *Language perspectives, acquisition, retardation and intervention*, pp. 505–528. Baltimore, MD: University Park Press.

SIMON, C. (1985). The language-learning disabled student: Description and therapy implications. In *Communication skills and classroom success: Therapy methodologies for language-learning disabled students*, pp. 1–58. San Diego: College-Hill Press.

SPECKMAN, N. (1981). Dyadic verbal communication abilities of learning disabled and normally achieving fourth- and fifth-grade boys. *Learning Disability Quarterly, 4*(2), 139–151.

STROMINGER, A. Z., & BASHIR, A. S. (1977). A nine-year follow-up of language delayed children. Presented at the annual convention of the American Speech Language and Hearing Association, Chicago.

WALLACH, G., & LIEBERGOTT, J. (1984). Who shall be called "Learning Disabled": Some new directions. In G. Wallach & K. Butler (eds.), *Language learning disabilities in school-age children*, pp. 1–14. Baltimore, MD: Williams & Wilkins.

WESTBY, C., & ROUSE, G. (1985). Culture in education and the instruction of language-learning disabled students. *Topics in Language Disorders, 5*(4), 15–28.

YOSHINAGO-ITANO, C., & DOWNEY, D. (1986). A hearing-impaired child's acquisition of schemata: Something is missing. *Topics in Language Disorders, 7*(1), 45–57.

Words/Sentences

BLISS, L., ALLEN, D., & WALKER, G. (1978). Sentence structures of trainable and educable mentally retarded subjects. *Journal of Speech and Hearing Research, 21*(4), 722–731.

CARROW-WOOLFOLK, E., & LYNCH, J. (1982). Learning words: Semantic development. In *An integrative approach to language disorders in children*, pp. 133–151. New York: Grune and Stratton.

CONDUS, M., MARSHALL, K., & MULLER, S. (1986). Effects of keyword mnemonic strategy on vocabulary acquisition and maintenance by learning disabled children. *Journal of Learning Disabilities, 19*(10), 609–613.

NIPPOLD, M. (1985). Comprehension of figurative language in youth. *Topics in Language Disorders, 5*(3), 1–20.

PAGE, J., & CULATTA, B. (1986). Incorporating relational vocabulary teaching into daily classroom activities. *Journal of Childhood Communication Disorders, 9*(2) 157–168.

SEIDENBERG, P., & BERNSTEIN, D. (1986). The comprehension of similes and metaphors by learning-disabled and nonlearning-disabled children. *Language, Speech & Hearing Services in the Schools, 17*(3), 219–229.

WALLACH, G. (1977). The implications of different language comprehension strategies in learning disabled children: Effects of thematization. Unpublished doctoral dissertation, City University of New York. As reported in G. Wallach and K. Butler (eds.), (1984), *Language learning disabilities in school-age children*, pp. 26–27. Baltimore, MD: Williams & Wilkins.

Conversation

BRINTON, B., FUJIKI, M., LOEB, D., & WINKLER, E. (1986). Development of conversational repair strategies in response to requests for clarification. *Journal of Speech and Hearing Research, 29*(1), 75–81.

ROSINSKI-McCLENDON, M. K., & NEWHOFF, M. (1987). Conversational responsiveness and assertiveness in language-impaired children. *Language, Speech and Hearing Services in the Schools, 18*(1), 53–62.

SPECKMAN, N. (1983). Discourse and pragmatics. In C. Wren (ed.), *Language learning disabilities*, pp. 157–172. Boulder, CO: Aspen Press.

TERRELL, B. (1985). Learning the rules of the game: Discourse skills in early childhood. In D. Ripich & I. Spinelli (eds.), *School discourse problems*, pp. 13–28. San Diego: College-Hill Press.

Narratives

CRAIS, E., & CHAPMAN, R. (1987). Story recall & inferencing skills in language-learning disabled and non-disabled children. *Journal of Speech & Hearing Disorders, 52*(1), 50–55.

Garnett, K. (1986). Telling tales: Narratives and learning disabled children. *Topics in Language Disorders, 6*(2), 44–56.

MANDLER, J., SCRIBNER, S., COLE, M., & DeFOREST, M. (1980). Cross-cultural invariance in story recall. *Child Development, 51,* 19–26.

PAGE, J., & STEWART, S. (1985). Story grammar skills in school-age children. *Topics in Language Disorders, 5*(2), 16–30.

ROTH, F., & SPECKMAN, N. (1986). Narrative discourse: Spontaneously generated stories of learning-disabled and normally achieving students. *Journal of Speech and Hearing Disorders, 51*(1), 8–23.

STEIN, N., & GLENN, C. (1979). An analysis of story comprehension in elementary school children. In R. O. Freedle (ed.), *Advances in discourse processing*, Vol. 2. *New directions in discourse processing*, pp. 53–120. Norwood, NJ: Ablex.

WESTBY, C. (1984). Development of narrative language abilities. In G. Wallach & K. Butler (eds.), *Language learning disabilities in school-age children*, pp. 103–127. Baltimore, MD: Williams & Wilkins.

Language at School

Discourse

BERLIN, L., BLANK, M., & ROSE, S. (1980). The language of instruction: The hidden complexities. *Topics in Language Disorders and Learning Disabilities* 1, 47–58.

BLANK, M., & WHITE, S. (1986). Questions: A powerful but misused form of classroom exchange. *Topics in Language Disorders*, 6(2), 1–12.

CUDA, R. A., & NELSON, N. (1976). Analysis of teacher speaking rate, syntactic complexity and hesitation phenomena as a function of grade level. Presented at the annual meeting of the American Speech-Language-Hearing Association, Houston. As reported in G. Wallach & K. Butler (eds.), (1984), *Language learning disabilities in school-age children*, pp. 158–160. Baltimore, MD: Williams & Wilkins.

DAMICO, J. (1985). Clinical discourse analysis: A functional approach to language assessment. In C. Simon (ed.), *Communication skills and classroom success assessment of language-learning disabled students*, pp. 165–206. San Diego: College-Hill Press.

RIPICH, D., & SPINELLI, F. (1985). *School discourse problems*. San Diego: College-Hill Press.

TATTERSHALL, S., & CREAGHEAD, N. (1985). A comparison of communication at home and school. In D. Ripich & F. Spinelli (eds.), *School discourse problems*, pp. 29–52. San Diego: College-Hill Press.

WELLS, G. (1986).*The meaning makers: Children learning language and using language to learn*. Portsmouth, NH: Heinemann.

WESTBY, C. (1985). Learning to talk—talking to learn: Oral-literate language differences. In C. Simon (ed.)., *Communication skills and classroom success: Therapy methodologies for language-learning disabled students*, pp. 181–218. San Diego: College-Hill Press.

Reading, Writing, Academic

CARLSON, J., GRUENEWALD, L., & NYBERG, B. (1980). Everyday math is a story problem: The language of curriculum. *Topics in Language Disorders*, 1(1), 59–70.

CATTS, H., & KAMHI, A. (1986). The linguistic basis of reading disorders: Implications for the speech-language pathologist. *Language, Speech and Hearing Services in the Schools*, 17(4), 329–341.

DARCH, C., & CARNINE, D. (1986). Teaching content area material to learning disabled students. *Exceptional Children*, 53(3), 240–246.

GRUENEWALD, L., & POLLACK, S. (1984). *Language interaction in teaching and learning*. Austin, TX: Pro-Ed.

JOHNSON, D. (1985). Using reading & writing to improve oral language skills. *Topics in Language Disorders*, 5(3), 55–69.

LASKY, E., & CHAPADY, A. (1976). Factors affecting language comprehension. *Language, Speech, and Hearing Services in the Schools*, 7(3), 179–184.

LIBERMAN, I., LIBERMAN, A., MATTINGLY, I., & SHANKWEILER, D. (1980). Orthography and the beginning reader. In J. F. Kavanagh & R. L. Venezsky (eds.), *Orthography, reading, and dyslexia*. Baltimore, MD: University Park Press.

LIBERMAN, I. & SHANKWEILER, D. (1979). Speech, the alphabet and teaching to read. In L. Resnick & P. Weaver (eds.), *Theory and Practice of Early Reading,* Vol. 2, pp. 109–132. Hillsdale, NJ: Erlbaum.

MENYUK, P. (1983). Language development and reading. In T. Gallagher and C. Prutting (eds.), *Pragmatic assessment and intervention: Issues in language,* pp. 151–170. San Diego: College-Hill Press.

REID, E. (1986). Practicing effective instruction: An exemplary center for reading instruction approach. *Exceptional Children, 52*(6), 510–519.

TUNMER, W., & COLE, P. (1985). Learning to read: A metalinguistic act. In C. Simon (ed.), *Communication skills and classroom success: Therapy methodologies for language-learning disabled students,* pp. 293–314. San Diego: College-Hill Press.

VANKLEECK, A. (1984). Metalinguistic skills: Cutting across spoken and written language and problem-solving abilities. In G. Wallach & K. Butler (eds.), *Language learning disabilities in school-age children,* pp. 128–154. Baltimore, MD: Williams & Wilkins.

WIIG, E., & SEMEL, E. (1980), 1984). *Language assessment and intervention for the learning disabled.* Columbus, OH: Charles E. Merrill.

Computers and Language

JOHNSON, B., & JOHNSON, R. (1984). *Computer courseware for the exceptional student.* Tucson, AZ: Communication Skill Builders.

LARSON, V. L., & STEINER, S. (1985). Language intervention using microcomputers. *Topics in Language Disorders, 6*(1), 41–55.

PETERSON, D., & KREIT, A. (1986). *Language activity booklet for KIDWRITER.* Tucson, AZ: Communication Skill Builders. (KIDWRITER is a trademark of Spinnaker Software Corporation.)

ROESSLER, M., & ROESSLER, M. (1987). *The STORYTELLER: Interactive fiction integrating the computer with language arts, reading and creative writing.* Freeport, NY: Educational Activities.

SMITH, D. D., SMITH, J. O., MAXWELL, B., THOMPSON, B., & CHAFFIN, J. (1985). *MicroSoc thinking games: SocSort.* Circle Pines, MN: American Guidance Service.

TORGESEN, J. K. (1986). Computers and cognition in reading: A focus on decoding fluency. *Exceptional Children, 53*(2), 157–162.

Instructional Programs and Materials

BLANK, M., & MARQUIS, A. M. (1987). *Directing discourse.* Tucson, AZ: Communication Skill Builders.

GLASER, A., JOHNSTON, E., & WEINRICH, B. (1987). *A sourcebook of remediating language.* Tucson, AZ: Communication Skill Builders.

SIMON, C. (1981). *Communicative competence: A functional-pragmatic approach to language therapy.* Tucson, AZ: Communication Skill Builders.

SIMON, C. (1980). *Communicative competence: A functional-pragmatic language program.* Tucson, AZ: Communication Skill Builders.

Primary Level

CAMP, B., & BASH, M. (1975). Think aloud program: Group manual revised. Denver: University of Colorado, Medical School, ERIC Document Reproduction Service No. ED142024.

DINKMEYER, D., & DINKMEYER, D. (1982). *DUSO-Revised: Developing understanding of self and others.* Circle Pines, MN: American Guidance Service.

DUNN, L., DUNN, L., SMITH, J. O., SMITH, D. D., & HORTON, K. (1983). *Peabody picture collection.* Circle Pines, MN: American Guidance Service.

DUNN, L. M., SMITH, J. O., DUNN, L. M., HORTON, K., & SMITH, D. D. (1981). *Peabody language development kits (Revised), Levels P-3.* Circle Pines, MN: American Guidance Service.

JOHNSTON, E., WEINRICH, B., & JOHNSTON, A. (1984). *A Sourcebook of pragmatic activities.* Tucson, AZ: Communication Skill Builders.

PLOURDE, L. (1985). *Classroom listening and speaking (CLAS).* Tucson, AZ: Communication Skill Builders.

Adolescents

BOURGAULT, R. (1985). Mass media and pragmatics: An approach for developing listening, speaking and writing skills in secondary school students. In C. Simon (ed), *Communication skills and classroom success: Therapy methodologies for language-learning disabled students,* pp. 241–272. San Diego: College-Hill Press.

BOYCE, N., & LARSON, V. (1983). *Adolescents' communication: Development and disorders.* Eau Claire, WI: Thinking Publications.

HOSKINS, B. (1987). *Conversations: Language intervention for adolescents.* Allen, TX: DLM-Teaching Resources.

MARQUIS, A. (1985). *Pragmatic language trivia.* Tucson, AZ: Communication Skill Builders.

SCHWARTZ, L., & MCKINLEY, N. (1984). *A daily communication: Strategies for the language disordered adolescent.* Eau Claire, WI: Thinking Publications.

WEINRICH, B., GLASER, A., & JOHNSTON, E. (1986). *A sourcebook of adolescent pragmatic activities.* Tucson, AZ: Communication Skill Builders.

WIIG, E. (1982). *Let's talk: Developing prosocial communication skills.* Columbus, OH: Charles E. Merrill.

ZACHMAN, L., JORGENSEN, C., BARRETT, M., HUISINGH, R., & SNEDDEN, M. K. (1986). *MEER: Manual of exercises for expressive reasoning.* Moline, IL: LinguiSystems.

ZAKIM, S. (1986). *Communication workshop.* Moline, IL: LinguiSystems.

7

Generic Interventions that Improve Academic Performance

In general, when children achieve overall academic success, both teachers and students work in partnership. The teacher's role is to present a curriculum that helps students to acquire knowledge of many subjects as well as to learn a wide variety of complex skills. For this to occur efficiently, the teacher must create a positive learning environment and select the effective interventions. The student, ultimately, must not only possess the skills needed to perform the task, but also must perform these functions:

Understand the requirements of a task.
Use an appropriate strategy for solving the problem or doing the task.
Know which of their skills they must use to perform the task.
Use the appropriate strategy in an organized, rather than random, fashion.
Assess how well they applied their skills to requisite steps in the task or problem's completion.

These goals of instruction can be achieved when a positive learning environment exists, where students' curricula are well planned, and when teaching tactics are selected to produce maximal learning. This chapter summarizes a number of interventions that research and practice have shown facilitate learning. The purpose is to provide teachers with a number of intervention strategies so those can be matched with diverse students who have individual learning styles and needs.

There are many ways to organize information about general remedial interventions. One way is to classify interventions by the time they are usually applied (e.g., before, during, or after the student performs the task). Another way is by the purpose of the procedure. Using this system, tactics would be discussed by whether they increase or decrease the occurrences of the target behavior. Although both are functional methods of organizing interventions, to rely on either of these schemes is to fail to recognize the complexity of educational situations.

 When teachers are helping students increase their academic skills, further classification that assists in the selection of interventions is useful. Both research and practice have shown that the effectiveness of many interventions depends on the student's entry level or stage of learning. Certain tactics are most effective when a youngster is first learning how to perform a task; others seem to be influential only when that student needs to become more skilled in its execution. For example, the tactics teachers use to teach sight words or arithmetic facts are different from those used to teach fluency in reading or computation. The probability of achieving the greatest improvement is increased when the student's stage of learning is matched with an intervention.

Some tactics are more influential in specific stages. There is a relationship between students' entry levels and the selection of the most effective intervention procedures. As discussed in Chapter 1, if a student is just learning how to perform a skill, the teacher should consider that student in the acquisition stage of learning. An intervention that has the greatest influence in that stage should then be applied. For these reasons, discussions of tactics are presented by stage of learning. Tactics specific to certain academic tasks are discussed in later chapters of this text.

INITIAL ACQUISITION STAGE

As discussed in Chapter 1, the initial acquisition stage of learning occurs when an individual is beginning to learn a skill. Here, the student's entry level might be as low as 0%, indicating that the entire skill must be learned and mastered. Some students might be able to perform part of the skill, but because they cannot complete the entire task, initially their correct scores are low. The tactics discussed in this section are most appropriately applied when the student needs to learn how to execute a task or answer the material presented. In these cases, most teachers evaluate the influence of their instructional programs by measuring student performance in terms of percent correct scores (see Chapter 3 for a review of evaluation procedures).

Physical Guidance

This tactic is used when motor skills are involved. Physical guidance, sometimes referred to as molding or manual guidance, requires the teacher actually to participate in the execution of the skill. When teachers take preschool children's hands to help them cut paper, the tactic of physical guidance is being used. Handwriting, assembly tasks, and many vocational skills can be acquired initially through the use of physical guidance. A speech clinician helping a student to pronounce a deficient articulation sound often physically guides the correct formation of the student's lips. This direct contact with students should be used only in the early phases of acquiring a skill and should be *faded* (gradually eliminated) as soon as possible.

Shaping

This procedure involves the careful reinforcement of successive approximations of the target response. The student is rewarded first for attempting to perform the new skill. Gradually, rewards are offered only as closer and closer approximations of the skill are performed by the student. Finally, only accurate responses are rewarded.

Elaine is learning how to play tennis. She is learning how to swing the racket. At first, her coach praises her for any swing in the right direction. Soon, she is praised only when the racket is positioned correctly and the swing is straight. After awhile, praise is only given when the swing is correct and Elaine follows through with the racket. Gradually, her coach shapes an accurate or correct swing, and eventually she is praised only for completely accurate (although not yet proficient) swings of the racket.

Shaping can be useful in building new skills. Certainly handwriting is a prime target for the application of shaping procedures. At first, an approximation of the correct formation of a letter is rewarded; later only better and better attempts at letter formation are rewarded. Clearly, the use of shaping, rather than allowing students to learn through trial and error, allows less chance of learning incorrect responses.

Modeling

Demonstrating or showing someone how to perform a skill is a most efficient tactic when attempting to teach new response patterns to individuals. Modeling is used to advantage when academic subjects need to be learned. Modeling simply involves the active participation of at least two individuals: one demonstrates the desired behavior to one or more observers. The observers then are required to imitate or copy the target skill. The ability of the observer to imitate is crucial to the process. Because the imitative skill is innate and comes early in normal human development, teachers normally do not have to teach it.[1] Most children come to school already possessing a developed set of imitative skills. It is primarily through the modeling-imitation paradigm that infants, toddlers, and

---

[1]Those interested in developing imitative repertoires in deficient students should refer to procedures texts in the area of moderately handicapped (see Snell, 1987).

preschool children learn a wide variety of language, social, and academic skills before they come to school.

Since showing someone else how to do a task is probably the most natural teaching skill that humans possess, it is one that is unnecessary for teachers to learn how to use. It is important, however, to remember to demonstrate the task to be learned by the observer carefully, completely, and slowly. In many cases, verbalizing the steps that must be followed to execute the skill accurately is helpful. Having the learner repeat the modeled steps before completing the skill independently ensures accuracy.

Modeling can be used with either groups or individuals. If used with a group, however, the teacher should be certain that all the students are at the same stage of learning. If the students are at different levels, instruction appropriate for one youngster might not be for another. A pupil who is more advanced than the others in the group will be wasting instructional time. In these situations, it is best to individualize.

Since in academic situations modeling is most thoroughly researched in computational arithmetic, this tactic is discussed in more detail in Chapter 11. Modeling is appropriately applied in other areas as well. Whether the new skill is how to use a new software program, how to compute arithmetic problems, how to write cursively, or how to use a learning strategy, modeling can be a most effective instructional tool.

Match-to-sample

This initial acquisition tactic is included in many commercially available workbooks. The student is provided with the correct answer and is required to select from a number of choices the item matching the one provided initially. For example, in a letter identification worksheet, the student is shown a series of letters in the first column and must circle its match in the corresponding row.

Another form of match-to-sample is the cue sheet. Sample letters written in cursive above the blackboard allow students to match their letters to the properly formed ones on the cue sheet. Multiplication tables where students can look for the problem they are solving on another sheet also is a variation of this tactic. Match-to-sample interventions are appropriate only in the initial phases of acquisition and should be gradually eliminated so the student is required to perform the skill independently.

Telling

Verbal directions or instructions to help students acquire new skills have always been used in education. Unfortunately, many youngsters seem not to profit from instructions or directions. Most likely, this is due to adults' careless application of instructions. Telling students how to perform the target skill can be efficient when students are acquiring skills, but communication must be conveyed with more care and concern than usually is the case. Instructions must be consistent and specific to the goals the instructor has for the student. For example, for students learning to write better themes, teachers might instruct them to vary their sentence beginnings, expand the length of their sentences, and use more elaboration.

Lovitt and Smith (1972) found that teachers have a propensity for using instructions. They have estimated that many teachers make more than 200 instructional statements a day. Most of these, however, are not specific to either student or situation. When instructions are provided systematically, they can serve efficiently to direct the student to perform the desired skill without the necessity of scheduling time-consuming, elaborate, or expensive educational procedures.

Cueing and Prompting

These procedures are used during the early acquisition phase, but do not necessarily stimulate first occurrences of the target behavior. Both cueing and prompting help students to make a correct response and can be added to the tactics just discussed.

There are three kinds of cues: movement, position, and redundancy. When movement cues are provided, the teacher points to, touches, or taps the item that represents the correct choice. When position cues are used, the correct choice is placed closest to the student. Redundancy cues pair the correct response with a particular property. For example, the correct choice might be physically larger than the other items.

Prompts often are used in reading. Here, teachers first form their lips as though to say the correct initial sound, then actually say the first sound of the unknown word, then sound out the word in its phonetic units. At any time students have figured out the correct response, they are encouraged to provide it. Prompts provide students with "hints" in the hope that the correct response will be uttered before the answer must be provided.

Time Delay

In many remedial classroom situations, teachers need to find procedures that students can use without the teachers' assistance. Such tactics are useful for work performed independently or at work stations. Time delay can be employed in this way by preparing audiotapes for students to use in their assignments. Anyone who has studied a foreign language by listening to audiotapes has experienced the time delay procedure. The voice on the tape says the word or phrase in a foreign language; in the segment of silence the student is to provide the answer or repeat what was previously heard, and the audio then restates the original word or phrase.

This tactic can easily be used in spelling or arithmetic. In spelling, for example, the teacher dictates a word. During the silence of 20 to 25 seconds, the student is to spell the word. The correct spelling is then provided on the tape. After the day's spelling list is presented in this fashion once, the process is repeated on the tape. In these ensuing trials, the time for the student to spell each word correctly is reduced. Time delay has considerable potential because of several important advantages. It is easy for the teacher to administer, it places the student in control of the instructional situation, and it can be discontinued easily when the skill is mastered.

Flow Lists

Some students have difficulty memorizing large amounts of information, but can remember items if presented in small groups. Many teachers have found flow lists most useful with such children in subjects like spelling and arithmetic. When this tactic is used, the student's daily spelling list might comprise only five words. Once any word is spelled correctly three days in a row, it is dropped from the daily spelling list and another one is added. Using this system ensures that the student knows the information taught before instruction is discontinued. However, many teachers also schedule periodic review tests to be certain that learning is maintained. If a student forgets a word, the word is recycled through the flow list. An example of a flow list data sheet for addition facts is found in Figure 7.1.

Advance Organizers

The research conducted at the Kansas University Institute for Research and Learning Disabilities (KUIRLD) revealed that few teachers provide students with advance organizers (Deshler et al., 1983); that is, teachers do not tell students what the lecture or lesson is about and why the information presented is important. However, when informed instruction (Paris & Jacobs, 1984) is used, it has been found that students who are made aware of a reading task before they read a passage, for example, score higher on comprehension tests over those passages. Simply stated, teachers who introduce their lectures or assignments clearly find that their students learn the information better whether the subject to be learned is history, science, or English (Lenz, Alley, & Schumaker, 1987).

Reinforcement (Rewards)

Reinforcement procedures were discussed in some depth in Chapter 4 (see Chapter 4 for a review of reinforcement theory, selecting reinforcers, and cautions teachers should take). Regardless of the specific form that reinforcement takes (praise, tokens, privileges), it is delivered according to a schedule. These schedules vary in appropriateness depending on the characteristics of the learner and the stage of learning in which the reinforcement is being applied. For example, the continuous reinforcement (CRF) schedule is only appropriately applied in the initial acquisition stage of learning. In this situation, the student

NAME _John_____   ADDITION FACT FORM

Fact	Pretest	9/10	9/11	9/12	9/13	9/4		9/17	9/18	9/19	9/20	9/21
4+ 1												
2	+											
3	+											
4	+											
5	−	+	+	+								
6	−	−	+	+	+							
7	−	−	−	+	+	+						
8	−	+	+	−	+	+		+				
9	−	+	+	+								
0	+											
5+ 1	+											
2	+											
3	−				−	+		+	+			
4	−			+	+			+	+			
5	+											
6	−				−			−	+	+	+	
7	−							−	−	−	+	+
8	−								−	+	+	+
9	−									+	+	+
0	+											
6+ 1	+											
2	+											
3	−								+	−	−	
4	−										+	
5	−											
6	−											
7	−											
8	−											
9	−											
0	+											
7+ 1	+											
2	−											
3	−											
4	−											
5	−											
6	−											
7	−											
8	−											
9	−											
0	+											

Figure 7.1 Addition fact flow list data sheet.

earns a unit of reinforcement for each occurrence of the target behavior. With other fixed ratio (FR) schedules, the student earns rewards after so many occurrences of the target behavior. For example, John might earn one unit of reinforcement for every ten correct arithmetic problems because his schedule of reinforcement was set at an FR of 10 : 1. FR schedules are most commonly used to help students become motivated for academic learning, and for that purpose, they are most useful.

ADVANCED ACQUISITION STAGE

Many times students learn academic tasks rather efficiently. At first they cannot perform the task correctly, indicating that they are in the initial acquisition stage of learning. They receive carefully planned instruction, and then indicate by their percent correct scores (90–100%) that they have mastered the skill that was targeted for them to learn. Sometimes, the percent correct scores indicate that the students have learned most of the skill, but have not mastered it. In these cases, students seem not to be able to meet mastery criterion (three days above 90%) due to either inefficient learning or careless errors. The tactics described earlier were insufficient to elicit sufficient learning for the students to advance. They failed to prepare these students for instruction aimed at making them proficient at a given task; they failed also in preparing them to address the next skill in the curriculum. The tactics described next are usually ineffective in the initial acquisition period, but help students achieve mastery. They are frequently referred to as *refinement tactics.*

Feedback

Knowledge of results can come in a variety of forms. Regardless, the purpose of feedback is to inform students about the accuracy of their responses. Feedback tactics form a category that falls along a continuum (ranging from a simple yes or no, right or wrong, to more thorough and complex forms reminiscent of instructional tactics). Some of these versions of feedback are more effective than others. Knowledge about which answers are correct and which are incorrect is far superior to only identifying correct answers. Although many teachers of handicapped youngsters feel that these students have already experienced too much failure and therefore their errors should be ignored, excusing errors constitutes an unnecessary form of overprotection. Student performance improves more when correct and incorrect responses are identified.

For many students, an additional variety of feedback is most helpful. As indicated, correct answers are so noted, but answers that are incorrect are re-instructed. The teacher might demonstrate, again, how to solve a long division problem or punctuate a compound sentence.

Telling

Specific instructions carefully applied can be useful in increasing student's academic performance. Simply telling youngsters to be more careful as they do their assignments can contribute to increases in their percent correct scores. Smith and Lovitt (1975) found that some of their students made careless errors in their arithmetic assignments and, therefore, did not reach percentage scores that indicated mastery. These students' scores averaged about 75%. Telling the students to be more careful as they computed the problem was sufficient, and the students obtained scores indicating mastery (in these cases, three consecutive days at 100%).

For students who have acquired the basic processes involved but whose accuracy is still of concern, further explanation or redirection might be helpful. Sometimes only minor instructional statements relating to the way the student is completing the assignment facilitate final acquisition of the task. Once this is accomplished, proficiency can become the target.

Drill

Drill can also bring about necessary increases in accuracy. There are several varieties of drill that, when specifically applied, can facilitate mastery of many academic areas such as sight words, arithmetic facts, spelling, handwriting, and punctuation. For students who are unsure of the correct answer and get the correct solution one day and not the next, error drill specifically on those items not definitely mastered can be sufficient to increase accuracy. New response drill can also be helpful. Here, the teacher might select words from the upcoming reading passage that students have a high probability of missing, and drill students on those words before they read independently. Both these forms of drill, new response and error, can be accomplished through the use of flashcards, language master machines, or computer software programs (e.g., shell games).

Positive Practice Overcorrection

In Chapter 4, two forms of overcorrection (restitution and positive practice) were discussed. One of these procedures, positive practice, has application to academic instruction. When students have not completely acquired a skill, and exhibit inconsistent results, this form of overpractice can be helpful. For example, for students who misspell words written in themes or reports, their teachers have required those students to write each word correctly five times, look up and rewrite those words' definitions in the dictionary, and break them into syllables. This is the application of positive practice overcorrection for spelling. Similar applications can be made for most academic situations, and they have proven effective in eliminating many errors made by students.

Reward for Accuracy

Sometimes students need an extra incentive to encourage them to put out the extra effort required to achieve mastery level percentage scores. Various incentive systems can be applied to increase accuracy. Students could receive extra bonuses or privileges for perfect papers. Special certificates of commendation, perfect papers placed on a bulletin board, notes home to parents, extra recess or leisure time, and other special activities could be scheduled for final mastery of academic tasks.

Fines

For some students, directions, drill, or rewards do not achieve the aim of increased accuracy. For those who seem to have a motivational problem, and make inconsistent and careless mistakes, withdrawing the opportunity for privileges contingent upon errors is one way to stimulate increased percentage scores. This tactic of fining students for unsatisfactory performance, also referred to as *response cost,* can be most effective for some students. Withdrawing minutes from recess or loss of privileges can encourage students to reduce errors in arithmetic, spelling, or written composition. One caution about this technique should be noted, however. The teacher must be certain that the student can perform the desired task before fines are levied. It is unfair to punish students for things they are incapable of doing. When the teacher is certain that the reason for unsatisfactory scores is not a lack of ability or knowledge, but rather an unwillingness to provide the correct answer, fines might well be a beneficial tactic to select.

Peer Tutoring

As discussed in Chapter 4, using children to teach their classmates is not a new concept. When its purpose is to improve academic performance, it is called tutoring. Many such systems have been explored in schools. Probably the most common is *cross-age tutoring.* Here, an older student teaches a younger one. *Same-age* or *classmate tutoring* also is effective when arrangements cannot be made for an older student to tutor. Regardless, tutoring can be applied in a wide variety of academic situations: written expression, arithmetic computation and problem solving, reading orally and answering comprehension questions, studying for tests in content subjects such as history or social studies, and completing homework assignments.

If peer tutoring is to be employed successfully, several things must be considered. First, the tutors must be carefully selected. There must be a good fit between the two students (it is best if tutors work in pairs and not with small groups). The tutors must be trained. They need to be proficient in the skills they are to teach as well as in teaching skills. Tutors should participate in training sessions where they learn how to use instructions, feedback, praise, and reinforcement properly. Tutors also need to receive rewards themselves for being tutors.

In classrooms where students' abilities vary widely, teachers should consider tutoring for the faster and slower students. Tutoring may also be helpful for classes with a large number of students. One-to-one or individualized instruction is beneficial for most students, but is expensive in teacher time. Therefore, in many classrooms, individualization is viewed as unfeasible. Using peer tutors allows teachers to individualize instruction for those students who need extra assistance to master academic skills.

The Puzzle or Jigsaw Technique

Using this intervention, a group of students solve a problem or complete a task together with each member assigned a specific activity. For example, three high school students are assigned the group task of proofing and correcting a poorly written term paper by an anonymous person (perhaps the teacher). One student is assigned the job of correcting all capitalization errors, another is to correct the punctuation, and the other the spelling mistakes. When they have each completed their corrections, they discuss the reasons for their corrections and go through the paper together as a group.

This intervention has several advantages in addition to its effectiveness. It encourages group involvement and increased attention to the learning task. In many cases, it can also lead to a better understanding of assignments because the students share, discuss, and model the steps followed to arrive at the correct solution to the problem or task.

PROFICIENCY STAGE

A number of instructional tactics facilitate proficiency or fluency. Modeling, telling, drilling, and reinforcement can improve both the quality and quantity of students' academic performances. This, of course, is the aim of instruction once students have acquired or learned how to perform the targeted skill. While in the proficiency stage of learning the interventions scheduled should help students to retain their high levels of accuracy while increasing their speed. To judge the effectiveness of these interventions, teachers evaluate student performance in terms of correct and error rate scores (see Chapter 3 for a review).

Modeling

Modeling was discussed in some detail in the acquisition section of this chapter and is most commonly and appropriately applied there. However, modeling has proven to be instrumental in building proficiency in some students' academic performances. Smith (1978, 1979), for example, used a modeling tactic to increase students' oral reading proficiency. The students had to increase their correct rates of oral reading. During the intervention conditions, the teacher read the first passage from the students' basal text at the desired rate (approximately 100 words per minute). The students then continued reading from the text for the allotted time. Modeling substantially and positively influenced the students' oral reading performances. Although there are few examples of the use of modeling in proficiency building situations, modeling is natural to the instructional situation; it is easy to schedule and might be a worthwhile tactic to try.

Telling

Another simple tactic natural to instructional situations frequently is underused. Sometimes students do not know what is expected of them. Are they supposed to fill the math period with the seatwork given to them at the beginning of the period? Are they supposed to concentrate on accuracy? If students are privy to the teacher's aims, improved performance in line with the desired outcome might occur without the scheduling of elaborate techniques. Some teachers report that simply clarifying goals for students when they are told to work faster helps students to achieve desired results. This technique works particularly well when students are told to read faster or compute as many problems as they can. Often teachers forget to tell their students what is expected of them in academic situations. This might be a good first tactic to apply when fluency or proficiency must be enhanced.

Drill

A tactic used in schools for many, many years to improve fluency is drill and practice. Music teachers help students become more proficient at playing musical instruments by insisting on drill and practice. The purpose of these tactics is to get the target skill at an automatic level of functioning. Handwriting is taught almost exclusively through the use of these tactics. Drill on errors seems to enhance oral reading, handwriting, and computational arithmetic. Error drill can improve fluency or rates of performance because errors often interrupt individuals' flow of responding. Without these interruptions, students move through academic tasks more proficiently.

To help students become more proficient at basic academic tasks, many teachers schedule time for speed building activities. For example, in reading, many teachers use a procedure called repeated readings. Here, for the purpose of building fluency, the student rereads the same passage orally until a desired rate is achieved. Gradually, improvement noted while repeated reading was in effect transfers to reading of new material. Flashcards—commercially available or teacher- or student-made—are also used to increase students' rates of producing correct answers.

Many students, however, find drill uninteresting and refuse to practice tasks over and over when drill alone is scheduled. Some teachers add incentives to the drill procedures so that these students will practice sufficiently. Others vary the drill and practice activities so they are more interesting and gamelike. It is not uncommon to have a mathematics teacher say long series of arithmetic facts rather quickly. The student who can arrive at the solution, despite the rather fast delivery of the problems, is the winner.

The introduction of microcomputers to schools has many advantages. One of these is the opportunity for drill and practice. A number of microcomputer games, most notably the *Arcademic* materials (e.g., *Alien Addition, Master of Mathomatics*), allow youngsters to practice arithmetic facts in gamelike situations. Such programs encourage accuracy and fluency on what are frequently laborious tasks.

Reinforcement

Reinforcement procedures were discussed in some detail in Chapter 4 (on generic interventions that improve social performance) and earlier in this chapter. Here, reinforcement procedures that are typically used to increase proficiency are discussed.

Premack Principle

This principle, sometimes called Gramma's rule, arranges the time in which activities are scheduled. Those activities the student likes to engage in (high strength) follow those activities the student does not like or voluntarily engage in very much (low strength).

In some cases, rescheduling the academic routine can effect positive changes in student performance. Some students while away time when given an assignment they do not like. If that assignment were scheduled first, and activity enjoyable to the students followed, they would have an incentive to complete the tedious activity so they could move on to one they liked. For example, if Ruth hates arithmetic and loves reading, arithmetic seatwork would be given to her first. The longer she spends on the arithmetic assignment (both completing it and correcting errors made), the less time left for reading. Before resorting to more complicated or elaborate intervention procedures, teachers might consider trying an application of the Premack Principle by rescheduling academic assignments according to student preferences.

Freetime

Contingent freetime is the most common application of the Premack Principle in classroom situations. When contingent freetime is used, students earn minutes to spend in activities of their choice contingent upon improved academic performance. Freetime is earned by using an FR schedule of reinforcement (discussed in Chapter 4). Here, the teacher or student might have determined that for every two study questions found at the end of the social studies text that are answered correctly, the student can earn one minute of freetime (FR2). Once enough freetime minutes are accumulated, the student can choose an activity from a number of selections (working on a science project, leisure reading, programming the microcomputer).

Go-No Go Contingencies

These contingency arrangements are merely adaptions of FR schedules (see also discussion in Chapter 4). They are referred to in the research literature as differentially reinforcing higher rates of responding (DRH) and differentially reinforcing lower rates of responding (DRL) schedules. These schedules do not determine what (freetime, points, privileges) the student earns for improved performance, but rather how many units of reinforcement.

In FR schedules, reinforcement is earned for every set number of correct responses. If Billy is given an FR5 schedule for correctly spelled words on a weekly test, then for every five words correctly spelled he can earn one minute of freetime. If there are twenty words on the weekly test, he could earn four minutes of freetime each week. If he only spells five words correctly, he would earn one minute of freetime. This, however, is unfortunate, for he would receive reinforcement for unsatisfactory performance, and Billy's teacher wants him to score a minimum of 75% on those tests. By adding a go-no go contingency, reinforcement is given only when his score surpasses a certain level. Billy would earn his minutes of freetime only when he correctly spells at least fifteen words. Thus, reinforcement is earned only when a minimally acceptable level of performance is achieved.

Go-no go contingencies are used frequently in oral reading, where the teacher might be concerned about correct rate and error rate scores simultaneously. She wants a student's correct reading rates to increase and the error rates to decrease. Minimally acceptable scores can be set for both these rates. For example, it could be arranged that Tiffany would not receive any freetime unless her correct rate exceeded sixty-five, and her error rate was lower than five on any one day. Once her scores indicated improvement beyond these minimal levels, the FR schedules are applied.

MAINTENANCE STAGE

In the maintenance stage of learning, the aim is for the student to retain the mastery levels of performance attained when direct instruction was in effect. The goal is for both accuracy and proficiency to remain at acceptable levels. In some cases, maintenance conditions are conducted without any intervention scheduled to determine whether the student can actually perform the task or skill without any help from the teacher. In other cases, during the maintenance conditions the student receives reinforcement for satisfactory performance, but infrequently. Unfortunately, not many academic and behavioral researchers have devoted their energies to the study of retention.

Once mastery levels are achieved, it is important that students maintain them. For example, once a youngster reaches a mastery level of performance in oral reading, in order to keep up with the peer group, fluency must be retained.

Of course, merely practicing oral reading skills should help to retain satisfactory reading levels. Certainly, if once reading is "mastered" it is dropped from the curriculum and no longer receives attention from the teacher or student, performance levels will decrease. Academic learning, particularly for those who have had difficulty mastering a given academic skill in the first place, is not like riding a bike. Once students learn how, they might not remember. Therefore, one important key to retention is continued practice, although on a periodic basis. For many students, however, practice alone is not enough. For them, direct though infrequent intervention is required for some time to ensure that learning is retained. Following is a summary of some tactics that facilitate maintenance and retention.

Overlearning

This procedure has received little attention from researchers lately, but it has merit and should be reinvestigated as a maintenance procedure. The concept of overlearning requires the learner to practice a task well beyond the level of mastery. Probably the concept of overlearning gave rise to the notion that three or even five consecutive scores be above a predetermined level before the student can move on to learn more difficult tasks. If a teacher were to incorporate overlearning into the teaching process, students would have to demonstrate mastery for a longer time than is typically used. Snell made the point that if overlearning is used, "repeated practice or review distributed over time rather than massed into a brief time period" should facilitate long-term retention (1978, p. 363). Overlearning should be an integral part of the teaching routine for handicapped learners because it tends to improve retention and generalization.

Variable Ratio Schedules

In fixed ratio schedules of reinforcement, rewards are delivered after a set number of correct responses or a set amount of time have been recorded. Variable schedules provide students with reinforcement in such a way that the student cannot predict when the opportunity for reinforcement will occur. In a sense, this keeps the student on guard, performing as best as possible. Usually, variable schedules lead to consistent performance with higher and more constant rates.

Variable ratio (VR) schedules are not usually recommended for direct application to academic subjects, for if the ratio changed daily, one day's performance would be worth more units of reinforcement than another day's performance. However, an interesting application of VR schedules can be applied to academic subjects when long-term maintenance is of concern. For example, Steve was a poor reader but finally reached his long-term goal score. His teacher was afraid that he would not maintain his now proficient rate of oral reading.

During intervention, Steve received reinforcement using a fixed ratio of 15 : 1 for correct rate. During long-term follow-up, the teacher read with Steve three days a week. She told him that they were going to play a game. Some days he would receive reinforcement for his reading assignment and some days he would not. He would never know in advance which days "counted." Initially, she applied a VR of 2 : 1 to his reading sessions, so on the average every other reading session earned him reinforcement (using the fixed ratio schedule of the intervention condition to determine the exact amount of reinforcement earned). Gradually, the VR scheduled was leaned. By the end of the school year, reinforcement was earned only periodically. Through the use of this technique, however, Steve not only maintained his proficient oral reading rate, but also continued to improve.

VR schedules for academic situations must be carefully applied. Using such schedules for cases such as Steve's, however, might facilitate the maintenance of desirable performances.

Social Reinforcement

Social reinforcement (praise and adult and peer approval) is underutilized as a planned intervention. Often, after months and months of direct instruction, acquisition, and proficiency mastery levels are achieved. These accomplishments are put behind both student and teacher. All intervention is discontinued; no reminders are provided to use these newly mastered skills. No wonder teachers frequently note that once instruction is completed, academic performance decreases. In particular, for youngsters who seem to have retention problems, continued and periodic feedback and praise for using their newly learned skills are warranted.

Statements like "Gee, you remembered to borrow here," possibly would alleviate this situation. The power of praise is well-documented. If used on a variable schedule, praise can serve to remind the student of what the desired behavior actually is, provide feedback about the fine points of the newly mastered skill, and show the teacher's approval of the student's efforts to use academic skills appropriately. In some situations, the peers can be encouraged to praise classmates for continued academic improvement. Social reinforcement might well be sufficient to keep a former target behavior within a youngster's repertoire.

Intrinsic Reinforcement

The hope is that students will eventually work to maintain proficient levels of basic skills because they enjoy the product of those skills. All teachers hope that their students eventually will enjoy reading, that they will read without outside encouragement. Certainly, this is the ultimate goal of the educational process. Unfortunately, many students do not achieve this goal in all school-related areas. Teachers must strive continually to help their students attain such proficient levels of performance that intrinsic reinforcement will in fact guarantee maintenance.

GENERALIZATION STAGE

As discussed in Chapter 1 in the section on stages of learning, many students with special needs do not automatically generalize or transfer their learning to new settings or situations. In some cases, researchers have found that careful, direct instruction on the target skill will cause some students to generalize that skill to others that are closely related. For example, a number of studies (Blankenship & Baumgartener, 1982; Lloyd, Saltzman, & Kauffman, 1981; Smith & Lovitt, 1975; Rivera & Smith, 1987) have shown that some tactics such as modeling and demonstration promote generalization in computational arithmetic. However, it does not happen for all children in this way. For many youngsters, generalization needs to be a target for instruction in and of itself. Stokes and Baer (1977) postulate that generalization might well be a skill that must be taught to those who are deficient in its application.

There are several guidelines about generalization that may be helpful:

1. Do not expect it to occur.
2. Extend the contingencies used in the teaching situation to the generalization settings also.
3. Plan to implement the original, effective intervention procedure in the generalization situations.

Once students do generalize, teachers must remind, reinforce, and praise them, for generalization is an important aspect of academic achievement.

Rationales

Many teachers have found that when students understand the importance of applying newly mastered skills to different settings or situations, generalization is more likely to occur. Deshler and Schumaker, through their work at the KU-IRLD, found that many students who had mastered various learning strategies that would help them to improve their grades and learning in regular classroom settings did not use their new learning skills in those settings. The students did not generalize. However, when students were given the reasons why they should apply learning strategies to these settings, and accepted these rationales, they did generalize.

Transfer Activities

After students have mastered a skill or the use of a learning strategy and have demonstrated that mastery in the special setting, they need to use their newly learned skills in other settings. If, for example, students have learned a strategy that will improve their theme-writing abilities, they need to apply that strategy in history and English classes. If students do not generalize their strategy use, the following techniques might be helpful. Cue cards, which summarize a learning strategy, can serve as reminders to apply the strategy in the regular education setting. Also, group discussions and making lists about classes and situations where this technique would be useful encourages generalization. The special education teacher can arrange for practice sessions where assignments similar to those given in the history class are completed with guided practice in a more controlled setting.

Varying Stimulus Conditions

Generalization may be facilitated by varying stimulus conditions—introducing extraneous, irrelevant, or distracting stimuli; changing instructors and instructional settings; and changing class size. Teaching the student what and what not to respond to and reinforcing only correct responses in a variety of settings in the presence of different people also seem to promote generalization. If those in the youngster's environment (parents, siblings, other teachers) do not carry out and extend remedial efforts consistently, little maintenance or generalization will occur.

Self-management

Self-control procedures (discussed in detail in Chapter 4) also foster generalization. For those students who have great difficulty generalizing from one setting to another, they and their teacher could mutually set a goal to generalize a specific skill in a particular setting. They might develop a behavioral contract to implement this goal. Then, the students would monitor their own behavior, take data on their performance, and reward themselves for meeting their goals.

Cooperative Planning

Too often special education and regular education teachers do not share information about the progress made by individual students with special needs whom they both serve. In part, this is because of the busy schedules that teachers keep. Sometimes it is due to the unfortunate distance between these two fields and their administrative organizations. It is important for special educators to communicate with the other teachers who work with their pupils. Communication will lead to better academic programming for the student, for the teachers can discuss individuals' strengths, weaknesses, and recent progress. With an open dialogue, cooperative planning about students' programs can occur.

As discussed in this section, many students with special needs do not generalize or transfer their learning from one setting to another. When special and regular education teachers hold periodic conferences about those students with whom they are mutually concerned, they can share information about what particular students have learned in each classroom. The special education teacher, for example, can indicate what skills and strategies students have mastered in the special education setting. If students are not applying those skills in the regular education setting, the teachers can discuss ways they can both encourage generalization. The regular education teacher might cue a student to use a strategy when appropriate; the special education teacher might provide specific instructions, arrange for practice sessions, or train a peer tutor to assist the special education student.

PROBLEM SOLVING (ADAPTION)

Problem solving is the ability to extend knowledge and skills to novel situations. The inability to solve problems might be one of the greatest weaknesses of students with special needs (Havertape & Kass, 1978) and is an area that must gain more attention from researchers, curriculum materials developers, and teachers. Problem solving involves a number of skills that fall on a continuum. The dimensions of problem solving range from being able to figure out how to perform an academic task to solving the most pressing problems facing humankind. Although the depth of abilities to solve problems probably relates to the innate characteristics of individuals, various degrees of problem solving can be taught.

There are many components or individual skills that are used when people solve problems. Awareness of requisite elements, such as those listed on Table 7.1, might help teachers to plan more complete educational programs for their students. For example, if Crista has difficulty solving problems because she cannot categorize information, direct instruction on that skill is warranted. She might be assigned to work on a microcomputer game like *Soc Sort* to improve her categorization skills. Eric, who cannot identify similarities among groups of items, could be asked to find the common elements of the things he has in his desk.

Table 7.1
Component Skills of Problem Solving

Flexibility
Categorizing
Persistence
Decision making
Recognizing patterns
Determining relationships
Identifying irrelevant items
Finding similarities
Analyzing
Estimating

Table 7.2
Conditions and Activities that Improve Problem Solving

Have a plan of attack.
Have an overall approach.
Practice generating and testing solutions.
Retell problem in your own words.
Use imagery.

Guided Instruction

When teachers hold guided group discussions, students are taught to understand the problem, relate it to a simpler one, find different ways to solve it, and check their solutions. Although youngsters probably need some adult guidance, teachers must be cautious not to dominate the discussions. Rather, through open-ended questions, they should guide the students when they need direction.

Students seem to develop better problem solving skills when they work in small groups. Problem solving instruction might provide good opportunities to integrate group activities into the instructional routine. In most special education classrooms, instruction is individualized and group activities are limited. Although individualization produces excellent academic improvement, it does not foster cooperation and communicative interaction. Group activities centered on solving problems could alleviate this situation.

A number of conditions exist that can improve children's abilities to solve problems. Some of those are found on Table 7.2. Also, guidelines are available for teachers to follow as they plan and conduct problem-solving activities; those are found on Table 7.3. It is important to remember that above all, students need to have continued practice in generating and testing solutions to solve problems. This means that time needs to be devoted to this important stage of learning.

Table 7.3
Teacher Guidelines for Problem-Solving Activities

Present real-life problems.
Present problems with several or no solutions.
Present problems within the experiences of the students.
Provide many opportunities to solve problems.
Allow students to experiment and discover.
Ask open-ended questions.
Assist students in collecting data.
Reward different methods of approaching the problem.
Reward different solutions.

Cognitive Modification

Cognitive modification combines the techniques of behavior therapy with those of cognitive therapy by using a person's inner speech to guide behavior. Students learning to write often tell themselves how to form letters as they perform the task. While writing the letter *t* a student might say, "swing up, swing down, and make a cross."

This teaching sequence can be applied to a variety of instructional situations. Once children have had experience with this teaching method, it can be applied to more and more complex problems, like the problem-solving strategy described next.

Problem-Solving Strategy

The steps used in the problem-solving process are sequential. Children first must be able to get the information required to solve the problem. The second step is to understand what is to be solved; they must also determine what information and what techniques for solution the problem demands. The third step, actually solving the problem, has three general substeps and an infinite number of specific parts. The general substeps are generating hypotheses, evaluating hypotheses, and implementing the solution. To generate hypotheses, individuals need to use systematic, organized strategies rather than impulsive or random ones. For many students with special needs, this will require substantial guidance from the teacher. Figure 7.2 is helpful in teaching and having youngsters remember the strategy.

SUMMARY

As students learn new skills, they pass through several stages of learning. Many instructional procedures are effective in only one of these stages and are ineffective in the others. Table 7.4 lists tactics that tend to be most effective in each stage of learning. Unfortunately, teachers cannot simply match their students' behavioral descriptions to the categories provided in this table and be guaranteed successful remediation programs. All students are individuals, and what is effective for one student might not be for another. The purpose of this chapter has been to help teachers better select those procedures with the highest *probability* of affecting improvement by reviewing those basic, generic procedures that can be applied across a variety of academic skills. Tactics limited to one particular academic subject (reading, mathematics) are described in later chapters.

STUDY AND DISCUSSION QUESTIONS

1. Discuss the role of the stages of learning theory as applied to academic instruction.
2. Describe three tactics applicable in each stage of learning; provide classroom examples for each.
3. Develop lesson plans for a problem-solving unit.

1

What is my problem?

2

How can I do it?

3

Am I using my plan?

4

How did I do?

Figure 7.2 An illustration from a comprehensive problem-solving program. (*Source:* B. Camp & M. Bash, *Think aloud program: Group manual, revised* (Denver: University of Colorado Medical School, 1975), ERIC Document Reproduction Service No. ED 142 024. Reprinted by permission of the authors.)

Table 7.4
Generic Academic Tactics by Stage of Learning

ACQUISITION		PROFICIENCY	MAINTENANCE	GENERALIZATION	PROBLEM SOLVING (ADAPTION)
Initial	*Advanced*				
Physical guidance	Feedback	Modeling	Overlearning	Rationales	Guided instruction
Shaping	Telling	Telling	Intermittent reinforcement	Reinforcement	Cognitive modification
Modeling	Drill	Drill	VR schedules	Instructions	Problem-solving strategy training
Match-to-sample	Error drill	Error drill	Speed drill	Social reinforcement	Transfer activities
Telling	New response drill	New response drill	Praise	Self-management	
Cues	Positive practice	Repeated practice	Adult and peer approval	Cooperative planning	
Movement	Overcorrection	Flashcards	Feedback		
Position	Puzzle technique	Microcomputer games	Intrinsic reinforcement		
Redundancy	Reward for accuracy	Reinforcement			
Prompts	Fines	Premack principle			
Time delay	Peer tutoring	Freetime			
Flow list	Cross-age tutoring	FR			
Advanced organizers	Classmate tutoring	Go-no go contingencies			
Reinforcement	Self-management				
	Self-instruction				
	Self-correction				

REFERENCES AND SUGGESTED READINGS

General Academic Remediation

AFFLECK, J. Q., LOWENBRAUN, S., & ARCHER, A. (1980). *Teaching the mildly handicapped in the regular classroom* (2nd ed.). Columbus, OH: Charles E. Merrill.

HARING, N. G., LOVITT, T. C., EATON, M. D., & HANSEN, C. L. (1978). *The fourth R: Research in the classroom.* Columbus, OH: Charles E. Merrill.

LOVITT, T. C. (1984). *Tactics for teaching.* Columbus, OH: Charles E. Merrill.

MERCER, C. D. (1983). *Students with learning disabilities.* Columbus, OH: Charles E. Merrill.

Modeling

BANDURA, A. (1965). Behavioral modifications through modeling procedures. In L. Krasner & L. P. Ullmann (eds.), *Research in behavior modification.* New York: Holt, Rinehart and Winston.

BANDURA, A. (1969). *Principles of behavior modification.* New York: Holt, Rinehart and Winston.

CULLINAN, D., KAUFFMAN, J. M., & LaFLEUR, N. K. (1975). Modeling: Research with implications for special education. *The Journal of Special Education, 9,* 209–221.

HENDRICKSON, J. M., & GABLE, R. A. (1981). The use of modeling tactics to promote academic skill development of exceptional learners. *Journal of Special Education Technology, 4*(3), 20–29.

SMITH, D. D. (1978). The influence of modeling on children's oral reading performance. In A. H. Fink (ed.), *International perspectives in future special education.* Reston, VA: Council for Exceptional Children.

SMITH, D. D. (1979). The improvement of children's oral reading through the use of teacher modeling. *Journal of Learning Disabilities, 12,* 172–175.

SMITH, D. D., & LOVITT, T. C. (1975). The use of modeling techniques to influence the acquisition of computational arithmetic skills in learning-disabled children. In E. Ramp & G. Semb (eds.), *Behavior analysis: Areas of research and application.* Englewood Cliffs, NJ: Prentice-Hall.

SNELL, M. E. (ed.) (1978). *Systematic instruction of the moderately and severely handicapped.* Columbus, OH: Charles E. Merrill.

SNELL, M. E. (1987). *Systematic instruction of persons with severe handicaps.* (3rd ed.). Columbus, OH: Charles E. Merrill.

Previewing

SINGH, N. N., & SINGH, J. (1984). Antecedent control of oral reading errors and self-corrections by mentally retarded children. *Journal of Applied Behavior Analysis, 17,* 111–119.

Telling

KRAETSCH, G. (1981). The effects of oral instructions and training on the expansion of written language. *Learning Disability Quarterly, 4,* 82–90.

LOVITT, T. C. (1978). *Managing inappropriate behaviors in the classroom.* Reston, VA: The Council for Exceptional Children.

LOVITT, T. C., & SMITH, J. O. (1972). Effects of instructions on an individual's verbal behavior. *Exceptional Children, 38,* 685–693.

Time Delay

SNELL, M. E., & GAST, D. L. (1981). Applying time delay procedure to the instruction of the severely handicapped. *Journal of the Severely Handicapped, 6*, 3–14.

STEVENS, K. B., & SCHUSTER, J. W. (1987). Effects of a constant time delay procedure on the written spelling performance of a learning disabled student. *Learning Disability Quarterly, 10*, 9–16.

Drill

HARING, H. G., LOVITT, T. C., EATON, M. D., & HANSEN, C. L. (1978). *The fourth R: Research in the classroom.* Columbus, OH: Charles E. Merrill.

Feedback

ANDERSON, R. C., & FAUST, G. W. (1974). *Educational psychology: The science of instruction and learning.* New York: Dodd, Mead.

BRUNI, J. V. (1982). Problem solving for the primary grades. *Arithmetic Teacher, 24*, 10–15.

BUSS, A. H., BRADEN, W., ORGEL, A., & BUSS, E. H. (1956). Acquisition and extinction with different verbal reinforcement combinations. *Journal of Experimental Psychology, 52*, 288–295.

BUSS, A. H., & BUSS, E. H. (1956). The effect of verbal reinforcement combinations on conceptual learning. *Journal of Experimental Psychology, 52*, 283–287.

BUSS, A. H., WEINER, M., & BUSS, E. (1954). Stimulus generalization as a function of verbal reinforcement combinations. *Journal of Experimental Psychology, 48*, 433–436.

GABLE, R. A., & HENDRICKSON, J. M. (1979). Teacher feedback: Its use and impact on learner performance. *Journal of Special Education Technology, 3*, 29–35.

KULHAVY, R. W. (1977). Feedback in written instruction. *Review of Educational Research, 47*, 211–232.

KULHAVY, R. W., & ANDERSON, R. C. (1972). Delay-retention effect with multiple-choice tests. *Journal of Educational Psychology, 63*, 505–512.

McGEE, J. E. (1970). Moderate failure as an instructional tool. *Exceptional Children, 36*, 757–761.

SAUDARGAS, R. W., MADSEN, C. H., JR., & SCOTT, J. (1977). Differential effects of fixed- and variable-time feedback on production rates of elementary school children. *Journal of Applied Behavior Analysis, 10*, 673–678.

SWANSON, L. (1982). A multidirectional model for assessing learning disabled students' intelligence: An information-processing framework. *Learning Disability Quarterly, 5*, 312–326.

Rewards (See also Chapter 4)

KISTNER, J., HAMMER, D., WOLFE, D., ROTHBLUM, E. & DRABMAN, R. S. (1982). Teacher popularity and contract effects in a classroom token economy. *Journal of Applied Behavior Analysis, 15*, 85–96.

Premack Hypothesis

COWEN, R. J., JONES, F. H., & BELLACK, A. S. (1979). Grandma's rule with group contingencies—A cost-effective means of classroom management. *Behavior Modification, 3*, 397–418.

HOMME, L. E., DeBACA, P. C., DEVINE, J. B., STEINHORST, R., & RICKERT, E. J. (1963). Use of the Premack principle in controlling the behavior of nursery school children. *Journal of the Experimental Analysis of Behavior, 6,* 544.

PREMACK, D. (1959). Toward empirical behavior laws. I. Positive reinforcement. *Psychological Review, 66,* 219–233.

Contingent Freetime

HOPKINS, B. L., SCHUTTE, R. C., & GARTON, K. (1971). The effects of access to a playroom on the rate and quality of printing and writing of first- and second-grade students. *Journal of Applied Behavior Analysis, 4,* 77–87.

LOVITT, T. C., GUPPY, T. E., & BLATTNER, J. E. (1969). The use of a free-time contingency with fourth graders to increase spelling accuracy. *Behavior Research and Therapy, 7,* 151–156.

OSBORNE, J. G. (1969). Free-time as a reinforcer in the management of classroom behavior. *Journal of Applied Behavior Analysis, 2,* 113–118.

ROBERTS, M. B. (1977). The influences of increased correct and decreased error oral reading rates on the recall comprehension abilities of learning disabled children (doctoral dissertation, George Peabody College for Teachers, 1977). *Dissertation Abstracts International, 38,* 2706A. (Xerox University Microfilms No. 77-25, 125.)

ROBERTS, M., & SMITH, D. D. (1980). A study of the relationship among correct and error reading rate and comprehension. *Learning Disability Quarterly, 3,* 54–64.

SALZBERG, B. H., WHEELER, A. J., DEVAR, L. T., & HOPKINS, B. L. (1971). The effect of intermittent feedback and intermittent contingent access to play on printing of kindergarten children. *Journal of Applied Behavior Analysis, 4,* 163–171.

SMITH, D. D., & LOVITT, T. C. (1976). The differential effects of reinforcement contingencies on arithmetic performance. *Journal of Learning Disabilities, 9,* 21–29.

Fines

LOVITT, T. C., & SMITH, D. D. (1974). Using withdrawal of positive reinforcement to alter subtraction performance. *Exceptional Children, 40,* 357–358.

Tutoring

BLOOM, B. S. (1984). The 2 sigma problem: The search for methods of group instruction as effective as one-to-one tutoring. *Educational Researcher, 6,* 4–16.

CHIANG, B., THORPE, H. W., & DARCH, C. B. (1980). Effects of cross-age tutoring on word recognition performance of learning disabled students. *Learning Disability Quarterly, 3,* 11–19.

DELQUADRI, J., GREENWOOD, C. R., WHORTON, D., CARTA, J. J., & HALL, R. V. (1986). Classwide peer tutoring. *Exceptional Children, 52,* 535–542.

DEVIN-SHEEHAN, L., FELDMAN, R. S., & ALLEN, V. L. (1976). Research on children tutoring children: A critical review. *Review of Educational Research, 46,* 355–385.

EHLY, S., & LARSEN, S. C. (1980). *Peer tutoring for individualized instruction.* Austin, TX: Pro-Ed.

EVANS, G. W., & OSWALT, G. L. (1968). Acceleration of academic progress through the manipulation of peer influence. *Behavior Research and Therapy, 6,* 189–195.

FOWLER, S. A. (1986). Peer-monitoring and self-monitoring: Alternatives to traditional teacher management. *Exceptional Children, 52,* 573–581.

GREENWOOD, C. R., DINWIDDIE, G., TERRY, B., WADE, L., STANELY, S. O., THIBADEAU, S., & DELQUADRI, J. C. (1984). Teacher-versus-peer mediated instruction: An ecobehavioral analysis of achievement outcomes. *Journal of Applied Behavior Analysis, 17,* 521–538.

HOWELL, K. W., & KAPLAN, J. S. (1978). Monitoring peer tutor behavior. *Exceptional Children, 45,* 135–137.

JENKINS, J. R., & JENKINS, L. M. (1981). *Cross age and peer tutoring: Help for children with learning problems.* Reston, VA: Council for Exceptional Children.

JOHNSON, D. W., & JOHNSON, R. T. (1986). Mainstreaming and cooperative learning strategies. *Exceptional Children, 52*(6), 553–561.

KROUSE, J., GERBER, M. M., & KAUFFMAN, J. M. (1981). *Peer tutoring: Procedures, promises and unresolved issues.* Rockville, MD: Aspen Systems.

MANDOLI, M., MANDOLI, P., & McLAUGHLIN, T. F. (1982). Effects of same-age peer tutoring on the spelling performance of a mainstreamed elementary learning disabled student. *Learning Disability Quarterly, 5,* 185–189.

PIGOTT, H. E., FANTUZZO, J. W., & CLEMENT, P. W. (1986). The effects of reciprocal peer tutoring and group contingencies on the academic performance of elementary school children. *Journal of Applied Behavior Analysis, 19,* 93–98.

SINDELAR, P. T. (1982). The effects of cross-age tutoring on the comprehension skills of remedial reading students. *The Journal of Special Education, 16,* 199–206.

Self-Management

BLANDFORD, B. J., & LLOYD, J. W. (1987). Effects of a self-instructional procedure on handwriting. *Journal of Learning Disabilities, 20,* 342–346.

BRYANT, L. E., & BUDD, K. S. (1982). Self-instructional training to increase independent work performance in preschoolers. *Journal of Applied Behavior Analysis, 15*(2), 259–271.

KOSIEWICZ, M. M., HALLAHAN, D. P., & LLOYD, J. (1981). The effects of an LD student's treatment choice on handwriting performance. *Learning Disability Quarterly, 4,* 281–286.

KOSEIWICZ, M. M., HALLAHAN, D. P., LLOYD, J., & GRAVES, A. W. (1982). Effects of self-instruction and self-correction procedures on handwriting performance. *Learning Disability Quarterly, 5,* 71–79.

Maintenance

KELLY, M. L., & STOKES, T. F. (1984). Student-teacher contracting with goal setting for maintenance. *Behavior Modification, 8*(2), 223–244.

PATTERSON, G. R., & FLEISCHMAN, M. J. (1979). Maintenance of treatment effects: Some considerations concerning family systems and follow-up data. *Behavior Therapy, 10,* 168–185.

Generalization

BLANKENSHIP, C. S., & BAUMGARTENER, M. D. (1982). Programming generalization of computational skills. *Learning Disability Quarterly, 5,* 152–162.

BUCKLEY, N. K., & WALKER, H. M. (1978). *Modifying classroom behavior: A manual procedure for classroom teachers* (rev. ed.). Champaign, IL: Research Press.

DERMITT, M., EISENBERGER, R., MITCHELL, M., & MATERSON, F. A. (1984). Accuracy versus speed in the generalized effort of learning-disabled children. *Journal of Experimental Analysis of Behavior, 42,* 19–36.

DESHLER, D. D., ALLEY, G. R., WARNER, M. M., & SCHUMAKER, J. B. (1981). Instructional practices for promoting skill acquisition and generalization in severely learning disabled adolescents. *Learning Disability Quarterly, 4,* 415–421.

ELLIS, E. S. (1986). The role of motivation and pedagogy on the generalization of cognitive strategy training. *Journal of Learning Disabilities, 19,* 66–70.

ELLIS, E. S., LENZ, B. K., & SABORNIE, E. J., (1987a). Generalization and adaption of learning strategies to natural environments. Part 1. Critical Agents. *Remedial and Special Education, 8,* 6–20.

ELLIS, E. S., LENZ, B. K., & SABORNIE, E. J., (1987b). Generalization and adaption of learning strategies to natural environments. Part 2. Research into Practice. *Remedial and Special Education, 8,* 6–23.

LLOYD, J., SALTZMAN, N. J., & KAUFFMAN, J. M. (1981). Predictable generalization in academic learning as a result of preskills and strategy training. *Learning Disability Quarterly, 4,* 203–216.

MCLESKEY, J., RIETH, H. J., & POLSGROVE, L. (1980). The implications of response generalization for improving the effectiveness of programs for learning disabled children. *Journal of Learning Disabilities, 13*(5), 59–62.

NAGEL, D. R., SCHUMAKER, J. B., & DESHLER, D. D. (1986). *The first-letter mnemonic strategy.* Lawrence, KS: Excel Enterprises.

REESE, S. C., & FILIPCZAK, J. (1980). Assessment of skill generalization: Measurement across setting, behavior, and time in an educational setting. *Behavior Modification, 4*(2), 209–225.

RIVERA, D., & SMITH, D. D. (1987). Facilitating generalization for computational arithmetic. Albuquerque: University of New Mexico, Special Education Department.

SCHMIDT, J. L. (1983). Conditions that promote generalization. *The Pointer, 27*(2), 8–10.

SMITH, D. D., & LOVITT, T. C. (1975). The use of modeling techniques to influence the acquisition of computational arithmetic skills in learning disabled children. In E. Ramp & G. Semb (eds.), *Behavior analysis: Areas of research and application.* Englewood Cliffs, NJ: Prentice-Hall.

SNELL, M. E. (ed.) (1978). *Systematic instruction of the moderately and severely handicapped.* Columbus, OH: Charles E. Merrill.

STOKES, T. F., & BAER, D. M. (1977). An implicit technology of generalization. *Journal of Applied Behavior Analysis, 10,* 349–367.

THORPE, H. W., & CHIANG, B. (1981). Programming generalization when mainstreaming exceptional children. *Journal of Special Education Technology, 4,* 15–23.

WEHMAN, P., ABRAMSON, M., & NORMAN, C. (1977). Transfer of training in behavior modification programs: An evaluative review. *The Journal of Special Education, 11,* 217–231.

WILDMAN, R. W., II, & WILDMAN, R. W. (1975). The generalization of behavior modification procedures: A review—With special emphasis on classroom applications. *Psychology in the Schools, 12,* 432–448.

Problem Solving

BELMONT, J. M., FERRETT, R. P., & MITCHELL, D. W. (1982). Memorizing: A test of untrained mildly mentally retarded children's problem-solving. *American Journal of Mental Deficiency, 87,* 197–210.

HAVERTAPE, J. F., & KASS, C. E. (1978). Examination of problem solving in learning disabled adolescents through verbalized self-instructions. *Learning Disability Quarterly, 1,* 94–103.

KAHNEY, H. (1986). *Problem solving: A cognitive approach.* Philadelphia: Open University Press.

MAKER, C. J. (1981). Problem solving: A general approach to remediation. In D. D. Smith, *Teaching the learning disabled.* Englewood Cliffs, NJ: Prentice Hall.

SLIFE, B. D., WEISS, J., & BELL, T. (1985). Separability of metacognition: Problem solving in learning disabled and regular students. *Journal of Educational Psychology, 77*(4), 437–445.

SMITH, D. D., & ROBINSON, S. (1986). Educating the learning disabled. In R. J. Morris & B. Blatt (eds.), *Special education research trends.* New York: Pergamon Press.

Computer Applications

CHAFFIN, J., MAXWELL, B., THOMPSON, B., SMITH, D. D., & SMITH, J. O. (1985a). *MicroSoc thinking games: SocMatch.* Circles Pines, MN: American Guidance Service.

EDUCATIONAL INFORMATION SYSTEMS (1985b). *Arcademic drill builders.* Allen, TX: Developmental Learning Materials.

EDUCATIONAL INFORMATION SYSTEMS. (1985c). *U.S. atlas action.* Allen, TX: Developmental Learning Materials.

EDUCATIONAL INFORMATION SYSTEMS. (1985d). *Arcademic skill builders in language arts.* Allen, TX: Developmental Learning Materials.

HOWELL, R., SIDORENKO, E., & JURICA, J. (1987). The effects of computer use on the acquisition of multiplication facts by a student with learning disabilities. *Journal of Learning Disabilities, 20,* 336–341.

MAXWELL, B., THOMPSON, B., CHAFFIN, J., SMITH, D. D., & SMITH, J. O. (1985a). *MicroSoc thinking games: SocLink.* Circles Pines, MN: American Guidance Service.

MAXWELL, B., THOMPSON, B., CHAFFIN, J., SMITH, D. D., & SMITH, J. O. (1985b). *MicroSoc thinking games: SocPix.* Circles Pines, MN: American Guidance Service.

ROBINSON, P. W., NEWBY, T. J., & GANZELL, S. L. (1981). A token system for a class of underachieving hyperactive children. *Journal of Applied Behavior Analysis, 14,* 307–315.

SMITH, D. D., SMITH, J. O., MAXWELL, B., THOMPSON, B., & CHAFFIN, J. (1985a). *MicroSoc thinking games: SocSort.* Circles Pines, MN: American Guidance Service.

SMITH, D. D., SMITH, J. O., MAXWELL, B., THOMPSON, B., & CHAFFIN, J. (1985b). *MicroSoc thinking games: SocMate.* Circles Pines, MN: American Guidance Service.

THOMPSON, B., MAXWELL, B., CHAFFIN, J., SMITH, D. D., & SMITH, J. O. (1985). *MicroSoc thinking games: SocOrder.* Circle Pines, MN: American Guidance Service.

Advance Organizers

DESHLER, D. D., WARNER, M. M., SCHUMAKER, J. B., & ALLEY, G. R. (1983). Learning strategies intervention model: Key components and current status. In J. D. McKinney & F. Feagans (eds.), *Current topics in learning disabilities,* Vol. 1. Norwood, NJ: Ablex.

LENZ, B. K., ALLEY, G. R., & SCHUMAKER, J. B. (1987). Activating the inactive learner: Advance organizers in the secondary content classroom. *Learning Disability Quarterly, 10,* 53–62.

PARIS, S. G., & JACOBS, J. E. (1984). The benefits of informed instruction for children's reading awareness and comprehensions skills. *Child Development, 55,* 2083–2093.

8

Reading*

The ability to read and comprehend the written word has long been viewed in our society as an indicator of intellectual competence. More recently, reading has also come to be seen as a functional tool that allows each individual to develop and maintain employment skills and to participate more fully in the social and recreational activities of daily life. Since underachievement in reading is a common problem of students with special needs, the selection of appropriate reading strategies is a critical task in instructional planning.

This chapter describes the major components of the reading process, discusses the major areas of instruction, and reviews some procedures that have been found effective in obtaining student improvement in specific reading skills. Part of the chapter is devoted to a discussion of specific instructional techniques and procedures that have been validated by case study, sound research methodology, or student progress data.

TOPICS FOR INSTRUCTION

Reading involves a complex set of behaviors. To assist in understanding the scope of the task that is presented to the student, a lattice was developed (Figure 8.1). This lattice is not comprehensive in scope, but is intended to highlight the magnitude of the task before both the student and the teacher.

*This chapter was written by Carlene VanEtten.

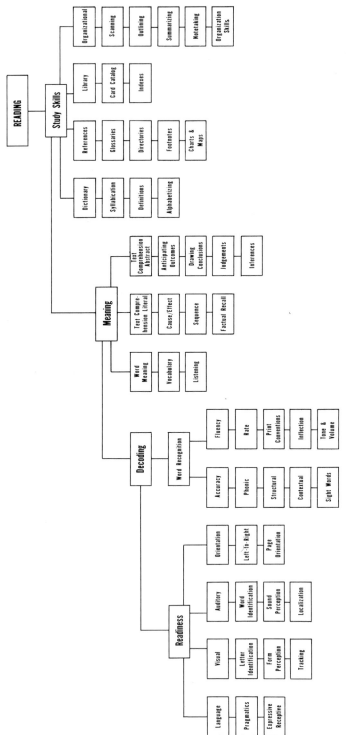

Figure 8.1 Component skills of reading.

The arrangement of the components on the lattice does not imply a rigid sequence or hierarchy. Many of the skills develop, or should develop, simultaneously. Carnine and Silbert (1979) present the task of learning to read as a two-step process. Acquisition of a set of subskills is the first step, followed by assimilation of those subskills into the holistic act of reading as the second step. Such a view does not assume that decoding is more important than comprehension. Instead, the focus is on analyzing both decoding and comprehension to create instructional procedures that will improve reading performance. The following section discusses the various component skills of reading.

Readiness Skills

Wilson and Cleland (1985) identify the basic readiness areas of reading as language, auditory, visual, and orientation.

Language

Many professionals assume that highly developed oral language skills must be present before initial reading instruction can proceed, though some research information questions this assumption. Hammill and McNutt (1981, p. 36) reviewed 322 studies that examined the correlation of reading with a variety of other variables. They found a strong relationship between written language and reading and a weak relationship between oral language and reading.

> Our analyses show only that reading correlates marginally well with spoken language. They do not necessarily support the idea that reading is a particular developmental level in a communication "hierarchy," that has spoken language at its base and writing at its top.

Strong faith in the "oral language first theory" has prompted some practitioners to delay instruction in reading until highly developed oral language is present. There is no requirement for an either/or choice. Language and reading instruction can and should proceed on a complementary and integrated basis.

Visual and Auditory

Discrimination skills must also be examined. Many students have intact vision and hearing, but poorly developed or utilized visual and auditory discrimination skills. It is commonly accepted theory that some level of visual and auditory functioning is directly related to a variety of school tasks, especially reading. The facts, however, are somewhat different if research data are considered (Kavale, 1982; Muehl & Kremenak, 1966).

Orientation Skills

These skills are concerned with the left-to-right movement required for efficient reading. The student with poor skills in this area exhibits letter and word reversals and frequently loses his or her place on the page. Fortunately, many of these problems can be remediated by specific practice.

Decoding Skills

Word Recognition (Accuracy)

The first problem in learning to read is that the learner must know some words. There is a considerable difference of opinion about exactly what strategies should be used to teach those initial words. Instruction in word recognition may focus on phonic, structural, or contextual analysis skills or simply upon learning a set of sight words without regard to the particular analysis strategy employed.

Phonic analysis is a systematic study of words by sound units (Otto & McMenemy, 1966). Phonic analysis should be used in conjunction with other word recognition techniques. Application of phonetic techniques assists the learner in decoding unknown written symbols that frequently match a familiar auditory representation.

Structural analysis (sometimes termed morphemic) focuses on the reader's use of the meaning units of words. These units typically include instruction in three areas: (1) roots, (2) inflected forms of words, and (3) affixes. A clear and concise description of these units can be found in Ringler and Weber (1984).

In *contextual analysis* the learner uses clues drawn from the nearby words or visuals in the text. Johnson and Pearson (1978) identified four types of clues: typographical, pictorial and graphic, syntactic, and semantic. These clues are provided as extra signals by authors to assist the reader in making decisions about unknown words. Many students with learning problems are unaware of such clues. Unless specific instructional procedures incorporate use of such clues, students may fail to realize the benefits intended by the authors.

Another aspect of decoding skills is *sight word* instruction. Ekwall (1977) recognized sight word development as a distinct subskill of word recognition. There is evidence that isolated words may be efficiently taught through specific error correction procedures (Fleisher & Jenkins, 1983; Jenkins & Larson, 1979; Jenkins, Larson, & Fleisher, 1983).

There are two instances when sight word instruction of limited duration may be appropriate. The first instance is for elementary students who possess a very limited sight vocabulary (fewer than sixty words). The development of a sight vocabulary of ninety to one hundred words provides a base for teaching many other skills. For secondary students with no functional reading skills, and for students who are more severely impaired, training in a minimum (fifty to one hundred words) sight word vocabulary might be most appropriate.

Word Recognition (Fluency)

Along with the development of specific word recognition skills that focus on accuracy, the acquisition of a broad range of oral reading skill with a focus on fluency is also taking place.

Reading rate is one aspect of building fluency. Carnine and Silbert (1979) describe the relationship between accuracy and fluency in the context of the stages of acquisition and proficiency. Though the stages overlap, the instructional intent of each differs. Acquisition focuses on developing the new skills to some basic level of response. After the skill has been presented and practiced, attention is directed toward proficiency (reading fluently). LaBerge and Samuels (1974) noted that movement from accuracy to automaticity was necessary to acquire both fluent reading and good comprehension.

A source of difficulty for many students is the arbitrary *conventions of print* used in written language (Samuels, 1981). Many students do not realize the significance, or the utility, of punctuation. Instruction may be necessary to ensure that students grasp the importance of such markers. Appropriate use of pitch, inflections, and intonations must also be demonstrated.

Several error correction procedures thought to be efficient in improving either, or perhaps both, accuracy and fluency have been identified (Jenkins & Larson, 1979; Rose, McEntire, & Dowdy 1982). Table 8.1 contains a brief description of some of the most commonly employed procedures. Specific application of a technique may have several variations.

Rose, McEntire, and Dowdy (1982) examined the effects of word supply and phonic analysis correction procedures with elementary-aged students who were classified as learning disabled. Under the word supply conditions, the teacher provided the correct word after each student error. When the phonic

Table 8.1
Common Error Correction Procedures for Reading Skills

Drill	Error words are noted and usually printed on individual index cards. Words are then presented individually to the student. The teacher supplies word, and the student repeats. Procedure continues until the student says all words correctly, usually to some criterion (certain number of errors, usually tied to some number of consecutive presentations).
Phonic analysis	The learner is directed to note specific phonetic elements of the error word and is told to sound out each element.
Sentence repeat	Each error word is supplied correctly by the teacher, followed by correct production by the student and completion of the sentence. The student then rereads the sentence containing the error word. If a second error occurs, the word correction by the teacher and student is repeated, but not the entire sentence.
Word meaning	Each error word is supplied by the teacher, with the student repeating the word. This is followed by the teacher asking, "What does this word mean?" If the student does not know, the teacher provides definition or synonym, and the student repeats meaning. Oral reading resumes at point of corrected word. If missed again, error procedure is repeated. At end of each page, a list of all words missed is presented. Student reads each word and repeats any definition provided earlier. If any word or meaning error occurs, the correction procedure is repeated.
Word supply	Any error word is supplied by the teacher. The student is usually required to focus visually on the error word and repeat it.

analysis technique was used, the student was directed to attend to specific phonetic elements of the error word and was told to sound out each element.

Though the findings were not consistent with all students, the word supply
correction was found to be more effective than the phonic analysis correction.
There was little difference between the no-correction condition and the phonic
analysis correction. This finding conflicts with earlier work of Jenkins and Larson (1979), in which they examined various procedures (Table 8.1) for correcting oral reading errors. No corrective feedback was only slightly inferior to word
supply across all students in this study, carried out with students of junior high
age. The other four correction procedures generally produced higher word
recognition scores than did the word supply method. Most correction procedures resulted in little improvement when compared with the no-feedback
condition. Every student in this study achieved his or her highest performance
level under the drill procedure.

Two more recent studies (Rosenberg, 1986; Singh & Singh, 1985) also
examined the effects of word supply and other error correction procedures.
Rosenberg's subjects were middle school students with learning disabilities, while
Singh and Singh's students were adolescents, who had moderate mental handicaps. All error correction procedures employed produced better results than
did word supply.

Based on their study, Jenkins and Larson (1979) concluded that word
supply has little effect on subsequent word recognition, a fact supported by their
work with junior high-aged students, but contradicted by Rose, McEntire, and
Dowdy (1982), whose subjects were elementary-aged students. The conflicting
results found in these two studies may be a result of the research design, or it
may indicate the need for differential application of various error corrections
procedures, depending on the age of the students and on their instructional
history.

More recently the role of computers in developing decoding fluency has
been investigated (Jones, Torgesen, & Sexton, 1987; Torgesen, 1986). Using a
commercially available program, designated to provide practice in recognizing
and analyzing words varying in medial vowels and vowel combinations, Jones et
al. (1986) found substantial improvements in a group of elementary students
who had been identified as learning disabled. This improvement was obtained
on words practiced in the program, but also occurred on words that were never
practiced during the training. Not only was improvement obtained in speed and
accuracy for context-free word reading, but speed and accuracy also improved
in oral reading of text materials.

Meaning Skills

Although comprehension skills are certainly recognized as important, most
reading programs serving students with mild handicaps have placed a heavy
emphasis on the decoding aspects of reading. Jenkins and Heliotis (1981) pro-

vide two explanations for the focus on decoding. First, decoding skills were assumed to be prerequisite to understanding, and, second, it was usually assumed that if efficient decoding skills were developed, comprehension would naturally follow. Fleisher, Jenkins, and Pany (1979) completed two investigations to determine if increased decoding speed of poor readers would lead to improved comprehension. Although students trained in rapid decoding developed substantially improved reading rates, performance on reading comprehension measures were comparable to those of another group of poor readers who did not receive the rapid decoding training. Dahl (cited in Jenkins & Heliotis, 1981), however, found significant improvement in comprehension skills as a result of a program that focused on increasing the rate of oral reading. There are two possible reasons for such conflicting results. Fleisher, Jenkins, and Pany (1979) used an isolated word procedure, while Dahl used a context format in an attempt to increase fluency. Dahl's data are the result of a year-long program, while the students in the Fleisher, Jenkins, and Pany study participated only for the short duration of the study.

A study by Roberts and Smith (1980) also focused on the connection between decoding skills and improved performance in comprehension. Mild improvement in comprehension was obtained as a result of improved correct or error rates. When comprehension was specifically targeted, correct and error rates remained at desired levels. This study suggests that selecting dual targets for instruction, which increases teaching efficiency, should be considered in planning instructional programs.

Extending earlier work, Jenkins, Larson, and Fleisher (1983) examined the effects of two error correction procedures on word recognition and reading comprehension. This was done with students labeled as "elementary," although the students were later described as being in the third through seventh grades. There are two important findings from this study. First, the drill correction again produced better results than did word supply. These effects were present on words read in isolation and on a measure of oral reading in context. These findings also support the assumption that appropriate word recognition intervention can also affect comprehension of text to a limited degree.

Fleisher and Jenkins (1983) made several observations in summary of a series of studies and as a result of a study that compared the effect of word and comprehension training on reading performance.

1. Word emphasis instruction did not seem to impair comprehension as predicted by some authorities.
2. Nor did it substantially aid comprehension as predicted by others.
3. Recognition of isolated words is improved by word drill.
4. Word emphasis approaches may be no more effective in teaching new words than use of context practice only.
5. Based on this study, there is a suggestion that students who read correctly fewer than 50% of the new words at the pretest may benefit from word emphasis instruction (error correction applied to isolated words).

These observations were offered with a "buyer beware" note. At present, results are conflicting, confusing, and frustrating to practitioners who seek to make judgments based on data. However, the line of research reported here, if continued and expanded, will provide some solid evidence upon which appropriate instructional programs can be developed.

Recent efforts to make comprehension a task that can be specifically defined, and therefore specifically taught, appear quite promising. More recent efforts to teach comprehension use an instructional format that includes a variety of direct instruction principles (Engelmann & Carnine, 1982). Such instruction might use lessons that present rules and examples for teaching a specific skill (Darch & Kameenui, 1987; Patching et al., 1983). Students participating in such instruction have shown significant gains when compared with students participating in more traditional discussion/workbook instruction. Other specific training programs, with somewhat less structure, have also obtained positive results (Chan, Cole, & Barfett, 1987).

Study and Content Area Skills

Study and content area skills tap the student's ability to use a variety of location and reference skills, to use library resources, to use and apply highly specific study, comprehension, and organizational skills. The student is required to use a variety of skills, to apply them to a variety of situations and materials, then, to organize and recall the material for later use.

These skills become more important as the student progresses through school. In the elementary grades the task is to learn to read from a textbook (Huhn, 1980). The task of the secondary student is to learn subject matter from a textbook.

Darch and Gersten (1986) compared two procedures designed to increase high school learning disabled students' comprehension of important concepts during content area instruction. One group received instruction typical of the kind found in most basal programs. The second group was instructed through advanced organizers, which was an outline/overview that provided students with important concepts of the lesson. Advanced-organizer group subjects almost reached mastery level performance of 75%, while those students in the basal group attained only 53% on the posttest measure. It appears that study or content area skills may be taught through direct instruction procedures, just as other reading skills.

CURRICULUM-BASED ASSESSMENT AND EVALUATION

In traditional assessment, tests are given in an effort to discover specific strengths and weaknesses or dysfunctions that relate to poor performance in reading. This particular approach does not usually lead to effective reading instruction (Engelmann, Granzin, & Severson, 1979). Engelmann, Granzin, and

Table 8.2
Suggested Performance Standards: Precision Teaching Project Reading

PINPOINT	STANDARD
See/Say isolated sounds	60–80 sounds/minute
See/Say phonetic words	60–80 words/minute
Think Alphabet (forward/backward)	400+ letters/minute
See/Say letter names	80–100 letters/minute
See/Say sight words	80–120 words/minute
See/Say words/context (Oral Reading)	200+ words/minute
See/Think words/context (Silent Reading)	400+ words/minute
Think/Say ideas or facts	15–30 ideas/minute

Source: Precision Teaching Project, *Training Manual,* 8th ed. (Great Falls, MT: Precision Teaching Materials, 1984). Used by permission.

Severson recommended that assessment should begin with instructional diagnosis. The purpose of this instructional diagnosis is to determine the extent to which a problem is caused by poor instruction and to determine what different teaching behaviors might be appropriate. This assessment includes looking at time, learning tasks, and materials and how students are grouped or structured for instruction (Ysseldyke & Algozzine, 1983).

Direct assessment of specific reading behaviors should be paired with the assessment of teaching behaviors. Measures of fluency (rate of response), oral reading errors, and comprehension will be required for planning appropriate instructional programs for most students in special education classrooms.

The Precision Teaching Project (1984) provides some suggested performance fluency standards for a number of specific reading behaviors (Table 8.2). Some suggestions have also been provided for oral and silent reading by grade level. McCracken (1967) suggested minimum oral reading speeds of 60 words per minute at grade 1, 90 at grade 3, and 150 words per minute by grade 6.

Direct assessment involves combining learning channels (input and output) to measure specific reading subskills. These combinations include See/Say, See/Point, See/Do/Write, Hear/Point, Hear/Say, Hear/Do/Write, Think/Say, Think/Do/Write.

This direct assessment, paired with efficient instructional tactics and appropriate teaching behaviors, can lead to reading improvement for individual students. Teachers must continually evaluate the effects of instruction by keeping percentage or rate data on a daily basis.

TEACHING TACTICS

Readiness Skills

Tactics that emphasize both oral language and reading skills offer advantages to both teachers and students. Use of such tactics increases teaching efficiency, since the focus of instruction is on both oral expression and reading skills. One such tactic is the *free description technique* (Hansen & Lovitt, 1977; Lovitt, 1984). Lovitt noted that this technique eliminates preparation of comprehension questions by teachers, requires students to make passage-dependent responses, rather than guess, and requires students to use language to describe what they read.

Steps follow for this simple and useful procedure. The teacher role and response is identified by *T* and the student response by *S*. This procedure requires solo and cooperative efforts by both the teacher and the student.

1. *T:* Defines response desired from the student. If the student is a young child, simply requiring that the student tell simple facts about the story is appropriate. Lovitt defined a fact as a comment about a story's theme, a noun plus an action verb (two facts), an adjective or adverb that describes a noun or verb, and a preposition that describes a location.
2. *T:* Provides examples and nonexamples of facts.
3. *T:* Models saying facts for child (i.e., the boy wore a red shirt, his dog was big and black, his bike was old).
4. *T & S:* Count facts together (those given by teacher).
5. *T & S:* Discuss correct/incorrect responses.
6. *S:* Reads passage; then says facts (thirty seconds to one minute).
7. *T:* Counts number of correct/incorrect facts, as they are provided by S.
8. *T:* Provides feedback to S at end of session. Indicates how present performance compared with previous efforts.
9. *T or S:* Plots numbers on chart.
10. *T:* Critiques student performance, provides feedback on errors, gives suggestions for improvement.

Another technique designed to provide students with a strategy for approaching a story is one that has been identified as "story grammars" or "story mapping" (Idol, 1987; Lovitt, 1984; Mandler & Johnson, 1977). The purpose of this technique is to provide students with a guide to understanding written narrative.

Mandler and Johnson (1977) identified six story elements:

Setting: Introduction of main characters, time, place.
Beginning: Event that triggers the story.
Reaction: Response of main characters, what they do—goal?
Attempt: What effort is made to attain goal?
Outcome: Results of attempt to reach goal.
Ending: Consequences of the action and the final response of main characters.

Several procedures have been suggested to assist students in mapping a story. One is a sorting task that requires students to arrange a jumbled short story in the correct order of the various elements as just indicated. Another task requires students to sort the sentences for each of the elements into separate piles. An application of the story mapping procedure with a focus on written language was reported by Idol (1987).

Both the free description and the story grammar tactics provide excellent examples of how to answer the question of whether oral language or reading is the most critical focus for instruction. These techniques require the student to use and develop skills important to both oral language and reading. Therefore, students receive skill building instruction in two important areas at the same time.

Decoding Skills

Word Recognition (Accuracy)

Competent readers usually possess a variety of strategies for identifying words. These strategies may focus on sound-symbol relationships (phonics), on analyzing the various parts of words (structural analysis), or on analysis of the words within phrases or sentences (contextual analysis).

Many traditional phonics programs begin with teaching letter-sound correspondence. Frequently, gamelike activities are employed in the initial teaching activities. Carnine and Silbert (1979) offer a direct instruction procedure for teaching letter-sound correspondence. An introductory format is used in the first one or two lessons in which a new letter appears. Following are the steps for the introductory format:

1. Teacher writes the letter/sound to be learned on the board and provides basic directions to students. "When I touch under the letter, you say the sound. Keep saying the sound as long as I touch it."
2. Teacher models the sound.
3. Teacher leads by responding with the group.
4. Teacher tests by having the group repeat sound several times, then prompts students with, "Your turn, say it by yourselves."
5. Teacher tests individuals in groups.

After the initial introduction of the new letters, the discrimination format is presented. In this format the students receive the practice they need to become fluent in letter-sound correspondence. Direct instruction procedures for teaching letter combinations have also been developed (Carnine & Silbert, 1979).

Flashcards, drills, lists, and games and exercises of a wide variety, focusing on various aspects of structural or contextual analysis, have traditionally been used as a part of a total instructional program (Ekwall, 1985). However, direct instruction procedures have also been developed for these areas (Carnine & Silbert, 1979). The format is much like that described under phonics tactics.

Building sight word vocabulary through word expansion techniques was described by Lovitt (1984). Word expansion techniques use known words to teach new words, through the addition of prefixes, suffixes, and inflectional endings. This tactic incorporates aspects of both structural and contextual analysis into a three-step teaching procedure:

1. Six to ten words not instantly recognized by the student are printed on individual index cards, with a sentence containing the selected word written on the back of each card. The students are to practice the sentences.
2. The identified words are systematically expanded by adding inflectional endings, suffixes, and prefixes. Drawing on the work of Floriani (1979), a word expansion chart was provided as a reference to levels of development. Level 1 contains the simpler endings of s, ed, d, and ing, while level 4 contains a number of more difficult affixes, such as ex, pre, sion, and ness.
3. In this step the children use the words in a variety of contexts. As an example, Lovitt (1984) suggested that if the emphasis was on semantic variables, the students might be asked to classify the sight words and their expansions into categories.

A variety of other tactics may be used to teach sight words to students. Some focus on words that are selected by the students themselves (Ashton-Warner, 1963). Another approach is a compare/contrast procedure that requires the students to use known words to decode unknown words (Guthrie & Cunningham, 1982). Also available are procedures using some direct instruction techniques, which are designed for group instruction (Lovitt, 1984). A taped word procedure for teaching sight words has also been described (Freeman and McLaughlin, 1984). Students practice isolated words presented on a tape recorder; then the teacher takes a daily one-minute sample to measure progress. This procedure was reported to be highly successful with high school-age students with learning disabilities.

The following section focuses on techniques for improving fluency and oral reading expression. Concurrent instruction in both aspects of decoding, along with instruction in meaning skills, is required to develop a competent reader.

Word Recognition (Fluency)

A variety of procedures have been identified as potentially helpful in improving oral reading fluency. Included are previewing techniques, error correction procedures, preteaching of target words, phonics, modeling, and repeated readings. Some techniques focus more on the affective aspects of fluency, attempting to focus students' attention on the linguistic features of the language. More recently, computers have received attention as a possible resource in improving reading fluency.

Previewing has been used to describe a wide range of procedures (Lovitt, 1984; Rose, 1984; Rose & Beattie, 1986). Lovitt described a technique where students practice on either error words or new words. For example, if a student reads a passage and misses five words, those five words are practiced for five minutes following the reading session. These cards are added to words missed in other reading sessions. Before the next reading session, the students identify all words a few times. The student then reads the assigned text. Missed words are identified and the cycle of error word practice is again completed.

Rose (1984) described two previewing (sometimes termed prepractice) procedures: silent and listening. Following are descriptions of the two procedures:

Silent:

1. Student reads passage silently.
2. Student tells teacher when silent reading is completed.
3. Student reads passage to teacher.

Listening:

1. Teacher reads assigned passage orally to student, who follows along as teacher reads.
2. Student reads passage to teacher.

Repeated readings (rereading of the same material) has been described as a method for improving fluency (Lauritzen, 1982; Lovitt, 1984; Samuels, 1979). This tactic is supported by the automaticity theory proposed by LaBerge and Samuels (1974). The assumption is that once the reader can decode fluently, then effort can be devoted to comprehending what is read. Although there are many slight variations, the following are steps for the repeated readings procedure.

1. Determine the student's average correct word-per-minute (wpm) rate, over a two- or three-day period.
2. Set a target that is 10–15% higher than the best rate or the average rate.
3. Tell the student his or her present rate and the target rate.
4. Have the student read the passage. Collect a one-minute sample, but have the student complete the entire passage selected.
5. Tell the student the results of the reading. a. If the target was obtained, move to the next passage and set a new target. Repeat the process.
   b. If the target is not reached, then practice takes place. Practice may focus on specific errors, rereading of the most difficult spots, or any other type of practice thought to be appropriate for the student. Coaching by the teacher, such as "Look ahead as you read" or "Skip the words you don't know," may also be provided.

After practice the student reads again and is timed. This process is continued for five readings (others use as few as three or as many as seven). Depending on results, the student returns to more practice or moves to the next passage. Students move to the next passage after ten attempts, even if criterion is not met.

Modeling has also been investigated as a method to promote fluency in reading. The purpose of this tactic is to demonstrate how the passage sounds, or how it should be read. The teacher may read for only a minute (Smith, 1979) or may read an entire passage of a story (Lovitt, 1984). When the student completes the assigned passage, the teacher points out differences between the readings and then may ask the student to again repeat a portion, following another passage modeled by the teacher.

Choral reading is an activity designed to provide practice for students in reading for meaning and in reading with expression (Tierney, Readence, & Dishner, 1980). This procedure provides needed practice in oral expression and is an excellent group experience. The careful use of choral reading requires the student to integrate both speaking and listening skills. Dallman (1976) and Tierney, Readence, and Dishner (1980) provide clear guidelines for introducing choral reading.

Meaning Skills

One suggestion for improving comprehension skills is simply to schedule time for teaching reading comprehension (Jenkins, Stein, & Osborn, 1981). Although instruction in reading is usually included as part of the overall program, actual instruction in how to learn to comprehend encompasses a very small portion of instructional time (Durkin, 1978–1979). Frequently, students are instead simply tested to see if they comprehended the assigned reading task.

Applied behavior analysis techniques have been investigated as a procedure for indirectly improving performance in reading comprehension. One area of focus has been the effect of vocabulary instruction on several types of reading comprehension tasks (Pany, cited in Jenkins & Heliotis, 1981; Pany & Jenkins, 1978). These studies used applied behavior analysis procedures to compare indirect and direct vocabulary instruction procedures. They found that direct vocabulary instruction procedures were far more successful than were indirect procedures, when compared on all measures of vocabulary acquisition. However, although some improvement was obtained on measure of sentence comprehension, overall passage comprehension did not improve.

Some specific strategies have been developed in an attempt to improve comprehension. One example is the *cloze technique* (Bloomer, 1962; Goodman, 1967; Gove, 1975), which indirectly attempts to build comprehension skills. The cloze strategy requires students to use the context of a sentence or passage to determine replacements for deleted words. Goodman (1967) describes these clues as either syntactic or grammatical word order clues, semantic or meaning clues, or sound-symbol clues. The level of difficulty may be varied by altering the graphic structure of the words and the parts of speech selected as foils. Although many commercial materials are now available, teachers may easily construct their own cloze materials.

Limited results have been obtained with many of the indirect methods used to improve comprehension. Therefore, more recent efforts have been directed toward developing procedures that provide students with a strategy for learning how to approach text in a systematic manner. One such example is the *Paraphrasing Strategy* (Schumaker, Denton, & Deshler, 1984), developed by the University of Kansas Institute for Research in Learning Disabilities (KU-IRLD) researchers.

Table 8.3
Steps for Paraphrasing

Step 1	**R**ead a paragraph.
Step 2	**A**sk yourself, "What were the main ideas and details in this paragraph?"
Step 3	**P**ut the main idea and details into your own words.

Source: J. B. Schumaker, P. H. Denton, & D. D. Deshler, *The Paraphrasing Strategy* (Lawrence, KS: University of Kansas, 1984), p. 58.

The paraphrasing strategy is a technique designed to help students improve recall of main ideas and specific facts. This strategy requires students to complete three activities for every paragraph they read. They must find the main idea, identify at least two details that relate to the main idea, and restate (paraphrase) the content of the main idea and details in their own words. As with all the learning strategies developed at the KU-IRLD, to help students remember the steps that must be followed to complete the strategy accurately, a mnemonic device (RAP)[1] is used. (See Table 8.3 for a description of the steps used in the RAP (*r*ead, *a*sk, *p*ut) strategy.)

To help students learn this strategy, many teachers model the application of the strategy. They read the first paragraph of a chapter in one of the student's textbooks outloud. Then, the teachers show students how to use the RAP strategy with that paragraph.

The process is repeated with the second paragraph, with the students participating in some of the RAP steps. Throughout the lesson, the students apply more and more of the strategy to ensuing paragraphs. Some teachers use the jigsaw technique (see Chapter 7) while teaching RAP to their students. Each student is assigned a part of the strategy to complete for each paragraph read. One student might identify the main idea, several others might identify the details about the main idea, and another student might paraphrase the paragraph.

Students who have been taught this strategy to mastery, through all the acquisition and generalization steps, have substantially improved their reading comprehension scores. During the pretest, for example, students' average comprehension percentage score from reading passages from their assigned grade-level texts was only 48%. However, after learning the RAP strategy, these students obtained an average score of 84%. Clearly, this strategy can assist students in understanding and remembering information presented in typical high school social studies and science books. Such ability contributes to students' ability to succeed in regular education classes where students are expected to gain information from books often written above their reading abilities.

---

[1]For more information or training about this or other learning strategies developed by the KU-IRLD, contact Dr. Fran Clark, University of Kansas, Institute for Research in Learning Disabilities, 223 Carruth-O'Leary Hall, Lawrence, KS 66045.

Other researchers have also devised programs to focus students' attention on text structure and to teach the students to monitor their comprehension (Chan, Cole, & Barfett, 1987; Darch & Kameenui, 1987; Englert & Thomas, 1987; Wong & Jones, 1982). These procedures provide students with direct and explicit step-by-step instructions in how to comprehend. This emphasis on active involvement and monitoring is important since students with learning disabilities have been described as inactive learners (Torgesen, 1986) and deficient in self-monitoring skills (Flavell, 1970).

Direct instruction techniques focus careful attention on program design and on presentation techniques. Carnine and Silbert (1979) specified six features of direct instruction program design: specifying objectives, devising problem-solving strategies, developing teaching procedures, selecting examples, providing practice-and-sequencing skills, and supplying examples. Although exact presentation procedures change with the stages of reading instruction, there are several aspects of the presentation of information that are important. First, initial instruction is carried out in small groups, with students responding orally and in unison. Both signals and pacing are used to keep the students actively involved and responding frequently. Progress is continually assessed, and specific diagnosis and correction procedures are followed.

Carnine and Silbert (1979) present direct instruction procedures for teaching vocabulary and language skills, along with directions for teaching higher-level, complex comprehension skills, such as inference, critical reading, and content area–related comprehension and study skills. They have provided procedures for teaching vocabulary by modeling, synonyms, and definitions. They suggest that much of the vocabulary teaching be done orally.

Study and Content Area Skills

There is convincing evidence that focusing students' attention through the use of advance organizers (mapping, visual displays, networking, outlines) may lead to improvement in the amount of material students retain (Klauer, 1984). The purpose of these various techniques is to aid students in organizing information that they read. More recently, attention has been focused on procedures that incorporate advance organizers but also provide the students with a step-by-step strategy that teaches them to be responsive to various elements of the text structure. These techniques are especially helpful in aiding students who experience great difficulty with reading in content areas. One such technique is *Multipass* (Schumaker et al., 1982).

Multipass is a complex strategy that is taught through a ten-step process. The strategy involves modeling, verbal rehearsal practice, feedback, and testing at various points. The three substrategies (survey, size-up, and sort-out) focus student attention on the material for a particular purpose.

Because each strategy requires discrete behaviors, each is taught as a unit. It is this specificity that makes this strategy potentially useful for many students with learning problems. Brief descriptions of the substrategies follow.

Survey Pass

This pass (movement through the text) is to familiarize the student with the chapter's organization and main ideas. Students complete seven steps, including reading the title, introductory paragraph, and the major subtitles.

Size-up Pass

This pass is designed to help students gain specific information. Four steps are required here, including paraphrasing and looking for textual clues, such as italics, subtitles, or boldface print.

Sort-out Pass

This part of the strategy requires the students to test themselves over the material in the chapter. Students follow four steps that require them to focus on thinking about where answers to a question would be found and on learning how to skim to locate needed information.

SUMMARY

Learning to read is a complex process, laden with frustrations for students who encounter many difficulties, and filled with rewards for those who quickly and easily master the task. Students arrive at the schoolroom door with the expectation that they will learn to read. National literacy statistics clearly indicate that this goal is not attained by all individuals, even though they may possess a high school diploma. Although experts disagree as to the exact percentage, a substantial number of the students referred for special education services will exhibit moderate to severe disabilities in the area of reading. Therefore, provision of a structured and comprehensive program of reading instruction is of critical importance.

A successful reading program must include consideration of the basic visual, auditory, and language abilities of the individual student. However, waiting for the student to develop some prescribed level of functioning in these areas, before beginning formal instruction in reading, will delay his or her learning to read. The student may also fall behind in content area subjects which require reading. There are many programs and techniques that may be used to increase both general language skills and specific reading skills. The first part of the "teaching tactics" section of this chapter offers some specific suggestions for providing such instruction.

The decoding versus meaning debate, which has continued endlessly in texts and journals, has done little to instruct professionals in how to teach either skill. A comprehensive and effective reading program must include specific instruction in both areas. Instruction in decoding must focus on both accuracy and fluency, while instruction in meaning must move from word comprehension to literal and abstract comprehension of sentences and paragraphs. This chapter's sections about decoding and meaning provide specific procedures for teaching these skills, including some techniques for direct instruction.

Students in special education classes frequently obtain fluency in narrative reading, but are unable to transfer this newly learned skill to content area reading. An effective reading program must include specific instruction in content area reading skills and study skills to ensure the transfer and generalization of newly learned skills. Specific strategies for obtaining meaning from content materials must be taught. Specific instruction in how to use the library in general, including the various reference materials, should also be part of a comprehensive reading program.

Although Figure 8.1 indicates four component skills (readiness, decoding, meaning, study skills), acquisition of reading skills is not a simple linear process. The reader does not suddenly acquire readiness, then move to decoding, then to comprehension, and finally to study skills. Acquisition of that skill which we call reading is the end result of simultaneous and carefully structured instruction in each component area described.

STUDY AND DISCUSSION QUESTIONS

1. Describe/discuss the basic components of reading.
2. List and describe three procedures for improving fluency in oral reading.
3. Develop a lesson plan to improve teaching of comprehension skills.

REFERENCES

General Reading Remediation

ASHTON-WARNER, S. (1963). *Teacher.* New York: Simon & Schuster.

CARNINE, D., & SILBERT, J. (1979). *Direct instruction.* Columbus, OH: Charles E. Merrill.

EKWALL, E. E. (1977). *Teacher's handbook on diagnosis and remediation in reading.* Boston: Allyn & Bacon.

EKWALL, E. E. (1985). *Locating and correcting reading difficulties* (4th ed.). Columbus, OH: Charles E. Merrill.

HAMMILL, D. D., & McNUTT, G. (1981). *The correlates of reading: The consensus of thirty years of correlational research.* Austin, TX: Pro-Ed.

JENKINS, J. R., & HELIOTIS, J. G. (1981). Reading comprehension instruction: Findings from behavioral and cognitive psychology. *Topics in Language Disorders, 1*(2), 25–41.

LOVITT, T. C. (1984). *Tactics for teaching.* Columbus, OH: Charles E. Merrill.

OTTO, W., & McMENEMY, R. A. (1966). *Corrective and remedial teaching: Principles and practices.* Boston: Houghton Mifflin.

TIERNEY, R. J., READENCE, J. E., & DISHNER, E. K. (1980). *Reading strategies and practices: Guide for improving instruction.* Boston: Allyn & Bacon.

WILSON, R. M., & CLELAND, C. J. (1985). *Diagnostic and remedial reading for classroom and clinic* (5th ed.). Columbus, OH: Charles E. Merrill.

Readiness

CARNINE, D., & SILBERT, J. (1979). *Direct instruction.* Columbus, OH: Charles E. Merrill.

HAMMILL, D. D., & McNUTT, G. (1981). *The correlates of reading: The consensus of thirty years of correlational research.* Austin, TX: Pro-Ed.

HANSEN, C., & LOVITT, T. (1977). An applied behavior analysis approach to reading comprehension. In J. T. Guthrie (ed.), *Cognition, curriculum, and comprehension.* Newark, DE: International Reading Association.

IDOL, L. (1987). Group story mapping: A comprehension strategy for both skilled and unskilled readers. *Journal of Learning Disabilities, 20,* 196–205.

KAVALE, K. (1982). Meta-analysis of the relationship between visual perceptual skills and reading achievement. *Journal of Learning Disabilities, 15,* 42–51.

LOVITT, T. C. (1984). *Tactics for teaching.* Columbus, OH: Charles E. Merrill.

MANDLER, J., & JOHNSON, N. (1977). Remembrance of things passed: Story structure and recall. *Cognitive Psychology, 9,* 111–151.

MUEHL, S., & KREMENAK, S. (1966). Ability to match information within and between auditory and visual sense modalities and subsequent reading achievement. *Journal of Educational Psychology, 57,* 230–239.

WILSON, R. M., & CLELAND, C. J. (1985). *Diagnostic and remedial reading for classroom and clinic* (5th ed.). Columbus, OH: Charles E. Merrill.

Decoding Skills

Word Recognition (Accuracy)

ASHTON-WARNER, S. (1963). *Teacher.* New York: Simon & Schuster.

CARNINE, D., & SILBERT, J. (1979). *Direct instruction.* Columbus, OH: Charles E. Merrill.

EKWALL, E. E. (1985). *Locating and correcting reading difficulties,* 4th ed. Columbus, OH: Charles E. Merrill.

EKWALL, E. E. (1977). *Teacher's handbook on diagnosis and remediation in reading.* Boston: Allyn & Bacon.

FLEISHER, L. S., & JENKINS, J. R. (1983). The effect of word- and comprehension-emphasis instruction on reading performance. *Learning Disability Quarterly, 6,* 146–153.

FLORIANI, B. P. (1979). Word expansions for multiplying sight vocabulary. *The Reading Teacher, 33,* 155–157.

FREEMAN, T. J., & McLAUGHLIN, T. F. (1984). Effects of a taped-words treatment procedure on learning disabled students' sight-word oral reading. *Learning Disability Quarterly, 7,* 49–54.

GUTHRIE, F. M., & CUNNINGHAM, P. M. (1982). Teaching decoding skills in educable mentally handicapped children. *The Reading Teacher, 35,* 554–559.

JENKINS, J. R., & LARSON, K. (1979). Evaluating error-correction procedures for oral reading. *Journal of Special Education, 13,* 145–156.

JENKINS, J. R., LARSON. K., & FLEISHER, L. (1983). Effects of error correction on word recognition and reading comprehension. *Learning Disability Quarterly, 6,* 139–145.

JOHNSON, D. D., & PEARSON, T. D. (1978). *Teaching reading vocabulary.* New York: Holt, Rinehart and Winston.

JONES, K. M., TORGESEN, J. K., & SEXTON, M. A. (1987). Using computer guided practice to increase decoding fluency in learning disabled children: A study using the Hint and Hunt I Program. *Journal of Learning Disabilities, 20,* 122–128.

LOVITT, T. C. (1984). *Tactics for teaching.* Columbus, OH: Charles E. Merrill.

OTTO, W., & MCMENEMY, R. A. (1966). *Corrective and remedial teaching: Principles and practices.* Boston: Houghton Mifflin.

RINGLER, L. H., & WEBER, C. K. (1984). *A language-thinking approach to reading: Diagnosis and teaching.* San Diego: Harcourt Brace Jovanovich.

SAMUELS, S. J. (1981). Some essentials of decoding. *Exceptional Education Quarterly, 2*(1), 11–25.

Word Recognition (Fluency)

CARNINE, D., & SILBERT, J. (1979). *Direct instruction.* Columbus, OH: Charles E. Merrill.

DALLMAN, M. (1976). *Teaching the language arts in the elementary school.* Dubuque, IA: Wm. C. Brown.

JONES, K. M., TORGESEN, J. K., & SEXTON, M. A. (1987). Using computer-guided practice to increase decoding fluency in learning disabled children: A study using the Hint and Hunt I Program. *Journal of Learning Disabilities, 20,* 122–128.

LABERGE, D., & SAMUELS, S. J. (1974). Toward a theory of automatic information processing in reading. *Cognitive Psychology, 6,* 293–323.

LAURITZEN, C. (1982). A modification of repeated readings for group instruction. *The Reading Teacher, 35,* 456–458.

LOVITT, T. C. (1984). *Tactics for teaching.* Columbus, OH: Charles E. Merrill.

ROSE, T. L. (1984). The effects of two prepractice procedures on oral reading. *Journal of Learning Disabilities, 17,* 544–548.

ROSE, T. L., & BEATTIE, J. R. (1986). Relative effects of teacher-directed and taped previewing on oral reading. *Learning Disability Quarterly, 9,* 193–199.

ROSE, T. L., MCENTIRE, E., & DOWDY, C. (1982). Effects of two error-correction procedures on oral reading. *Learning Disability Quarterly, 5,* 100–105.

ROSENBERG, M. S. (1986). Error-correction during oral reading: A comparison of three techniques. *Learning Disability Quarterly, 9,* 182–192.

SAMUELS, S. J. (1979). The method of repeated readings. *The Reading Teacher, 32,* 403–408.

SAMUELS, S. J. (1981). Some essentials of decoding. *Exceptional Education Quarterly, 2*(1), 11–25.

SINGH, J., & SINGH, N. N. (1985). Comparison of word-supply and word-analysis error-correction procedure on oral reading by mentally retarded children. *American Journal of Mental Deficiency, 90,* 64–70.

SMITH, D. D. (1979). The improvement of children's oral reading through the use of teacher modeling. *Journal of Learning Disabilities, 12,* 172–175.

TIERNEY, R. J., READENCE, J. E., & DISHNER, E. K. (1980). *Reading strategies and practices: Guide for improving instruction.* Boston: Allyn & Bacon.

TORGESEN, J. K. (1986). Computers and cognition in reading: A focus on decoding fluency. *Exceptional Children, 53,* 157–162.

Meaning Skills

BLOOMER, R. H. (1962). The cloze procedure as a remedial reading exercise. *Journal of Developmental Reading, 5,* 173–181.

CARNINE, D., & SILBERT, J. (1979). *Direct instruction.* Columbus, OH: Charles E. Merrill.

CHAN, L. K. S., COLE, P. G., & BARFETT, S. (1987). Comprehension monitoring: Detection and identification of text inconsistencies by LD and normal students. *Learning Disability Quarterly, 10,* 114–124.

DALLMAN, M. (1976). *Teaching the language arts in the elementary school.* Dubuque, IA: Wm. C. Brown.

DARCH, C., & KAMEENUI, E. J. (1987). Teaching LD students critical reading skills: A systematic replication. *Learning Disability Quarterly, 10,* 82–91.

DURKIN, D. (1978–1979). What classroom observations reveal about reading comprehension instruction. *Reading Research Quarterly, 14,* 481–533.

ENGELMANN, S., & CARNINE, D. (1982). *Theory of instruction.* New York: Irvington.

ENGLERT, C. S., & THOMAS, C. C. (1987). Sensitivity to text structure in reading and writing: A comparison between learning disabled and non-learning disabled students. *Learning Disability Quarterly, 10,* 93–105.

FLAVELL, J. H. (1970). Developmental studies of mediated memory. In H. W. Reese & L. P. Lippitt (eds.), *Advances in child development and behaviour,* Vol. 5, pp. 181–221. New York: Academic Press.

FLEISHER, L. S., & JENKINS, J. R. (1983). The effect of word- and comprehension-emphasis instruction on reading performance. *Learning Disability Quarterly, 6,* 146–153.

FLEISHER, L. S., JENKINS, J. R., & PANY, D. (1979). Effects on poor readers' comprehension of training in rapid decoding. *Reading Research Quarterly, 15,* 30–48.

GOODMAN, K. S. (1967). Reading: A psycholinguistic guessing game. *Journal of the Reading Specialist, 4,* 126–135.

GOVE, M. K. (1975). Using the cloze procedure in a first-grade classroom. *The Reading Teacher, 29,* 36–38.

HANSEN, C., & LOVITT, T. (1977). An applied behavior analysis approach to reading comprehension. In J. T. Guthrie (ed.), *Cognition, curriculum, and comprehension.* Newark, DE: International Reading Association.

IDOL, L. (1987). Group story mapping: A comprehension strategy for both skilled and unskilled readers. *Journal of Learning Disabilities, 20,* 196–205.

JENKINS, J. R., & HELIOTIS, J. G. (1981). Reading comprehension instruction: Findings from behavioral and cognitive psychology. *Topics in Language Disorders, 1*(2), 25–41.

JENKINS, J. R., LARSON, K., & FLEISHER, L. (1983). Effects of error correction on word recognition and reading comprehension. *Learning Disability Quarterly, 6,* 139–145.

JENKINS, J. R., STEIN, M. L., & OSBORN, J. R. (1981). What next after decoding? Instruction and research in comprehension. *Exceptional Education Quarterly, 2*(1), 27–39.

LOVITT, T. C. (1984). *Tactics for teaching.* Columbus, OH: Charles E. Merrill.

MANDLER, J., & JOHNSON, N. (1977). Remembrance of things passed: Story structure and recall. *Cognitive Psychology, 9,* 111–151.

PANY, D., & JENKINS, J. R. (1978). Learning word meanings: A comparison of instructional procedures and effects on measures of reading comprehension with learning disabled students. *Learning Disability Quarterly, 1,* 21–32.

PATCHING, W., KAMEENUI, E., CARNINE, D., GERSTEN, R., & COLVIN, G. (1983). Direct instruction in critical reading skills. *Reading Research Quarterly, 18,* 406–418.

ROBERTS, M., & SMITH, D. D. (1980). The relationship among correct and error oral reading rates and comprehension. *Learning Disability Quarterly, 3,* 54–64.

SCHUMAKER, J. B., DENTON, P. H., & DESHLER, D. D. (1984). *The paraphrasing strategy.* Lawrence: University of Kansas Press.

TORGESEN, J. K. (1986). Computers and cognition in reading: A focus on decoding fluency. *Exceptional Children, 53,* 157–162.

WONG, B. Y. L., & JONES, W. (1982). Increasing metacomprehension in learning disabled and normally achieving students through self-questioning training. *Learning Disability Quarterly, 5,* 228–240.

Study and Content Area Skills

DARCH, C., & GERSTEN, R. (1986). Direction-setting activities in reading comprehension: A comparison of two approaches. *Learning Disability Quarterly, 9,* 235–243.

HUHN, R. H. (1980). Readiness as a variable influencing comprehension in content-area reading at the secondary level: A cognitive view. *Learning Disability Quarterly, 3,* 29–33.

KLAUER, K. J. (1984). Intentional and incidental learning with instructional texts: A meta-analysis for 1970–1980. *American Educational Research Journal, 21,* 323–339.

SCHUMAKER, J. B., DESHLER, D. D., ALLEY, G. R., WARNER, M. M., & DENTON, P. H. (1982). Multipass: A learning strategy for improving reading comprehension. *Learning Disability Quarterly, 5,* 295–304.

Curriculum-Based Assessment

ENGELMANN, S., GRANZIN, A., & SEVERSON, H. (1979). Diagnosing instruction. *Journal of Special Education, 13,* 355–363.

McCRACKEN, R. (1967). The informal reading inventory as a means of improving instruction. In T. Barrett (ed.), *The evaluation of children's reading.* Newark, DE: International Reading Association.

PRECISION TEACHING PROJECT. (1984). *Training manual* (8th ed.). Great Falls, MT: Precision Teaching Materials.

YSSELDYKE, J. E., & ALGOZZINE, B. (1983). Where to begin in diagnosing reading problems. *Topics in Learning Disabilities, 2*(4), 60–69.

9

Written Communication

Writing is the process of organizing, clarifying, and perfecting one's thoughts on paper and storing those thoughts for later use and reference. Writing is a highly important skill, as proof of students' learning academic subjects often rests upon their ability to communicate in writing.

Most students with special needs are deficient in writing. Because they can communicate with others orally, their inabilities to transmit thoughts in a logical, orderly fashion becomes apparent only when they are required to write. In this chapter, a range of written communication skills are discussed, from succeeding in the mainstream (regular education curriculum) to survival writing.

TOPICS FOR INSTRUCTION

Being able to communicate in written form requires mastery of a number of different skills. To help conceptualize the skills that constitute written communication, consider the lattice in Figure 9.1. In this case, however, although the lattice does imply a sequence or hierarchy, many of the targets placed high on the lattice should be taught concurrently with skills found lower on this visual display. Also, some students with special needs might not master or be presented with all of the skills listed on the lattice. Regardless, it does provide a visual representation of the major components of the written language curriculum.

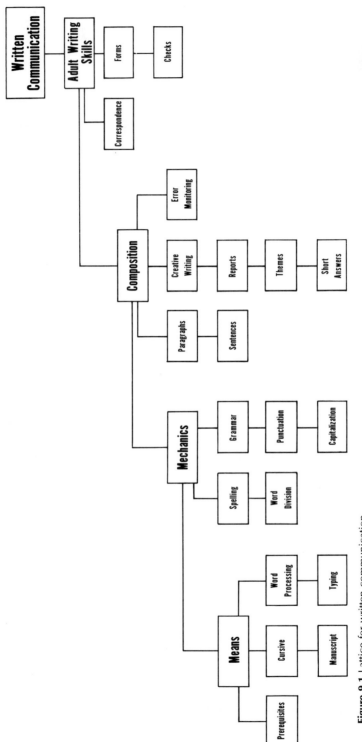

Figure 9.1 Lattice for written communication.

Means of Written Communication

This section is devoted to the foundation skill of written communication: the formation of letters and symbols. There are various means of putting information into the written mode. At school, handwriting is the most commonly used form; certainly, it is the means used by students to take notes, write in-class themes and term papers, and take tests. At home, business, and schools, typing and word processing have gained in popularity and are becoming the norm. For students whose handwriting is poor—and this is particularly true for most students with special needs—knowing how to type and use a microcomputer and a word-processing program can compensate for their poor handwriting; moreover, these skills allow them to concentrate their efforts on content rather than form. Students freed from the constraints of handwriting often improve the spelling, grammar, and organization of their written assignments.

Prewriting Skills

Before children can learn to write letters and symbols, they must possess some prerequisite skills. For example, students must be able to hold a pencil correctly, draw straight lines at different angles, draw curved lines at different angles, draw freehand lines, and draw a variety of shapes in which lines are joined and crossed at specific points. Students also need good spatial orientation and directional sense to succeed in handwriting. It is important, for example, for students to understand the concepts of left-to-right sequencing, up and down, and around. It is possible to teach these concepts concurrently with letter formation, but instruction proceeds most efficiently if these skills are already mastered.

Before handwriting instruction is actually initiated, the teacher must determine the handedness of each student. Some 11% of the population is left-handed, and accommodations must be made for those students. For example, when writing at a blackboard, the right-handed student stands to the left and the left-handed student to the right of the letters or symbols being written. The left-handed student should place the top of the paper in a clockwise position (to the right), while the right-handed child should place the paper square to the body or turned slightly to the left. Since the writing motion for left-handed persons requires them to push rather than pull their pens, care must be taken to find a pen with a point that moves easily across paper. Left-handed youngsters should not be allowed to cup their hands over the letters being formed; first because this is not a comfortable position and second because it impairs later speed and proficiency. Enstrom (1968) even suggests that during the initial period of handwriting instruction, left-handed students be separated from right-handed students to avoid unnecessary confusion. Regardless of the precautions taken, it is important for teachers to be aware of the handedness of their students and plan instruction accordingly.

Some students have difficulty holding a pencil correctly; their hands slip too far down. Turnbull and Schulz (1979) suggest that a grip be placed on a pencil for students with poor motor abilities. A ball of clay or piece of sponge molded around the pencil approximately three-quarters of an inch from the pencil point might help students with this problem. Other students with minor motor problems find that writing with larger pencils is easier than writing with standard-sized pencils. Teachers should allow students to find and use the size most comfortable for them until later, when their fine motor skills are better developed.

Manuscript (Printing)

The debate about the merits of teaching students to write using the manuscript form seems perpetual. Although it is relatively easy to teach to young children and does more closely match the print that appears in basal readers, it is a skill that is taught and used for only a few years and then dropped from the curriculum. Long ago, Strauss and Lehtinen (1951, p. 187) suggested that learning disabled students not be taught manuscript writing but instead learn only the cursive.

> We have found it advantageous for several reasons to make an early start in teaching connected writing to the brain-injured child and to omit specific instruction in the manuscript form. The perceptional disturbances of the brain-injured child act as a definite handicap in acceptably spacing letters and words. Perception of a word form as a unified whole is aided when the letters of the word are actually joined to form a whole. Connected or cursive writing also seems to lend itself more effectively to developing a kinesthetic perception of word forms.

Also, for students who have a propensity to reverse letters, instruction in manuscript should be discontinued and instruction in cursive initiated. Because of the way letters are formed and joined in cursive writing, the opportunity for making reversals is reduced. The frequency of writing a letter *b* backwards in the cursive form is substantially lower than is printing a *b* in reverse. The confusion between *b* and *d,* and *p* and *q,* is not as common when using the cursive means of writing because the letters have more definitive characteristics.

One other reason for not teaching manuscript printing to academically deficient youngsters is efficiency of learning and instruction. Why spend time teaching a skill that is soon discontinued from the school curriculum? For students who have a difficult time mastering academic tasks, it is more beneficial to spend classroom instructional time on the skill expected in the later school years. Unfortunately, for some students, there is no choice. If a student must use manuscript in the regular education setting, then that student needs to acquire and become proficient in its use.

Cursive

Whether students begin learning to write using the manuscript or cursive mode seems to be more of an administrative decision than one based on empirical findings. In some school districts, children first learn to print. In others, manuscript is not presented and students begin their writing experiences with the cursive form. There is not a definite instructional sequence that begins with manuscript writing and terminates with mastery of the cursive system. When manuscript is taught first, usually instruction on cursive begins in the middle of the second grade. Regardless, there is no evidence that mastery of manuscript writing is a prerequisite to success in learning the cursive form.

As with all other academic areas, there are at least three stages of learning that teachers must address when teaching students to write: acquisition, proficiency, and maintenance. A substantial amount of time is spent in schools teaching students how to write using the cursive system. Children spend hours practicing correct letter formation. Once the skill is acquired, however, teachers must help students become proficient. Youngsters must be able to write fast enough to be able to complete assignments in other academic areas (history, social studies, literature). If a student is not proficient in writing skills, other subject areas will suffer. For example, if a student is too slow in forming letters, dictation is an impossible task. Spelling assignments are unfinished, possibly not because of a spelling deficiency, but because of a writing deficiency.

Typing

Researchers still have not carefully studied how students with special needs benefit from learning how to type. There is little evidence to guide teachers on many important aspects relating to the relationship between written communication skills and typing. For example, at what point are students ready to learn to type? Does typing positively influence students' writing form and content? Since the introduction of microcomputers into school settings, however, there is growing clinical evidence that being able to type enhances written communication skills.

Individuals for whom handwriting is laborious and difficult frequently avoid all writing tasks. This ultimately could lead to the selection of careers that do not require them to write, not because their interests direct them to those occupations, but because they seek to avoid writing.

Word Processing

Although one does not have to be a proficient typist to use a word-processing program with a microcomputer, as with handwriting, proficiency is ultimately necessary. Without proficiency in typewriting, attention cannot be focused on the content of what is being written.

Because of the availability of microcomputers in schools, many youngsters are learning to use the computer as a writing tool. A number of easy-to-use word-processing programs are available. Probably, the most popular one developed for child use is *Bankstreet Writer*. Once this program is mastered, the transition to more powerful and complex programs is relatively easy.

Mechanics of Written Communication

Possessing manuscript, cursive, typing, or word-processing skills certainly does not guarantee proficiency in written communication. They are only the means by which information is put onto paper. When at least one skill has been mastered, instruction can be initiated on the mechanics of written communication; the way words are put together to communicate with others.

Unfortunately, mastery of oral communication does not ensure mastery of written communication. Although the basic rules used to communicate orally are the same as those for writing, tolerance for incorrect usage is greater in oral communication. When words are put on paper, correct spelling, grammar, and punctuation, variation in sentence construction, and some consistency in style are expected. The youngster's writing shown in Figure 9.2 shows phonetic spelling and grammar correlated to his oral language. This child grew up in the Ozark region of Missouri, and his written communication abilities reflect his regional upbringing. Regardless of where individuals are from, they are expected to use standard English in their written communication. The mechanics

I wint on The flote trip. Tharr wase a worldpool in The mitl. a man wase in The world pool and I wint in The tree house. in The tree house you cood see yorself in parpl. Then I wint in The fluded mins and a man skard me.

Figure 9.2 Sample of a child's writing that reflects his oral language dialect.

of written communication are fairly precise, and the demands on the learner are considerable.

Spelling

Spelling is difficult for many youngsters because standard English does not follow consistent rules. There seem to be as many exceptions to the rules as there are rules. For students with learning disabilities, spelling should be a particular area of concern because they are much poorer spellers than other students, even low achievers (Carpenter & Miller, 1982; Gerber, 1984; Moran, 1981).

Recently, many teachers have changed their spelling curriculum so that it includes words students hear and use daily. Most teachers, however, have retained the traditional approach for teaching spelling, a critical part of which is the spelling workbook. Although a number of different publishers have their own versions, they are remarkably similar. A list, usually twenty to twenty-five words, is generally presented on Monday. Every day a different type of exercise is followed (one day a paragraph with the new words is read and dissected, dictionary and phonetic spellings are practiced another day). The weekly culminating experience usually is a Friday test. Such has been the practice for years, and probably will remain so. There are several reasons for retaining the status quo. First, for many youngsters the procedure works and they become better spellers. Second, at least thirty minutes of the school day is planned for the teacher; the lesson plan and student materials are provided.

For students who are unable to learn to spell through the traditional approach, even with added interventions such as those discussed in the "teaching tactics" section found later in this chapter, a radically different program is available. *Corrective Spelling Through Morphographics* has been remarkably successful with a variety of students above the fourth grade level. This packaged program consists of 140 lessons and includes student workbooks, daily lessons, and a student evaluation system. The program teaches spelling through morphographs: prefixes, suffixes, and root words. For groups of students who have difficulty in mastering spelling, this program and its approach might be an excellent alternative to the spelling tradition.

Word Division

Breaking words into syllables is a useful skill. It can help students spell better. Also, it is required when a word is broken at the end of a line of writing and is completed on the following line. Although most word-processing programs automatically move whole words to the next line of type, students must still complete many assignments in manuscript or cursive writing and, consequently, must learn to divide words. Some teachers have students say the word aloud and clap with each sound unit to learn how a word is broken. However, the most reliable method of word division is to use a dictionary or word guide. Teaching students to use these two kinds of reference books is important because they are indispensable when writing compositions.

Capitalization

Capital letters are used to distinguish proper nouns and adjectives from common nouns and adjectives and to indicate the beginning of new sentences, salutations, and direct quotations. The rules for capitalizing the first letter in specific words are straightforward and are the simplest mechanical form for students to learn. Direct instruction on capitalization should begin in the early elementary grades. Practice materials can be easily adapted from standard English texts and workbooks.

Grammar

This is probably the most difficult component of the mechanics of written communication. Although the rules of grammar provide general guidelines, exceptions and variations make mastery difficult. Even academically talented youngsters often do not master these skills until early adulthood. No student will learn the vast number of grammatical subskills without considerable practice and guided instruction.

A number of newly developed programs and strategies teach grammatical skills as they teach sentence and paragraph writing (see "topics of instruction" section for more details). However, each of these has as a prerequisite the ability to identify parts of speech. In particular, students must know nouns and verbs or subjects and predicates. Activities where students identify these components of sentences can begin early with simple sentences, usually by fourth or fifth grade. Once students can identify nouns and verbs, they then should be taught to identify other parts of speech (pronouns, adjectives, adverbs, conjunctions, prepositions, and interjections).

Although many students with special needs will not become sophisticated writers, they can develop adequate writing skills. To do so, however, they must at least be able to use correctly the basic parts of speech necessary to form simple and compound sentences.

Punctuation

As with grammar, punctuation is now taught through structured instruction about sentence and paragraph writing (see "topics of instruction"). Punctuation follows consistent rules of application. As students learn to write a compound sentence, for example, they are taught that a comma is placed before the conjunction, and they learn that a period ends all sentences. As with all writing, however, if opportunities to write are not provided, if instruction is not direct, and if corrective feedback is infrequent, punctuation will not be mastered.

Composition

Students do not master written communication if they are not required to write. Although writing is not as important in today's society as it once was, it is still a vital process used in daily life. Writing essays is not the typical leisure pastime of most Americans. In some professions, however, it is a requirement, and for success in school it is a necessity. To write in composition format, a means of written communication must be selected and the mechanics of writing employed. In Figure 9.3 a high school senior's handicap is particularly apparent because of faulty mechanical elements in his written communication.

A norm-referenced test of written language is available (Hammill & Larsen, 1978) that directly measures students' writing abilities by utilizing both contrived and spontaneous writing samples to assess students' performance levels in the following areas: vocabulary, thematic maturity, thought units, handwriting, spelling, word usage, and style. The test areas could easily be transformed into instructional areas for those who wish to develop their own instructional sequence in the area of written communication.

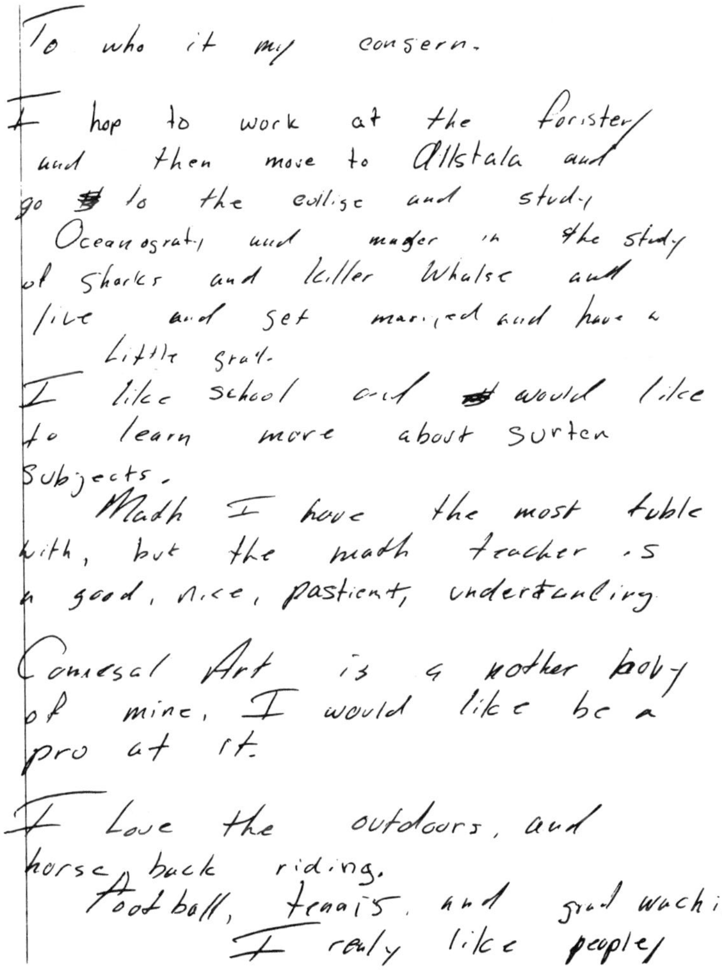
To who it my consern.

I hop to work at the foristery and then move to Allstala and go to the cullige and study Oceanogratly and mader in the study of Sharks and killer Whalse and live and get maried and have a Little girl.
I like school and would like to learn more about surten Subjects.
Math I have the most tuble with, but the math teacher is a good, nice, pastient, understanding.

Comesal Art is a nother hoby of mine, I would like be a pro at it.

I Love the outdoors, and horse back riding.
Foot ball, tennis, and girl waching.
I realy like people

Figure 9.3 A high school senior's plans for after graduation.

Functional Composition

Functional composition—writing themes, short answers, and reports—is the writing most commonly used in school and business. In high school, for example, students must express themselves and demonstrate their knowledge by writing book reports, themes, research papers, answers to questions at the end of chapters, and answers to questions on tests. Evaluation of the written content is biased by quality of the means used (legibility), accuracy of the mechanics used (correct spelling, punctuation, grammar), and the logical presentation of the information. Students who cannot write legibly should be allowed to type or use a word-processing program, so the means of writing does not negatively influence their work's evaluation. When students can see the written product clearly, often improvement in the mechanics of their writing occurs. When students are taught to write with structure (using topic sentences, examples and explanations, and summary or concluding sentences), often the form of writing is better.

One important key to improving functional composition is the ability to monitor one's own errors (referred to in the research literature as *error monitoring*). Writing improves when writers use self-correction procedures (see "teaching tactics" for more details). Students must learn to proof and correct their written work. This is an important aspect in the writing process. Therefore, teachers should not only allow students to monitor for errors, but also insist upon it. Accepting first drafts of students' functional writing is only the first step in writing instruction. Working in class individually or in groups using the jigsaw technique (where one student checks for capitalization, another for spelling errors, another for punctuation) to correct drafts of student writing is a critical learning activity. Unfortunately, it is often omitted from writing instruction.

Creative Writing

The problems of defining creativity are not of concern here. Probably a better topic heading would be *Interesting Writing*. The writing of many students with special needs can be typified by its shortness, use of few words over and over again, and illogical ordering of thoughts. In school, writing judged as "creative" is marked by its difference in vocabulary and variation in themes. Although many teachers believe that creativity and, thereby, creative writing cannot be taught, recent research indicates otherwise. Fortner (1986), for example, showed that students who were exposed to daily problem-solving activities, such as brainstorming sessions, do write with more expression on a greater variety of topics. She cautions teachers that students need to be encouraged to take risks and share their thoughts, even if they might be unusual or incorrect.

In another study, Kraetsch (1981) also showed that written productivity and diversity can be greatly influenced by direct instructions. When her subject was told to "write as many words and ideas as you can about the picture," he did so. When told to write more, using more adverbs and adjectives, each time he responded significantly to the teacher's directions.

Some older studies have also shown that students' writing can become more diverse. Maloney and Hopkins (1973) gave fourth, fifth, and sixth graders a topic noun and told the students to write a ten-sentence story. Each student's story was rated and points were given for each of the following: each adjective, adverb, action verb, different sentence beginning, different adjective, different adverb, prepositional phrase, compound sentence, and sentences over eight words in length. The classes were divided into two teams, and a modified version of the good behavior game (see Chapter 4) was employed. The students competed against each other, and whichever team received the most points on a given day could leave for recess five minutes early. Interestingly, raters judged the students' writing subjectively to be more creative when the above variables were increased.

Glover and Sautter (1977) took a slightly different tack to improve the creative writing of junior and senior high school students. They define creativity as having four different components: fluency (number of different responses, points, or illustrations), elaboration (number of words per response, point, or illustration), originality (responses different from classmates), and flexibility (number of different response forms: analogies, syntheses, comparisons). Reinforcement, practice, and instructions were given for each of the four components. Although all the variables did change, elaboration was the most responsive and originality the least subject to improvement.

Survival (Adult) Writing

There are a number of writing skills all people should possess if they are to cope successfully in everyday life. For many adults, the use of written communication markedly decreases once the school years are over. Some basic writing abilities, however, are required by society. If students are to be independent adults, these skills must be mastered. Unforunately, many of these writing skills are not taught in most school settings. Only a slight modification of the educational curriculum, however, is required for them to be included.

One writing skill that is very important in modern society is the signature. Not only must students learn to write their names, but they should also understand the implications of placing their signatures at the bottom of documents. Another commonly needed skill is check writing. This requires not only a signature, but also the ability to write dates and money amounts using both symbols and number names. Correct spelling of numbers often is not included in our educational curriculum, but it is a common requirement of daily life. The spelling of some numbers causes students particular difficulty. There is no reason why they could not be written down somewhere in the checkbook for reference. Some junior and senior high school teachers who use various token or reinforcement systems have their students write checks to purchase freetime and other privileges.

People must fill out various forms periodically (job applications, loan and credit applications). Most forms require that the individual print (or type) his or her name, address, phone number, social security number, and employer's name and address. Job applications ask the individual to list former employers, personal references, and school attended. Classroom instruction on how to fill out forms and applications is advisable, and certainly a worthwhile expenditure of instructional time. There are even commercially available workbooks for students to use to gain accuracy and some proficiency in these tasks. For many youngsters, a prepared sheet listing all their previous employers' names and addresses and other required information is helpful for completing various forms.

Being able to write simple letters and notes is useful. Many people with special needs have relatives and friends who live in other parts of the country and find that long-distance phone calls are too expensive. Being able to write simple notes and knowing the proper form to address envelopes are valuable skills.

Notetaking is another related writing skill that is both useful and necessary. Being able to write down the time and place of various appointments is useful for success in daily life, as is taking down information over the phone, including directions to places of business or friends' homes. In school, being able to take notes during classes is essential for receiving passing grades.

CURRICULUM-BASED ASSESSMENT AND EVALUATION

For instructional planning, teachers must know which skills their students possess and which they do not. This is true for all curriculum areas, but is extremely important for written communication. Students must possess the basic tools of written language if they are to write at even a functional level. They should acquire and become proficient in handwriting. A number of desired rates or aim scores have been suggested. The following letter-writing rates per minute are the most commonly used by teachers as goals: twenty-five letters for first graders, forty for third graders, forty-five for fourth graders, fifty for fifth graders, seventy for sixth graders, and eighty for eighth graders.

Hall (1981), through her study of numerous writing samples, found seven types of writing errors (see Table 9.1) that inhibit students' acquisition and proficiency in handwriting. Identifying these and then targeting instruction on errors should facilitate mastery of this component of written communication. For students whose errors are concentrated in several of these areas, teachers should evaluate the effectiveness of instruction by keeping daily percentage scores (except for speed when rate should be the measure used) on each of the error types receiving direct instruction.

A relationship exists between quality of student writing and rate of performance (Van Houten, Hill, & Parsons, 1975; Van Houten et al., 1974). Second, fourth, and fifth graders participated in their studies. Instead of using points or tokens as the intervention strategy, they utilized precise academic feedback and public posting of the children's scores. The children were told to beat their own writing rate (repetitious and nonsense sentences were not counted). In both

Table 9.1
Error Analysis for Handwriting

TYPE	DEFINITION
Letter formation	The letter is not correctly formed (an "a" is not closed, and "i" is not dotted, a "t" is not crossed).
Letter substitution	A letter or stroke is substituted for another (a capital for a lowercase letter, an "e" for an "i".
Spacing	Letters or words are either too far apart or too close together.
Spatial organization	Words or letters are not written on lines of the paper; letter size is inconsistent.
Slant	Letters are written in a variety of directions.
Illegibility	The written product is messy, with many erasures, strike-overs, and write-overs.
Speed	The product is incomplete because the student took too long to write the assignment.

studies, increased rate of writing correlated with improved quality of the children's stories. Through this research, some information about desired rate for story writing can be gleaned. During intervention, the second graders' mean writing rate was twelve words per minute; the fourth graders' averaged nine words per minute (one class achieved thirteen and the other five); and the fifth graders' mean was fourteen. Although no normed data are available, these mean scores might give some indication of acceptable limits.

TEACHING TACTICS

If students are to develop the skills required to communicate in writing their thoughts and knowledge, they must first become proficient in using handwriting, spelling, and grammar. Instruction in these prerequisites must be efficient so that students are adequately prepared to write themes, compositions, and reports required in the study of such subjects as literature, history, and social studies. Tactics that lead some youngsters to efficient mastery of these skills do not lead to mastery for others. Therefore, teachers need to be aware of a variety of proven teaching tactics for written language. Table 9.2 lists a number of different instructional interventions for written language. Also, the narratives in this section give more detail on selected tactics and strategies that are particularly applicable in this curriculum area.

Handwriting Acquisition

Handwriting is a component of written language that teachers—particularly at the elementary level—consider highly important. Although its importance seems to diminish as individuals get older, it is an instructional topic that con-

Table 9.2

Tactics for Written Communication

INSTRUCTIONAL TARGET	STAGE OF LEARNING	POSSIBLE TACTICS

Prewriting skills
  Identify letters
    orally
  Gross writing
    movements
	Acquisition	Drill
		  Group
		  Individual
		Fingerpainting
		Painting with a brush
		Coloring
		Practicing writing movements
		  In sand or on sandpaper
		  with finger

Hold a stylus		Painting Coloring Scribbling with a pencil Writing on a magic slate

Draw straight and
  curved lines at
  different angles
		Use geometric templates
		Tracing
		Copying

Draw freehand
  lines
		Joining two preprinted places on
		  paper (travel from the house to
		  the school)
		Dot-to-dot exercises

Left to right
  sequence
		Drawing lines from go sign to
		  stop sign
		Block designs

Manuscript and
  cursive
	Acquisition	Drill practice
		  List copying
		  Paragraph copying
		Cover-copy-write
		Trace letters
		  With fingers
		  With stylus
		  That are incomplete
		Demonstration plus permanent
		  model
		Special writing paper
		Space gauges
		Arrows on where to start letters
		Slant indicators
		Large to small lines
		Error drill

	Advanced
	  acquisition
		Self-management
		  Self-evaluation
		  Self-instruction
		  Self-correction
		  Self-selection of daily
		    procedure

	Proficiency	Freetime Rewards Beat Your Own Rate game Shorten session time

(continued)

Table 9.2 (*Continued*)

INSTRUCTIONAL TARGET	STAGE OF LEARNING	POSSIBLE TACTICS
Reversals	Acquisition	Instructions
		Demonstrations
Typing/word processing	Acquisition	Instruction on typing programs
		Instruction on computer programs
	Proficiency	Computer games
		Rewards
Spelling	Acquisition	Flow list
		Overcorrection (positive practice)
		Parent tutoring
		Distributed practice
		Cover-copy-compare
		Rewards
		Freetime
		Privileges
		Group contingencies
		Behavior games
		Modeling
		Error drill
		Self-correction
		Self-questioning
		strategy
		Dictionary skills
		Typing
		Time delay
Composition	Acquisition	PENS strategy
		11-sentence paragraph
		Demonstration
		Group writing
		Practice
		Instructions
		Jigsaw technique
		Self-monitoring
		Generalization
		Self-correction
		Error monitoring
		COPS
		WRITER
Creative writing	Acquisition	Praise for risk taking
		Brainstorming activities
		Behavior games
		Group sharing sessions
		Instructions
		Rewards

sumes a considerable amount of school time. With a more precise sequence and more efficient instruction, students require less instructional time to acquire and become proficient in handwriting. This savings in instructional time could then be reallocated to other written communication topics.

Towle (1978) offers a ten-part instructional sequence for handwriting instruction:

1. Copy straight lines.
2. Copy curved lines.
3. Copy letters from a model in close proximity to the student.
4. Write letters from memory (after just seeing the correct formation).
5. Copy letters from a model placed at some distance from the student (on the blackboard).
6. Write letters from memory.
7. Copy letters sequenced in words from a model in close proximity to the student.
8. Copy letters sequenced in words from a model placed at some distance from the student.
9. Copy sentences in close proximity to the student.
10. Copy sentences from a model placed at some distance from the student.

Some researchers (Towle, 1978) suggest that letters be taught in clusters; letters with common characteristics (swing up, swing over) are taught as units. Hansen and her colleagues (Hansen, 1978), however, could not give validity to this system of letter presentation through their research, which found no pattern of how children acquired correct letter formation. There were no consistently troublesome letters, and no definite pattern of specific letters acquired first. All of her students learned to write, but each mastered letters in a different order.

Hansen describes a five-level cursive writing program developed at the Experimental Education Unit of the University of Washington:

1. Say letter names (and print them if the child knows how).
2. Write lowercase letters.
3. Connect letters.
4. Write capital letters.
5. Write in context.

Each day while the program was in effect, the student wrote the alphabet. A maximum of five letters drawn from a pool of letters the student could not form legibly was taught and drilled daily. Once a letter was mastered (written legibly two out of three days), it was dropped from the daily list and another one added. If a student mastered a letter without direct instruction, it was no longer included in the pool of letters from which the daily lists were drawn. Connecting letters and writing sentences were taught in similar fashion.

There are other, less comprehensive tactics teachers have used to help children acquire legible handwriting. For example, students who do not use the correct slant often are given writing paper with slant indicators preprinted on the page. Students who have a tendency to write too large are given paper on which the top lines are some distance apart; as the child works down the page the distance between the lines decreases, forcing the student to write smaller. Space gauges can be placed on a writing worksheet to help students judge the appropriate width of letters and the proper space to be left between words.

When specific letters are in error, teachers often resort to the "copy-cover-write" technique as a form of error drill. Often times an index card with problem letters correctly formed is taped to the student's desk so the student can have a referent as writing assignments are produced. For students who have a direction problem, arrows and starting indicators can be added to the index card.

Reversals

Written reversals are most predominant when students print. It is important for teachers to remember that most young children make reversals when first learning to write. This is part of the normal developmental process and should not be viewed as unacceptable. Several early studies of young children's academic performance clearly indicate that reversals correlate with age (the younger the student, the higher the probability of reversals in written work). Davidson (1934, 1935) and Hildreth (1934) demonstrated that with increasing maturity and experience, children's frequency of reversing letters and symbols decreased. In those studies, practically all kindergarten children confused *b* and *d,* and *q* and *p.* This tendency was still prevalent among first graders, but to a lesser degree. Whether these data suggest that no direct remediation efforts should be initiated until second grade has not been answered through research. Logically, it seems that teachers should not adopt a laissez-faire attitude about reversals in young children and should at least provide corrective feedback when they occur. On the other hand, referral to a class for learning disabled students merely because a kindergartener reverses letters does not seem reasonable either.

A substantial amount of literature is available indicating that reversal problems in students' written work can be remediated through direct instructional techniques. Through modeling and corrective feedback, Stromer (1975, 1977) remediated several students' number and letter reversal tendencies. Hasazi and Hasazi (1972) remediated a student's digit reversals (writing 21 for 12) through an ignoring and praising procedure. Smith and Lovitt (1973) remediated a boy's b/d reversal problem by showing him an error (written by the teacher on an index card) and instructing the boy not to write a *b* for a *d.* One interesting feature of this study is the finding that, at least for this child, the frequency of reversals related to the position the letter had in the word (initial, medial, or final). During instruction, they targeted for remediation the letter (d) and the position (initial) most frequently in error. As that letter in that position was corrected, the student's pervasive b/d reversal problem was eliminated.

More recently, Deno and Chiang (1979) demonstrated that letter reversals can be ameliorated through the use of reinforcement contingencies. They believe that "reversal errors can be explained in educational rather than neurological terms" (p. 45). Certainly the data available indicate that teachers should try direct remediation efforts with students who have a tendency to reverse letters or numbers.

Handwriting Proficiency

Fluency in handwriting (or its substitutes, such as typing and word processing) is important, for without it, mastery of written language is impossible. Without this proficiency, students are unable to succeed in spelling, dictation, note taking, or other vital areas in upper elementary, middle, or high school. Besides the tactics listed in Table 9.2, teachers have found two other tactics invaluable in helping students increase their writing speed. One of these is that teachers gradually shorten the time scheduled for completing writing assignments in class. The other is that teachers allow freetime for students who have completed and corrected their assignments early. With this tactic, the remainder of a time period allotted for writing is given to students to use as they please. Other teachers have used games, such as Beat Your Own Rate, where students evaluate and graph their daily writing performance and are rewarded for increasing the number of words written in a set amount of time. Regardless of the tactic used, it is important that once letters and symbols are formed correctly, and legibility is no longer an issue, quality and quantity (proficiency) of writing become a target of instruction.

Spelling Acquisition

Spelling is a well-researched topic within the written communication curriculum. A large number of tactics have proven effective to improve students' spelling scores. Table 9.2 lists many of these. Further details are provided here about four more tactics.

Some tactics modify or adapt the traditional spelling approach and are effective in increasing students' spelling scores. Many are easy to implement and make an academic subject that is often boring to students a little more interesting. In one of these tactics, four spelling tests are given each week (Tuesday through Friday). Once students score 100% on that week's list, they are excused from spelling for the rest of the week and can use the time allotted for spelling in free activities.

Many teachers who use a positive practice overcorrection procedure also give more than one spelling test per week. For any word missed on a test, the student must use the word correctly in five sentences and provide the correct spelling, its correct phonetic spelling, its part of speech, and its complete dictionary definition. Although this tactic is drastic, teachers nevertheless often incorporate it in homework assignments. Students work long hours on such assignments, but the payoff is big: students significantly reduce their spelling errors when this instructional tactic is used.

Considerable evidence exists that the number of words presented to students each day can influence how well they remember the correct spellings. For many, presenting twenty or more words at one time is too difficult. When, however, distributed practice is used, only five or six words are presented daily, and students show great improvement on weekly spelling tests covering the entire list of words.

The last tactic does not adopt the traditional spelling approach. Rather, it requires teachers to create their own spelling lists, but its power and potential for enhanced generalization warrants consideration. Recently, cognitive training has received considerable attention in the research literature. Through this method students are taught specific information and are then taught a strategy that focuses their attention so they can apply this information correctly. Wong (1986) describes such a cognitive strategy for spelling. In her training procedure, students were taught to break words into syllables. They then learned about the structure of words (root words and suffixes) and how spelling changes according to the word's part of speech. She then taught the students the self-questioning strategy shown in Figure 9.4 and found that the students' spelling scores improved greatly.

Knowing about tactics proven influential in improving students' spelling is important, but knowing about those tactics proven ineffective is important as well. Two such instructional techniques, which research has shown to be of no instructional value, are the following:

(1) Vocabulary is first presented to students in sentences or paragraphs, with the supposition that if students understood a word in context, they could learn its spelling more easily (however, that has not been the case). And (2) students are made to write their spelling words in the air, on the supposition that they would be helped to visualize the words as they traced letters and thus would be able to spell the words correctly (this also has not been the case). Unguided study, as well, has proven to be of little or no instructional value. On the other hand, the tactics listed in Table 9.2 are verified through research and clinical practice. When seeking tactics to improve spelling performance, these techniques should prove to be effective.

---

1. Do I know this word?
2. How many syllables do I hear in this word? (Write down the number.)
3. I'll spell out the word.
4. Do I have the right number of syllables down?
5. If yes, is there any part of the word I'm not sure of the spelling? I'll underline that part and try spelling the word again.
6. Now, does it look right to me? If it does, I'll leave it alone. If it still doesn't look right, I'll underline the part I'm not sure of the spelling and try again. (If the word I spelled does not have the right number of syllables, let me hear the word in my head again, and find the missing syllable. Then I'll go back to steps 5 and 6.)
7 When I finish spelling, I tell myself I'm a good worker. I've tried hard at spelling.

Figure 9.4 Wong's self-questioning strategy. (*Source:* B. Y. L. Wong, A cognitive approach to teaching spelling, *Exceptional Children* (Council for Exceptional Children), *53*(2), (1986), 172.)

Simple sentences:		Compound sentences:
S	V	I, cI
SS	V	
S	VV	I; I
SS	VV	

Figure 9.5 PENS sentence formulas for simple and compound sentences, where I stands for independent clause; S for a subject; V, a verb; and c, conjunction. (*Source:* J. B. Schumaker & J. Sheldon, *The Sentence Writing Strategy*: Instructor's Manual, Lawrence, KS: University of Kansas, 1985).

Sentence Writing Acquisition and Generalization

The University of Kansas Institute for Research in Learning Disabilities (KU-IRLD) recently developed a comprehensive instructional program that teaches students a strategy for writing sentences ranging from simple to compound-complex.[1] The strategy, referred to as PENS (*p*ick a formula, *e*xplore words to fit the formula, *n*ote the words, *s*ubject-verb identification), provides structure to the mechanics of writing. A prerequisite for entering the program is the ability to identify nouns and verbs or subjects and predicates. The students are taught formulas for sentence constructions, such as those shown in Figure 9.5. After considerable instruction with student workbooks that provide practice and drill to encourage mastery of subskills through criterion performance tests, students are taught a strategy to form their own sentences. The cognitive strategy, shown in Figure 9.6, is then taught to the students. They are encouraged to use this strategy in all situations where it can be applied, to subjects such as history, social studies, and English. Students are allowed to use cue cards to help them remember the strategy in as many classroom settings as possible.

The field test data from this program are most exciting. High school students' written assignments from their regular education classes were scored for both pre- and posttests. Using a strict scoring system, both the percentages of complete and complicated sentences were judged, with remarkable increases noted on the posttests. Students in the first experimental groups did not often apply this strategy learned in the special education classes to their regular education classes. Therefore, several components were added to the program. Among these components are teaching students rationales for using the strategy in a regular education setting. Also, students are encouraged by their regular classroom teachers to apply the strategy. When they do so, their special education teacher rewards and praises them for appropriate application.

As students learn to write sentences, and use correct grammar and punctuation for their sentences, they also learn to write paragraphs. Once students have mastered the use of the formulas and the PENS strategy, they are then given topics to write about. The improvement in the students' writing clearly

---

[1]Teachers are required to receive intensive training in the PENS strategy before they are allowed to receive teacher's manuals or student workbooks. For information about the required training, contact Dr. Fran Clark, University of Kansas Institute for Research on Learning Disabilities, 206 Carruth-O'Leary Hall, University of Kansas, Lawrence, KS 66045.

1. **P**ick a formula.
2. **E**xplore words to fit the formula.
3. **N**ote the words.
4. **S**ubject-verb identification
   a. Look for the action or state-of-being word(s) to find the verb.
   b. Ask the "who" or "what" question to find the subject.

Figure 9.6 The mnemonic for the sentence writing strategy developed by KU-IRLD. (*Source:* J. B. Schumaker and J. Sheldon, *The sentence writing strategy* (Lawrence, KS: University of Kansas, 1985).)

indicates that most students with special needs can learn to write well enough to succeed in the regular education curriculum when instruction is carefully controlled and evaluated.

Paragraph Writing Acquisition

For the highly successful PENS and WRITER strategies to work, specialized teacher training to use the strategy and its related materials is required. For those who cannot arrange for this training, another excellent strategy, developed by Ray (1986) and called the *eleven-sentence paragraph,* provides structure to students' writing (see Table 9.3). Whether they are given a topic or are using one of their own, students begin their paragraphs with an opening topical sentence. Within the body of the paragraph, they provide three reasons that justify the opening statement. For each reason, an example is given and an additional sentence that supports the example is included. The paragraph concludes with a summary statement or a rephrasing of the opening topic sentence. This paragraph writing technique is particularly helpful to students who have difficulty organizing their thoughts or presenting their ideas logically. For example, a sample paragraph, written using this technique, is found on Figure 9.7. Before learning to write an eleven-sentence paragraph, this child's written work was unorganized and incomplete.

Self-Management

Students need to check their own work or proof their own written products. Low-achieving students tend not to check their work because they might not understand the importance of the appearance of their products, they do not focus attention, or they do not know how to do so (Schumaker, Nolan, & Deshler, 1985). For these reasons, the KU-IRLD developed a program to teach students to *error monitor.* The error monitoring strategy, often referred to as COPS (*c*apitalization, *o*verall appearance, *p*unctuation, *s*pelling) and WRITER,[2] teaches

---

[2]Teachers are required to receive intensive training in the WRITER strategy before they are allowed to receive teacher's manuals or student workbooks. For information about this training, contact Dr. Fran Clark, University of Kansas Institute for Research on Learning Disabilities, 206 Carruth-O'Leary Hall, University of Kansas, Lawrence, KS 66045.

Table 9.3
The Eleven-Sentence Paragraph

SENTENCE	WORDING AND PUNCTUATION	EXAMPLE
1. Write topic sentence.	There are three reasons why . . .	There are three reasons why dance is a challenging art.
2. State the first of the three reasons. (Be sure to include comma in structure.)	First, . . .	First, dance is physically demanding.
3. Give an example.	For example, . . .	For example, it requires a great deal of physical coordination and endurance.
4. Support the example.		The dances taught require intense balancing, lifting, bending, and stretching of the body.
5. State the second reason.	Second, . . .	Second, dance is mentally stimulating.
6. Give an example.	For example, . . .	For example, it tests the dancer's ability to recall movement quickly.
7. Support the example.		It is important to have total concentration to accomplish the task well.
8. State the third reason.	Third, . . .	Third, dance is emotionally challenging.
9. Give an example.	For example, . . .	For example, the perseverance necessary is tiring.
10. Support the example.		The repetition required of the same pattern to achieve perfection is phenomenal.
11. Conclude with a summary or restate topic sentence.		Dance is truly a mentally, physically, and emotionally demanding art.

Source: R. A. Ray, unpublished manuscript (1986), University of New Mexico, Albuquerque, NM. Used by permission.

students to correct their written paragraphs. To learn the strategies (*w*rite, *r*ead, *in*terrogate, *e*xecute, *r*eread) (see Figure 9.8), students must pass a pretest that requires a spelling and reading ability of at least fourth grade level. As with several other instructional programs developed by the KU-IRLD, the program is complete with teacher manuals and student workbooks. The students are taught to use COPS and WRITER through a series of exercises that are taught sequentially as students demonstrate mastery of each step.

The field test data on this program are remarkable and support the program's effectiveness. When students' final drafts of papers were scored during pretesting, one error for every five written words was found. On the posttest, these students made one error for every thirty-three words written.

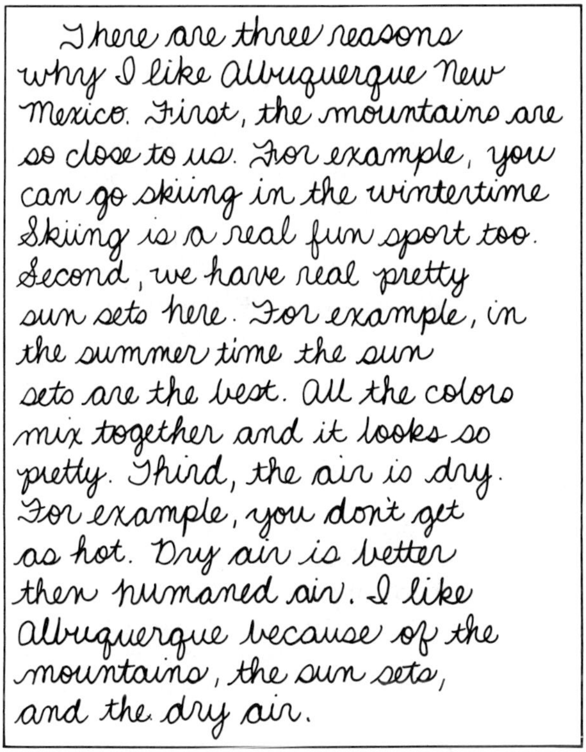

There are three reasons why I like Albuquerque New Mexico. First, the mountains are so close to us. For example, you can go skiing in the wintertime Skiing is a real fun sport too. Second, we have real pretty sun sets here. For example, in the summer time the sun sets are the best. All the colors mix together and it looks so pretty. Third, the air is dry. For example, you don't get as hot. Dry air is better then humaned air. I like Albuquerque because of the mountains, the sun sets, and the dry air.

Figure 9.7 Writing sample of a student using the eleven-sentence paragraph technique.

The Most Common Mistakes in Writing (COPS)

Capitalization
- Have I capitalized the first word of the sentence?
- Have I capitalized all the proper nouns in the sentence?

Overall Appearance
- Is my handwriting easy to read, on the line, and not crowded?
- Are my words and sentences spaced correctly?
- Did I indent and write close to the margin?
- Are there any messy errors?

Punctuation
- Did I use the right punctuation mark at the end of each sentence?
- Did I use commas and semicolons where necessary?

Spelling
- Does it look right?
- Can I sound it out?
- Have I used the dictionary?

Steps for Error Monitoring (WRITER)

1. Write on every other line using "PENS."
2. Read the paper for meaning.
3. Interrogate yourself using the "COPS" questions.
4. Execute a final copy.
5. Reread your paper.

Figure 9.8 Error monitoring strategies developed by KU-IRLD. (*Source:* J. B. Schumaker, S. M. Nolan, & D. D. Deshler, *The error monitoring strategy* (Lawrence, KS: University of Kansas, 1985).)

Besides this comprehensive strategy approach for students to manage their own writing, other strategies for self-monitoring and self-correcting writing have proven effective in helping students improve their writing. For example, Hayward and Le Buffe (1985) taught deaf students to note and code their errors in the margins of their written assignments. The identification of only one type of error was taught at a time. As students became proficient in finding one kind of error (spelling), identification of more kinds of errors types (capitalization, lowercase, awkward wording, subject-verb agreement) were taught successively. It is apparent that systematic instruction can lead to improved writing by students with special needs.

SUMMARY

Being able to write, whether to express oneself or to store information, is a highly important and useful skill. The ability to write well requires the use of highly structured rules about the mechanics of our written language. For example, people need to know how to use and apply the rules of grammar, punctuation, and spelling. They need to know how to use those rules to form compositions, as well as to select and use a means so that others can understand the communication.

Writing is a necessary skill at school, home, and later in adult life. Facility with this skill can contribute to an individual's success in the workplace also. Everyone needs to develop some level of competence in communicating through the written mode, even if the skills developed are as simple as being able to write and sign checks, fill out job applications, take messages, or write reminders to oneself. The degree of mastery of this curriculum area can relate directly to the degree of independence in adult life.

STUDY AND DISCUSSION QUESTIONS

1. Define the basic components of written communication.
2. Maggie, age 10, is a poor speller. She receives poor grades on her weekly spelling test in the regular education classroom, and her written assignments are replete with misspelled words. Develop a lesson plan aimed at remediating Maggie's spelling deficits. Justify your intervention selection.
3. List targets for survival (adult) writing. Suggest interventions that you would use to teach these skills.
4. Discuss the benefits of teaching students to monitor for errors in their written assignments.

REFERENCES AND SUGGESTED READINGS

Handwriting

ENSTROM, E. A. (1968). Left-handedness: A cause for disability in writing. *Journal of Learning Disabilities, 1,* 410–414.

HANSEN, C. L. (1978). Writing skills. In N. G. Haring, T. C. Lovitt. M. D. Eaton, & C. L. Hansen, *The fourth R: Research in the classroom.* Columbus, OH: Charles E. Merrill.

KOSIEWICA, M. M., HALLANAN, D. P., & LLOYD, J. (1981). The effects of an LD student's treatment choice on handwriting performance. *Learning Disability Quarterly, 4,* 281–286.

KOSIEWICA, M. M., MALLANAN, D. P., LLOYD, J., & GRAVES, A. W. (1982). Effects of self-instruction and self-correction procedures on handwriting performance. *Learning Disability Quarterly, 5,* 71–78.

STRAUSS, A. A., & LEHTINEN, L. E. (1951). *Psychopathology and education of the brain injured child.* New York: Grune and Stratton.

TOWLE, M. (1978). Assessment and remediation of handwriting deficits for children with learning disabilities. *Journal of Learning Disabilities, 11,* 370–377.

TURNBULL, A. P., & SCHULZ, J. B. (1979). *Mainstreaming handicapped students: A guide for the classroom teacher.* Boston: Allyn & Bacon.

Curriculum Based Assessment and Evaluation

HANSEN, C. L. (1978). Writing skills. In N. G. Haring, T. C. Lovitt, M. D. Eaton, & C. L. Hansen, *The fourth R: Research in the classroom.* Columbus, OH: Charles E. Merrill.

IVARIE, J. J. (1986). Effects of proficiency rates on later performance of a recall and writing behavior. *Remedial and Special Education, 7,* 25–30.

Spelling

BRODEN, M., BEASLEY, A., & HALL, R. V. (1978). In-class spelling performance: Effects of home tutoring by a parent. *Behavior Modification, 2,* 511–530.

BRYANT, N. D., DRABIN, I. R., & GETTINGER, M. (1981). Effects of varying unit size on spelling achievement in learning disabled children. *Journal of Learning Disabilities, 14*(4), 200–203.

CARPENTER, D., & MILLER, L. J. (1982). Spelling ability of reading disabled LD students and able readers. *Journal of Learning Disabilities, 5,* 65–70.

DIXON, R., & ENGLEMANN, S. (1979). *Corrective spelling through morphographs.* Palo Alto, CA: Science Research Associates.

FOSTER, K., & TORGESEN, J. K. (1983). The effects of directed study on the spelling performance of two subgroups of learning disabled students. *Learning Disability Quarterly, 6,* 253–257.

FOXX, R. M. & JONES, J. R. (1978). A remediation program for increasing spelling achievement of elementary and junior high school students. *Behavior Modification, 2,* 211–230.

GERBER, M. M. (1987). Information processing approaches to studying spelling deficiencies. *Journal of Learning Disabilities, 20*(1), 34–41.

GERBER, M. M. (1984). Investigations of orthographic problem-solving ability in learning disabled and normally achieving students. *Learning Disability Quarterly, 7,* 157–164.

GETTINGER, M., BRYANT, D. N., & FAYNE, H. R. (1982). Designing spelling instruction for learning disabled children: An emphasis on unit size, distributed practice, and training for transfer. *Journal of Special Education, 16*(4), 440–446.

HANSEN, C. L. (1978). *Writing Skills.* In N. G. Haring, T. C. Lovitt, M. D. Eaton, & C. L. Hansen, *The fourth R: Research in the classroom.* Columbus, OH: Charles E. Merrill.

KAUFFMAN, J. M., HALLAHAN, D. P., HAAS, K., BRAME, T., & BOREN, R. (1978). Imitating children's errors to improve their spelling performance. *Journal of Learning Disabilities, 11*, 217–222.

LOVITT, T. C., GUPPY, T. E., & BLATTNER, J. E. (1969). The use of a free-time contingency with fourth graders to increase spelling accuracy. *Behavior Research and Therapy, 7*, 151–156.

MANDOLI, M., MANDOLI, P., & McLAUGHLIN, T. F. (1982). The effects of same-age peer tutoring on the spelling performances of a mainstreamed elementary LD student. *Learning Disability Quarterly, 5*, 185–189.

MORAN, M. R. (1981). A comparison of formal features of written language of learning disabled, low-achieving and achieving secondary students. Research Report No. 34. Lawrence: University of Kansas Institute for Research in Learning Disabilities.

OLLENDICK, T. H., MATSON, J. L., ESVELDT-DAWSON, K., & SHAPIRO, E. S. (1980). Increasing spelling achievement: An analysis of treatment procedures utilizing an alternating treatments design. *Journal of Applied Behavior Analysis, 13*, 645–654.

RIETH, H., AXELROD, S., ANDERSON, R., HATHAWAY, R., WOOD, K., & FITZGERALD, C. (1974). Influence of distributed practice and daily testing on weekly spelling tests. *Journal of Educational Research, 68*, 73–77.

SIDMAN, M. T. (1979). The effects of group free time and contingency and individual free time contingency on spelling performance. *The Directive Teacher, 1*, 4–5.

STEVENS, K. B., & SCHUSTER, J. W. (1987). Effects of a constant time delay procedure on the written spelling performance of a learning disabled student. *Learning Disability Quarterly, 10*, 9–16.

VALLECORSA, A. L., ZIGMOND, N., & HENDERSON, L. M. (1985). Spelling instruction in special education classrooms: A survey of practices. *Exceptional Children, 52*(1), 19–24.

WONG, B. Y. L. (1986). A cognitive approach to teaching spelling. *Exceptional Children, 53*(2), 169–173.

Reversals

DAVIDSON, H. P. (1934). A study of reversals in young children. *Journal of Genetic Psychology, 45*, 452–465.

DAVIDSON, H. P. (1935). A study of the confusing letters b, d, p, and q. *Journal of Genetic Psychology, 47*, 458–468.

DENO, S. L., & CHIANG, B. (1979). An experimental analysis of the nature of reversal errors in children with severe learning disabilities. *Learning Disability Quarterly, 2*, 40–45.

HASAZI, J. E., & HASAZI, S. E. (1972). Effects of teacher attention on digit-reversal behavior in an elementary school child. *Journal of Applied Behavior Analysis, 5*, 157–162.

HILDRETH, G. (1934). Reversals in reading and writing. *Journal of Educational Psychology, 25*, 1–20.

SMITH, D. D., & LOVITT, T. C. (1973). The educational diagnosis and remediation of written b and d reversal problems: A case study. *Journal of Learning Disabilities, 6*, 356–363.

STROMER, R. (1975). Modifying letter and number reversals in elementary school children. *Journal of Applied Behavior Analysis, 8,* 211.

STROMER, R. (1977). Remediating academic deficiencies in learning disabled children. *Exceptional Children, 43,* 432–440.

Creative Writing

FORTNER, V. L. (1986). Generalization of creative productive-thinking training to LD students' written expression. *Learning Disability Quarterly, 9,* 274–284.

GLOVER, J. A., & SAUTTER, F. (1977). Procedures for increasing four behaviorally defined components of creativity within formal written assignments among high school students. *School Applications of Learning Theory, 9,* 3–22.

HALL, J. K. (1988). *Evaluating and improving written expression.* (2nd ed.). Boston: Allyn & Bacon.

KRAETSCH, G. (1981). The effects of oral instructions and training on the expansion of written language. *Learning Disability Quarterly, 4,* 82–90.

MALONEY, K. B., & HOPKINS, B. L. (1973). The modification of sentence structure and its relationship to subjective judgments of creativity in writing. *Journal of Applied Behavior Analysis, 6,* 425–433.

STODDARD, E. P., & RENZULLI, J. S. (1983). Improved writing skills of talent pool students. *Gifted Child Quarterly, 27*(1), 21–27.

Composition

HALL, J. K. (1981). *Evaluating and improving written expression.* Boston: Allyn & Bacon.

HAMMILL, D. D., & LARSEN, S. C. (1978). *The test of written language (TOWL).* Austin, TX: Pro-Ed.

HAYWARD, L. R., & LeBUFFE, J. R. (1985). Self-correction: A positive method for improving writing skills. *Teaching Exceptional Children, 18,* 68–72.

KRAETSCH, G. A. (1981). The effects of oral instructions and training on the expansion of written language. *Learning Disability Quarterly, 4,* 82–90.

POPLIN, M. S., GRAY, R., LARSEN, S., BANIKOWSKI, A., & MEHRING, T. (1980). A comparison of components of written expression abilities in learning disabled and non-learning disabled students at three grade levels. *Learning Disability Quarterly, 3,* 46–53.

RAY, R. (1986). The eleven-sentence paragraph. Working paper. Albuquerque: University of New Mexico, Special Education Dept.

SCHUMAKER, J. B., NOLAN, S. M., & DESHLER, D. D. (1985). *The error monitoring strategy.* Lawrence: University of Kansas Press.

SCHUMAKER, J. B., & SHELDON, J. (1985). *The sentence writing strategy.* Lawrence: University of Kansas Press.

THOMAS, C. C., ENGLERT, C. S., & GREGG, S. (1987). An analysis of errors and strategies in the expository writing of learning disabled students. *Remedial and Special Education, 8*(1), 21–20, 46.

VAN HOUTEN, R., HILL, S., & PARSONS, M. (1975). An analysis of a performance feedback system: The effects of timing and feedback, public posting, and praise upon academic performance and peer interaction. *Journal of Applied Behavior Analysis, 8,* 449–457.

VAN HOUTEN, R., MORRISON, E., JARVIS, R., & McDONALD, M. (1974). The effects of explicit timing and feedback on compositional response rate in elementary school children. *Journal of Applied Behavior Analysis, 7,* 547–555.

Computers (Word Processing)

BANK STREET COLLEGE OF EDUCATION, F. E. SMITH, & INTENTIONAL EDUCATIONS, INC. (1984). *Bankstreet writer*. San Rafael, CA: Broderbund Software.

KERCHNER, L., & KISTINGER, B. (1984). Language processing/word processing: Written expression, computers and learning disabled students. *Learning Disability Quarterly, 7,* 329–335.

VACC, N. N. (1987). Word processor handwriting: A comparative study of writing samples produced by mildly mentally handicapped students. *Exceptional Children, 54*(2), 156–165.

10

Mathematics

Although reading often dominates instructional time in classrooms for children with special needs, mathematics is an important topic of instruction that must be stressed. Mathematics provides learners with many basic skills needed for successful adult life. Managing a personal budget, shopping, and making simple home repairs require mastery of mathematical skills. Although research has shown that 33% of instructional time in resource rooms is spent on mathematics (Carpenter, 1985), the majority of effort is spent on computation. Unfortunately, this expenditure of instructional time is not highly successful. Secondary teachers report that the mathematical abilities of academically delayed students typically are no greater than third or fourth grade level (McLeod & Armstrong, 1982). It could be argued that the entire mathematics curriculum should be rethought. Certainly, for students with special needs, real-life mathematical applications, rather than mere computation, should be emphasized.

Experts in mathematics have questioned the content and sequence of the standard curriculum for normal students as well as for students with handicaps. Only skills (numeration, computation, measurement, and simple problem solving) usually acquired by students in fourth grade are necessary to succeed in most jobs. Now, with the advent of hand-held calculators, many mathematical functions used in life can be performed easily. Recently microcomputers have gained wide acceptance and are used at home and in the workplace. Mathematical instruction must change to meet the needs of students who will seek employment in a largely technological society. New, highly efficient instructional procedures that can greatly reduce the instructional time spent on computation are already available for implementation.

Several recent national mathematics assessments have revealed important information that teachers and curriculum planners should consider. Modern mathematics instruction has not lowered students' achievement in computation. Students are able to add, subtract, multiply, and divide, but they are weak in problem solving abilities. Proficiency in computational arithmetic alone is inadequate for functioning in the adult world. If youngsters cannot apply mathematical skills to situations outside of the traditional arithmetic worksheet or textbook assignments, what are the benefits of the curriculum? Emphasis must be placed on problem-solving and real-life applications of mathematical skills.

What should constitute the mathematics curriculum for students with special needs? Should there be two curricula—one for regular education and another for special education? Should there be one overall curriculum, with special education students leaving the sequence at an earlier point than others who have a proclivity for mathematics? If there are two curricula, at what point should students be placed into one or the other? There are no definitive or nationally agreed-upon answers to these questions; regardless, these are vital issues that special educators need consciously to address.

TOPICS FOR INSTRUCTION

Most instructional topics can be discussed from a mathematical perspective. Although educators have yet to reach a consensus about where instructional emphasis should be placed, most agree that showing students the relationship of these topics to mathematics will illustrate why they must learn math. Discussion of how mathematics relates to every aspect of daily life also may capture students' attention and instill in them a desire to learn. Nevertheless, different professional organizations and individual researchers have identified various skills that they think should constitute the mathematics curriculum. Table 10.1 lists skills used by the National Institute of Education (NIE), the National Council of Teachers of Mathematics (NCTM), and the Key Math test. These lists indicate what a federal agency, a professional organization, and test developers feel are the essential elements of mathematics.

No optimal, unanimously agreed-upon system is available. Special education teachers, therefore, are left to use their training and skills to plan the most appropriate instructional sequences for each student. To assist teachers in conceptualizing instructional programs for their individual students, a lattice (see Figure 10.1) was developed that highlights topics that might constitute students' mathematics programs throughout the school years. This lattice is not entirely sequential. Many of the skills found high on the lattice should be taught concurrently with others found earlier. For example, each year, basic consumer skills should be reintroduced as practical examples and applications of computation and problem solving. The importance of this lattice is to illustrate that numeration and computation are only components of the mathematics curriculum; they should not be considered as a total mathematics program. Unfortunately, for

Table 10.1
Organizational Schemes for Mathematics Curricula

NCTM CONTENT MATRIX	NIE 10 BASIC SKILLS	KEY MATH ORGANIZATIONAL AREAS
Numbers and numeration concepts	Problem solving	Content
Properties of numbers and operations	Apply math to everyday situations	Numeration
Arithmetic computations	Alertness to reasonableness of results	Fractions
Sets	Estimations and approximations	Geometry and symbols
Estimation and measurement	Appropriate computational skills	Operations
Exponents and logarithms	Geometry	Addition
Algebraic expressions	Measurement	Subtraction
Equations and inequalities	Reading, interpreting, and constructing tables, charts, and graphs	Multiplication
Functions	Using mathematics to predict	Division
Probability and statistics	Computer literacy	Mental computation
Geometry		Numerical reasoning
Trigonometry		Applications
Mathematical proofs		Word problems
Logic		Missing elements
Miscellaneous topics		Money
Business and consumer mathematics		Measurement
Attitude and interest		Time

many students with special needs, they are the only topics addressed during the school years.

Students whose disabilities do not preclude success with mathematics should be placed in the regular mathematics classes (algebra, geometry, trigonometry) with their nonhandicapped peers. For others, instructional time should be spent on mastering skills needed in adult life. In the following sections, discussion focuses on numeration, computation, measurement, problem solving, and consumer mathematics.

Numeration

There are a number of skills children should master before they begin to use numbers to calculate or solve problems. For example, they must understand that objects and things in their environment are related to each other. Many children master numerical concepts before they come to school. Others, however, need direct instruction concerning one-to-one correspondence, counting, quantitative relationships, and other topics. Because these concepts are difficult for many students with special needs to learn, some discussion is provided in the following sections.

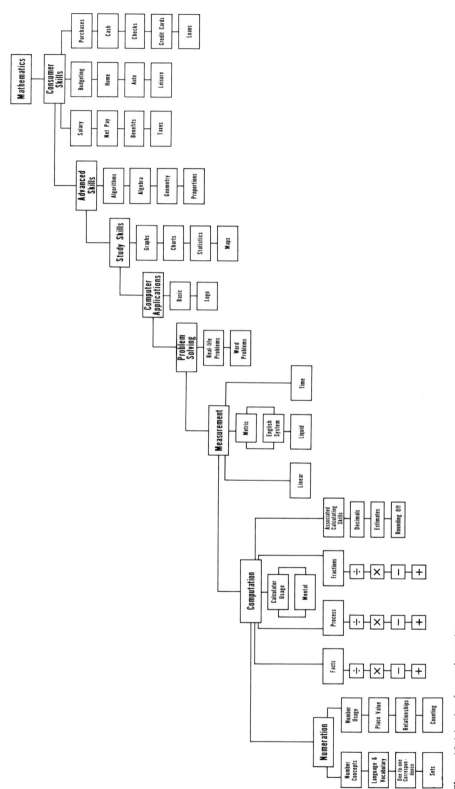

Figure 10.1 Lattice for mathematics.

Number Concepts

Very young children seem interested in number concepts (how many, how old) almost naturally. Because the concept of numbers is based on an abstraction related to quantity, however, some children with handicaps have difficulty with it from the outset.

Classification and grouping of objects is an early requisite skill. The notion of sets or clusters should come early in the instructional sequence. To be able to group things together requires an ability to discriminate and comprehend the properties of objects. Because shapes are rather easy to discriminate, they are usually taught during this initial period. Circles, for example, can become a set separate from triangles and squares. Size is another discriminating feature used in instruction about sets. Once children have learned to discriminate objects with several variables (shape, size, color), instruction about one-to-one correspondence can be initiated.

Other number concepts are important in students' early contact with mathematics. Students should develop a numerical vocabulary early. Words like most, few, many, big, little, heavy, long, short, top, and bottom must become part of young children's usable vocabulary. Such word knowledge and usage facilitates the development of more difficult numerical concepts. When one-to-one correspondence is taught, for instance, the phrases "one too many" and "one more than" are important to learn, for later concepts are related to the notion of "greater than." Once these foundation skills are mastered, students move easily to the use of numbers in their environment.

Number Usage

As with many numerical concepts, a large number of students come to school already possessing an ability to use simple numbers. A standard instructional sequence is often used to teach number usage. It usually starts with rote counting by ones (to ten or twenty), number recognition of simple (one-digit) numbers, and number writing (if the students possess the necessary prerequisite writing skills—see Chapter 9). Whether the student matches, says, or writes numbers, the skill of indicating how many objects are within a set usually is the next one in the sequence.

Once counting objects is mastered, students are taught to count and compare. Relationships between sets (greater than, less than, and equal to) become the topic of instruction. Many teachers have found that the concrete representation of sets and their composition is a prerequisite to paper and pencil worksheet activities.

Other general number usage skills must be mastered before computational instruction is initiated. Whether these miscellaneous skills are taught concurrent with or subsequent to the skills listed above is up to the teacher and the performance of the student. Regardless, at some time early in the mathematics curriculum, students should be able to count by ones, twos, fives, and tens, and should also master ordinal numbers (first, second, third).

The exact and precise sequence of these precomputational skills is not definite. Clearly, however, these skills should be mastered before computation is presented in any concentrated way. Many youngsters possess "spotty" skills. Teachers of students having difficulty with computation and other mathematical skills should assess their students' abilities in numeration, to be certain that these prerequisite skills are definitely part of their repertoires.

Computation

Computation has received considerable attention from teachers and researchers. In fact, most of this attention has centered on addition and subtraction. NCTM (1979) estimates that students devote at least 1,000 classroom hours during elementary school to mathematics, with most of that time spent on computation. Unfortunately for many students with handicaps, the only mathematics instruction they receive during their entire school career is in computational arithmetic.

The overemphasis on computation can be observed through the following example. Ron is a high school student who receives help from the special education teacher. Thirty minutes each day is devoted to mathematics. He spends ten minutes putting cards with multiplication facts written on them through a Language Master machine and twenty minutes computing problems on a worksheet. Sometimes these problems are only multiplication; other days the processes are mixed. Day in and day out, for the eleven years he has spent in school, mathematics instruction has been composed of similar activities. This is a travesty for all parties involved: Ron is still not proficient in computational skills, and the teacher is not providing an appropriate educational program. This overemphasis on the importance of computational arithmetic leaves a student with no usable mathematics skills.

Today, with our knowledge of well-researched interventions that can make computational instruction more efficient and less time consuming (see the "Teaching Tactics" section later in this chapter), and the availability of the hand-held calculator, such situations should not occur. Instruction in computational arithmetic should not be eliminated, for computation constitutes the basic tool skills of all mathematics. For those, however, who cannot master it within a reasonable time—even when efficient, researched procedures are applied—supplemental aids or compensating devices such as calculators or computers should be made available. Regardless, more emphasis must be placed on problem solving and life skills.

Computational Facts and Processes

There are four computational areas: addition, subtraction, multiplication, and division. Each can be further divided into two general types of problems: facts and process problems. The facts (7×8, $5 + 2$, $7 - 4$), consisting of 100 problems per operation, are those problems to be committed to memory. The process problems ($74 - 27$, 68×84) are solved by utilizing the facts and following operational rules. Usually, the first computational area taught is addition. Once addition is mastered, subtraction is taught, then multiplication, followed by division. For each area, the facts are taught first, followed by the larger process problems.

Fractions

Fractions often present a problem to both students and teachers. Many youngsters have great difficulty understanding and using fractions. Most seem to develop the concept of simple fractions and are able to divide circles and other geometric figures into halves, thirds, fourths, and even eighths. Using fractions in computations, however, can become an insurmountable task for many students with special needs. Adding and subtracting fractions with uncommon denominators, for example, is laborious for many youngsters. Some also find this function incomprehensible.

Fraction instruction presents two problems to teachers. First, often a substantial amount of instructional time is spent on fractions, but with little success. Second, whether more instructional time should be spent after students learn simple fractions needed in cooking is an issue for debate. With the national move toward the metric system (which does not utilize fractions) and the advent of the handheld calculator, the place of fractions in special education students' curriculum is questionable. (Of course, those students who are mainstreamed for mathematics might need assistance from the special education teacher in fractional computations.) If decimals were introduced earlier and students were taught to round off to the hundredth place (which correlates to our currency system), instruction on complicated fractional computations seems unnecessary.

Calculators

Computation is complicated and, consequently, in most elementary and middle school classes, receives the majority of time allotted for mathematics instruction. For students who are academically delayed, computational arithmetic has taken the place of all mathematics instruction, even in high school.

If more emphasis is to be placed on developing mathematical skills needed in daily life, less time must be spent on computation. Apportioning instructional time to adapt to this new emphasis presents a problem. Computation cannot be ignored: Students must be able to add, subtract, multiply, and divide. The handheld calculator could well provide a solution. Rather than struggling to acquire computational skills, which require continual practice to be retained, students could learn the simple computational functions of a pocket calculator. No longer would they waste their time on complicated, laborious computations; instead, they would spend their limited class time solving mathematical problems encountered in real life. These problems, such as developing a personal budget, calculating monthly wages from hourly wages, comparing unit pricing, computing gasoline mileage, and figuring tips and shared costs for a dinner, include computations that are often difficult and time consuming. If students first master computational functions on their calculators, they can achieve greater success in solving problems they will face every day of their lives. Even students in early grades can benefit from instruction in how to use handheld calculators and how to solve story problems. When the tediousness of computation is removed and real-life problems are presented, students should come to understand the importance of mathematics and be more motivated to learn it.

Teachers must provide such basic instruction as how to enter problems on the calculator and how to clear those problems after each calculation. For example, they must teach students which number to enter first in a subtraction problem, which number represents the minuend, and which represents the subtrahend. Students cannot be expected to develop calculator skills by chance.

The introduction of calculators into classrooms could cause some important curricula changes, including the early introduction of decimals and the concept of rounding off. Should calculators be adopted for routine classroom use, students must become familiar with their calculators' basic functions. They must learn to recognize decimals and know their meaning. And, since many calculators conclude answers with more than two decimals numbers, they must learn to round off. They also must learn to estimate the results of their computations so that they can be reasonably confident about the accuracy of the answers they later obtain. Exposing students to a variety of mathematical problems would help them gain experience needed to judge when solutions indicated on the answer display are reasonable.

Measurement

With the move to a more practical mathematics curriculum, measurement becomes a vital component of the instructional sequence. Rather than being relegated to the back of mathematics textbooks, linear and liquid measurement should become integral parts of the instructional sequence. So, too, should the measurement of time. Students with special needs, in particular, need direct instruction on these topics. Results from standardized tests show that many of these students cannot measure or tell time; these skills are needed in most jobs and in many aspects of adult daily life.

Continuous measurement (variables represented on an uninterrupted scale) include time, height, weight, temperature, volume, and distance. Although things can be measured differently (hands, fathoms, meters), standard units of measurement are used for uniform communication. Rulers, clocks, and thermometers are some instruments used to obtain standard measurements. In addition to instrument use, students need to develop a sense or concept of measurement.

Linear and Liquid Measurement

Measurement topics of practical importance are (1) converting and comparing units of measure; (2) estimating and measuring length; (3) determining perimeter, area, and volume; and (4) using measurement instruments. Students need to learn how to use various linear and liquid measurement devices, such as rulers, thermometers, and measuring cups. Since measuring length is the easiest skill, it should be presented first, followed by determining volume and area.

Measurement skills are difficult to master for many students with special needs. For those who have difficulties conceptualizing, instructional units should be carefully planned and sequenced. Instruction should contain many redundant experiences to permit opportunities for youngsters to manipulate and experiment. For example, students might first visually compare the size of objects, estimating length and height. Students can build block towers, compare heights, learn to make them equivalent, and use primitive measurements (three blocks high, two blocks high). A sense of height and length can be developed gradually using these kinds of teaching procedures. Others might seek to develop these concepts through continued practice in games and other independent and group activities. Regardless of the philosophy employed, exposure, contact, and instruction in measurement are vital.

During the past decade, increased discussion has focused on the use of the metric system of measurement. The NCTM has endorsed the inclusion of metric measurement in school and has encouraged a national conversion to this system. If metrics are adopted, more efficient instruction will occur, since many of the difficult elements of measurement will be eliminated (conversion to inches, feet, yards; use of fractions; cups, pints, quarts). Some school district officials have even suggested that only metric measurement be taught. Unfortunately, conversion to the metric system has not been speedy. Students who possess only knowledge of metrics will be as handicapped as those who possess only knowledge of our current standard measurement systems. Therefore, although confusing to many, it is advisable to teach both systems (at least for the present).

Time

Many special education teachers find that their students do not tell or understand time as well as their normal counterparts. Many students with special needs perform at least three grade levels below normal children on time-related items on standardized tests. When asked simple questions such as "How long does it take you to brush your teeth?" "How long does it take to send a letter from one town to another?" "How long does it take for a broken bone to mend?" answers from many students with handicaps, at all ages, are unrealistic. Often, these students respond that it takes anywhere from twenty seconds to an hour to brush their teeth, from five minutes to nine hours to ski downhill, and from ten minutes to a year to get a letter from one town to the next.

Before students can understand time (beyond the gross distinctions of morning, afternoon, night, lunchtime, and dinnertime), they must be able to tell time. Many supplemental aids are available that teachers can use in their instruction about time telling. Matching digital clock faces with traditional clocks, for example, can facilitate mastery. Students must be able to tell time and use time wisely if they are to live independently. To help students achieve mastery and later independence, teachers should make digital clocks available to those who have great difficulty understanding standard clock faces.

Throughout the school years, teachers should stress concepts about telling time and budgeting time because these concepts have been shown to be highly correlated to job success. As youngsters grow older and become more independent, they should be allowed to decide for themselves how to spend part of their day. (See Chapter 4 for a review.) With teacher guidance, students may gradually take more responsibility for scheduling their time. Eventually, routine self-management of daily schedules will foster students' better understanding and use of time.

Problem Solving

As emphasized throughout this text, more time and attention should be spent in developing instructional programs that address problem solving. Members of the NCTM have reached the same conclusion. In fact, in their recommendations for the focus of mathematics education in the 1980s, problem solving is listed first. Problem solving is particularly important for students with special needs. These students need problem solving skills not only to solve word (story) problems, but to deal effectively with nonroutine functions in daily life. In many instances, problem solving involves applying mathematics to problems encountered in the real world. Students who learn to solve mathematical problems may find that they can solve other kinds of problems as well.

Problem solving requires a wide variety of skills and knowledge. Individuals must generalize knowledge to new and novel situations; find relationships among skills, concepts, and principles; make decisions; be flexible; identify irrelevancies; seek similarities; estimate; and determine the reasonableness of their answers. They need to formulate questions, analyze and conceptualize problems, define problems, discover patterns and similarities, experiment, and transfer skills and strategies to new situations.

For youngsters to learn how to solve problems, they must have practice. Throughout the school years, many opportunities for youngsters arise at school to solve problems. These opportunities, which include routine events involving direct application of mathematics (dividing the class into teams during physical education period), can be used to teach mathematics. Rather than the adults always handling difficult or novel situations, students should become involved in their solutions. For example, problems like dividing the delivery of construction paper among the fourth grade teachers could be left to the children to solve. Using real situations, at the children's level of understanding, is more meaningful and serves well to illustrate problems for instructional purposes. Certainly, such problems are more interesting for groups of youngsters than determining the price of four different kinds of nuts when they are mixed together.

Computer Applications

Over the last few years, American schools have invested substantial resources to acquire computer equipment. Some local schools have set a goal for every classroom to be equipped with at least one microcomputer for student use. Others aim at acquiring computer banks or labs for use in regularly scheduled classes. Regardless of specific goals, the hope is that both teachers and students will become computer literate.

There are at least three ways that computers can be integrated into the curriculum. First, youngsters can be taught to program by learning either BASIC or Logo. Many handicapped youngsters are quite successful in learning these programs; later, programming could become a vocational skill. Second, computer-assisted instruction (CAI) can be used to teach students academic content, such as mathematics. Of course, CAI is only as effective as the available software. If the software is of high quality with the program field tested, CAI has proven to be superior to the traditional classroom approach (Trifiletti, Frith, & Armstrong, 1984). Microcomputers are also used to support the ongoing instructional program. In these instances, they are supplemental to the curriculum and are often used for drill and practice. For example, the *Arcademics* games are quite useful in helping children learn arithmetic facts through a format similar to those found in video arcades. Such instructional games provide an interesting and novel way for students to learn information that is usually taught through drill, a technique most students find tedious.

Study Skills

Study skills involve the use of information organizers to present materials. Graphs, charts, and tables are examples of organizers used in a wide variety of reading material found both in and outside of school. Many students with special needs do not become familiar with these information formats and, thus, cannot function as well in the regular curriculum. All students need to use some of these devices, particularly maps. Students who are mainstreamed for mathematics classes must become competent in using many of these organizers. The acquisition of these study skills has been too often ignored and now needs attention from both students and teachers.

Students who graph their academic improvement (see Chapter 3 for review) learn important study skills. Small groups of youngsters can work together to interpret charts and tables found in newspapers or sports magazines. With the advent of easy-to-use computer software programs that create graphs and charts, students can collect data from their school environments to organize in one of these concise formats. Study skills are important tools that facilitate problem solving. Many experts believe that making tables, charts, and diagrams of problems helps students to find solutions. Therefore, time spent teaching students to read, interpret, and create these information organizers is justified and could lead to the development of better problem solving abilities.

Advanced Mathematics

Most students with special needs are not exposed to this section of the mathematics curriculum. Those whose handicap does not preclude learning mathematics, however, should participate in standard algebra and geometry classes. If they need extra assistance to understand and master these more advanced classes, peer tutors, special education teachers, or others can help them.

Consumer Skills

All individuals living in our society must be able to select, evaluate, and use information relevant to purchasing and use the money available to them wisely and within their individual budgetary limitations. Americans are faced with almost unlimited choices of goods to buy. These range from purchasing items and activities required for simple survival to those that bring pleasure. Most children's experience in making monetary choices begins early. If given a set amount of money to spend, children need to decide if one expensive toy is preferable to two cheaper toys. As adults, choices become more complex. Most of these decisions are made using basic mathematical knowledge. Therefore, preparation for independent adult living must begin early. This curriculum strand should be incorporated into children's educational programs throughout the school years. Unfortunately, consumerism has received little attention from researchers, instructional materials writers, or curriculum developers.

The mathematics lattice (Figure 10.1) indicates some general areas where instruction might be targeted to prepare students better in the consumer skills needed in adulthood. Units on money use, banking skills, making major purchases (cars, houses), and setting up a household could become practical exercises to teach problem solving and applications of computation. For example, in a unit on buying a car, groups of students could discuss such questions as, What is the purpose of owning a car? What is the cost of the car you want? How much can you afford to pay? How will you pay for it? What if you want a new car? What if you want a used car? How much does it cost you to operate a car? Because money skills are necessary for the more complex consumer decision-making abilities, the following section discusses some of its components.

Money

As with time telling and other measurement skills, making change and money management are often neglected yet vital areas that should be topics of instruction for students with special needs. A number of different skills are required for proficiency in the use of money. At least the following skills should be incorporated into the mathematics curriculum: coin value and identification, counting money, making change, using money to make purchases, interpreting a budget, and having knowledge and understanding of checks and checking accounts. Also, in today's society it is important for students to understand the use of credit cards and develop a concept of credit.

At present, no comprehensive money management program is available. Splinter skills usually are taught in isolated units. Making change, for example, is commonly presented in arithmetic texts. Interestingly, that skill often is taught through subtraction (the amount given to the clerk minus the price of the item).

In real-life situations, however, change is obtained through a counting process (counting up from the price of the item to the amount given the clerk). Therefore, students do not need to know how to subtract to make change, and change making and other simple money usage activities can be introduced early in the student's educational career.

Teachers who include a token economy facet in their classrooms have an excellent opportunity to teach such money-related skills as comparing the amount of money (or points) one possesses with the cost of an item (or privilege). Some teachers of middle and secondary school students even capitalize on this situation by setting up banking procedures, in which students make deposits into their accounts and write checks to purchase items or privileges they have earned through good work.

Dahlquist (1977) described a learning experience for fifth graders that taught money management as well as economics. These students were taught to run the school store (which sold school supplies and other sundries). Every customer filled out preprinted order forms for desired purchases, and the students had to keep an inventory, price the items, and deliver purchase orders. This provided a unique and productive opportunity for these students to practice money management skills.

Money management should include information about such topics as budgeting, consumer awareness, and comparison shopping. Before students can learn about these advanced topics, they must be able to identify money (coins and bills), make change, and make value judgments about purchases in relation to their own financial situation. Although these topics normally are not part of the elementary or middle school curriculum, teachers should at least be aware of their importance and begin to include related topics in their instructional day. By the high school years, money management should become an emphasized topic of instruction.

CURRICULUM-BASED ASSESSMENT AND EVALUATION

In all curriculum areas, teachers must know which skills their students possess and which they do not. Otherwise, students without the necessary prerequisite skills might be assigned work too difficult for them to complete successfully. This is particularly true in mathematics. If a student does not know how to multiply or subtract, mastery of long division will be difficult. So instruction can be planned to best advantage, students' current functioning levels should be assessed. The best way to accomplish this is to test them with classroom materials. In computation, for example, students should be assigned all kinds of problems to see what facts and processes they know. The results of this kind of assessment leads to the best decisions about placement and instructional intervention.

Many students who have not mastered computation make consistent errors. For example, students who do not know how to regroup in subtraction problems, often merely subtract the smaller from the larger number in each column. In these instances, students follow standard, but incorrect rules for solving these problems. Systematic error patterns tend to be persistent. In many cases, what initially appears to be random errors might be the consistent application of a faulty rule. Knowing what kinds of errors students make can assist in the selection of an instructional procedure that has the highest probability of success. For example, if a student is applying a faulty rule, the teacher might demonstrate how to use the proper rule to solve the problem. If the student is writing random numbers and has previously indicated that he or she knows how to solve the problem, a motivational technique might prove sufficient to bring about academic improvement. Figure 10.2 displays several common error patterns.

More is known about how children perform in computation, so some instructional guidelines are provided about that curriculum area. According to Mercer (1979) students need to become proficient in writing numerals. He suggests that kindergarteners through second graders should aim at writing numbers at a rate of twenty-five per minute. Older elementary students should be able to write numbers between the rates of forty and sixty per minute. Students need to acquire and become proficient in their knowledge of the basic facts. Instruction for these problems needs to address both accuracy and speed. Therefore, correct and error rate scores are the data systems that should be used in student evaluations. In a study that included fifty teachers from three states, regular education students' rates of computing facts were assessed. For each fact group, students who were currently learning their solutions were tested, as were

1. $47 + 62 = 118$

2. $$\begin{array}{r} 249 \\ -\ 192 \\ \hline 157 \end{array}$$

3. $$\begin{array}{r} 429 \\ +\ 179 \\ \hline 5918 \end{array}$$

4. $$\begin{array}{r} 420 \\ -\ 179 \\ \hline 359 \end{array}$$

5. $$\begin{array}{r} 52 \\ -\ 16 \\ \hline 12 \end{array} \qquad \begin{array}{r} 64 \\ -\ 17 \\ \hline 34 \end{array} \qquad \begin{array}{r} 72 \\ -\ 22 \\ \hline 56 \end{array} \qquad \begin{array}{r} 89 \\ -\ 46 \\ \hline 78 \end{array}$$

1. In problem 1, the child added 4 and 7, then 6 and 2.
2. In problem 2, the child subtracted the smaller number from the larger number in each column.
3. In problem 3, the child added without carrying.
4. In problem 4, the child subtracted the larger number in each column from the smaller one.
5. In the series in problem 5, the child simply wrote as answers the numbers 1 to 8 in sequence.

Figure 10.2 Common errors in computation.

Table 10.2
Criteria Rates for Arithmetic Fact Proficiency

PROBLEM TYPE	SAMPLE	GRADE	CORRECT RATE	ERROR RATE
Addition facts	2 +3 ‾‾ 5	1 6	19.8 82.0	0.2 0.8
Addition carry facts	9 +9 ‾‾ 18	1 6	3.1 45.3	1.5 0.2
Mixed addition facts	4 5 +6 +1 ‾‾ ‾‾ 10 6	1 6	8.4 55.5	1.1 1.2
Subtraction facts	8 −2	1 6	12.9 51.5	0.5 0
Subtraction borrow- ing facts	17 −9	1 6	2.5 33.8	0.8 0.8
Mixed subtraction facts	16 5 −8 −3	1 6	4.8 44.8	0.8 0.3
Multiplication facts	3 ×3	3 6	43.4 68.2	0.8 5.0
Multiplication carry facts	7 ×6	3 6	21.3 40.0	0.3 0
Mixed multiplica- tion facts	4 9 ×2 ×8	3 6	31.3 52.7	0.5 2.0
Division facts	8 ÷ 1	3 6	12.6 47.0	1.7 3.3
Division facts	14 ÷ 2	3 6	8.3 39.3	0.7 0
Mixed division facts	6 ÷ 2 64 ÷ 8	3 6	11.4 45.0	0.7 0.7

Source: Adapted from D. D. Smith & T. C. Lovitt (1982). *The Computational Arithmetic Program*. Austin, TX: Pro-Ed, Inc.

students from sixth grade. The results from this research are shown on Table 10.2 and could be used as criteria or aim scores for instructional purposes.

When teaching the larger process problems, like those that require carrying in multiplication, teachers should be concerned with accuracy. Most students who are proficient in answering facts become proficient automatically in solving process problems, once they have acquired the rules followed to arrive at the correct answers. Therefore, most teachers only address acquisition of these computations and use percentage correct scores as their measurement system to judge the adequacy of their instructional procedures.

TEACHING TACTICS

Teachers should be aware of a wide variety of teaching tactics available for mathematics instruction. Sometimes, a tactic initially scheduled is insufficient to bring about the learning necessary to master the skill. Other times, teachers should vary their instructional methods. Table 10.3 summarizes a number of different instructional procedures that have proven successful in specific mathematical situations in both research and practice. Also, narratives are provided to give more detail on selected tactics. The tactics discussed are quite effective either in a particular stage of learning or for the development of a specific skill.

Fact Acquisition

Many different interventions are used to teach students the four hundred facts, one hundred per operation, that are the smaller components of larger computations. A number of those are highlighted in Table 10.3. Two highly effective tactics are described in further detail here. The first involves the use of a cue sheet; the second utilizes a counting method to answer multiplication and division facts.

Many teachers have found that cue sheets facilitate students' memorization of arithmetic facts. To use this technique, the teacher needs to prepare or have available two sets of worksheets. One set is composed of facts for the students to solve; the other set provides the student with the problems and their solutions. It is advisable to have at least three different versions of each set so the students cannot memorize the location of specific problems.

While answering facts on their worksheets, the students are encouraged to find those problems for which they do not know the answers. After using this search-and-find method for several days, the students are then rewarded for completing their pages more and more quickly, thereby discouraging them from looking for each problem and its solution. When instructed to answer problems from memory and to look only for those they cannot remember, students become less dependent on the cue sheet and complete their assignments more quickly.

The counting method is a strategy approach for answering multiplication and division facts. First, the students are taught to count each number by rote (by 2s, 3s, 4s, 5s). By demonstration, choral counting, and filling in numbers missing in the strands, students learn each sequence of numbers. Once the sequences are mastered, the students are taught the strategy shown on Table 10.4 for multiplication and then the one found on Table 10.5 for division.

Fact Proficiency

Students must become proficient in their knowledge and use of basic arithmetic facts (see Table 10.2 for criterion rates). If they are not fluent in solving these problems, the task of mastering larger computations is much more difficult and

Table 10.3
Mathematics Teaching Tactics

INSTRUCTIONAL TARGET	STAGE OF LEARNING	POSSIBLE TACTICS
Numeration		
Number concepts	Acquisition	Manipulatives
		Demonstration
		Guided practice
	Proficiency	Drill and practice
		Rewards
Number usage	Acquisition	Manipulatives
	Proficiency	Drill and practice
		Rewards
Computation		
Facts	Initial acquisition	Manipulatives
		Abacus
		Rods
		Counting devices
		Hatch marks
		Number lines
		Time delay
		Audiotapes
		Tutoring
		Cue sheets
		Flow sheets
		Self-correction
		With calculator
		With answer keys
		Self-talk
		Verbalize problem
		Drill
		Flashcards
		Language master
		Computer games
		Reward for accuracy
		Individual
		Group contingencies
		Tutoring
		Study groups
		Drill
	Advanced acquisition	Error drill
		Telling
		Rewards
		Praise
		Fines
		Self-correction
		With calculators
		With answer keys
		Tutoring
		Peer drill
		Peer correction
		Study groups
	Proficiency	Telling
		"Work faster"
		Goal

(continued)

Table 10.3 (*Continued*)

INSTRUCTIONAL TARGET	STAGE OF LEARNING	POSSIBLE TACTICS
		Pacers
		Metronome
		Feedback
		Today's score compared to goal
		Today's score compared to yesterday's
		Circle goal problem
		Computer games
		Competition
		Team
		Class
		Self
		Drill
		Tutoring
		Rewards
		Praise
Processes and fractions	Initial acquisition	Demonstration plus permanent model
	Advanced acquisition	Redemonstration of errors
		Telling
		"Be more careful"
		Add cues
	Proficiency	Fluency on facts
	Generalization	Sequence of instruction
		Telling
Calculator usage	Acquisition	Jigsaw technique
		Tutoring
		Study groups
		Peer
		Demonstration
Problem solving	Acquisition	Demonstration
		Manipulatives
		Blocks
		Physical model
		Student-made visuals
		Models
		Charts
		Diagrams
		Tables
		Pictures
		Graphs
		Write number sentences
		Personalize the problem
		Use problems that are experimentally-based
		Restate problems with smaller numbers
		Study (solution) groups
		Guess and verify
		Discovery approach
		Self-talk

Table 10.4
Attack Strategy for Multiplication Facts

Attack Strategy: Count by one number the number of times indicated by the other number.

Steps in Attack Strategy:	Example:
1. Read the problem.	2 × 5 = ____
2. Point to a number that you know how to count by.	student points to 2
3. Make the number of marks indicated by the other number.	2 × 5 = ____
4. Begin counting by the number you know how to count by and count up once for each mark, touching each mark.	/ / / / / "2, 4 . . ."
5. Stop counting when you've touched the last mark.	" . . . 6, 8, 10"
6. Write the last number you said in the answer space.	2 × 5 = ____ 10 / / / / /

Source: D. Cullinan, J. Lloyd, & M. H. Epstein (1981), Strategy training: A structured approach to arithmetic instruction. *Exceptional Education Quarterly, 2* (1), p. 44. Used by permission of Pro-Ed, Inc.

Table 10.5
Division Fact Strategy

1. Look at the problem.
2. Find the number to "divide by."
3. Count by that number.
4. Make a hatch mark or use a counting device for each number counted.
5. Stop at the other number in the problem.
6. Write the answer.

time consuming. When youngsters are proficient in the use of facts, once they master a more complex process such as regrouping in subtraction, those problems automatically indicate proficiency also.

The most commonly applied tactics to encourage proficiency are rewards. Two other proven tactics are described here. Pacing devices, which make a sound at adjustable intervals, have facilitated fact proficiency. Pacers come in a variety of forms, ranging from metronomes to prerecorded audiotapes. The students are instructed to write an answer with each sound while working on their assigned fact worksheets. Once they can answer the problems at the pacer's rate, the speed is gradually increased until the student reaches the desired rate or aim score.

Computer games are a fun and novel way for students to practice arithmetic facts. The most recent version of the *Arcademic* arithmetic games, *Master of Mathomatics,* incorporates many outstanding features. The speed of problem presentation can be set by either the teacher or the student. The program also keeps data on student performance and can even make graphs of individual

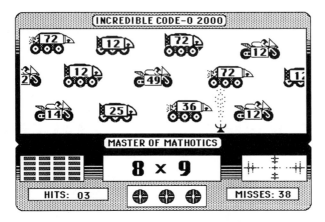

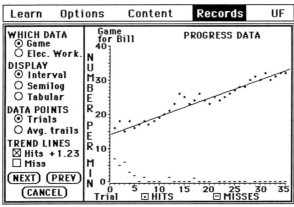

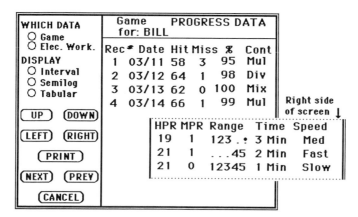

Figure 10.3 Sample screens from *Master of Mathomatics*. (*Source:* From *Chaffin & Maxwell's Math Mastery: Multiplication and Division.* © 1988 DLM, Teaching Resources, Allen, TX 75002.)

student performance. Sample screens of the game and data management system serve as an illustrative example of arithmetic computer games and are shown in Figure 10.3.

Process Acquisition

Time after time, the *demonstration plus permanent model technique* has proven exceptionally effective in teaching students how to solve those problems that include the operations of addition, subtraction, and multiplication. This technique takes approximately forty-five seconds of instructional time, is best applied individually, and can greatly facilitate mastery of computation. It is common for teachers using this procedure to report that students mastered an entire operation (subtraction) in only one school month.

When using this tactic, the teacher instructs and demonstrates before the student completes the arithmetic assignment for the day. The student is given a worksheet containing problems from the same response class (all three-digit problems containing zeros in the minuend's units and tens columns). Before the student solves the problems on the page, the teacher comes to the student's desk and computes a sample problem. Throughout this demonstration, the teacher verbalizes the steps used to arrive at the correct solution. The teacher then has the student solve another problem on the page to be certain that he or she can do so accurately. If that problem is correctly computed, the student completes the worksheet independently. This routine is followed for a minimum of three days or until the student reaches the criterion (three scores above 90%).

For long division, this procedure needs to be adapted slightly. Because of the complexity of long division and the number of steps involved in their solutions, some students need more assistance than a single demonstration. The script to follow when demonstrating long division to students is found on Table 10.6. In addition, some students become confused while solving these multistep problems, and the teacher asks the following (strategy) key questions:

1. What is the problem?
2. What are the steps?
3. What did you just do?
4. What do you do next?

Process Generalization

Recent research (Rivera & Smith, 1987a; Rivera & Smith, 1987b; Rivera & Smith, 1988) suggests that the sequence of instruction can facilitate both computational mastery and response generalization. Traditionally, special education teachers present information to students in a sequenced format. Students are taught the easiest skill in a task-analyzed sequence first. Once that skill is mastered, the next one is presented, and so on. In their research, students were taught how to compute long division problems that were neither the hardest nor

Table 10.6
Daily Procedures and Script to Teach Long Division

Step 1	
Teacher:	Shows students how to use fact table.
Step 2	
Teacher:	Shows graphs to each student. Points out changes on graph.
Step 3	
Teacher:	Implements intervention on demonstration problem (e.g., $5\overline{)1240}$).
	"Does 5 go into* 1? Does 5 go into 12?"
	"Place dot. $5\overline{)12.40}$ How many numbers are in the answer?"
	"Divide. How many times does 5 go into 12?" (Student says and writes answer.)
	"Multiply."
	"Subtract."
	"Check. Is the subtraction answer smaller than divisor? Yes, continue. No, check work."
	"Bring down." (Student brings down next number.)
	"Repeat."
	"Put up remainder, even if zero."
Step 4	
Student:	Solves a sample problem and verbalizes steps.
	If student completes problem correctly, then completes worksheet independently.
	If problem computed incorrectly, Steps 3 and 4 are repeated with different problems.

*Underlined words are key words emphasized by data collector.

Source: D. Rivera & D. D. Smith (1988), Using a demonstration strategy to teach learning-disabled midschool students how to compute long division, *Journal of Learning Disabilities, 21*(2).

easiest in the sequence. The students generalized their learning in both direc-tions, resulting in substantial savings in instructional time required to master the entire long division sequence. Although this study has not yet been replicated with the other arithmetic operations (addition, multiplication), the sequence of instruction may, in fact, facilitate generalization.

Problem Solving

Answering word problems and solving problems are not synonymous. Answer-ing word problems relies on the application of a formula when the worded problem so indicates, while problem solving is much broader and more complex. Students can be trained to solve arithmetic word problems. Although not the best approach because it does not lead to understanding and can mislead stu-dents to use the word method, teachers can drill students on key words con-tained in word problems. This method cannot be used to teach problem solving. For example, learning to look for the numbers in the sentences and key words (return, sell, buy, give) might lead to the wrong solution. Although a correlation exists between solving word problems and reading, eliminating the reading diffi-culty does not guarantee correct solutions.

To help students answer word problems, many teachers have found that students have more success if they are allowed to use manipulatives, such as blocks, to count out the problem's solution. For some youngsters, being able to

Table 10.7
Strategy for Approaching Word Problems

Are there words I do not know?
Restate the problem.
What's the problem's question?
What's the important information?
What are the key words?
Is there unnecessary information?
What numbers do I use?
Choose the operation to perform.
Do it!

verbalize the problem as they either count up (to add) or down (to subtract) helps them answer the problem. For others, being able to use a calculator removes the difficulty of having to compute the answer and allows the student to focus on the problem's demands. Some teachers have found that the questions cited in Tables 10.7 and 10.8 aid some children in solving word problems.

Table 10.8
Areas to Consider When Solving Word Problems

What information is needed?
  Highlight the information that is needed.
  List needed, missing information.
What operation will solve the problem?
  Mentally picture the problem.
Is the answer reasonable?
  Estimate before computing.

When teaching problem solving, there are some general notions (besides those found in Tables 7.2 and 7.3) that teachers should keep in mind. To become good problem solvers, students need to have many opportunities to solve problems. They need sufficient time to think, plan, discuss, and test their solutions. Problem solving requires a great deal of thinking and decision making. To help students approach problems, teachers should emphasize the three areas where they will have to make decisions (see Table 10.9). These questions can become an overall strategy to help students approach and solve problems.

Besides strategy approaches, it is most important that students have considerable practice in solving math-related problems. Groups of youngsters could be

Table 10.9
Problem-Solving Strategy

1. Get the information.
2. Understand the problem.
3. Solve the problem.

given many different problems throughout the school years that match their interests and experience. They could be asked to divide a roll of construction paper among all the fourth grade teachers, find possible ways to arrange five square blocks, or write the numbers from 1 to 25 as the sums of consecutive numbers. Have a group of three children share a banana. A group could be asked to cover a supermarket box so it can be used for classroom storage. The number of practical examples of problem-solving activities that are available in school settings is almost unlimited. It is important for students to develop these skills through instruction and practice.

SUMMARY

Mathematics is an important curricular area for all students—the skills it is composed of are important to independent adult living as well as to academic success. As teachers plan instruction, they must remember that mathematics is a complex area made up of many diverse skills. Although many students with special needs receive instruction predominately on arithmetic computation, instructional balance should be sought. All students should be exposed to a wide variety of topics, such as consumer skills, measurement, problem solving, numeration, and computation. They should also be taught to use calculators and computers, which might facilitate reasoning skills.

Research provides considerable information about many instructional tactics that are effective in assisting students to master mathematical concepts and skills (see Table 10.3 for a review). These procedures include modeling, drill and practice, computer-assisted instruction, and problem solving strategies. Throughout the instructional process, however, teachers must remember to apply the stages of learning theory as they help children master mathematics. Unless students have acquired requisite skills in mathematics and can maintain their proficient use, they will be unable to think through situations requiring mathematics, which are routinely encountered in daily life.

STUDY AND DISCUSSION QUESTIONS

1. Provide three reasons for changing the orientation of the traditional mathematics curriculum for students with special needs.
2. Discuss how to decide how much emphasis should be placed on teaching computation to specific youngsters. Develop a case study.
3. What are the purposes of curriculum-based assessment for mathematics?
4. Describe ways to integrate calculators into the instructional program.
5. Prepare a lesson plan to teach a group of students how to solve a mathematically based problem.
6. List the steps followed when applying the demonstration plus permanent model technique. When and how is it best applied?

REFERENCES AND SUGGESTED READINGS

General Mathematics Remediation

BLEY, N. S., & THORNTON, C. A. (1981). *Teaching mathematics to the learning disabled.* Rockville, MD: Aspen Systems.

BROWN, V. L. (1985). Direction mathematics: A framework for instructional accountability. *Remedial and Special Education, 6*(1), 53–58.

CARPENTER, R. L. (1985). Mathematics instruction in resource rooms: Instruction time and teacher competency. *Learning Disability Quarterly, 8,* 95–100.

CARPENTER, R. L., COBURN, T. G., REYS, R. E., & WILSON, J. W. (1978). *Results from the first mathematics assessment of the National Assessment of Educational Progress.* Reston, VA: National Council of Teachers of Mathematics.

CARPENTER, T. P., COBURN, T. G., REYS, R. E., & WILSON, J. W. (1975a). Results and implications of the NAEP mathematics assessment: Elementary school. *The Arithmetic Teacher, 22,* 438–450.

CARPENTER, T. P., COBURN, T. G., REYS, R. E., & WILSON, J. W. (1975b). Notes from national assessment: Basic concepts of area and volume. *The Arithmetic Teacher, 22,* 501–507.

CARPENTER, T. P., CORBITT, M. K., KEPNER, H., LINDQUIST, M. M., & REYS, R. E. (1980). Results and implications of the second NAEP mathematics assessment: Elementary school. *Arithmetic Teacher, 27,* 10–12, 44–47.

CAWLEY, J. F., FITZMAURICE, A. M., SHAW, R., KAHN, H., & BATES, H. (1979). LD youth and mathematics: A review of characteristics. *Learning Disability Quarterly, 2,* 29–44.

CHANDLER, H. N. (1978). Confusion compounded: A teacher tries to use research results to teach math. *Journal of Learning Disabilities, 11,* 361–369.

CONNOLLY, A. J., NACHTMAN, W., & PRITCHETT, E. M. (1988). *KeyMath revised: A diagnostic inventory of essential mathematics* (manual). Circle Pines, MN: American Guidance Service.

COPELAND, R. W. (1970). *How children learn mathematics: Teaching implications of Piaget's research.* New York: Macmillan.

JOHNSON, S. W. (1979). *Arithmetic and learning disabilities: Guidelines for identification and remediation.* Boston: Allyn & Bacon.

McLEOD, T. M., & ARMSTRONG, S. W. (1982). Learning disabilities in mathematics—Skill deficits and remedial approaches at the intermediate and secondary level. *Learning Disability Quarterly, 5,* 305–311.

NATIONAL COUNCIL FOR TEACHERS OF MATHEMATICS (1980). *Agenda for action: Recommendations for school mathematics.* Reston, VA: National Council for Teachers of Mathematics.

REISMAN, F. K., & KAUFMAN, S. H. (1980). *Teaching mathematics to children with special needs.* Columbus, OH: Charles E. Merrill.

SUYDAM, M. N. (1979). The case for a comprehensive mathematics curriculum. *Arithmetic Teacher, 26,* 10–11.

Numeration

HAMRICK, K. B. (1979). Oral language and readiness for written symbolization of addition and subtraction. *Journal for Research in Mathematics Education, 10,* 188–194.

Computation

BLANKENSHIP, C. S. (1978). Remediating systematic inversion errors in subtraction through the use of demonstration and feedback. *Learning Disability Quarterly, 1,* 12–22.

BRIGHT, G. W., HARVEY, J. G., & WHEELER, M. M. (1979). Using games to retrain skills with basic multiplication facts. *Journal for Research in Mathematics Education, 10,* 103–110.

COX, L. S. (1975). Diagnosing and remediating systematic errors in addition and subtraction computations. *The Arithmetic Teacher, 22,* 151–157.

CULLINAN, D., LLOYD, J., & EPSTEIN, M. H. (1981). Strategy Training: A structured approach to arithmetic. *Exceptional Education Quarterly, 2,* 41–49.

ENGLEMANN, S., & CARNINE, D. (1972). *Distar II.* Chicago: Science Research Associates.

ENGLEMANN, S., & STEELY, D. (1981). *Corrective math.* Chicago: Science Research Associates.

FIRL, D. H. (1977). Fractions, decimals, and their futures. *The Arithmetic Teacher, 24,* 238–240.

KILLIAN, L., CAHILL, E., RYAN, C., SUTHERLAND, D., & TACCETTA, D. (1980). Errors that are common in multiplication. *Arithmetic Teacher, 27,* 22–25.

KIRBY, F. D., & SHIELDS, F. (1972). Modification of arithmetic response rate and attending behavior in a seventh-grade student. *Journal of Applied Behavior Analysis, 5,* 79–84.

LOVITT, T. C. (1984). *Tactics for teaching.* Columbus, OH: Charles E. Merrill.

LOVITT, T. C., & CURTISS, K. A. (1968). Effects of manipulating an antecedent event on mathematics response rate. *Journal of Applied Behavior Analysis, 1,* 329–333.

LOVITT, T. C., & ESVELDT, K. A. (1970). The relative effects on math performance of single- versus multiple-ratio schedules: A case study. *Journal of Applied Behavior Analysis, 3,* 261–270.

LOVITT, T. C., & SMITH, D. D. (1974). Using withdrawal of positive reinforcement to alter subtraction performance. *Exceptional Children, 40,* 357–358.

MAERTENS, N., & JOHNSTON, J. (1972). Effects of arithmetic homework upon the attitudes and achievement of fourth, fifth, and sixth grade pupils. *School Science and Mathematics, 72,* 117–126.

MERCER, C. D. (1979). *Children and adolescents with learning disabilities.* Columbus, OH: Charles E. Merrill.

MEYER, P. I. (1980). When you use a calculator you have to think! *Arithmetic Teacher, 27,* 18–21.

PETERSON, D. L. (1973). *Functional mathematics for the mentally retarded.* Columbus, OH: Charles E. Merrill.

REISMAN, F. K. (1972). *A guide to the diagnostic teaching of arithmetic.* Columbus, OH: Charles E. Merrill.

SCHOEN, H. L., & ZWENG, M. J. (1986). *Estimation and mental computation: 1986 yearbook.* Reston, VA: National Council for Teachers of Mathematics.

SMITH, D. D., & LOVITT, T. C. (1975). The use of modeling techniques to influence the acquisition of computational arithmetic skills in learning-disabled children. In E. Ramp & G. Semb (eds.), *Behavior analysis: Areas of research and application.* Englewood Cliffs, NJ: Prentice Hall.

SMITH, D. D., & LOVITT, T. C. (1976). The differential effects of reinforcement contingencies on arithmetic performance. *Journal of Learning Disabilities, 9,* 32–40.

SMITH, D. D., & LOVITT, T. C. (1982). *The computational arithmetic program.* Austin, TX: Pro-Ed.

SMITH, W. D. (1978). Minimal competencies: A position paper. *Arithmetic Teacher, 26,* 25–26.

STEVENSON, H., & FANTUZZO, J. W. (1986). The generality and social validity of a competency-based self-control training intervention for underachieving students. *Journal of Applied Behavior Analysis, 19,* 269–276.

TRANTHAM, P. R. (NATIONAL COUNCIL OF TEACHERS OF MATHEMATICS). (1979). Toward a better balanced curriculum. *Arithmetic Teacher, 26*(6), 2, 59.

WOOD, S., BURKE, L., KUNZELMANN, H., & KOENIG, C. (1978). Functional criteria in basic math skill proficiency. *Journal of Special Education Technology, 2,* 29–36.

Facts

BRULLE, A. R., & BRULLE, C. G. (1982). Basic computational facts: A problem and a procedure. *Arithmetic Teacher, 29*(7), 34–36.

CULLINAN, D., LLOYD, J., & EPSTEIN, M. H. (1981). Strategy training: A structured approach to arithmetic instruction. *Exceptional Education Quarterly, 2,* 41–49.

GARNETT, K., & FLEISCHNER, J. E. (1983). Automatization and basic fact performance of normal and learning disabled children. *Learning Disability Quarterly, 6,* 223–231.

LLOYD, J., SALTZMAN, N. J., & KAUFFMAN, J. M. (1981). Predictable generalization in academic learning as a result of preskills and strategy training. *Learning Disability Quarterly, 4,* 203–216.

Process Computation

BLANKENSHIP, C. S., & BAUMGARTNER, M. D. (1982). Programming generalization of computational skills. *Learning Disability Quarterly, 5,* 152–162.

RIVERA, D., & SMITH, D. D. (1988). Using a demonstration strategy to teach learning disabled midschool students how to compute long division. *Journal of Learning Disabilities, 21*(2), 77–81.

RIVERA, D., & SMITH, D. D. (1987a). Facilitating generalization for computational arithmetic. Albuquerque: University of New Mexico, Special Education Department.

RIVERA, D., & SMITH, D. D. (1987b). Influence of modeling on acquisition and generalization of computational skills: A summary of research findings from three sites. *Learning Disability Quarterly, 10,* 69–80.

Systematic Errors

ASHLOCK, R. B. (1986). *Error patterns in computation: A semi-programmed approach* (4th ed.). Columbus, OH: Charles E. Merrill.

BLANKENSHIP, C. S., & KORN, J. (1980). *Differential effects of antecedent and consequent events on two types of arithmetic errors.* Unpublished manuscript. Champaign-Urbana: University of Illinois.

ENGELHARDT, J. M. (1982). Using computational errors in diagnostic teaching. *Arithmetic Teacher, 29*(8), 16–18.

SHAW, R. A., & PELOSI, P. A. (1983). In search of computational errors. *Arithmetic Teacher, 30*(7), 50–51.

Calculator Usage

BEARDSLEE, E. C. (1978). Teaching computational skills with a calculator. In M. Suydam & R. Reys (eds.), *Developing computational skills: 1978 yearbook*. Reston, VA: National Council of Teachers of Mathematics.

BELL, M. S. (1976). Calculators in elementary schools? Some tentative guidelines based on classroom experience. *The Arithmetic Teacher, 23*, 502–508.

CAPPS, L. R., & HATFIELD, M. M. (1977). Mathematical concepts and skills: Diagnosis, prescription, and correction of deficiencies. *Focus on Exceptional Children, 8*, 1–8.

CARAVELLA, J. R. (1977). *Minicalculators in the classroom*. Washington, D.C.: National Education Association.

CARPENTER, T. P., CORBITT, M. K., KEPNER, H. S., LINDQUIST, M. M., & REYS, R. E. (1981). Calculators in testing situations: Results and implications from national assessment. *Arithmetic Teacher, 28*(5), 34–37.

CRESWELL, J. L., & VAUGHN, L. R. (1979). Hand-held calculator curriculum and mathematical achievement and retention. *Journal for Research in Mathematics Education, 10*, 64–67.

GALLERY, M. E., & RICKERT, D. C. (1978). It figures. A program to teach calculator skills to the mildly handicapped. *Journal of Special Education Technology, 2*, 15–21.

GAWRONSKI, J. D., & COBLENTZ, D. (1976). Calculators and the mathematics curriculum. *Arithmetic Teacher, 23*, 510–512.

MILLER, D. (1982). *Motivational activities for low (and higher) achievers*. Columbus, OH: Calculator Information Center.

MORRIS, J. (1981). *How to develop problem solving using a calculator*. Reston, VA: National Council of Teachers of Mathematics.

O'NEIL, D. R., & JENSEN, R. (1982). Let's do it: Let's use calculators. *Arithmetic Teacher, 29*, 6–9.

REYS, R. E. (1980). Calculators in the elementary classroom: How can we go wrong! *Arithmetic Teacher, 29*, 38–40.

REYS, R. E., BESTGEN, B. J., RYBOLT, J. F., & WYATT, J. W. (1980). Hand calculators: What's happening in school today? *Arithmetic Teacher, 27*, 38–43.

SHULT, D. L. (1978). Calculators, computers, and exceptional children. *Journal of Special Education Technology, 2*, 59–65.

SHUMAY, R. S., WHEATLEY, G. H., COBURN, T. G., WHITE, A. L., REYS, R. E., & SCHOEN, H. L. (1981). Initial effect of calculators in elementary school mathematics. *Journal for Research in Mathematics Education, 12*, 119–141.

TEITELBAUM, E. (1978). Calculators for classroom use? *Arithmetic Teacher, 26*, 18–20.

TRINGO, J. L., & ROIT, M. L. (1977). *Telling time—Time instruction by modular elements*. Northbrook, IL: Hubbard.

VAN ETTEN, C., & WATSON, B. (1978). Arithmetic skills. Assessment and instruction. *Journal of Learning Disabilities, 11*, 155–162.

VAN HOUTEN, R., MORRISON, E., BARROW, B., & WENAUS, J. (1975). The effects of daily practice and feedback on the acquisition of elementary math skills. *School Applications of Learning Theory, 7*, 1–16.

VASTA, R., & STIRPE, L. A. (1979). Reinforcement effects on three measures of children's interest in math. *Behavior Modification, 3*, 223–244.

WHEATLEY, G. H., SHUMWAY, R. J., COBURN, T. G., REYS, R. E., SCHOEN, H. L., WHEATLEY, C. L., & WHITE, A. L. (1979). Calculators in elementary schools. *Arithmetic Teacher, 27*, 18–21.

Computer Applications

EDUCATIONAL INFORMATION SYSTEMS. (1982a). *Alien addition,* Allen, TX: Developmental Learning Materials.

EDUCATIONAL INFORMATION SYSTEMS. (1982b). *Demolition division.* Allen, TX: Developmental Learning Materials.

EDUCATIONAL INFORMATION SYSTEMS. (1982c). *Meteor multiplication.* Allen, TX: Developmental Learning Materials.

EDUCATIONAL INFORMATION SYSTEMS. (1982d). *Minus mission.* Allen, TX: Developmental Learning Materials.

EDUCATIONAL INFORMATION SYSTEMS. (1983). *Alien action.* Allen, TX: Developmental Learning Materials.

EDUCATIONAL INFORMATION SYSTEMS. (1987a). *Decimal discovery.* Allen, TX: Developmental Learning Materials.

EDUCATIONAL INFORMATION SYSTEMS. (1987b). *Fast track fractions.* Allen, TX: Developmental Learning Materials.

EDUCATIONAL INFORMATION SYSTEMS. (1988). *Master of Mathomatics.* Allen, TX: Developmental Learning Materials.

TRIFILETTI, J. J., FRITH, G. H., & ARMSTRONG, S. (1984). Microcomputers versus resource rooms for students: A preliminary investigation of the effects on math skills. *Learning Disability Quarterly, 7,* 69–76.

Study Skills

CHRISTOPHER L. (1982). Graphs can jazz up the mathematics curriculum. *Arithmetic Teacher, 30*(1), 28–30.

NIBBELINK, W. (1982). Graphing for any grade. *Arithmetic Teacher, 30*(3), 28–31.

Consumer Mathematics

DAHLQUIST, J. (1977). Playing store for real. *The Arithmetic Teacher, 24,* 208–210.

DOEBLING, M. J. (1981). The mathematics of buying a car: A basic skills unit. *Mathematics Teacher, 74*(3), 184–186, 238.

LANGE, W. H., MASON, R. D., & ROUSOS, T. G. (1982). *Consumer mathematics.* Atlanta: Houghton Mifflin.

WARD, S., WACKMAN, D. B., & WARTELL, E. (1977). *How children learn to buy.* Beverly Hills, CA: Sage.

Problem Solving

BLANKENSHIP, C. S., & LOVITT, T. C. (1976). Story problems: Merely confusing or downright befuddling. *Journal for Research in Mathematics Education, 7,* 290–298.

BRUNI, J. V. (1982). Problem solving for the primary grades. *Arithmetic Teacher, 29*(6), 10–15.

BURNS, M. (1982). How to teach problem solving. *Arithmetic Teacher, 29*(6), 46–49.

CARLSON, J., GRUENEWALD, L. J., & NYBERG, B. (1980). Everyday math is a story problem: The language of the curriculum. *Language Disorders and Learning Disabilities, 1,* 59–70.

CARPENTER, T. P., MOSER, J. M., & ROMBERG, T. A. (1982). *Addition and subtraction: A cognitive perspective.* Hillsdale, NJ: Erlbaum.

CAWLEY, J. F., FITZMAURICE, A. M., GOODSTEIN, H. A., LEPORE, A. V., SEDLAK, R., & ALTHAUS, V. (1976a). *Project math* (Level 1). Tulsa, OK: Educational Development.

CAWLEY, J. F., FITZMAURICE, A. M., GOODSTEIN, H. A., LEPORE, A. V., SEDLAK, R., & ALTHAUS, V. (1976b). *Project math* (Level 2). Tulsa, OK: Educational Development.

FISHER, B. (1979). Calculator games: Combining skills and problem solving. *Arithmetic Teacher, 27,* 40–41.

FLEISCHNER, J. E., NUZUM, M. B., & MARZOLA, E. S. (1987). Devising an instructional program to teach arithmetic problem-solving skills to students with learning disabilities. *Journal of Learning Disabilities, 20,* 214–217.

LARSEN, S. C., PARKER, R. M., & TRENHOLME, B. (1978). The effects of syntactic complexity upon arithmetic performance. *Learning Disability Quarterly, 1,* 80–85.

LOVITT, T. C. (1978). Managing inappropriate behaviors in the classroom. Reston, VA: Council for Exceptional Children.

MALETSKY, E. M. (1982). Problem solving for the junior high school. *Arithmetic Teacher, 29*(6), 20–24.

MEYER, P. I. (1980). When you use a calculator you have to think! *Arithmetic Teacher, 27,* 18–21.

MOSER, J. M., & CARPENTER, T. P. (1982). Young children are good problem solvers. *Arithmetic Teacher, 30*(3), 24–26.

MOYER, J. C., MOYER, S. B., SOWDER, L., & THREADGILL-SOWDER, J. (1984). Story problem formats: Verbal versus telegraphic. *Journal for Research in Mathematics Education, 15*(1), 64–68.

NATIONAL COUNCIL FOR TEACHERS OF MATHEMATICS. (1979). Toward a better balanced curriculum. *Arithmetic Teacher, 26,* 2, 59.

NATIONAL COUNCIL FOR TEACHERS OF MATHEMATICS (1980). *An agenda for action: Recommendations for school mathematics of the 1980s.* Reston, VA: National Council of Teachers of Mathematics.

PELLEGRINO, J. M., & GOLDMAN, S. R. (1987). Information processing and elementary mathematics. *Journal of Learning Disabilities, 20,* 23–32, 57.

PETERSON, D. L. (1973). Functional mathematics for the mentally retarded. Columbus, OH: Charles E. Merrill.

REISMAN, F. K. (1972). *A guide to the diagnostic teaching of arithmetic.* Columbus, OH: Charles E. Merrill.

RILEY, J. G., GREENO, J. G., & HELLER, J. I. (1983). Development of children's problem solving ability in arithmetic. In H. P. Ginsburg (ed.), *The development of mathematical thinking.* New York: Academic Press.

SCHOEN, H. L., & ZWENG, M. J. (1986). *Estimation and mental computation: 1986 yearbook.* Reston, VA: National Council for Teachers of Mathematics.

SUYDAM, M. N. (1982). Update on research on problem solving: Implications for classroom teaching. *Arithmetic Teacher, 29*(6), 56–60.

THORNTON, C. A., & BLEY, N. S. (1982). Problem solving: Help in the right direction for LD students. *Arithmetic Teacher, 29*(6), 26–27, 38–41.

TOBIN, A. (1982). Scope and sequence for a problem solving curriculum. *Arithmetic Teacher, 29*(6), 62–65.

WORTH, J. (1982). Problem solving in the intermediate grades: Helping your students learn to solve problems. *Arithmetic Teacher, 29*(6), 16–19.

11

Study Skills

Being able to study independently is an important skill, particularly for those students who try to compete successfully in regular education classes at the middle and secondary levels. The setting demands (discussed in Chapter 1) of regular education's content subject courses are difficult for many students with special needs. Most middle and high school teachers expect students to gain information from textbooks that are often beyond their reading abilities and from lectures that surpass their auditory comprehension abilities. If students with special needs are to pass classes in history, social studies, and science, they need to develop the skills that allow them to organize and remember vast amounts of information. Students also must demonstrate their knowledge by writing reports, taking tests, and participating in class discussions.

Many special education teachers of middle and high school students engage in "crisis teaching." They help students complete homework assignments. They tutor youngsters so they have a better chance of passing upcoming tests in their regular education classes. This approach is not highly successful for most students with special needs; at best, it is only a temporary solution to academic difficulties. For such students to be more successful in regular education classes, they must learn strategies that they can use to meet more advanced curricular demands. They need to develop study, test-taking, and theme and report writing skills. As more and more strategies for these skill areas are developed, the content of many middle and secondary special education classes should change. For those students who remain in regular education content courses, the teaching approach of special education classes should shift away from crisis teaching or tutoring to a learning strategies approach.

Special education teachers and parents need to consider whether maintaining students in the regular education curriculum is appropriate for all students with special needs. For some, success in later life might be enhanced if they were placed in a curriculum option oriented to career education and independent living skills (see Chapter 12). Issues surrounding the tracking of students into various curriculum options are complex. Once students are placed, they are usually bound to that curriculum track. Flexibility is lost. If more curricular options are made available, how will decisions about which students should receive what type of instruction be determined? Who should take the responsibility for making conscious, placement decisions that could become prophecies self-fulfilled?

The information presented in this chapter reflects recent interests of researchers, curriculum developers, and teachers. Considerable development activity is currently underway. The intervention strategies described here reflect only a sampling of tactics aimed to improve students' abilities to cope with regular education classes and content subject information presented in the later years of school. Although most of these strategies were developed for students who have at least a fourth grade reading level, some of these concepts can be adapted for younger children as well. Teaching students how to study and learn independently should begin early in students' school careers. These skills are particularly related to students' successful coping with the academic demands of least restrictive environments.

TOPICS OF INSTRUCTION

For students to learn from textbooks, teachers' lectures, and class discussions, they must develop a number of skills. They must learn to think, organize information so it is useful, discriminate important from irrelevant information, gain knowledge, and remember it. They must demonstrate their mastery of content by taking objective tests, writing themes and reports, and answering short answer essays found on tests. In this section some aspects of these study skills are discussed (see Chapter 8 for information about improved reading and comprehension skills and Chapter 9 for writing skills).

Thinking Skills: Classification, Association, Sequencing

A prerequisite to efficient studying is being able to think. Students must organize information into usable units and know when and how to use that information. Several thinking skills are particularly relevant to organizing and relating information: classifying, associating, and sequencing. These skills can be taught to students through direct instruction, drill, and practice. Classification, categorizing, and grouping items and information together by relevant characteristics allows individuals to "chunk" information so it is more easily remembered. Being able to associate items by some common denominator helps individuals to see the relationships that exist among and between different knowledge bases. Sequencing allows individuals to put things, items, and concepts into an order that may be rather concrete (size, volume) or abstract (complexity). These skills could be viewed as prerequisite to advanced learning, complex memorization, and study skills.

Thinking skills are related to academic success. Being able to categorize or "chunk" information into usable units helps people to remember large amounts of information that otherwise could not be remembered. For example, knowing that a list of forty items belongs to five common categories (fruits, vegetables, meats, types of cars, kinds of dogs) facilitates remembering long lists. Being able to associate items along various dimensions also facilitates memory but, more important, allows information to be used in meaningful ways. Through associations, students find the connections or common elements that units of information possess. They are able to recognize common attributes that facilitate memory and problem solving. For example, being able to relate items or things that are fast, cold, hard, tall, or sharp allows people to relate information on different dimensions. Being able to sequence allows people to put things into an order or hierarchy as another way to organize information.

These thinking skills are often not taught directly in school. Students do not have the opportunity to experiment in classifying, finding relationships, sequencing, determining the common attributes of items and information, clustering information, or identifying a category and its elements. With practice and guided instruction, thinking skills can be developed. An example of one microcomputer software program that allows students to practice and use these skills in gamelike situations is shown in Figure 11.1. Regardless of how the material is presented, students need opportunities to think about and use information that exists in the world around them. These experiences can and should be planned for throughout the school years. The development of these skills facilitates an ability to think, learn, and organize the content presented in school.

Learning and Remembering Content Information

Through their comprehensive research, the University of Kansas Research Institute on Learning Disabilities (KU-IRLD) researchers found that many students are unable to meet the demands of secondary schools. Some of those demands are gaining information and knowledge from textbooks and lectures. To pass tests given by secondary teachers, students must organize and memorize information. They need to be aware of how bits of information are related and associated (that, for example, Huron, Ontario, Michigan, Erie, and Superior—HOMES—are the Great Lakes). Finally, they need to approach studying in an organized fashion, so they collect and treat the information for later use. The KU-IRLD researchers have developed a number of learning strategies that rely on the use of mnemonics (like HOMES). These strategies help students to remember information. Details about specific study strategies (taking notes, taking tests, and remembering content information) are found later in this chapter.

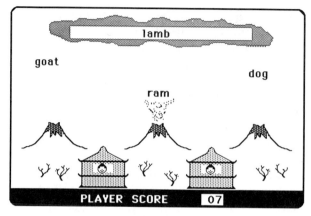

Figure 11.1 MicroSoc Thinking Games' game and words missed screen. (*Source:* Reproduced by permission of American Guidance Service, Inc., Circle Pines, MN 55014. *MicroSoc Thinking Games* by B. Maxwell, B. Thompson, J. Chaffin, D. Smith, J. O. Smith. © 1985. Rights reserved.)

Information about other learning strategies (error monitoring, paraphrasing) also developed by KU-IRLD is found elsewhere in this book.

Besides teaching students learning strategies, teachers can facilitate learning and memory through their mode of presentation. Darch and Carnine (1986) found that teachers can help students to remember content information by using particular instructional formats. In their study, the group of students whose teachers used visual aids that categorized and organized information surpassed another group who studied the material from a textbook. As discussed earlier (see Chapter 7), advance organizers—where teachers introduce lessons and instructional topics well—also facilitate comprehension and memory. Clearly, the ways in which teachers present content information to students influences how well students learn.

Maintenance and Generalization

Unless teachers promote and encourage maintenance and generalization of study skills, these skills will probably not be remembered or used when appropriate (Borkowski & Varnhagen, 1984; Borkowski, Weyhing, & Turner, 1986; Ellis, 1986). Considerable discussion about maintenance and generalization of skills is presented throughout this text, but it is important to remember that skills do not become or remain useful automatically. As with all academic and social targets, study skills must be acquired by students, brought to a level of proficient use that must be maintained, and then used when appropriate (generalized). Unless teachers help students to generalize their learning of study skills, the probability is that they will not apply this knowledge in regular education content courses.

Ellis (1986) maintains that some interventions commonly used by teachers impede generalization. Tactics such as feedback, when overly relied upon, reinforce dependency, learned helplessness, and learning inactivity (see Chapter 1 for more details). On the other hand, some interventions, such as self-management, enhance the likelihood of generalization.

Students must understand that learning how to study can be difficult and time consuming. Teachers need to prepare students for their learning of study skills. They must indicate to their students that considerable work is required to master study skills and additional efforts are necessary for them to persist in using them so their performance in content subject courses will be more successful. In this regard, it is often helpful to provide students with rationales (reasons) for expending the energy necessary to learn and apply these skills. These rationales need to be given as students acquire and begin to generalize their application of study skills. Self-management tactics, where students are actively involved in the learning situation, facilitate generalization. These tactics require students to regulate and monitor their own behavior and reward themselves for achievement. Also, some teachers have found that once students have mastered a particular study technique, cueing them to use that strategy helps with generalization. These cues, or reminders, should be given by the special educator who taught the student the strategy and by the regular educator who can help the student remember to use the technique when appropriate in that setting as well. Possessing skills and applying them in the proper situations are two different aspects of learning. Teachers must be vigilant and continually monitor students' application of study skills to ensure that they are used to advantage.

TEACHING TACTICS

Several specific strategies and procedures that are used to teach students various study skills are discussed in this section. As stated previously, work in this area is in the formative stages. As interest in the area of study skills gathers momentum, more interventions will be developed and verified through research. Three important study skills areas—taking notes, learning and remembering content, and taking tests—are discussed in the following sections.

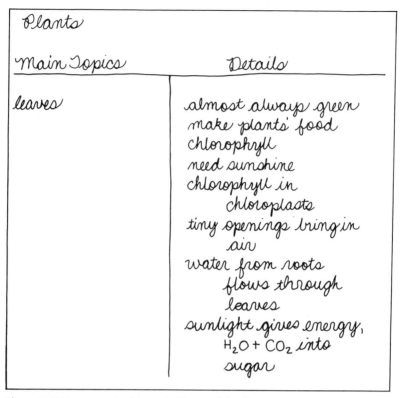

Plants

Main Topics | Details

leaves | almost always green
make plants' food
chlorophyll
need sunshine
chlorophyll in
chloroplasts
tiny openings bring in
air
water from roots
flows through
leaves
sunlight gives energy,
$H_2O + CO_2$ into
sugar

Figure 11.2 Notes organized by main ideas and details.

Taking Notes

Students need to gain information from teachers' lectures. In secondary schools, one important setting demand (see Chapter 1) is an ability to listen and remember information given primarily in lectures. Teachers give students many subtle cues (both verbal and nonverbal) to indicate important information that will be on tests. For example, one teacher might underline important points written on the blackboard or an overhead projector. Another might tell students, "This is important information to remember. It will be on the test." To help students take notes, the KU-IRLD[1] researchers have developed a notetaking method whereby students write the main ideas in one column and the details in another. Figure 11.2 shows student's notes that were organized in this fashion. These topic and information organizers are like those used in the paraphrasing strategy described in Chapter 8.

[1]For more information or training about the use of specific learning strategies developed by KU-IRLD, contact Dr. Fran Clark, University of Kansas Institute for Research in Learning Disabilities, 223 Carruth-O'Leary Hall, Lawrence, KS 66045.

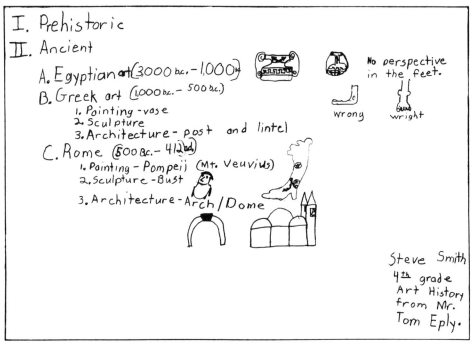

Figure 11.3 A fourth grader's art history notes using the traditional outlining method.

Also, many teachers teach students to take notes by the more traditional outlining method, having students place short descriptors of each major topic next to a roman numeral (I, II, III) and detail information beneath each main heading. To use the outlining methods requires students to categorize and associate information, the prerequisite skills to studying that were discussed earlier in this chapter. In Figure 11.3, a fourth grader's notes taken from an art history lecture are shown as an example of the outlining method.

Learning and Remembering Content Information

Students need to gain information from textbooks, frequently written at a level higher than their reading ability. They also need to organize that information and memorize it so they can pass tests and participate in class discussions. Without these skills, they cannot function adequately in regular education classes. The KU-IRLD researchers developed procedures that help students improve their abilities in these areas. The FIRST[2] Letter Mnemonic Strategy (known to students as FIRST) is a strategy that helps students learn and relate content information. The steps used in this strategy are found in Table 11.1.

To learn and use the FIRST strategy, students must be able to discriminate

[2]Ibid.

Table 11.1
FIRST-Letter Mnemonic Strategy

STEPS FOR DESIGNING A MNEMONIC DEVICE

Step 1: **F**orm a word.
Step 2: **I**nsert a letter(s).
Step 3: **R**earrange the letters.
Step 4: **S**hape a sentence.
Step 5: **T**ry combinations.

Source: D. R. Nagel, J. B. Schumaker, & D. D. Deshler, *Learning Strategies Curriculum: The FIRST-letter Mnemonic Strategy* (Lawrence, KS: Excel Enterprises, 1986), p. 101.

main ideas from details. They must be able to identify a topic (deserts) and find the details (Mohave, Arabian, Thar, and Sahara). To help them remember the information, students develop mnemonic devices (MATS) for each group or cluster of information. Then to help students know which mnemonic device relates to specific information, students are taught to associate their mnemonic with a picture they can visualize in their minds (mats on the desert). Some students who have mastered the FIRST strategy have improved their grades in regular education classes from F's to B's.

Taking Tests

At school, being able to pass tests is an important ability. Tests become more and more complicated. By high school, they can be quite difficult. Even students who have studied well and know the content that the test covers might not receive a passing grade if they cannot handle the testing situation. Secondary school teachers often create tests that use different types of questions: true/false, multiple choice, matching, and short answer. To help students take tests, the KU-IRLD researchers developed a test-taking strategy, PIRATES.[3] Table 11.2 shows the steps used in this strategy.

PIRATES does not help children memorize or learn the content found on tests. It does help students learn how to handle the testing situation, particularly for social studies and science. Students who cannot successfully answer short answer questions because they cannot write coherent paragraphs should be taught the writing strategies discussed in Chapter 9 of this book. To teach this strategy, the developers have created several tests that allow students to answer questions written in the same format as tests used by secondary teachers. For example, students can practice test-taking skills on such questions as: Guyems who live in the Land of Ponch are this tall: (a) one foot, (b) about two and a half feet, (c) twelve inches, (d) ninety-two inches. Through a process of elimination, students should select item (b) as their choice for these reasons: items (a) and (c)

[3]Ibid.

Table 11.2
The PIRATES Test-Taking Strategy

Step 1: Prepare to succeed.

Put "PIRATES" and name on the test.
Allot time and order to sections.
Say something positive.
Start within 2 minutes.

Step 2: Inspect the instructions.

Read the instructions carefully.
Underline how and where to respond.
Notice special requirements.

Step 3: Read, remember, reduce.

Read the whole question.
Remember with memory strategies.
Reduce choices.

Step 4: Answer or abandon.

Answer the question.
Abandon the question if you're not sure.

Step 5: Turn back.

Turn back to abandoned questions when you get to the end of the test.
Tell yourself to earn more points.

Step 6: Estimate.

Estimate unknown answers using the "ACE" guessing techniques:
Avoid absolutes.
Choose the longest or most detailed choice.
Eliminate identical choices.

Step 7: Survey

Survey to ensure that all questions are answered.
Switch an answer only if you're sure.

Source: C. A. Hughes, J. B. Schumaker, D. D. Deshler, & C. Mercer, The test-taking strategy (cuecard 1) (Lawrence, KS: Excel Enterprises, 1987). Used by permission.

are the same answer, and item (d) is too exact to describe the height of a group of people.

SUMMARY

As discussed in the first chapter of this book, the demands of settings in middle schools and high schools are quite substantial. Students are expected to gain information from textbooks and lectures. They need to organize, remember, and use that information to pass tests and write themes and reports. Although study skills are not always taught directly at school, they are required to cope with the secondary school curriculum.

Some special educators would argue that not all students with mild handicaps should be retained in the regular education curriculum. They believe that other, perhaps several, alternative curriculum tracks should be available for students, particularly those with special needs. However, students who are able to or who wish to compete with their normal counterparts in traditional history, English, and literature courses must develop the abilities to take notes, tests, and write themes and reports.

STUDY AND DISCUSSION QUESTIONS

1. Develop a practice test for students to use when learning the test-taking strategy PIRATES.
2. In your opinion should there be different curricular options for students with special needs? If so, what should they be and how should students be selected for these options? If not, provide your reasons.
3. Plan at least one lesson to teach association, categorization, or sequencing thinking skills.
4. Create a test to use in a lesson to teach students how to answer true/false, matching, and multiple choice questions.
5. Using a chapter from a social studies or history text, create mnemonics to help remember the content.

REFERENCES AND SUGGESTED READINGS

Study Skills

DESHLER, D. D., WARNER, M. M., SCHUMAKER, J. B., & ALLEY, G. R. (1983). Learning strategies intervention model: Key components and current status. In J. D. McKinney & F. Feagans (eds.), *Current topics in learning disabilities,* Vol. 1. Norwood, NJ: Ablex.

SCHUMAKER, J. B., DESHLER, D. D., ALLEY, G. R., & WARNER, M. M. (1983). Toward the development of an intervention model for learning-disabled adolescents: The University of Kansas Institute. *Exceptional Education Quarterly, 4,* 45–74.

WALLACE, G., & KAUFFMAN, J. M. (1986). *Teaching students with learning and behavior problems.* Columbus, OH: Charles E. Merrill.

Thinking Skills: Classification, Associations, Sequencing

CHAFFIN, J., MAXWELL, B., THOMPSON, B., SMITH, D. D., & SMITH, J. O. (1985). *MicroSoc Thinking Games: SocPix.* Circle Pines, MN: American Guidance Service.

MAXWELL, B., THOMPSON, B., CHAFFIN, J., SMITH, D. D., & SMITH, J. O. (1985). *MicroSoc Thinking Games: SocOrder.* Circle Pines, MN: American Guidance Service.

SALATAS, H., & FLAVELL, J. H. (1976). Behavioral and metamnemonic indicators of strategic behaviors under remember instructions in first grade. *Child Development, 47,* 81–90.

SMITH, D. D., SMITH, J. O., MAXWELL, B., THOMPSON, B., & CHAFFIN, J. (1985). *MicroSoc Thinking Games: SocSort.* Circle Pines, MN: American Guidance Service.

SMITH, D. D., SMITH, J. O., MAXWELL, B., THOMPSON, B., & CHAFFIN, J. (1985). *Microsoc Thinking Games: SocMate.* Circle Pines, MN: American Guidance Service.

THOMPSON, B., MAXWELL, B., CHAFFIN, J., SMITH, D. D., & SMITH, J. O. (1985). *MicroSoc Thinking Games: SocMatch.* Circle Pines, MN: American Guidance Service.

Learning and Memorizing Content Information

DARCH, C., & CARNINE, D. (1986). Teaching content area material to learning disabled students. *Exceptional Children, 53,* 240–246.

NAGEL, D. R., SCHUMAKER, J. B., & DESHLER, D. D. (1986). *Learning strategies curriculum: The FIRST-letter mnemonic strategy.* Lawrence, KS: Excel Enterprises.

Taking Tests

HUGHES, J., SCHUMAKER, J., DESHLER, D. D., & MERCER, C. (1987). *The test-taking strategy: PIRATES.* Lawrence: University of Kansas—Institute for Research in Learning Disabilities.

Strategy Maintenance and Generalization

ANDERSON-INMAN, L. (1986). Bridging the gap: Student-centered strategies for promoting the transfer of learning. *Exceptional Children, 52,* 562–572.

BORKOWSKI, J. G., & VARNHAGEN, C. K. (1984). Transfer of learning strategies: Contrast of self-instructional and traditional training formats with EMR children. *American Journal of Mental Deficiency, 88,* 369–379.

BORKOWSKI, J. G., WEYHING, R. S., & TURNER, L. A. (1986). Attributional retraining and the teaching of strategies. *Exceptional Children, 53,* 130–137.

DESHLER, D. D., & SCHUMAKER, J. B. (1986). Learning strategies: An instructional alternative for low-achieving adolescents. *Exceptional Children, 52,* 583–590.

ELLIS, E. S. (1986). The role of motivation and pedagogy on the generalization of cognitive strategy training. *Journal of Learning Disabilities, 19,* 66–70.

12

Transition Education*

Not too long ago, students, parents, and professionals began to recognize and discuss the continued presence of difficulties among secondary and post-secondary students with special needs. It became apparent that traditional curricula were not preparing many students for adult life. Hope for improvement increased as simple, creative modifications (e.g., taped books and advance organizers) demonstrated that some people could fully benefit from their educational programs. The passage of P.L. 94-142 illustrated the potential capabilities of persons with disabilities when given proper support and that services throughout life are important (Weicker, 1987). As a result, concentrated efforts to establish individualized, appropriate services for adolescents and young adults with special needs began during the late 1970s. These endeavors continue to increase in number and comprehensiveness today.

The assessment that students need to be prepared for adult life, work, and independence (White, 1987) has resulted in changes in the orientation of many students' instructional programs. Study of the educational needs of persons with mild to moderate difficulties reveal that many are likely to aim toward college at some point in their lives (Vocational Committee Survey, 1982). For example, 67% of adults with learning disabilities surveyed in one study indicated plans for future education (White et al., 1982). These individuals appear to fit into secondary core curricula with success, with minor accommodations. However, for a large number of secondary students, a separate curriculum is needed for at least

*This chapter was written by Ginger Blalock.

a portion of their educational experiences to help them gain independence as adults.

Over the past twenty-five years, several service delivery systems have emerged to prepare persons with disabilities for transition to employment. Vocational education has offered training in job skills to some mainstreamed students at secondary and postsecondary levels. Special education has provided prevocational skills classes and work-study experiences for many secondary students. Vocational rehabilitation agencies have served many youth and adults in vocational assessment, job readiness, counseling, training, and job placement areas. In addition, generic adult services such as two-year colleges, military training, and job corps programs have been utilized by many young adults with disabilities. However, professionals from these systems have infrequently coordinated their efforts. A consistent, comprehensive continuum of services has not evolved in most local communities. Recent follow-up studies of special education graduates show that graduates with mild handicaps often have great difficulty with competitive employment and independent living, even though their needs for supportive services may be minimal (Fafard & Haubrich, 1981; Hasazi, Gordon, & Roe, 1985; Mithaug, Horiuchi, & Fanning, 1985). In response to these findings, in the last five years Congress allotted greater federal support for personnel preparation, research, and demonstration projects to aid the transition of the population from school to adult life. Many of the approaches that bear promise for special adolescents and adults are the focus of this chapter.

THEORETICAL FRAMEWORK

Discussion of effective contemporary approaches requires a foundation that yields a broad-based and historical perspective. This section summarizes the developmental process faced by all adolescents and adults, the options traditionally available to these groups when disabilities are present, and the transition models under which the field operates.

Life Span Development and Demands

Adolescence has long been studied as a period of complex and unique development, described as a "state of dynamic limbo" (Cullinan & Epstein, 1979). Developmental tasks during this stage include establishing one's identity and interaction style, setting goals, developing mental and physical coping strategies, defining one's points of view on social and moral issues, and planning for vocational activities (D'Alonzo, Arnold, & Yuen, 1986; Grinder, 1980). In contrast, adulthood has only recently achieved a status of its own as a "qualitatively distinct" developmental period (Bova, 1979). Several theories about development at various stages of life are suggested by work completed in the past fifteen years. These theories seek to explain the roles and responsibilities shared by most individuals as they mature (Gould, 1972; Havighurst, 1972; Knowles, 1979; Knox, 1977; Levinson, 1978).

Life Span Developmental Theories

Most adolescents and adults live their lives in patterns that alternate between stable periods and periods of change. The former allow solidification and enjoyment of competence in some form; the latter period brings new challenges and directions (Aslanian & Brickell, 1980; Knox, 1977). Havighurst's (1972) "developmental task" schema is widely used to explain the reasons underlying these alternating stages. Havighurst's three major stages of adulthood and the developmental tasks of each are outlined in Table 12.1. While not exhaustive, the list suggests the principal demands made upon adults at various stages in their lives. They illustrate the importance of striving for intellectual and social/emotional independence as well as occupational integrity.

Career/vocational concerns are critically significant during late adolescence and adulthood. Thus, a greater understanding of adolescent/adult demands is offered by a frequently utilized vocational development theory. Super (1953) validated and refined his own developmental model of occupational maturity, based upon Ginzberg's (1952) occupational choice and life-stage theory and

Table 12.1
Havighurst's Developmental Tasks

STAGE/AGE RANGE	DEVELOPMENTAL TASK
Early adulthood (Ages 18–30)	Selecting a mate
	Learning to live with a marriage partner
	Starting a family
	Rearing children
	Managing a home
	Getting started in an occupation
	Taking civic responsibility
	Finding a congenial social group
Middle age (Ages 30–60)	Assisting teen-age children to become responsible and happy adults
	Achieving adult social and civic responsibility
	Reaching and maintaining satisfactory performance in one's occupation/career
	Developing adult leisure time activities
	Relating to one's spouse as a person
	Accepting and adjusting to physiological changes of middle age
	Adjusting to aging parents
Late maturity (Ages 60+)	Adjusting to decreasing physical strength and health
	Adusting to retirement and reduced income
	Adjusting to death of spouse
	Establishing an explicit affiliation with one's age group
	Adopting and adapting social roles in a flexible way
	Establishing satisfactory physical arrangements

Source: From Robert J. Havighurst, *Developmental Tasks and Education.* Copyright © 1972 by Longman, Inc. Reprinted by permission of Longman, Inc., New York.

Table 12.2
Super's Stages of Vocational Development

STAGE/SUBSTAGE	AGE	MAJOR TASKS OR ACTIVITIES
Growth Stage	Birth–14	Self-concept developed
a. Fantasy	4–10	Needs dominate; role playing
b. Interest	11–12	Likes are major determinants of aspirations, activities
c. Capacities	13–14	Abilities given more weight; job requirements considered
Exploration	15–24	Self-examination, role tryouts, and occupational exploration in school, leisure activities, and part-time work
a. Tentative	15–24	Tentative choices made, tried out in fantasy, talk, courses, work
b. Transition	18–21	Implement self-concept via training/work; more thought given to reality
c. Uncommitted trial	22–24	First job tried
Establishment	25–44	Permanence sought
a. Committed trial and stabilizing	25–30	May undergo 1–2 changes before establishment
b. Consolidation and advancement	31–44	Efforts to solidify; usually most creative years
Maintenance	45–64	Concern about holding on; continuation of established lines; some innovation
Decline Stage	65+	Work activity changes with declines in mental and physical power; new roles
a. Deceleration	65–70	
b. Retirement	71+	

Source: D. E. Super (1953), A theory of vocational development. *American Psychologist, 8,* 185–190. Copyright 1953 by the American Psychological Association. Adapted by permission of the publisher and the author.

Havighurst's developmental tasks. Super proposed that one's self-concept is developed through each stage of childhood and drives one toward particular occupational decisions (see Table 12.2).

Super's model depends heavily upon the idea of individual differences (abilities, interests, and personalities) and, therefore, readily accommodates those with special needs. He stresses that a range of occupations suits each individual and conversely that many variations are seen among people in any given occupation.

Characteristics of Adolescents and Adults with Special Needs

Studies of this population have indicated particular areas of concern (see Table 12.3) that can help guide educators in curricular and other decisions (Blalock & Dixon, 1982; Clark, 1980; Cronin & Gerber, 1982; Jackson, Enright, & Murdock, 1987; Masters & Mori, 1986; Patton & Polloway, 1982). The list reflects

Table 12.3
Problem Areas Among Adolescents and Adults with Special Needs

Academic Domain
  Academic achievement
  Intellectual functioning/learning rate
  Oral language
  Thinking/reasoning skills
  Organization and study skills
  Memory and attention

Emotional-Social Domain
  Emotional stability
  Self-esteem/expectations for success
  Self-trust
  Personal maturity
  Social experience
  Social perception
  Making/keeping friends
  Recreation/leisure life-styles
  Independent living skills

Vocational Domain
  Career attitudes
  Career/vocational information
  Realistic goal setting
  Choosing satisfying vocations
  Long-range preparation

problems that warrant specific interventions to assist in the development of academic, social and emotional, independent living, and career/vocational skills. More recently, Johnson and Blalock (1987) found that problems in academic and vocational skills were predominant with the ninety-three adults with learning disabilities they studied. The skills, delineated in Table 12.4, are significant areas that require attention from both professionals and the students themselves. Unfortunately, not until recently have alternatives been available to individuals with special needs.

Traditional Secondary and Postsecondary Options

Since the early 1970s, professionals have addressed the educational needs of youth and adults generally in a reactionary manner. This section surveys the alternatives typically extended to teens and young adults as they prepare for gainful activities.

Secondary Options

The range of secondary program offerings still varies greatly across the nation. According to Deshler, Lowrey, and Alley (1979), five major service options traditionally are offered to youth with special needs. Their national survey

Table 12.4
Characteristics of 93 Adults with Learning Disabilities

CHARACTERISTIC	NO. REPORTING
Academic Problems Reported	
Written language	72
Reading	62
Oral language	26
Organization/planning	15
Mathematics	12
Attention	7
Nonverbal abilities	6
Conceptual thinking	4
Vocational Achievements Reported	
Students	26
Unemployed	18
Clerical/sales workers	13
Professional/technical workers	12
Laborers	8
Service workers	6
Craftsmen/foremen	4
Operatives	3
Managers/officials	3

Source: D. J. Johnson & J. W. Blalock (eds.), *Adults with Learning Disabilities: Clinical Studies* (Orlando, FL: Grune & Stratton, 1987). Used with permission of Grune & Stratton, Inc.

found that academic remediation programs were the most common (45% of those surveyed), while others (24%) stressed tutoring in regular content subjects. Three stressed other areas: functional life skills (17%), work-study (5%), and learning strategies (4%). In far too many instances, only one curricular option is available to students with educational difficulties. At least three distinct options (particularly survival skills, supervised work experiences, and study/learning strategies) should be offered by every setting to best meet individuals' needs and goals.

Postsecondary Options

Patton and Polloway (1982) describe the typical opportunities available to young adults after high school (see Table 12.5). Having a disability may present problems in satisfactory functioning within some of these options.

Data from follow-up studies of students with special needs indicate that most do not fare well as adults. Far too many end up unemployed or underemployed. Many describe their lack of satisfaction with work, interpersonal relationships, and recreation/leisure life-styles. A large number remain living with their parents in dependent arrangements. Many of today's adults with special needs were not served adequately when they were children. For many, their disorders were often undisclosed or even unknown by the individuals involved.

Table 12.5
Postsecondary Options for Young Adults in General

Work (full time or part time)
Education/training (trade or technical schools; adult education; CETA programs, which are no longer
   available; two- and four-year colleges)
Military service
Volunteer service (community, VISTA, Peace Corps)
Housewifery/househusbandry
Absence of gainful activity

Source: J. R. Patton & E. A. Polloway, The learning disabled: The adult years, *Topics in Learning and Learning Disabilities,* 2(1982).

These factors have contributed to incomplete services being provided to these adults. Assistance for difficulties in educational, social/interpersonal, independent living, and occupational realms are inconsistently available, and only from a few sources. Vocational rehabilitation agencies, colleges (especially community colleges), and advocacy organizations have created more and more appropriate options for adults with special needs. These offerings are described in greater detail in the "Intervention Tactics" section of this chapter.

Transition Models

Ianacone (1987, p. 1) offers an expanded definition of transition:

> Transition is conceptualized as a process of movement through life phases or a methodology associated with the life development process of persons as they move from one service delivery system to another. This process encompasses the compendium of those activities which lead to independent living, employment and other productive life situations.

Several transition models are currently used throughout the United States. Four approaches have been selected to discuss here. These approaches respond to the range of transition issues identified earlier. The newness of these models is due to the fact that little attention has been paid to students moving into postsecondary training and work before the 1980s (D'Alonzo, Owen, & Hartwell, 1985).

Halpern's (1985) Transition Model

Halpern suggests that the foundation of successful transition lies at the time of secondary school, with the desired outcome being community adjustment. Adult adjustment includes three broad areas: employment, social and interpersonal networks, and residential environments. His data-supported rationale suggests that successful interventions in one life area does not necessarily yield improvements in the other dimensions. Without direct programming, generalization does not occur.

Brolin's (1985) *Life-Centered Career Education Model*

This approach teaches work preparation in four major areas of adult productivity: occupational, domestic, avocational, and preparation for voluntary work. Within these areas, critical steps begin with developing a "work personality" (unique abilities, needs, interests, work ethics, work motivation, work values, work goals, and work habits and behaviors). These facets are similar to Super's (1953) work-related self-concept. From these, Brolin developed 22 major competencies (see Table 12.6) and 102 subcompetencies that interface on two critical dimensions: (1) school, family, and community experiences and (2) the four stages of career development (awareness, exploration, preparation, and placement/follow-up/continuing education).

Table 12.6
Life-Centered Career Education Competencies, Revised 1988

DAILY LIVING SKILLS
  1. Managing personal finances
  2. Selecting and managing a household
  3. Caring for personal needs
  4. Functioning in adult living situations
  5. Buying, preparing, and consuming foods
  6. Buying and caring for clothing
  7. Exhibiting responsible citizenship
  8. Utilizing recreational facilities and engaging in leisure
  9. Getting around the commmunity

PERSONAL-SOCIAL SKILLS
  10. Achieving self-awareness
  11. Aquiring self-confidence
  12. Achieving socially responsible behavior
  13. Maintaining good interpersonal skills
  14. Achieving independence
  15. Achieving problem-solving skills
  16. Communicating with others

OCCUPATION SKILLS
  17. Knowing and exploring occupational possibilities
  18. Selecting and planning occupational choices
  19. Exhibiting appropriate work habits and behaviors
  20. Exhibiting sufficient physical manual skills
  21. Obtaining specific occupational skills
  22. Seeking, securing, and maintaining employment

Source: D. E. Brolin, Life-centered career education: A competency-based approach (Reston, VA: The Council for Exceptional Children, 1988). Used by permission.

Clark's (1980) Career Preparation Model

Clark views individualized career preparation as the optimal mechanism for enhancing adult adjustment for all students. Four components receive varying degrees of emphasis as students progress: (1) identification of one's values, attitudes, and habits, and the relationships among these personal characteristics; (2) human relationships and the roles that communication and acceptance play in these relationships; (3) occupational information (work roles, job-specific language, employment alternatives, and basic "realities" about the work world); and (4) acquisition of critical skills for daily living related to work (transportation).

University of Kansas Life-Planning Program

Schumaker, Hazel, and Deshler (1985) offer a cognitive skills program to address transitional needs of adolescents with learning problems. These activities include problem solving, goal setting, and goal implementation (see Figure 12.1) in three content areas: career/educational plans, independent living, and social interactions. The program connects solidly with IEP planning and implementation and with community resources.

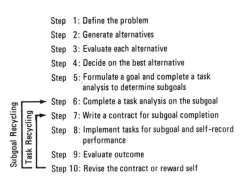

Step 1: Define the problem
Step 2: Generate alternatives
Step 3: Evaluate each alternative
Step 4: Decide on the best alternative
Step 5: Formulate a goal and complete a task analysis to determine subgoals
Step 6: Complete a task analysis on the subgoal
Step 7: Write a contract for subgoal completion
Step 8: Implement tasks for subgoal and self-record performance
Step 9: Evaluate outcome
Step 10: Revise the contract or reward self

Subgoal Recycling / Task Recycling

Figure 12.1 The life-planning process. (*Source:* J. B. Schumaker, J. S. Hazel, & D. D. Deshler, A model for facilitating postsecondary transitions, *Techniques, 1* (1985), 442.)

CURRICULAR MODELS

The question remains: What should the content of secondary and postsecondary instruction for special learners be? The developmental models, prevalent options, and transitional approaches provide guidelines for selecting appropriate curricula for each individual. These frameworks illustrate the diversity of all people's educational, social, and vocational needs, made more complex by the presence of disabilities. Thus, demands by people with learning problems on the educational system are great, making obvious the need for numerous intervention alternatives. A continuum of options that begins at the preschool level and flows through postsecondary opportunities, branching off into many directions along the way, is clearly indicated for these individuals (Blalock, 1988; Brolin, 1985).

Mainstream Preparation for Postsecondary Education

Issues about academic and cognitive development are presented throughout this text and are critical topics for enhancing success in higher education. Remediation of basic skills continues, but should be used only with content that relates to life or other school demands (avoiding unimportant subject matter or skills in isolation). Compensatory strategies, tutorial support, survival skills, learning strategies, social skills, and communication competencies comprise a critical repertoire that students need in moving from secondary to postsecondary environments.

Silagyi (1986) offers a thorough list of questions intended to help parents match the requirements and offerings of prospective colleges to their students' abilities and limitations. The questions are targeted at parents, high school personnel, and college staff. McGuire and Shaw (1987) provide specific forms for assessing the potential match among learner, institution, and educational program.

Career Education Model

The goal of career education is the development of general career competencies (knowledge, skills, aptitudes, attitudes) that are useful within any vocational area and enhance individuals' overall growth. Specific features of an individual's career education are:

1. Purposeful sequence of planned educational activities that is systemwide (integrated into all curricula).
2. Systematic coordination of all school, family, and community components toward the student's personal, social, and occupational development.
3. Focus on both paid and unpaid (volunteer, internship) work.
4. Emphasis on a broad scope of abilities.
5. Instruction at all age levels.
6. Instruction by educators from all areas. (Rusch, Mithaug, & Flexer, 1986)

Content areas within career education curricula include generic work behaviors approved by most employers: emergency and safety skills, awareness of work, appropriate behavior, listening skills, interpersonal relationships, prevocational skills, awareness of aptitudes and abilities, following instructions, and information about job choices (White, 1983). Community input must be solicited for more specialized topics to ensure relevancy. Mithaug, Martin, and Agran (1987) offer a strategy that teaches students to adapt to diverse work situations. The *adaptability model* specifically prepares students to deal effectively with five typical problem areas: tasks that workers may or may not enjoy, earning wages, tasks that match employees' skills and abilities, quick and accurate task completion, and prioritizing tasks for completion. Strategies for advancement and mobility leading to the development of independent living skills should also be addressed. Students with mild to moderate disabilities seem to require at least a minimal level of assistance in identifying and acting upon alternatives in living.

Mori (1980) suggests a structure for career education that is flexible and provides sufficient alternatives to meet the diverse needs of persons with learning disabilities. His plan serves as a useful model for all youth and adults with mild to moderate disabilities.

Super's (1953) vocational development theory more closely agrees with the career development model than with any other option. Super stated that one's development through each life stage can be guided by enhancing growth of one's abilities and interests and through reality testing and work on self-concept. Super's (1953) description of the importance of role playing may be a signal to educators to refine and evaluate more carefully ongoing aims and uses of this technique with special populations.

Vocational/Occupational Education Model

One goal of vocational and occupational education is to help students select and acquire marketable skills in a vocational field that leads toward successful job placement (Renzaglia, Bates, & Hutchins, 1981). It begins with broad exposure to a variety of occupations in middle or junior high school and narrows to more selective, in-depth training in specific vocations at high school and postsecondary levels. It has several important features, including vocational assessment, vocational counseling, and occupational exploration that should begin in earlier grades (e.g., middle school). Also, tasks learned should relate directly to the student's occupational choice. With options dependent upon local job opportunities, vocational training is provided in more than one occupational area (office occupations, home economics or child development, industrial arts, agriculture). Broadening an individual's vocational experiences are viewed as much more important for special students than are academics. However, vocational and occupational education includes academic work and laboratory experiences, with the latter designed to aid transfer to the worksite. Cooperative work programs that provide training and experience in actual job sites also are offered. Frequently, assistance in finding jobs is available upon completion. There are drawbacks to this model. Although teachers are experienced in the occupation being taught, they typically are not trained to accommodate students with special needs. Also, occupations taught may be in demand currently, but not in the future. Nevertheless, efforts are made to see that the jobs are challenging and pay moderate to better than average wages (Greenan, 19S2; Renzaglia, Bates, & Hutchins, 1981; Rusch, Mithaug, & Flexer, 1986).

Enrollments in vocational education have increased sixfold from 1976 to 1983 (White, 1987). However, several issues impair effective integration of students with special needs into vocational education programs (Minner & Beane, 1983). Negative attitudes and expectations of content area teachers appear to stem from their perceived inability and lack of preparation to teach this population effectively. Continued overreliance on academic remediation by special educators may result from their lack of knowledge about vocational education and older students' needs. Finally, organizational and administrative barriers to integrating special students often exclude vocational educators from planning and IEP meetings. These barriers also hinder vocational educators from getting accurate information and help for students mainstreamed into their classes.

Special strategies by which students with special needs are more readily accommodated in regular vocational education classes are numerous. For example, peer tutors (Asselin & Vasa, 1983) and vocational-technical aides have helped to maintain such secondary and postsecondary students. Horton (1983) suggests several useful techniques, such as mnemonic devices coupled with condensed material to help many students achieve the required equipment safety certifications. Daily logs may include printed activity items accompanied by related drawings. Of great importance is a modified grading system, often jointly planned by special and vocational educators. A grading system chart can be used to specify all targeted tasks, outcomes expected, possible points, and measurement schedules so that the student clearly understands employers' expectations (Horton, 1983). Contracts stating requirements for achieving each letter grade can guide students in their classroom efforts without penalizing them unfairly. Renzaglia, Bates, and Hutchins (1981) describe strategies for teaching specific work skills that may be helpful to vocational educators unfamiliar with special education technology.

Special Education Work-Study Model

The goals of work-study programs include more than the acquisition of job skills and work-related behaviors. They also seek to enhance individuals' awareness of different jobs available in the community. Rusch, Mithaug, and Flexer (1986) describe several components inherent within most secondary work-study programs for special students:

1. Simultaneous classroom instruction in prevocational skills and survival skills related to jobs and daily living.
2. Placement and supervision by special education teacher (typically untrained and inexperienced in the world of work).
3. Part-time (half-day) worksite placement, usually beginning in junior year; sometimes full-day placement in senior year.
4. Placement either on campus or in community (typically whatever is available).
5. Vocational assessment procedures conducted by school or vocational rehabilitation personnel, or both.
6. Jobs usually unskilled or low-level, semiskilled; often "terminal" placements in the past (i.e., no exposure to other jobs).
7. Linkages to aid transition to rehabilitation services, in many communities.

Brolin (1985) says that academic and work-study experiences planned years ago fell short of preparing special students for successful adult adjustment. Students' training and employment opportunities are more limited with this model because the work-study teachers have a narrow world of work experiences. Also, the focus is generally on employment only, excluding daily living and social skills. However, for certain students at particular points in their development, work-study programs may be the least restrictive approach.

Postsecondary versions of the work-study model are found in at least two self-contained programs for adults with moderate to severe learning disabilities. Both Adelphi University and City University of New York offer highly structured training in which students are immersed in vocationally oriented remedial classes, tutoring, supervised field placements, and weekly group therapy (Barbaro, 1982; Blalock & Dixon, 1982).

INTERVENTION TACTICS

Important approaches for adolescents with special needs include individualized content and methods, vocational assessment, affective strategies and clarification of work-related values (Daniels & Wiederholt, 1986), community-based instruction, and job coaching. Guidelines for teaching in these areas follow.

Encouraging Individualization

Clark (1980) calls for a full commitment to individualization of appropriate education plans for secondary students with handicaps. He proposes that the career preparation model offers the best means for true individualization.

Content

In addition to diverse service delivery options, the instructional content available must be flexible. One tutorial or remedial period per day might be sufficient for some students to make continued progress in the regular education program. Special accommodations could be necessary (such as special materials or modified course objectives). A substantial few continue to fail in the regular setting, as this is the best that mainstreaming provides. For these students, alternatives to standard content classes must be provided. These options may take the form of separate, unique curricula or creative combinations of traditional academic, vocational, and special education. Emphasis should center on skills that enhance achievement of the person's basic goals. Formal academic achievement tests, standardized interest inventories, and informal assessment strategies, all addressed in the next section, are important sources for planning. In addition, students' parents and previous teachers, employers, service agency personnel, and adults with disabilities outside one's service delivery system are additional resources for perspectives on curricular decisions. However, the key resource for all assessment, programming, and evaluation decisions is the person who has the difficulties. Including the student in all decision making not only ensures critical input, it also greatly increases the student's motivation to participate in the educational program and enhances his or her understanding and acceptance of their handicap.

Approach

As with selection of content, identification of the optimal approach or combination of approaches depends upon the person's background, abilities, limitations, interests, and goals. Results from the process described in the "Vocational Assessment" section help target the most promising instructional and study arrangements for the individual.

Institutions of higher education are obliged by Section 504 of the Vocational Rehabilitation Act of 1973 to make programs fully accessible to "otherwise qualified disabled individuals." Postsecondary educators tend to use two major approaches to serve these students. The *selective environments* mode (Blalock & Dixon, 1982), called the "fit-the-system" option by Wiederholt and McEntire (1980), helps students to meet the institution's existing curricula, requirements, and standards. Such settings offer a limited number of instructional options that work well only for students with certain traits and abilities, often those with fairly mild deficits. Table 12.7 outlines some selective strategies that many individuals use to compensate for their disabilities to succeed in their educational programs. Patton (1987) offers ways to teach listening, speaking, reading, and writing skills to adults with special needs. These strategies include direct instruction with modeling, relating to real life situations, sufficient practice with feedback, and strategies to increase understanding and memory.

The other approach, *adaptive environments*, combines Wiederholt's and McEntire's (1980) "change-the-system" and "ignore-the-system" options. Its aim is to shape the system to meet students' individual needs. A variety of instruc-

Table 12.7
Selective Educational Strategies to Compensate for Special Needs

---

Extra instructions.

Oral examinations.

Readers.

Taped textbooks and other reading materials, tape libraries.

Extended time limits on tests and assignments.

Free typing, xeroxing services.

Free use of tape recorders, typewriters, word processors.

Tape recording of lectures; if copyrighted videotaped or audiotaped materials are used, permission may need to be obtained from the distributor.

Encouraging students to request copies of notes from another student if real problems exist in this area; NCR paper automatically makes carbon copies (found at office supply stores).

Encouraging use of yellow or blue tinted transparencies when reading purple ditto copies (also found helpful with regular black and white print, for many students).

Remedial instruction in reading, writing, spelling, and/or mathematics, when (1) the learning disability specialist believes strongly in the approach and (2) program materials are novel to the students (Blalock & Dixon, 1982); even then, one must caution the learner about problems in expecting significant gains.

Academic tutoring, either by trained peer tutors or professional staff.

Study skills instruction—note taking, reading comprehension strategies, outlining, questioning, listening, test-taking, time management, analytical skills, use of tape recorders, retrieval of usable notes from lectures.

Table 12.8
Adaptive Educational Strategies to Accommodate Special Needs

Provision of note-taking guides, lists of key terms, outlines prior to session.

Presentation of information as clearly as possible and using more than one channel (visual, auditory, manual, etc.).

Teaching use of memory/learning strategies as pertinent content is presented.

Allowing use of dictionaries (particularly spelling dictionaries) or of calculators in activities where actual spelling or computational skills are not being assessed.

Changing grading standards and/or required formats so that students are not penalized for their disabilities but are still expected to demonstrate mastery.

Development of an individual education plan for each student with special learning needs.

Waiving certain required courses if they conflict with the student's area of disability.

Changes in or exemptions from regular semester load requirements, grade point average requirements, admissions requirements that rely heavily on GPA or standardized test scores, and academic probation procedures.

Inclusion of the student in all assessment, programming, and evaluation decisions and findings, so that the student is fully aware of and agrees with strengths, weaknesses, goals, progress, and procedures and so that the instructor can utilize his or her knowledge of self as the best resource for accommodation ideas.

An instructional process that leaves little or no room for failure, inherent within the learning strategies approach presented throughout the text.

Links across community service providers, educational institutions, businesses, and citizens to ensure that all areas of the learning disabled adult's development receive necessary attention.

---

tions and administrative options are provided, based on each person's past performance, learning strengths and weaknesses, and interests. Few educational institutions are prepared to totally accommodate all students using this approach. Table 12.8 lists some of the ways instructors and administrators may help students succeed. Educators should examine features of both models to select those strategies best suited for their particular settings and students.

Despite their difficulties, many adults successfully adjust to the demands of adult life, such as college, work, and family. Often they develop specific coping strategies such as spelling logs of frequently used words, getting speakers to slow down, and seeking help on reading or writing tasks from secretaries, spouses, and friends.

Deciding When to Switch Priorities

Decisions about the most appropriate educational aims, approaches, settings, and materials for each adolescent or adult with special needs must be made continually. At the secondary level, major changes in educational programs must be considered from mainly academic curricula to a more functional or vocational emphasis. Variables to consider for such decisions are:

1. Student's steady progress in present coursework.
2. Student's and parents' expressed aims and interests regarding future vocational and life activities.
3. Instructional program's relevance to those future aims.
4. Input from all persons involved about future options.

The National Joint Committee on Learning Disabilities (NJCLD, 1987a) offers a range of additional considerations for placement decisions. Individualized attention to short- and long-term needs, coupled with using older students as their own primary resources, remain the most critical guidelines for helping them to move forward. The following intervention tactics constitute a broad spectrum of alternatives for special populations.

Vocational Assessment and Evaluation

Super (1953) cites several factors of importance in occupational choice and work adjustment, all of which are targets in vocational assessment. These include vocational preferences and competencies, living and work situations, family socioeconomic level, mental ability, personality characteristics, and available opportunities. Stodden (1986, p. 68) presents this perspective:

> *Vocational assessment* is the collection of data/information contributing to a description of a person's performance in a career/vocational program or the world of work. *Vocational evaluation* is the process of reviewing/interpreting assessment information to provide meaning and significance in placement and programming decisions.

Peterson (1985) describes both center-based and curriculum-based models of vocational assessment. The primary applications of center-based assessment information in school settings are (1) programming for skill development, (2) integrating classroom tryouts and work samples into training programs, and (3) support services (e.g., compensatory strategies) for special needs students.

The curriculum-based model involves collecting information in special and regular education classrooms, thus increasing relevancy to students' instructional needs and reducing unnecessary costs. This model stems from a developmental perspective that considers student skills, interests, values, and personalities throughout the life span, providing important information for generating IEPs. A comprehensive or combined model of vocational assessment is advocated by Peterson (1985), drawing upon the strengths of both the evaluation centers and the curriculum-based processes. The most critical information comes from real work settings (Glascoe & Levy, 1985). Initial rotated training placements followed by extended training or work experiences provide much important data about the worker (situational assessment), the jobs (job analysis), the job sites (site analysis), and employment options in the community (labor market analysis).

Identification of who best conducts vocationally related assessment varies from community to community, depending upon certification requirements, available talent, and local politics. The responsible party may be the counselor, the school psychologist, the special education teacher, or the vocational evaluation specialist in some instances (Peterson, 1985). Roberts, et al. (1983) outline the assessment-related roles and responsibilities of each of the entire school staff (i.e., administrators, counselors, and teachers from all disciplines) in their vocational assessment model.

Emotional and Social/Interpersonal Development

A multitude of social and emotional development issues were discussed earlier in the text. However, two broad facets of affective development that are major concerns among youth and adults are self-esteem and adjustment, for which informed guidance and counseling are helpful. In particular, interventions aimed at improving self-concept and social perception skills show great promise.

Guidance and Counseling

Teachers, parents, and other significant adults often do not realize their effect on these students, both positive and negative. A continuum of individual and group counseling should be available to special learners. For those with more moderate difficulties, numerous counseling contacts over extended periods should be heavily encouraged. In addition, anxiety management training to deal with tension is recommended, in combination with programmed successful events to aid self-confidence (Miller, McKinley, & Ryan, 1979). Teachers can easily learn to model and supervise practice in relaxed breathing techniques, visualization, and cognitive counteractions to negative thinking.

Career/vocational counseling, as well as personal and academic counseling, are strongly advocated from the early years. Direct instruction and role-playing in active listening strategies and assertiveness offer several benefits, such as fostering autonomy and independent living skills as well as self-advocacy (Brown, 1984; NJCLD, 1987a). Print, audiovisual, and personal resources to assist young adults with disabilities to understand and compensate for their problems should be readily available in schools, community programs, and postsecondary institutions (Brown, 1981; Patton & Polloway, 1982).

Developing Identity and Self-Concept

Schmitt and Hall (1986) state that barriers to identity and self-concept development among special needs learners are lack of acceptance of one's own disability and little or no knowledge of self. Their recommendations include (1) providing information about specific learning problems and their relationships to employability within the regular curriculum and (2) training in interpersonal skills, including exploration of life span issues through problem-solving, role-playing and peer evaluation techniques. Sachs, Iliff, and Donnelly's (1987) learning disabilities seminar in high school greatly helped students to accept and understand their disabilities and to become more productive, active learners.

Social Perception Improvement

Many adolescents with special needs have social perception problems, a fact supported empirically (Jackson, Enright, & Murdock, 1987). Use of a greater range and number of situational cues and structuring more practice opportunities in natural settings appear helpful in improving important interaction behaviors in social and work settings.

Interdisciplinary/Interagency Collaboration

Cooperative planning and program implementation must be developed among a variety of agencies: between secondary and postsecondary vocational programs, between secondary and postsecondary vocational programs and cooperative job sites, between vocational and special education at both levels, between education and community services, and among educators, service providers, and employers. Research continues to demonstrate that programs for special needs learners do not work in isolation.

Cobb and Hasazi (1987) identify eight exemplary program elements as necessary support for students with mild disabilities making successful transitions. These include an individualized transitional plan (ITP), integrated vocational education experiences in high schools, paid work experiences, training in job-seeking skills, flexible staffing patterns, active parent and student involvement, follow-up studies of former special education students, and a system for managing and transferring student and consumer data from agency to agency.

A recent study by Benz and Halpern (1986) addresses vocational preparation opportunities for students with mild disabilities, as reported by LEA administrators, teachers, and parents. Findings indicate that communication and collaboration between special and vocational educators must increase if students are to make successful transitions to work. Suggestions include exchange of new mainstreaming and materials technology from each other's disciplines, interagency agreements, collaboration at the preservice training level, and, particularly effective, cross-disciplinary inservice training. Greenan (1982) advocates IEP development, assessment, least restrictive environment, and program evaluation as targets for interagency collaboration.

The major responsibility for changing secondary operations to meet the needs of special students better appears to lie with two groups. First, administrators must provide the leadership to facilitate communication and cooperation between regular and special education. Only when special education teachers and students are considered an integral part of the school will effective collaboration occur. Also, a reciprocal consultant relationship between regular and special educators is helpful. Professionals from both groups must learn about each other's disciplines, how to seek each other's expertise, and how to serve as resources toward accomplishing their shared goals (Minner & Beane, 1983). Cross-disciplinary staff development has been proposed as an effective facilitator of such collaboration (Benz & Halpern, 1986; Greenan, 1982).

Planning Teams and IEP/ITP Development

As a general rule, vocational educators are not included in individual education plan or individual transition plan planning meetings (Greenan, 1982). Students suffer as a result, by either exclusion from or failure in vocational programs. As a team, vocational and special educators can and must develop very useful programs for students. Special education personnel can only guess at the value and demands of particular classes pertinent to certain students. Therefore, firsthand information is required from vocational teachers. In turn, special education teachers can share information about effects of disabilities, functioning levels, and techniques for instructional and behavioral mainstreaming. Special educators have a responsibility to help prepare content area teachers to serve students with disabilities appropriately in the mutually agreed least restrictive environment (Brolin, 1983).

Interagency Agreements

Cooperative agreements among participating agencies are crucial to communication and planning efforts. Important features in their development include delineation of (1) basic values and assumptions shared by the group, to serve as guidelines for all planning and service provision activities, (2) roles and responsibilities of each participant, (3) overall scope of activities, and (4) establishment of a common language and data base (Stodden & Boone, 1987). Agreements may be part of the IEP. Several benefits of such articulation agreements have been outlined (Johnson, 1981).

Parental Involvement in Transition Education

The importance of maximum involvement by parents and students themselves in planning intervention programs has been stressed by numerous authorities (Fafard & Haubrich, 1981; NJCLD, 1987b; Patton & Polloway, 1982). Recent research confirms that parental support of transition programs is critical to success (Johnson, Bruininks, & Thurlow, 1987). Other data also indicate that many parents think little or not at all about their child even having a career; they are unaware of the home activities that could enhance students' independence (Kokaska & Hughes, 1985).

Public Awareness/Education

Public and professional awareness and understanding of special needs among adolescents and adults are often called for (NJCLD, 1987a). This particularly applies to employers whose misconceptions or ignorance often impede satisfying job opportunities (Patton & Polloway, 1982). Therefore, parents, consumers, and professionals must collaborate to disseminate accurate information about the abilities and needs of special learners.

Follow-up Studies/Program Evaluation

Professionals who work in secondary settings should be encouraged to evaluate adjustment of former students through follow-up studies, researching clear and consistently defined outcome variables. Of special significance are studies of well-adjusted adults with disabilities. Stodden and Boone (1987) propose nine areas of transition adjustment to serve as indicators of program success (see Table 12.9). Specific criteria for each variable need targeting to measure success.

Table 12.9
Outcome Indicators for Evaluating Transitional Programs

1. Occupational placement/maintenance
2. Income level
3. Continued education
4. Community leisure
5. Transportation
6. Residential arrangements
7. Advocacy arrangements
8. Medical/health needs
9. Personal/social adjustment

Source: R. A. Stodden,, & R. Boone, Assessing transition services for handicapped youth: A cooperative interagency approach, *Exceptional Children,*
53(1987), 542.

Community-Based Instruction/Job Coaching

In particular, approaches that help workers with disabilities obtain jobs in integrated settings and earn at least the minimum wage (competitive employment)
have gained considerable attention and praise in the past few years. Work activity centers and sheltered workshops should never be considered viable alternatives for anyone with mild or moderate disabilities. A recent model, originally
designed for persons with more severe needs, offers great promise for those who
have difficulty getting and keeping competitive jobs on their own. Community-
based instruction is a means of obtaining training in an integrated setting. Such
instruction involves learning and/or working alongside nondisabled workers,
engagement in functional activities, and learning actual job and daily living skills
in the natural environment. The training aspect during secondary or postsecondary schooling may not include salaries. With the eventual goal of fully competitive employment, however, earnings of at least minimum wage and chances
for more pay and responsibilities are sought.

The job coaching aspect of integrated employment includes a person
(teacher, paraprofessional, trained co-worker) who provides initial job skills
training and remains or visits on-site to intervene whenever needed. Frequently,
the job coach educates employers, supervisors, and/or co-workers about the
abilities of the worker with a disability and any accommodations needed.

Use of Available Nonschool Resources

One of the most critical strategies for preparing to make a transition from school
(or from more to less restrictive environments) is the ability to locate and effectively use area resources. Use of initial role-playing situations or simulations can
help students learn the types of services available, their nomenclature, and their
locations. Those classroom experiences should also teach students the content

and approach needed to solicit the services desired. Occasional community-based assignments, particularly if actual needs of students and families are involved, can ensure generalization of those strategies to later situations.

Vocational Rehabilitation

Two goals of vocational rehabilitation (VR) are employment and successful closure of individuals' cases. The services provided by VR agencies include vocational evaluation, vocational counseling, referrals to vocational training programs, rehabilitative services such as therapies, job placement, and follow-up services for a limited time. The Rehabilitation Services Administration agencies in each state have three basic eligibility criteria:

1. Formal diagnosis of mental or physical disability
2. Disability as a substantial barrier to full employment
3. Reasonable expectation of benefits toward employability from rehabilitation services

Many private rehabilitation services are also available in most urban areas and many rural areas.

Generic Adult Services

Many generic services available to all adults may fit the individual's needs (e.g., career counseling centers, state employment offices, community education programs, community college services or classes). Volunteer groups (such as advocacy or church organizations) may be particularly helpful in tape recording or otherwise modifying instructional materials. Other groups (e.g., Jaycees or Chamber of Commerce) may help teach appropriate social or occupational skills needed by some individuals. Volunteers or local literacy projects (often listed through the mayor's office) have been valuable tutoring resources for those unable to afford professional tutors. However, efforts should be made to ensure that professionals in those agencies are at least minimally informed about disabilities before referring students to those resources.

Self-help Groups

Peer groups are another beneficial coping technique in which adults with similar situations can help each other in a variety of ways (see Table 12.10).

Self-help groups are usually run by volunteers. Their formats and emphases vary, depending upon the leader's personality and the local needs. Memberships may range from three to a few thousand. Through sharing problems, solutions, and support, participants typically make significant progress in their life adjustments. Most rate peers as most helpful to them (Patton & Polloway, 1982). Self-help support groups for adults with learning disabilities have been established across the nation. A few national organizations are listed in Table 12.11.

Table 12.10
Benefits from Self-Help or Support Groups

Accept their disabilities, believe in themselves.
Make friends.
Find jobs.
Gain inspiration from role models with whom they identify.
Locate needed support services.
Seek parental support as needed.
Plan ahead—be prepared and organized, study ahead of time.
Learn how to seek help tactfully.
Request frequent feedback, especially early in a new class or job.
Find solutions to shared problems.
Develop leadership skills.
Participate in social activities, learn social skills.
Develop independence and carryover of learned skills.
Increase public awareness of their abilities and needs.

Table 12.11
Learning Disabilities Support Groups

Association for Children & Adults with Learning Disabilities (ACLD)
Youth & Adult Section
4156 Library Rd.
Pittsburgh, PA 15234   412/341-1515, 341-8077

Association of Learning Disabled Adults
P.O. Box 9722, Friendship Station
Washington, DC 20016

LAUNCH, Inc.
Dept. of Special Education
East Texas State University
Commerce, TX 75428

National Network of Learning Disabled Adults
808 W. 82nd St., F-2
Scottsdale, AZ 85257

Setting Adequate Standards

Special education, vocational education, vocational rehabilitation, and related professions currently face exciting challenges. Identification of broad, comprehensive guidelines for moving forward is critical and is evolving from three major directions of policy articulation, systems change, and rural implementation.

Policy Development and Articulation

Public Law 99-457 reauthorizes and expands transition programs mandated under the Education of All Handicapped Children Act of 1975. Funded activities must include students who have left school as well as those in secondary special education programs, stimulating inclusion of vocational and life skills in special education programs as well as follow-up studies of dropouts (Weicker, 1987). The Rehabilitation Act Amendments of 1986, P.L. 99-506, add supported employment services funding and continue funding for Centers for Independent Living and Projects with Industry for five more years. These activities appear in direct contradiction with national and state policy statements regarding excellence in education. This movement favors the college-bound student, ignoring the needs of less able students by requiring them to take more hours in problematic classes and to pass competency exams (Elrod & Lyons, 1987). Such practices appear likely to impede appropriate education for many special needs students (Knowlton & Clark, 1987). A recommitment to career education, alternative (not adjusted) diplomas, and expanded vocational opportunities are encouraged (Benz & Halpern, 1986; Elrod & Lyons, 1987).

Institutionwide policy decisions at the postsecondary level are urged by Blalock and Dixon (1982) to accommodate the needs of adults with learning disabilities. Policy determinations with meaning for this group include IEP or ITP development, specially designed courses, waivers on requirements that conflict with the disability, alterations in academic probation procedures, reduction of semester load requirements, changes in admissions requirements in special cases, and official administrative support at top levels. The California Community College have developed their own system for dealing with special needs students (Strategies Intervention Model Training Notes, 1987).

Changing Systems and Attitudes

A continuity of programs and services throughout the life span is now an accepted, albeit unrealized, aim of transition programs, necessitated by the long-term nature of disabilities (NJCLD, 1987b). Knowlton and Clark (1987) emphasize several considerations related to system change to improve transitional support: preparation and planning emerge as important themes—determining exactly what needs to change from a long-range perspective, determining ways for change to occur, soliciting local commitment to and participation in the change process. Johnson, Bruininks, and Thurlow (1987) outline the steps needed to improve transitional planning and coordination, highlighting the importance of values and goals articulation.

Rural Implementation Strategies

A variety of obstacles and issues (Clark & White, 1985) have been cited in provision of career and vocational programs for rural populations. Barriers include narrow program offerings, difficulties recruiting qualified staff, transportation problems, isolation, and few community services with which to link. Complicating factors are geographical locations, heterogeneity of rural residents, economic conditions, and language differences. Compensatory features unique to rural school districts include the rural work ethic, mutual family support traditions, children's early awareness of work, and family participation in determining community programs. Kasten and Squires (1983) identified four success factors common to programs in rural Nebraska: strong teaching staff, heavy administrative support, effective staff communication, and curricula focused on development of independent living skills and career-related preparation. External variables (facilities, transportation, materials) did not relate nearly as strongly to program success (Clark & White, 1985). Greenan (1982) and Peters, Templeman, and Brostrom (1987) offer further considerations for implementing rural transition programs.

It is obvious that numerous professionals across the nation are meeting the challenges presented by adolescents and adults with special needs. Working with the consumers themselves and with other educators and service providers increases the creativity and productivity of transitional support efforts. Prospects are indeed improving for maturing individuals who seek to learn and develop.

SUMMARY

School instruction is meant to prepare students to embrace the responsibilities and privileges of adulthood in a full and informed manner. Provision of a comprehensive curriculum with important content as well as instructional procedures that promote independent learning should accomplish this goal. By the time students reach adolescence, teachers' selection of the most important content and strategies becomes even more critical. Opportunities for learning are rapidly disappearing, and the time left should be spent on the most relevant skills possible. This is particularly true for students with special needs for whom such skill development may take longer. Follow-up studies of special education graduates indicate, however, that our instructional scope and procedures have been inadequate. These students, whose needs are quite diverse, are not fully prepared to make transitions into adult life. Consequently, a carefully planned continuum of meaningful instructional offerings is crucial at the secondary level.

Teachers must begin to shift their thinking from strictly a classroom perspective to a broader community scope. Careful matching of required competencies with the particular strengths and limitations of one's students helps to pinpoint specific areas for intervention. In addition, the teacher must consider all domains that research says are pertinent to school preparation: career and vocational development, personal and social growth, academic skills, independent living competencies, and community integration skills (e.g., leisure lifestyles). Curricular models offer an array of options for pertinent content related to these domains. The career education model promotes general competency development (i.e., generic work behaviors, education about all types of careers) through system-wide infused instruction at all age levels. In contrast, the vocational education model aims toward more specific job skills through features that are especially helpful for special needs students, such as laboratory experiences, cooperative work programs, and job placement. The special education work-study model offers an approach by which classroom instruction and training placements are coordinated to educate students about work demands, job skills, and occupational options.

Guidelines for selecting individualized content and appropriate approaches are outlined, as are numerous compensatory strategies and accommodations for mainstreaming into secondary and postsecondary classes. A variety of methods for vocational assessment and evaluation are included as intervention tactics due to their importance in planning programs and activities. Techniques for enhancing the affective skills of older students are presented in response to findings that social and emotional development remains a critical concern among this population. Finally, the reader is provided with a number of suggestions for establishing and strengthening interdisciplinary and interagency collaboration and for utilizing outside resources. Although not instructional in nature, these strategies facilitate the team-building and community involvement that must be present if secondary teaching with special students is to bear meaning and fruit.

STUDY AND DISCUSSION QUESTIONS

1. Interview an older friend or relative to determine the progression of his or her life tasks. Do they follow those suggested by Havighurst?

2. Apply your own occupational development to Super's theory. Outline specific events and activities in your life for each of the substages. How closely did you follow the same progression?

3. Describe the in-school resources required to best serve special needs students at your middle or high school. Who and what do you need? What must you do to find and obtain that support?

4. Give five examples of community resources that would be critical in a program in your school (e.g., people, equipment, facilities, experiences). Describe your plan for getting those resources involved.

5. Generate an approach for getting several of your students' parents committed to your transitional program. What do you see as your biggest hurdle?

6. Imagine that your superintendent has just given you the task of improving collaboration between vocational educators and special educators. What would you do?

REFERENCES AND SUGGESTED READINGS

Lifespan Development

ASLANIAN, C. B., & BRICKELL, H. M. (1980). *Americans in transition: Life changes as reasons for learning.* New York: College Entrance Examination Board.

BOVA, B. (1979). *Motivational orientation of adult learners in credit and non-credit classes at the University of New Mexico and Albuquerque Technical Vocational Institute.* Unpublished doctoral dissertation, University of New Mexico, Albuquerque.

BROWN, D. (1981). *Counseling and accommodating the student with learning disabilities.* Washington, DC: President's Committee on Employment of the Handicapped (ERIC Document Reproduction Service No. ED 214 338, EC 141 556).

CRONIN, M. E., & GERBER, P. J. (1982). Preparing the learning disabled adolescent for adulthood. *Topics in Learning and Learning Disabilities, 2,* 55–68.

GINZBERG, E. (1952). Toward a theory of occupational choice. *Personnel and Guidance Journal, 30,* 491–494.

GOULD, R. (1972). The phases of adult life: A study in developmental psychology. *The American Journal of Psychiatry, 129,* 521–531.

GRINDER, R. E. (1980). Adolescence in the United States: A review of contemporary research trends and problems. In *Status of children, youth and families.* Washington, DC: Administration for Children and Families.

HAVIGHURST, R. J. (1972). *Development tasks and education* (3rd ed.). New York: David McKay.

JOHNSON, D. J., & BLALOCK, J. W. (eds.) (1987). *Adults with learning disabilities: Clinical studies.* Orlando, Fl: Grune and Stratton.

KNOWLES, M. (1979). *The adult learner: The neglected species* (2nd ed.). Houston, TX: Gulf Publishing.

KNOX, A. B. (1977). *Adult development and learning.* San Francisco: Jossey-Bass.

LEVINSON, D. J. (1978). *The seasons of a man's life.* New York: Alfred A. Knopf.

SUPER, D. E. (1953). A theory of vocational development. *American Psychologist, 8,* 185–190.

Traditional Secondary and Postsecondary Options

CULLINAN, D., & EPSTEIN, M. H. (1979). *Special education for adolescents: Issues and perspectives.* Columbus, OH: Charles E. Merrill.

D'ALONZO, B. J., ARNOLD, B. J., & YUEN, P. C. (1986). Teaching adolescents with learning and behavioral differences. In L. F. Masters & A. A. Mori (eds.), *Teaching secondary students with mild learning and behavior problems: Methods, materials, strategies.* Rockville, MD: Aspen.

DESHLER, D. D., LOWREY, N., & ALLEY, G. R. (1979). Programming alternatives for learning disabled adolescents: A nationwide study. *Academic Therapy, 14,* 54–63.

MASTERS, L. F., & MORI, A. A. (1986). *Teaching secondary students with mild learning and behavior problems: Methods, materials, strategies.* Rockville, MD: Aspen Publishers.

MILLER, C. D., McKINLEY, D. L., & RYAN, M. (1979). College students: Learning disabilities and services. *Personnel and Guidance Journal, 58*(3), 154–158.

PATTON, J. R., & POLLOWAY, E. A. (1982). The learning disabled: The adult years. *Topics in Learning and Learning Disabilities, 2,* 79–88.

VOCATIONAL COMMITTEE SURVEY (1982). *Association for Children and Adults with Learning Disabilities Newsbriefs,* 20–23.

WHITE, W. J., ALLEY, G. R., DESHLER, D. D., SCHUMAKER, J. B., WARNER, M. M., & CLARK, F. L. (1982). Are there learning disabilities after high school? *Exceptional Children, 49,* 273–274.

WIEDERHOLT, J. L., & McENTIRE, B. (1980). Educational options for handicapped adolescents. *Exceptional Education Quarterly, 1,* 1–10.

Transition Models

BLALOCK, G. (1988). Transitions across the life cycle. In B. Ludlow, R. Luckasson, & A. Turnbull (eds.), *Transitions to adult life for persons with mental retardation: Principles and practices.* Baltimore, MD: Paul H. Brookes.

CLARK, G. M. (1980). Career preparation for handicapped adolescents: A matter of appropriate education. *Exceptional Education Quarterly, 1,* 11–17.

D'ALONZO, B. J., OWEN, S. D., & HARTWELL, L. K. (1985). Transition models: An overview of the current state of the art. *Techniques, 1,* 429–436.

DESHLER, D. D., LOWREY, N., & ALLEY, G. R. (1979). Programming alternatives for learning disabled adolescents: A nationwide study. *Academic Therapy, 14,* 54–63.

HALPERN, A. S. (1985). Transition: A look at the foundations. *Exceptional Children, 51,* 479–485.

IANACONE, R. N. (1987, April). Introduction: Expanding the definition of transition. In R. N. Ianacone (chair), *Next steps: A continuum of transitional training and services.* Paper presented at the International Conference of the Council for Exceptional Children, Chicago.

RUSCH, F. R., & PHELPS, L. A. (1987). Secondary special education and transition from school to work: A national priority. *Exceptional Children, 53,* 487–492.

SCHUMAKER, J. B., HAZEL, J. S., & DESHLER, D. D. (1985). A model for facilitating postsecondary transitions. *Techniques, 1,* 437–446.

Preparation for Postsecondary Education

BARBARO, F. (1982). The learning disabled college student: Some considerations in setting objectives. *Journal of Learning Disabilities, 15,* 599–603.

McGUIRE, J. M., & SHAW, S. F. (1987). A decision-making process for the college-bound student: Matching learner, institution, and support program. *Learning Disability Quarterly, 10,* 106–111.

PATTON, J. R. (1987). Disabled adults. In G. Wallace, S. B. Cohen, & E. A. Polloway, *Language arts: Teaching exceptional students.* Austin, TX: Pro-Ed.

SHAW, S. F., & NORLANDER, K. A. (1986). The special educator's role in training personnel to provide assistance to college students with learning disabilities. *Teacher Education and Special Education, 9,* 77–81.

SILAGYI, C. (1986). Finding the right college for your L.D. kid. *ED-PAC Newsletter.* Teaneck, NJ: Parent Information Center, pp. 8–9.

Career Education

ASSELIN, S. B., & VASA, S. F. (1983). The use of peer tutors in vocational education to assist mildly handicapped students. *Career Development for Exceptional Individuals, 6,* 75–83.

BROLIN, D. E. (1985). Preparing handicapped students to be productive adults. *Techniques, 1,* 447–454.

DANIELS, J. L., & WIEDERHOLT, J. L. (1986). Preparing problem learners for independent living. In D. D. Hammill & N. R. Bartel (eds.), *Teaching students with learning and behavior problems* (4th ed.). Boston: Allyn & Bacon.

KOKASKA, C. J. (1985). Perspectives: Position statement on career development. *Career Development for Exceptional Individuals, 8,* 125–129.

MITHAUG, D. E., MARTIN, J. E., & AGRAN, M. (1987). Adaptability instruction: The goal of transitional programming. *Exceptional Children, 53,* 500–505.

MORI, A. A. (1980). Career education for the learning disabled—Where are we now? *Learning Disability Quarterly, 3,* 91–101.

WHITE, W. J. (1983). The validity of occupational skills in career education: Fact or fantasy? *Career Development for Exceptional Individuals, 6,* 51–60.

Vocational Education/Work-Study

GREENAN, J. P. (1982). Problems and issues in delivering vocational education instruction and support services to students with learning disabilities. *Journal of Learning Disabilities, 15,* 231–235.

HORTON, S. (1983). Delivering industrial arts instruction to mildly handicapped learners. *Career Development for Exceptional Individuals, 6,* 85–92.

MINNER, S., & BEANE, A. (1983). Handicapped students in regular vocational education: Three issues. *Career Development for Exceptional Individuals, 6,* 25–30.

RENZAGLIA, A., BATES, P., & HUTCHINS, M. (1982). Vocational skills instruction for handicapped adolescents and adults. *Exceptional Education Quarterly, 3*(3), 61–73.

RUSCH, F. R., MITHAUG, D. E., & FLEXER, R. W. (1986). Obstacles to competitive employment and traditional program options for overcoming them. In F. R. Rusch, (ed.), *Competitive employment issues and strategies.* Baltimore, MD: Paul H. Brookes.

Vocational Assessment

BROLIN, D. E. (1983). Career education: Where do we go from here? *Career Development for Exceptional Individuals, 6,* 3–14.

BULLIS, M., & FOSS, G. (1986). Guidelines for assessing job-related social skills of mildly handicapped adolescents. *Career Development for Exceptional Individuals, 9,* 89–97.

GLASCOE, F. P., & LEVY, S. M. (1985). A multidimensional, observational approach to vocational assessment and placement. *Career Development for Exceptional Individuals, 8,* 73–79.

PETERSON, M. (1985). Model of vocational assessment of handicapped students. *Career Development for Exceptional Individuals, 8,* 110–118.

PETZY, V. (1983). Vocational assessment for special needs students in the middle/junior high school. *Career Development for Exceptional Individuals, 6,* 15–24.

ROBERTS, S., DOTY, D., SANTLEBEN, S., & TANG, T. (1983). A model for vocational assessment of handicapped students. *Career Development for Exceptional Individuals, 6,* 100–110.

STODDEN, R. A. (1986). Vocational assessment: An introduction. *Career Development for Exceptional Individuals, 9,* 67–68.

Emotional/Social Skills

BROWN, D. (1981). *Counseling and accommodating the student with learning disabilities.* Washington, DC: President's Committee on Employment of the Handicapped (ERIC Document Reproduction Service No. ED 214 338, EC 141 556).

BROWN, D. (1984). Employment consideration for learning disabled adults. *Journal of Rehabilitation, 50,* 74–77.

FAFARD, M. B., & HAUBRICH, P. A. (1981). Vocational and social adjustment of learning disabled young adults: A follow-up study. *Rehabilitation Counseling Bulletin, 4,* 144–155.

JACKSON, S. C., ENRIGHT, R. D., & MURDOCK, J. Y. (1987). Social perception problems in adolescents with learning disabilities: Developmental lag versus perceptual deficit. *Journal of Learning Disabilities, 20,* 361–364.

SACHS, J. J., ILIFF, V. W., & DONNELLY, R. F. (1987). Oh, OK, I'm LD! *Journal of Learning Disabilities, 20,* 92–93, 113.

SCHMITT, P., & HALL, R. (1986). About the unique vocational adjustment needs of students with a learning disability. *The Directive Teachers, 8,* 7–8.

Interdisciplinary/Interagency Collaboration

COBB, B., & HASAZI, S. B. (1987). School-aged transition services: Options for adolescents with mild handicaps. *Career Development for Exceptional Individuals, 10,* 15–23.

HASAZI, S. B., GORDON, L. R., & ROE, C. A. (1985). Factors associated with the employment status of handicapped youth exiting high school. *Exceptional Children, 51,* 455–469.

JOHNSON, C. (1981). Using the I.E.P. for postsecondary vocational programs: A reaction. *Career Development for Exceptional Individuals, 4,* 78–82.

JOHNSON, D. R., BRUININKS, R. H., & THURLOW, M. L. (1987). Meeting the challenge of transition service planning through improved interagency cooperation. *Exceptional Children, 53,* 522–530.

KOKASKA, C. J., & HUGHES, C. M. (1985). A parent handbook for life-centered career skills. *Career Development for Exceptional Individuals, 8,* 119–122.

MITHAUG, D. E., HORIUCHI, C. N., & FANNING, P. N. (1985). A report of the Colorado follow-up survey of special education students. *Exceptional Children, 51,* 397–404.

NATIONAL JOINT COMMITTEE ON LEARNING DISABILITIES (1987a). Adults with learning disabilities: A call to action. *Journal of Learning Disabilities, 20,* 172–175.

NATIONAL JOINT COMMITTEE ON LEARNING DISABILITIES (1987b). Issues in the delivery of educational services to individuals with learning disabilities. *Journal of Learning Disabilities, 20,* 286–288.

PETERS, J. M., TEMPLEMAN, T. P., & BROSTROM, G. (1987). The school and community partnership: Planning transition for students with severe handicaps. *Exceptional Children, 53,* 531–536.

WHITE, S. (1987). Least restrictive environment: The challenge to special education. *Career Development for Exceptional Individuals, 10,* 33–41.

Policy Development and System Change

BENZ, M. R., & HALPERN, A. S. (1986). Vocational preparation for high school students with mild disabilities: A statewide study of administrator, teacher, and parent perceptions. *Career Development for Exceptional Individuals, 9,* 3–15.

BENZ, M. R., & HALPERN, A. S. (1987). Transition services for secondary students with mild disabilities: A statewide perspective. *Exceptional Children, 53,* 507–514.

BLALOCK, G., & DIXON, N. (1982). Improving prospects for the college-bound learning disabled. *Topics in Learning and Learning Disabilities, 2,* 69–78.

ELROD, G. F., & LYONS, B. A. (1987). A nation at risk or a policy at risk? How about career education. *Career Development for Exceptional Individuals, 10,* 10–14.

KNOWLTON, H. E., & CLARK, G. M. (1987). Transition issues for the 1990s. *Exceptional Children, 53,* 562–563.

STODDEN, R. A., & BOONE, R. (1987). Assessing transition services for handicapped youth: A cooperative interagency approach. *Exceptional Children, 53,* 537–545.

STRATEGIES INTERVENTION MODEL TRAINING NOTES (1987, May). Who's LD in the California community colleges? Lawrence: University of Kansas Institute for Research in Learning Disabilities.

WEICKER, L. P., JR. (1987). A look at policy and its effect on special education and vocational rehabilitation services. *Career Development for Exceptional Individuals, 10,* 6–9.

Rural Strategies

CLARK, G. M., & WHITE, W. J. (1985). Issues in providing career and vocational education to secondary-level mildly handicapped students in rural settings. *Career Development for Exceptional Individuals, 8,* 42–49.

KASTEN, K., & SQUIRES, S. (1983). *Nebraskans serving secondary special education students: Case studies of successful programs.* Omaha: University of Nebraska.

Author Index

Subject Index